THEORIES OF COLLECTIVE ACTION

Also by David Reisman

ADAM SMITH'S SOCIOLOGICAL ECONOMICS
*ALFRED MARSHALL: Progress and Politics
*THE ECONOMICS OF ALFRED MARSHALL
*GALBRAITH AND MARKET CAPITALISM
*THE POLITICAL ECONOMY OF JAMES BUCHANAN
 RICHARD TITMUSS: Welfare and Society
*STATE AND WELFARE: Tawney, Galbraith and Adam Smith

*Also published by Macmillan

Theories of Collective Action

Downs, Olson and Hirsch

David Reisman

MACMILLAN

First published 1990

Published by
THE MACMILLAN PRESS LTD
Houndmills, Basingstoke, Hampshire RG21 2XS
and London
Companies and representatives
throughout the world

Printed in Hong Kong

British Library Cataloguing in Publication Data
Reisman, David
Theories of collective action: Downs, Olson and
Hirsch.
1. Man. Collective action — Socio-economic
perspectives
I. Title
302.3
ISBN 0–333–49471–7

Contents

Acknowledgements   vi

1 INTRODUCTION   1

PART I   DOWNS

2 DEMOCRACY AND CONSENT   7
2.1 Methodology   9
2.2 Policies Supplied   24
2.3 Policies Demanded   44

3 ORGANISATIONS AND INTERESTS   60
3.1 Methodology   61
3.2 The Bureau: Responsibility and Responsiveness   79
3.3 The Bureau: Accountability and Action   95

PART II   OLSON

4 FREE RIDERS AND FREE MARKETS   141
4.1 Methodology   142
4.2 Group Size   149
4.3 The Prisoner's Dilemma   160

5 COLLECTIVE ACTION AND ECONOMIC GROWTH   210
5.1 Groups and Growth   212
5.2 Illustrations and Implications   229
5.3 The *Logic* and the *Nations*   246

PART III   HIRSCH

6 SOCIAL LIMITS AND COLLECTIVE ACTION   259
6.1 The Adding-Up Problem   259
6.2 The Moral Nexus   262
6.3 Policy Inferences   267
6.4 Hirsch and Collective Action   271

Notes and References   315

Index   339

Acknowledgements

This book was written during the period I spent as Hallsworth Fellow in Political Economy in the University of Manchester. I should like to thank all my colleagues in Manchester for making my stay so agreeable, and Ian Steedman in particular for his help and advice.

DAVID REISMAN

The author and publishers wish to thank the following who have kindly given permission for the use of copyright material:

Scott, Foresman and The RAND Corporation for permission for Anthony Downs, *Inside Bureaucracy*, copyright © 1967, 1966 by The RAND Corporation.

Yale University Press for short quotations from Mancur Olson, *The Rise and Decline of Nations*, Yale University Press, 1982.

Routledge & Kegan Paul Ltd and Harvard University Press for extracts from F. Hirsch, *Social Limits to Growth*, Routledge & Kegan Paul, 1977.

Harvard University Press for material taken from Mancur Olson, *The Logic of Collective Action*, Harvard University Press, 1965.

1 Introduction

Individuals make choices, reveal preferences and perform actions. Their subjectivity may be purposively self-interested and calculatively rational, but their calculus is still constrained and their freedom the plaything of others. From the past comes the multi-period constitutional conservatism of roles and rules, conventions and habits, the moral consensus and the traditional standard which stultify innovativeness even as they cocoon the socialised actor in an external web that is an ongoing culture. In the present there is the problem of interdependence of preferences and their consequences for, just as Robinson Crusoe and Friday cannot both win the race for relative standing purchased via conspicuous consumption of acknowledged status symbols, so Sir Robinson, immobilised in a monumental traffic-jam despite the fact that he himself is driving but one car, is bound to recall with some nostalgia the halcyon days alone on his island when his discrete and unique actions were not served up polluted with the actions of others. With respect to the future, finally, there is the uncertainty and unknowledge that is the inevitable concomitant of decisions made in advance of outcomes being known, both in the case of the isolated individual (as where the rational consumer must estimate the utility to him of the apple in advance of having established whether or not its taste actually satisfies his expectations) and *a fortiori* in the case of the individual who knows he is not alone (as where the rational oligopolist must decide whether to cut his price while dwelling behind a veil of ignorance so thick that he hasn't a clue as to how his cut-throat competitors will subsequently react). Individuals make choices, reveal preferences and perform actions, but they do so, evidently, subject to constraints so considerable that the Rousseauist natural man, upset by convention, is likely to return in disgust to the bush, the *enfant sauvage*, appalled by interdependence, to remain resolutely *sauvage*, Wild Peter of Hanover, unable to cope with uncertainty, to devote the rest of his life to teaching first-year economics courses to students of mathematics and engineering. Neither the natural man nor the *enfant sauvage* nor Wild Peter would feel entirely at home with the theories of collective action which form the subject matter of this book. The treble constraints upon individual action that are represented by convention, interdependence and uncertainty are so powerful, however, that it is much to be hoped that

1

they will ultimately overcome their commitment to the atomistic and the uni-disciplinary and venture into the maze of conjectural variation and strategic interaction where so much of the human drama is willy-nilly played out.

This book is divided into three parts. Part I, which deals with the theories of collective action that were developed by Anthony Downs, is concerned with the political market – with rational voters who judiciously squeeze the lemons in the Shop of Commons with a view to picking the fruit that yields the greatest pleasure; with rational politicians who sensibly sample the preferences of the median voter in order thereby to win the competition for the prize of power; with rational bureaucrats who, like all organisation men on a salary, have a personal incentive to rank expensive carpets for their offices above a high take-up rate for the benefits to which they are the gatekeepers. Imbued as it is with the ethos of self-seeking self-interest and cost-counting calculative rationality, it comes as somewhat of a surprise to learn that the Downsian system is capable of predicting and of explaining socio-political choices that are somewhat more sophisticated than is that, let us say, of maximal swill for minimal bill. One of these is the choice of the voter to donate his participation in an election on the outcome of which a single vote cannot be expected to have more than a token impact. Another is the choice of the politician to go to the country when he believes it to be essential to do so but when his action, he also anticipates, will cost him his mandate, his seat and his political career. A third is the choice of that bureaucrat known as the policeman to take risks that put his life on the line while simultaneously refusing bribes such as could buy health and happiness for himself and his family. These choices can, of course, be accounted for in terms of altruism of orientation, Downs concedes; but they can equally well be explained as the self-interested commitment of the rational democrat to the survival of the system. The Downsian distinction between altruism (as is typified by the charitable donation that benefits unknown others in the here-and-now) and egotism, broadly defined (in the sense of the long-term investment from which generations of strangers as yet unborn will draw the usufruct) is perhaps an artificial one. It does, however, provide a valuable link between Part I of the book and Part II by demonstrating that, in Anthony Downs' perspective at least, not every potential free rider will in practice opt to ride free.

Part II is concerned with the social market and deals with the theories of collective action of Mancur Olson. The representative actor is taken to be self-interested and calculatively rational – and fully aware, therefore, of the significance of being insignificant. Wild Peter, a citizen, can enjoy the benefits of the democratic system without himself having to abstain from profit-seeking activity in order to vote. The *enfant sauvage*, a registered client of the National Health Service, can consume a transfusion without having to prove that he has himself previously played the Blood Samaritan. The natural man, a perfect competitor, can cut his charges to increase his sales without having himself the least impact upon the public good of the going price. Wild Peter, the *enfant sauvage* and the natural man, fully aware as they are that one is never so unimportant as in a crowd, are led as if by an Invisible Hand to opt out of the costs in the expectation that others will supply the benefits. Should those others harbour the same expectation, needless to say, then not a vote will be cast, not a pint will be gifted, not a price will be stable, for the simple truth is, present the large group situation and absent the coordinative direction of wise leadership, that what one can do, all cannot. Not that the small-group situation can reasonably be regarded as a risk-free environment for the actor who hasn't a script: the evocative illustration of Jack and Jill, suspected criminals and bilateral monopsonists with respect to the implications, bears eloquent witness to the dilemma faced by the rational collaborator when imprisoned in a cell of which the windows are guesses and the doors are gambles. Whether in large groups or in small, one fears, the collective actor's lot is not a happy one. Since Olson also seeks to demonstrate that a nation's rate of economic growth is inversely correlated *ceteris paribus* with the significance of the special-interest groups and distributional coalitions that operate within its territory, the rational response for the friend of national affluence, assuming only that he is entirely convinced by Olson's arguments and evidence, would seem to be to offer the free rider a drink. Perhaps so. Not, however, always so – since the nation is itself an organisation and an alliance, and the free rider is none other than the oarsman who relies upon his team-mates to pull his weight. The strict moralist will find it deeply reprehensible that the free rider should elect to progress on the efforts of others. The strict economystic, more sceptical about the coarse clay that has been human nature ever since the apple and the Fall, will call instead for the privatisation of public goods such as the vessel rowed by the team, and therewith the proportioning of pay to product. That being done, the economystic will say, if the free rider opts not to row, neither shall he eat.

Part III brings together the discussion of the political and the social market and does so with particular reference to the theories of collective action that were developed by Fred Hirsch when that sensitive interpreter of history-to-come turned his mind to social limits to economic growth. One limit has to do with positional goods such as top jobs or second homes in secluded areas – utilities, in short, which are more and more in demand as a nation grows rich but of which the quantity supplied cannot be expanded sufficiently, if at all. The second limit has to do with the decay in personal morality that sets in when a society, growing up, renounces God and rejects convention – a decay that will be particularly deplored, it is clear, by the strict moralist with a firm conviction that the strict economystic's bag of tricks contains no functional equivalent whatsoever for self-policing conduct and internalised standards of right and wrong. Laws and State directives may, of course, relieve the strains and reduce the tensions – a Hirschian defence of the pragmatic response on the middle ground which will, one suspects, have a greater appeal to readers who attempt the present book from Index to Acknowledgements than to those who, beginning at the beginning with the politicians and the bureaucrats, will by the end have begun to wonder if those self-interested and calculatively rational agents are genuinely to be trusted with the resolution of a problem of which they may themselves most conspicuously be a manifestation. Thus it is that this book would end on a sombre note indeed, were it not for the fact that the title refers, reassuringly, to *theories* of collective action, the sub-title, more specifically, to Downs, Olson and Hirsch. Other authors have advanced other hypotheses. The reader with adequate evidence in his or her computer to be able to say with absolute certainty whether the blood donor or the free rider is properly to be regarded as the typical member of the modern community may legitimately be excused the laborious task of examining the various theories and studying the alternative hypotheses. For the rest of us, however, the outlook is less settled. The single-valued truth is somehow never in stock, external reality reveals itself to be complex, opaque and ever-changing, and it is all-too-frequently the case that a comparison of ideas and insights is the nearest we can approach to the hard facts which are denied us by the Great Computer-maker who in compensation endowed us with the logic, the tolerance and the curiosity that impel and permit us to hone and refine our own world-views through debate and discussion with the intellectual systems of our fellow men.

Part I
Downs

2 Democracy and Consent

Much of traditional economic theory is predicated on the proposition that individual self-interest, operating through the self-regulating market mechanism and guided as if by an Invisible Hand, has the welcome if unintended function of significantly advancing the economic welfare of the community. It was clearly this beneficence of outcome which Adam Smith had in mind when he spoke as follows of the appeal to what many would undoubtedly castigate as mean rapacity: 'It is not from the benevolence of the butcher, the brewer, or the baker, that we expect our dinner, but from their regard to their own interest. We address ourselves, not to their humanity but to their self-love, and never talk to them of our own necessities but of their advantages.'[1] Mean rapacity it may be, but the fact remains that filthy pigs can and do produce better ham than may reasonably be expected from, let us say, the polished elegance of the Angora cat: 'The natural effort of every individual to better his own condition, when suffered to exert itself with freedom and security, is so powerful a principle, that it is alone, and without any assistance, not only capable of carrying on the society to wealth and prosperity, but of surmounting a hundred impertinent obstructions with which the folly of human laws too often encumbers its operations.'[2] Thus the conclusion that private vices are public virtues and that theories which begin with individual self-interest need not end in tears.

Much of traditional economic theory adopts the constructs of self-interest and calculative rationality and proceeds thence, employing deductive logic and situating itself firmly within the maximising mind-set, to an equilibrium position generated spontaneously through the interaction of individual actors (not imposed from above by some exogenous authority) and not normally so repugnant to the representative member of the community as to render the whole process of searching and finding socially unacceptable. Yet the same cannot be said of much of traditional political theory, which demonstrates conspicuous reluctance to explain the behaviour of men in government – of politicians and bureaucrats – in the language of individuals maximising utility, of exchanges involving constraints, and which opts instead for an approach which views the State as made up in essence of depersonalised frictionless automatons with no life of their own independent of some Rousseauist General

Will which they are assumed obediently to serve, some Samuelsonian Social Welfare Function within the framework of which they passively maximise collective bliss.[3] Much of traditional political theory, it would appear, does not seek to explain the conduct of public officials (elected or appointed) by means of those key constructs – self-interest and calculative rationality – which traditionally constitute the meat and potatoes of the economist's argument when he strives to explain why it is in practice that the butcher, the brewer and the baker are ultimately persuaded to supply us with our dinner. This means in turn that the traditional *political* economist, charged as he is with explaining man's behaviour in more than one area of human life, must also be the master of more than one body of traditional theory.

The idea that the springs of action are different for the politician and the bureaucrat from those that account for the conduct of the butcher, the brewer and the baker has an intuitive appeal to the intellectual pluralist who senses that each of us behaves differently in the pub or on the beach from the way in which he behaves when in the chapel or on the bench. One such pluralist is Kenneth Boulding, who has criticised the totalitarian one-dimensionality which he identifies in the postulation of homogeneity – and who is particularly hostile to the manifestation that he calls 'economics imperialism' (i.e. 'the attempt on the part of economics to take over all the other social sciences').[4] Other writers have argued, however, that the duality between economic and political actions is in essence a false one and one which should not only be transcended but transcended quite specifically by means of a general theory modelled on the buying and selling of traditional textbook microeconomics. One such writer is Joseph Schumpeter, who pioneered the economic approach to politics in hypotheses such as the following: 'The incessant competitive struggle to get into office or to stay in it imparts to every consideration of policies and measures the bias so admirably expressed by the phrase about "dealing in votes" '.[5] A more recent advocate is Bruno Frey: 'There is little evidence for believing that the politicians and public bureaucrats involved in government intervention are interested in furthering abstract social welfare . . . It must rather be assumed that they are more concerned with their own welfare.'[6] Yet another advocate is Gordon Tullock, who, calculating with exemplary precision (and 'as a result of empirical research') that 'the average human being is about 95 per cent selfish in the narrow meaning of the term', states that this orientation is in fact the very reason why political democracy is so successful in ensuring that government policies are matched to popular preference: 'There is no reason why we should be disturbed by this phenomenon. The market operates by providing a structure in which individuals who simply want to make money end up by producing motor-cars that people want. Similarly, democracy operates so that politicians who simply want to hold public office end up by doing things the people want. Perhaps the people are badly informed in their choice of policies, but all a democracy can really guarantee is popular control.'[7] One of the most sophisticated contributors to the approach is Anthony Downs, whose analyses of the political market (principally in *An Economic Theory of Democracy*) and of thinking men within administrative structures (principally in *Inside Bureaucracy*) undeniably ask all the key questions even should they not ultimately provide all the final answers.

Downs' work is accordingly the central focus of this chapter and of the next. The next chapter examines the bureaucrat on the null assumption that he is an economic actor. The present chapter is concerned with the position of the politician in the democratic system characterised by free elections held at regular intervals and competition for power among teams of office-seekers called parties, each offering a differentiated menu of policy-options and each anxious first and foremost to win the prize of popularity that is the mandate. The chapter is divided into three sections, the first dealing with Methodology, the second with Policies Supplied, the third with Policies Demanded. The theme linking the three is the pragmatism of instrumentality; since democracy to Downs is desirable not because participative involvement is in some absolute sense a good thing in its own right but merely because no better way of registering and aggregating preferences has as yet been discovered. Were an omniscient computer or a beneficent despot to be able more effectively to perform the same task, the consistent Downsian would have to conclude, there would in those circumstances no longer be a need for a democratic system at all – or for an economic theory of political democracy such as that which is the central focus of the present chapter.

2.1 METHODOLOGY

The Downsian approach is the deductive one of the neo-classical orthodoxy. It begins with assumptions which have the force of axioms and then derives, by means of a long chain of logic and reasoning, a series of propositions and conclusions. It employs as its dual-faceted point of departure the two well-known *a prioris* of self-interest and calculative rationality which are the intellectual bedrock of modern market microeconomics. The propositions and conclusions which are derived from the initial assumptions may, at least conceptually, be regarded as testable hypotheses, inferences which can be broadly supported or broadly called into question by an appeal to empirical evidence. The accuracy and relevance of the axioms employed is, however, somewhat more difficult to confirm or refute: the actual content of men's minds being inaccessible even to the most sensitive of psychologists, the rationalisations which acting individuals provide (even where not accompanied by deliberate obfuscation and manipulative demi-mendacity) being unreliable guides at the best of times to their actual motivation, the theoretician has no inductive option and no alternative but to posit some *a priori* which he himself regards as reasonable – and to accept that one man's reasonable *a priori* may well be another man's arrant nonsense. The theoretician's lot is not a happy one.

The Downsian approach is the median methodology in the analysis of the economic market, the Downsian contention that the tools and techniques developed explicitly to account for the supply and demand of apples and nuts can usefully be employed in the political market as well, in an attempt to explain the policies supplied and policies demanded that are there seen to emerge. Many political scientists, comparing the inelegance and imprecision of their own tentative generalisations with the majesty of expression and determinateness of outcome that are the economist's undeniable selling-points when he mixes marginalism and maximisation, curves and calculus, equilibration and welfare, in such a way as to arrive at coordination without coercion and harmony amidst diversity, will no doubt wish most sincerely to *believe*, and *a fortiori* so if their own personal bias happens to be that of the classical liberal, in favour of conflict reduction without central direction and balance of power within the society as well as within the State. The classical liberal will also, it must be added, be much impressed by the individualism and the atomism with which the Downsian economic approach is imbued: just as there is no benevolent despot in the system, so there is no social class or multi-period grouping, but instead the isolated person equipped with a depersonalised vote which resembles nothing so much as the anonymity of money. Tribesmen in newly-industrialising countries will complain that their interdependence and solidarity are not picked up by such a perspective, while workers in the older industrialised countries will observe that, for them at least, self-interest and calculative rationality do nothing to obviate the fact that position on the social map is a shared attribute that is by no means easy to alter. It is in the circumstances not entirely surprising that the Downsian economic approach has enjoyed the greatest currency in the United States, where there is not only a widespread popular acceptance of the salesman-orientation to which the two axioms refer, but also the highly developed sense of self that characterises an expanding economy that sees itself as enjoying a relatively open and meritocratic social structure, that regards itself as having mercifully been spared the burden of inter-generational coalitions and the class monopoly of power that is the curse of less fortunate lands. Thus C. B. Macpherson says of the economic approach to politics that 'this kind of analysis is most developed in the United States but is still an imported academic luxury in Europe, where it has spread since the war at roughly the square root of the speed of Coca-Cola'.[1] John Toye is more explicit still in associating the Downsian world-view of self-interest and calculative rationality, possessive individualism and aggressive competitiveness, not with the optimistic capitalism of the American Dream in particular but with the specific historical phenomenon of capitalism *per se*: 'Economic theories of politics provide a crystalline example of the Marxist idea of "false consciousness". They are not merely an intellectual adventure that is likely to prove unfruitful; they are part of a much more general bias in present-day social science.'[2]

Toye would clearly take the view that the economic approach is inappropriate to politics for the simple reason that it is inappropriate to economics itself. Other – and more moderate – thinkers would have a certain sympathy with his position. Economists in the tradition of Galbraith, for example, would no doubt express some regret at the cultural lag which is involved when politics is asked to take over from economics a concept of equilibration which the emergence of power-blocs has rendered increasingly out of date; while economists in the tradition of Veblen would criticise the sheer nakedness of the disembodied abstractions that are the choices in the model for their conspicuous lack of sociological clothing (a lack of relatedness to the wider society which Macpherson has evocatively captured in the *dictum* that 'equilibrium is a nice tune for whistling in the dark'.[3]). It would have, therefore, to be conceded that not all economists, and certainly not all political scientists, would be prepared to share with Downs the conviction that deductions from the axioms of self-interest

and calculative rationality are a sound basis for a realistic theory of
political action. That some would be prepared to do so is not, however,
in dispute. Among their number are James Buchanan and Gordon
Tullock, whose *Calculus of Consent* contains the important observation that 'constitutional democracy in its modern sense was born as a
twin of the market economy'.[4] Two Enlightenment phenomena, one
Enlightenment body of theory – unification is at the heart of the
constitutionalists' enterprise, as it is at the heart of Downs'.
Unification is also the centrepiece of the account of the two axioms
which is undertaken in two sub-sections to which the discussion must
now turn.

2.1.1 Self-interest

Downs finds it implausible that the motivation of politicians should be
other-regarding in nature: despite their rhetoric of altruistic self-
sacrifice, he argues, and despite the fact that the outcome of their
actions is sometimes indeed improved social welfare, yet every
con-man knows that words are not indubitably the window to
thoughts, and every student of procreation among rabbits appreciates
that function is not to be confused with intent. Politicians, Downs
maintains, are no different in normative orientation from other actors
in a system of division of labour, and it is that primary selfishness above
all which causes them to rank policy A above policy B. Just as the
commercial entrepreneur maximises his profits by producing and
marketing those goods and services which most paying customers most
want to consume, so, Downs stresses, the political entrepreneur
maximises votes (he should presumably have said seats in Parliament,
but his meaning is clear enough) by offering those policies most likely
to prove popular with the electorate while rejecting those proposals
least like to find favour and please. Neither entrepreneur can, if he
genuinely wishes ongoing success in preference to spectacular
self-immolation, afford to supply a commodity for which there is no
demand, however much it may appeal to his own value-system and
outlook on life. Each, instead, must bow to revealed preferences and
articulated tastes (assumed, as in all neo-classical models of consumer
behaviour, exogenous to the process of want-satisfaction); and must
tailor his product accordingly if it is to be competitive (in free markets
or free periodic elections, respectively) for the custom of a
utility-maximising consumerhood/citizenry which itself is self-

interested. Politicians in the circumstances do not have a great deal of scope for the imposition on the community of their own private and personal notions of social utility. Other private and personal objectives remain, however, valid choices, and it is the very attraction of those rewards (power, prestige, income, love of conflict, access to the excitement of the Parliamentary game) which brings the self-interest of the politician into line with the self-interest of the voter to an extent that is not to be expected from benevolence alone.

This is not to say that Downs' conception of self-interest need be as cynically self-seeking, as narrowly hedonistic, as might on first acquaintance appear to be the case. Speaking of self-interest, after all, Downs quite clearly declares that 'in reality, men are not always selfish, even in politics. They frequently do what appears to be individually irrational because they believe it is socially rational – i.e., it benefits others even though it harms them personally.'[5] Yet he does at least argue that there is an asymmetry here. Voters, he points out, may and do make generosity and charity an object of utility and in that way compel politicians out of their own self-interest to opt for altruism in an attempt to capture votes; but a politician would not survive long in politics who, however noble and moral his intentions, independently introduced such policies. In saying that the principal (whether a voter or, say, a shareholder) can and does choose aid to developing countries in preference to a fourth colour television, but that the agent (whether a politician or, say, a salaried manager) is putting his job on the line if he gets into the habit of spending without legitimate authorisation monies which are not his own to spend, Downs is in a sense only making the most obvious point possible about accountability – that a shop-assistant will get the sack if she herself takes the decision to study rather than to assist, but that her employers have the right to offer her that option and may well feel that such a choice represents to them money well-spent. No employer wants to be bullied by his own employees, and that is why Downs is able to identify both other-regardingness on the part of principals and plasticity on the part of agents. As Tullock puts it: 'The people who are successful in moving up the hierarchy are those who are most likely to choose career-motivated action rather than action motivated by other things. As the economist likes to emphasize, everything in the world is obtained at a cost, and the politician who obtains satisfaction from extra-career motivations, must expect to pay for this in terms of a slower rate of advancement.'[6]

Even in the case of politicians, however, and similar in that respect to the case of voters, Downs appears in at least two instances himself to be on the point of broadening his concept of self-interest. In one, noting that the objectives of the politician include prestige, he reminds the reader that a man's behaviour might be governed by a desire to win the 'best reputation for service'[7]; and it is in such circumstances easy enough to imagine a scenario in which a far-sighted incumbent, out of devotion to the history-books as well as to the nation, deliberately administers a medicine so unpopular in the short run as to cost him the next election but from which untold benefits are ultimately seen to be reaped. In the second instance, speaking of the rule of law, he observes that politicians do not in a democratic system normally take bribes or employ violence to prevent elections, but provides no self-interested explanation for such self-denial. What he does say is that, quite simply, 'we do not assume that the private ambitions of party members are without bounds'[8] – an indication that hidden just behind the economic theory of democracy is implicit and tacit normative constraint so powerful that it limits the range of choices open to any and all politicians with a modicum of other-regarding sensibilities. Downs' democracy, one infers, is not 'new' democracy but *established* democracy, democracy built upon habits, traditions, conventions and culture favourable to that form of consultative and participative decision-making; and the obvious extension is to suggest that such a society might via the normal life-cycle conditioning and socialisation mechanisms have imposed invisible barriers to modes of action additional to those cited in connection with political corruption or the *coup d'état*. A sensitive politician deeply imbued with the values of a social consensus which extols human life and freedom to choose might prefer to resign rather than support popular pressures for capital punishment or immigration controls; and to describe his exit in this instance as an investment in his own career prospects (as where, say, he anticipates that the popular pressures in question will soon peter out and the electorate will then be in search of a new leader committed to the old ways) is to miss the point. The representative politician does not, in the work of Downs, take bribes or foment anti-democratic revolutions. It is likely, one must now add, that there are other things as well which the representative politician *qua* social actor will choose to do or not to do in an attempt to deserve self-congratulation and to avoid a badly-spoiled self-image. Self-interested this may be, but only in the tautologous sense that all conscious action is self-interested. What is important to note is that we have moved some way beyond the five ends – power, prestige, income, love of conflict, access to the excitement of the Parliamentary game – in terms of which Downs explains the self-interested behaviour of the elected official in the modern political democracy.

Politicians, certainly, have been among the first to point to the narrowness of the Downsian range of goals. Jo Grimond, for example, speaking from extensive personal experience in the House of Commons, has written as follows of the degree of conviction and responsibility which he had observed at Westminster: 'I was amazed by the altruistic outlook of many of my colleagues and, indeed, of bureaucrats . . . If you examine political decisions, a lot of them, I think, could only come from personal beliefs. Many Members of Parliament don't want power.'[9] And William Rodgers has returned a similar verdict on the actual motivation of real-world politicians: 'I doubt whether they can be easily classified as selfish careerists – interested only in office; or as ideological zealots – interested only in the rightness of their cause. I am not aware of any study that adequately considers the factors – psychological, environmental – that make some men and women politically active . . . I am not competent to explore this question of internal motivation. But I *am* clear that the idea of public service, old-fashioned although it may sound, has a role alongside ambition and ideology. There is genuine competition to "do good", and not only on the scale of constituency matters where the MP is more and more a cross between priest and social worker.'[10] Noting that for most British politicians the financial rewards from office are modest (particularly when one reflects that few are good at nothing else: many have other careers which they have had in whole or in part to give up, and almost all have the talents and potential to have at least equivalent success in a non-political setting), and convinced as well, one suspects, that, in Britain at any rate, politicians enjoy something less than the social status which they deserve, Rodgers makes clear that what many British politicians most want is the opportunity to get involved in good works and moral causes.[11] Witness the case of economic aid to Third World countries, supported in Britain, he says, by all the main political parties despite the general lack of support for such policies from the nation as a whole: 'The great majority of voters would not have noticed the omission of overseas aid from the Manifestoes and most of them would be neutral if not hostile to the idea. Commitments were included partly because the minority positively in favour of aid to the Third World is articulate and sympathetic, including the Churches; partly because on the left this minority includes many activists; and partly because of Britain's international reputation. But in addition there is the moral imperative felt by many Members of Parliament and senior officials. It is simply *right* to help relieve the most intolerable of world poverty.'[12] The libertarian critic will point out that this is an explicit defence of producer sovereignty which every conviction politician would instantly attack were it to arise in the economic rather than the political market (as where my MP quite rightly takes seriously my accusation of unfair and restrictive trade practices should the three main suppliers in the industry collude rather than compete and end up by offering me a car of any colour I like so long as it is black); while the concerned moralist will mutter darkly that the world would indeed be a better place if that which is 'simply *right*' were as unambiguously single-valued and straightforward as Rodgers himself would appear to think that it is (particularly since, in the case of foreign aid, he seems to be dismissing the attitudes of the great majority of voters as 'simply *wrong*'). What matters in the present context, however, is that Rodgers himself would not rank the objections of the libertarian critic or the concerned moralist any more highly than he would the contention of Downs that the self-interested politician is one who sets out to buy votes by selling *whichever* policies the citizen wishes to acquire.

Some popularity, Rodgers would hardly deny, is the *sine qua non* for the politician in a democracy to be in a position to do what is 'simply *right*'; and this pursuit of popularity is undoubtedly the reason why even conviction politicians have sometimes to employ cynically vote-seeking stratagems (the case of the 'election-year budget', for example, or the transfer of resources by a nervous governing party from areas of traditional support to marginal seats likely otherwise to fall to the Opposition) while guiltily suppressing vote-losing policies widely believed to be in the public interest (the most dramatic instance being that of tax-relief on mortgage interest: the libertarian Right believes it distorts the market for housing, the socialist Left sees it as regressive and a subsidy to privilege, but both Right and Left fully appreciate the serious implications of promising abolition in an electoral manifesto). Some popularity is the precondition for power; but power, Rodgers would say, is itself not end but means, and specifically the means to do that which is 'simply *right*'. To the extent that observers such as Grimond and Rodgers have the measure of the motivation of the present-day politician (at least of the contemporary *British* politician: there is no reason to suppose there is not considerable variation as between one culture and another), to that extent, of course, the positive value of Downs' deductions from his personal and private specification of the self-interest axiom are bound to be somewhat wide of the mark.

Thus it is that John Plamenatz, stressing that there is far more to life – and to *political* life – than is encompassed by conscious selection and attainment of goals based on the comparison of private costs and private benefits, pays tribute to Downs' work for being 'full of good ideas that throw light on many aspects of what political scientists like to call "the democratic process"', but also comments that its all but exclusive focus on interest and exchange significantly restricts its predictive power: 'Downs' model, admirable though it is in some ways as an intellectual exercise, is, so it seems to me, of limited use. It is much less useful than Downs meant it to be. What makes it of such limited use is precisely that it is an economist's model and therefore utilitarian.'[13] Plamenatz does not deny that some self-interest, narrowly defined, is to be observed in democratic politics. What he does say, however, is that Downs places too great an emphasis on self-interest, narrowly defined, and thereby compels his axiom to bear a burden of explanation and prediction which it is, in his view, demonstrably incapable of supporting.

The self-interest axiom in the work of Downs is employed principally with a view to explaining and predicting the behaviour-patterns of voters and politicians, but it is worth concluding our discussion of that axiom by reflecting that the self-interest of a third group as well is relevant in the present context – that, namely, of the party-activists who make the show possible without themselves ever once appearing on the stage. Typically unpaid volunteers with no personal aspirations to the privileges of power, party activists concentrate instead on maximising the ideological purity of the organisation and on ensuring that there is no sell-out of its traditional beliefs to vote-maximising policies calculated, in their eyes, to win power by running away from principle. Politicians know they are dependent on these loyalists (say, for canvassing in elections) and fear their censure (say, at the Party Conference), and this creates the curious phenomenon of the organisational part dominating the national whole which Robin Matthews has described as follows: 'As the views of party activists are likely to have a larger and possibly more extreme ideological content than those of the general public, a further result is to create a chronic tension: should policy be nearer to that of the median party activist, as being the line preferred within the party, or should it be nearer to that of the median voter in the electorate, so as to maximise the chances of winning the election? It is not surprising that the outcome has gone sometimes one way, sometimes the other.'[14] Nor is it enough simply to state that the parties cannot afford to alienate the enthusiasts who attempt to convince, on the doorsteps and in the High Street, the undecided and the indifferent. Should the winner-take-all voting rule of 51 per cent be employed both within the nation and within the parties, the outcome of this two-stage exercise in democracy can actually mean that the self-interest of quite a small minority comes to dictate the policies that are adopted for the nation as a whole – the phenomenon, as Matthews explains, of pyramiding, the '26 per cent' phenomenon: 'Given party discipline, a choice may be made that has the support of 51 per cent of the members of a party that itself has the support of 51 per cent of the electorate – even though the outcome is opposed by all but 26 per cent of the electorate.'[15] Indeed, should voting within the parties take the form of voting by representatives, the percentage in question can actually fall still further – as where, say, 51 per cent of union activists (themselves not necessarily a random cross-section of the union rank-and-file) succeed in appointing a delegate to the party congress who then forms part of a 51 per cent majority of delegates which selects a party programme for which 51 per cent of the voters in the nation as a whole will ultimately opt. Such a minority result is not inevitable (the proportion at each stage could *de facto* quite easily be 95 per cent or more). That it is possible, however, cannot be denied – one reason, one suspects, why some observers find representative government unrepresentative and wish to see a significant reduction in the role played by the State in social processes unless and until the voting-rule more nearly approximates the Wicksellian ideal *de jure* of 100 per cent.

2.1.2 Calculative rationality

Calculative rationality means the deliberate orientation of behaviour towards the attainment of consciously-selected, consistently-ranked and transitively-ordered objectives with the least possible input (to the economist in value terms, to the political scientist via simple addition) of scarce means per unit of output. It incorporates the notion of efficient deployment of means with a view to ends (an activity which, of course, could – assuming perfect information on the part of the observer – be independently estimated and objectively evaluated the moment that actors have provided the uniquely subjective component by revealing their preferences). It constitutes the second of the two assumptions from which the deductions of the Downsian model then follow as if guided by an Invisible Hand. It is also, as an intellectual construct, entirely separate from the first, in the sense that even a politician who is seen to rank aid to the people of Ethiopia above policies that yield benefits to him personally may nonetheless be assumed to prefer efficiency to waste and more to less. That having been said, it must immediately be conceded how seldom it is in practice in the Downsian model that calculative rationality puts in an appearance save in combination with the postulate of self-interest, narrowly defined.

No theory of rational action can be constructed without the postulation of rational calculation, but Downs is realistic enough to see that his assumption can all-too-easily degenerate, like that of self-interest, into a tautology. His technique for dealing with this problem and putting teeth into his axiom is, arguably, somewhat less realistic – as where he declares that he must suppress from his model the idea that citizens find the act of voting *per se* a source of prestige and then set out rationally to purchase for themselves that utility or satisfaction: 'If it is rational to vote for prestige, why is it not rational to vote so as to please one's employer or one's sweetheart? Soon all behavior whatsoever becomes rational because every act is a means to some end the actor values. To avoid this sterile conclusion, we have regarded only actions leading to strictly political or economic ends as rational.'[16] Such a declaration is unjustifiably arbitrary and one in addition which is capable of rendering the economic approach to democracy toothless in the face of potential real-world observations. If citizens genuinely regard it as desirable to vote for the prestige of having voted rather than after consideration of the issues, then the outcome of the election will be fully random but the election itself fully rational; and a similar comment must be made concerning the man who votes in such a way as to please his employer (thereby investing in a promotion), or his wife (thereby forestalling a marital dispute). What would be irrational in the former case would be to conceal the fact that one has gone to the polls at all; what would be irrational in the latter would be either to make a secret of the way in which one has voted (perhaps even going so far as to insist on a show of hands rather than a secret ballot as a public guarantee of non-duplicity) or to select a candidate who is other than the optimal means for the attainment of the desired objective. Where, however, social actors are seen carefully to rank ends and then efficiently to choose means, it is somewhat intolerant for the social scientist subsequently to dismiss their decision as irrational (however sincerely he may personally believe that it is irresponsible and wish that it be atypical). To the extent that Downs' theory abstracts from the non-political and the non-economic it becomes non-empirical and non-predictive; and for that reason his narrow focus with respect to rationality may legitimately be regarded as somewhat out of place in a model with avowedly scientific aspirations.

This is not to say that Downs is unaware of the broader considerations that influence the ranking of ends and the selection of means in the voting context – as where he states, for example, that a citizen 'might vote for the party whose leader has the most charming personality, or the one whose historic heroes appeal to him most, or the one his father voted for.'[17] Simply, Downs chooses deliberately to concentrate on issues-related rationality and to neglect influences other than issues that contribute to the shaping of perceived party differentials – influences such as product-image, charismatic personality, family tradition, peer-group pressures and even habit and inertia. He does so partly because of his appreciation that means-ends rationality is at some level so eternally true as to be eternally trivial, partly because he expects individual peculiarities to cancel one another out within the framework of large groups, partly because a high degree of problem-solving, issues-related rationality exists and must exist, in his view, if individuals and societies are to cope successfully with the exigencies of their situation, and partly because, as he puts it, 'this is a study of economic and political rationality, not of psychology.'[18] His reasons, clearly, are a mixed bag, ranging as they do from utilitarian philosophy to Weberian scientific method by way of statistical probability and casual empiricism, but it would appear that it is the economist's use of ideal types which in the last analysis is closest to his heart. Since he admits that it is 'erroneous as well as arbitrary'[19] to make the *ceteris paribus* assumption, one comes more and more to understand why Downs himself in one place characterises his theoretical approach as 'positive but not descriptive': 'The statements in our analysis are true of the model world, not the real world, unless they obviously refer to the latter.'[20] Downs himself would appear to entertain doubts concerning the extent to which his propositions are testable and predictive, and nowhere more so, one feels sure, than in the following defence of abstraction: 'We do not take into consideration the whole personality of each individual when we discuss what behavior is rational for him. We do not allow for the rich diversity of ends served by each of his acts, the complexity of his motives, the way in which every part of his life is intimately related to his emotional needs. Rather we borrow from traditional economic theory the idea of the rational consumer.'[21] Such doubts are a welcome corrective to the over-confidence of the rationality assumption. Sadly, they are also *obiter dicta* with little more than a walk-on role in the Downsian account of consumer rationality. They cannot be more: otherwise the predictions deduced from the axioms would be without meaning.

Even the rational consumer, however, may *rationally* choose to purchase on the basis of characteristics other than price, quantity and quality, and one is inclined to assert that Downs is actually being excessively modest with respect to the robustness of his rationality axiom when he limits its scope in the way that he does. Voting on the basis of tradition, for example, may itself turn out to be rationally issues-related, as where a given party has over the years built up so powerful an image of itself as the friend of trades unionism that the unionist sees no need to invest time and other resources in acquainting himself with precise policies and proposals; and a similar observation may even be made, surprising as it may at first seem, concerning voting on the basis of personalities and personal charisma. The reason is that every election (like any other contract, explicit or implicit) involves the institution of a monopoly of force for some period of time (long or short; fixed, as in the United States, or variable, as in the United Kingdom) of which Matthews writes as follows: 'During the tenure of the authority of the contract, competition is suspended and to that extent made less severe overall, though participants may doubtless be influenced in their conduct by consideration of the next round (the "reputation" factor). The duration of the time for which authority is conferred never approaches zero, unlike that of a transaction, because that would be inconsistent with the nature of authority itself.'[22] Yet a reference to time is a reference to change; the range of proposals in the manifesto, limited in number at the best of times, can never embrace the unforeseen contingency or the non-replicable emergency; and, save in a nation of which every citizen is a full-time politician and every issue is settled on the basis of a discrete referendum, much of the authority that is legitimately exercised by the leadership is by its very nature fiduciary authority, authority exercised on trust over the agreed-upon life-span of the monopoly. The comparison of an electoral victory to the victory of a runner in a marathon race is therefore a misleading one, since in the latter competition the victory is the proof of merit while in the former it is merely a licence to try. Given the extent to which an electoral victory is analogous to the signature of a blank cheque in favour of a favourite autocrat briefed to use his discretion, it is then, of course, hardly irrational for the concerned citizen to vote on the basis of personalities as well as (perhaps in preference to) issues. It is, in short, where so much of the job-description remains for the eventual appointee himself to specify,

highly *rational* for the concerned citizen to vote for what Downs
describes as 'the party whose leader has the most charming
personality' – provided only that the attractiveness in question is not
confined exclusively to politically-irrelevant characteristics such as the
chocolate-box good looks of the film star and derives principally from
politically-indispensable traits such as perceived strength of will,
clarity of objectives and general competence. This is not to say that the
individual voter will always make the right choice, only that it may be
at least as rational for him to try to do so on the basis of personalities as
it would be in the purest Downsian case where he would attempt to do
so on the basis of issues and little else.

Four or five years is a long time in politics, and that too has
significant implications for the assumption of calculative rationality in
view of the simple fact that, put bluntly, my consistency and my
transitivity are not for all seasons. Nor should it be forgotten how
frequently that ongoing alteration in tastes and preferences is itself a
function of governmental actions. Such endogeneity and malleability
of tastes may be associated with words (the cases of information,
exhortation, persuasion and propaganda, analogous to commercial
advertising and private-sector salesmanship even in the sense that
action is likely to provoke reaction from competitors in an attempt to
set the record straight), but it may also – perhaps more insidiously
because less clearly understood – be associated with deeds. As
Matthews explains, 'the implementation of policies may alter people's
preferences, in just the same way as consumers' preferences are
altered by the habits and aversions created by past purchases. If a given
policy is unwelcome both and before and after it is implemented,
deliberate adoption of it by the authority is clearly exploitative. But
the situation is less clear if it was unwelcomed beforehand but
welcomed in retrospect, or welcomed beforehand but regretted in
retrospect.'[23] Precisely because the political contract is to so great an
extent a blank cheque, the deliberate implementation of preference-
altering policies, although without any doubt *potentially* sinister, is
nonetheless not '*necessarily* sinister. In some areas the public may be
glad for governments to show "leadership", indeed expect it of them.
The difficulty is where to draw the line between leadership and
brainwashing.'[23] That 'the public should have a choice as to *who* is to
wash their brains'[25] is a *sine qua non* for political democracy in the
sense of Downs. That it is a sufficient as well as a necessary condition is
more debatable in view of the degree to which brains once washed then
remain washed because of the creation of a vested interest (frequently

pecuniary as well as intellectual) in the new institutional order – as where a right-wing party invests heavily in right-wing thinking (whether or not with the explicit intention of thereby augmenting the numbers of right-wing voters) by selling shares in denationalised industries to a broad cross-section of the population and converts a significant proportion of its council tenants into owner-occupiers, or where a left-wing party (perhaps one sincerely committed to social justice and totally unaware of the *de facto* manipulation of voting behaviour that is embodied in its *fait accompli*) introduces a lifetime minimum wage for the long-term unemployed that is equal to the national average level of earnings and is financed exclusively by confiscatory taxation on the top 1 per cent of wealth-holders. The point is that actions as well as ideas have consequences; and that tastes and preferences not only *change* over time but *are changed* by our servants when they become our masters. Such alterations do not invalidate the rationality axiom but they do cause it to be interpreted with caution – with great caution, in fact, if Schumpeter is correct in his assessment that, in the modern democracy at least, 'the will of the people is the product and not the motive power of the political process.'[26]

The Downs axiom of calculative rationality in the political market will have a strong intuitive appeal to the concerned citizen who has the interest and the background knowledge (and is prepared to find the time) to undertake the non-negligible task of extrapolating probable future party performance on the bases of electoral promises and the respective records when last in office (given that leaders may have changed, national circumstances may have altered, and experts may continue to disagree completely among themselves as to the proper means for dealing with major issues such as inflation and unemployment). Not every member of the community is, however, such a concerned citizen, and while Downs and other political economists who share his assumption of rationality in choice are sincerely to be congratulated on their confidence in the good common sense of their fellow-participants in the democratic enterprise, there are bound nonetheless to be less optimistic observers who will wonder if the floating voter ought to be likened not so much to the floating shopper (the sovereign consumer who meticulously maximises value for money) as to the floating husband or wife (the poor confused creature who is genuinely unstable). Thus Schumpeter at his most pessimistic was capable of conjuring up a nightmarish situation in which the bulk of voters mill aimlessly about the political marketplace furnished with nothing more than an 'indeterminate bundle of vague impulses loosely playing about given slogans and mistaken impressions',[27] while Brian Barry, after surveying the evidence on the high degree of inconsistency which appears to obtain in the field of voting behaviour, was forced to write as follows: 'It might perhaps be argued, desperately, that this simply reflects the fact that people "change their minds" with great frequency on these issues, but it is much more likely that many do not have a "mind" on them at all, in other words, that they do not think about them at all except when being interviewed, and then respond virtually at random.'[28] A vote for 'the party whose leader has the most charming personality' is – as we have seen – at least in certain circumstances fully compatible with the assumption of calculative rationality. A vote by guesswork on the part of an elector who doesn't really care about the policies being supplied and hasn't a clue as to the policies he would most like to demand is, however, less obviously so.

2.2   POLICIES SUPPLIED

Downs is, in general, reasonably content with his axioms – content enough, at any rate, to describe the hypotheses deduced from them as 'accurate representations of what happens in the real world most of the time'[1] In this section we shall be concerned with Downs' precise predictions concerning the nature of the product supplied. Parties are assumed to formulate policies in order to please as many voters as possible, and that is the message which underlies the four sets of observations about supply in democratic conditions which now follow.

2.2.1   Convergence and divergence

A businessman would be singularly inept if he did not make available *what* was demanded *where* it was demanded; and the product which he supplies is in that obvious and dual sense demand-determined. Harold Hotelling, building on the insights of Sraffa and other early Marshallians with respect to market-segmentation resulting from a number of differentiating characteristics including geographical location (and doing so four years in advance of the celebrated contributions of Joan Robinson and E.H. Chamberlin), was among the first to seek to apply the theory of quasi-monopoly based on characteristics to the political market. Hotelling, as it happens, was a teacher of Kenneth Arrow at Columbia and is singled out for special praise in *Social Choice and Individual Values* as the man 'to whom I owe my interest in economics and particularly my interests in problems of social welfare.'[2] Arrow in turn was Downs' teacher at Stanford and the source of 'many excellent ideas'.[3]

The Hotelling approach to differentiation based on characteristics is in two parts. The first part – the theoretical part – is an elaborate account of the extent to which each establishment has an absolute monopoly in being itself: 'If a seller increases his price too far he will gradually lose business to his rivals, but he does not lose all his trade instantly when he raises his price only a trifle. Many customers will still prefer to trade with him because they live nearer to his store than to the others, or because they have less freight to pay from his warehouse to their own, or because his mode of doing business is more to their liking, or because he sells other articles which they desire, or because he is a relative or a fellow Elk or Baptist, or on account of some difference in service or quality, or for a combination of reasons. Such circles of customers may be said to make every entrepreneur a monopolist within a limited class and region.'[4] The second part – the empirical part – is an assertion that, in America at least, (and fully in keeping with de Tocqueville's findings in that country almost exactly a century earlier), the standardised has the edge over the unique, the samey over the special, the agglomerative over the fissiparous. Many customers might prefer to trade with the small rural shopkeeper because he is conveniently local, but that does not mean that the would-be shopkeeper is prepared to trade with them. On the contrary: the greatest concentration of his potential customers being found in the town, it is in the financial interest of the rational new entrant to settle in the closest possible proximity to the old entrants, and to aim (while not precisely duplicating their appeal lest there then remain no alternative mode of competition to the beggar-my-neighbour destructiveness of the price-war) at maximising his trade by converging with his fellow-sellers on the hump of the frequency-distribution where the bulk of the buyers are situated. The odd Elk in the tails or Baptist at the fringe is no doubt a fine person in his own right, but there is not much money to be made from minorities, and that is why, in Hotelling's explanation of things as they are, 'as more and more sellers of the same commodity arise, the tendency is not to become distributed in the socially optimum manner but to cluster unduly'.[5] It is at this point that Hotelling makes his declaration that the 'agglomerative tendencies' which he had identified in the High Street are nothing short of 'strikingly exemplified' by the situation in the Shop of State: 'The competition for votes between the Republican and the Democratic parties does not lead to a clear drawing of issues, an adoption of two strongly contrasted positions between which the voters may choose. Instead, each party strives to make its platform as much like the other's as possible. Any radical departure would lose many votes, even though it might lead to stronger commendation of the party by some who would vote for it anyhow'.[6] Just as there is not much money to be made from minorities in the economic market, so in the political market, the rational vote-maximiser eschews controversy in the tails and differences at the fringe in favour of concentration of his appeal on the man in the middle – the median voter or representative consumer of political services. The resultant convergence on the middle ground will no doubt appear excessive to the social philosopher – and Hotelling is one of these – who believes that too much conformity and uniformity is a bad thing: 'All the shoes are too much alike . . . Methodist and Presbyterian churches are too much alike; cider is too homogeneous.'[7] A bad thing or a good thing, Hotelling would, however, argue, concentration on the hump is likely to remain the order of the day.

Downs was much influenced by Hotelling's approach. Like Hotelling he conceives of opinions and preferences in terms of a continuous political spectrum going from Left to Right; and like Hotelling he also anticipates convergence on the middle ground occupied by the median voter, provided that, empirically speaking, there is indeed a single hump in some bell-shaped frequency distribution of attitudes. Like Hotelling he predicts that there will be *some* differentiation between the parties (the logical precondition for the *multi*-party system); and like Hotelling he explains the very existence of non-perfect substitutability in terms of the desire of each party to minimise the loss of extremists as well as to maximise the adherence of moderates. Naturally, Downs, like Hotelling, would accept that each party will presume that its own extremists will prefer it to the opposition even if does move in the direction of the centre in an attempt to pick up additional voters; but nonetheless, Downs, like Hotelling, would stress, the brand-loyalty of even the most loyal of extremists cannot be presumed to extend to the case where the parties become absolutely identical in the course of their campaign to maximise their appeal to the median voter. This process of convergence without duplication is well-described by Hotelling as follows: 'The Democratic party, once opposed to protective tariffs, moves gradually to a position almost, but not quite, identical with that of the Republicans. It need have no fear of fanatical free-traders since they still prefer it to the Republican party, and its advocacy of a continued high tariff will bring it the money and votes of some intermediate groups.'[8] Downs would see no reason to dissent from this analysis of convergent tendencies around a representative median in a world characterised by a high degree of social consensus.

Hotelling believed that the frequency distribution of opinions and preferences in the world around us was genuinely uni-modal or single-humped. Arthur Smithies, writing twelve years later, was, however, less confident about convergence, and reported that the political parties, in his view, showed no signs of becoming more alike: the cross-elasticity of substitution, he argued, is not high but low and 'equilibrium is frequently established, with the competitors free to move but spatially separated.'[9] The reason which he gives for such divergence is one which, but less prominently, may be found in Hotelling's analysis as well, namely that 'neither party feels itself free to compete with the other for the undecided vote at the center, in full confidence that it will retain its support from the extremes of political opinion.'[10] One would have expected an author writing in the year of Pearl Harbor to be more optimistic about national unity than one writing in the year of the Great Crash, but the fact remains that the opposite was the case – and that the inference to be drawn from Smithies' work is that, if the parties do attribute such value to the extremes that they are prepared to sacrifice to the periphery the support which they might have gained at the centre, they must have identified very significant concentrations indeed of Hotelling shoppers dwelling at some distance from Hotelling towns. This insight, in the work of Downs, becomes the basis for the assertion that, while social consensus is likely to breed political convergence, yet life in society *per se* is not *prima facie* evidence for the existence of social consensus. The economic approach to politics, starting as it does with economist's usual postulate of scarcity, would indeed appear by its very nature to be at least as compatible with social conflict as it is with social integration: 'The fact that the world's resources are limited creates in every society an inherent tension among social groups',[11] and therewith the possibility of a frequency-distribution of attitudes which is not uni-modal with a single hump (the case of the normal distribution in statistical theory) but bi-modal with two humps (the case of a polarised polity with two parties, one serving the Right, the other the Left, and neither the middle ground) or, for that matter, poly-modal with numerous humps (the case where there are many parties because there are many divergent but strongly-held points of view). Whereas in the uni-modal case parties tend to resemble one another, in the bi-modal or the poly-modal case they do not, but rather strive to pick up votes through differentiating themselves as clearly as possible from their rivals.

The Downs model has the useful property that it can explain both political convergence and political divergence, but three comments by way of criticism must in conclusion be made.

The *first* concerns the extent to which it is legitimate to conceive of opinions and preferences as distributed from left to right along an ideological axis for which the electoral scale may be said to serve as a proxy. The problem here is that, while it is easy enough to name single issues in the case of which such an approach might be valid (the denationalisation of the coal industry or of the National Health Service, for example, or the imposition of a wealth tax), it is no less easy to name other issues – issues such as Sunday trading, nuclear power, race relations, the rights of women – which seem to have no natural habitat in the party-political forest. This distinction is particularly important in the light of the fact that few elections in any case are fought on single issues. Most elections are fought on packages of issues (a clear case of Marshallian joint supply); and where those packages contain proposals of a non-left-to-right as well as of a left-to-right nature (the protection of an endangered species, let us say, alongside an increase or a reduction in the highest rates of progressive income tax), the voter is undeniably faced with a choice which only with great difficulty may be squeezed into the corset of the Downsian left-to-right spectrum. Nor should it be forgotten just how many parties in the world today see themselves as actors in a drama far removed from the normal story of left and right – populist and nationalist parties in France, racialist parties in South Africa, religious parties in Israel, ethnic parties in Malaysia, to name but a few. And it is worth sparing a thought for the position of the voter who dares not vote on the basis of ideological preference for the simple reason that he regards the current leadership of what, intellectually speaking, would be his favoured party as, instrumentally speaking, inefficient, ineffective, and unlikely to be capable of reaching the stated goals if given the power to try: such a voter might wish to use 'voice' to displace such perceived incompetents, but 'exit' in the direction of a reasonable alternative is the easier option should a close, even if not a perfect, substitute be seen to exist. All of which will serve to remind us that there is far more to opinions and preferences than is encompassed in the one-dimensional scale.

The *second* comment that must be made about the Downs model and its explanation of convergence and divergence is that, like the economic approach to consumer behaviour, the economic theory of democracy treats tastes and preferences as exogenous, independent of the process of want-satisfaction – whereas, a point already noted, it is likely to be the study of the politician, analogous to that of any other producer in this respect, to seek to mould and shape those attitudes in the way that Mr Rodgers has in mind when he reveals himself to be an ideologue with a definite view on the nature of 'the good life': 'I believe that politicians should offer some vision and should raise the sights of voters beyond their immediate objectives and expectations.'[12] What this can mean is that the humps, the modes and the medians are not constant but variable, and that the reason for the shifting and the regrouping is nothing less than the persuasive force of on-going debate and discussion itself. This process of alteration and revision of rankings is well described by Duncan Black when, taking a more microscopic case than that of the nation as a whole, he shows how, 'for example, trade union representatives who are deciding on hours of labour or wage rates, may be influenced late in the meeting, after their preference schedules have already been formed, by another speaker; and their preference schedules may be formed anew. The comparison used by our theory would now be, not between one recorded decision and another, but between the decision reached after this speaker has addressed them and the decision which would have been reached had the representatives voted before his speech was made.'[13] It clearly matters who is allowed to speak before the vote is taken (and, by extension, who is denied the opportunity) – and this manifestation of power exercised by the chairman at the level of words is strongly reinforced by the power that he exercises at the level of deeds. All issues, after all, are not decided simultaneously, and – because, 'whether in politics or economics, complementary valuation is the rule and independent valuation the exception'[14] – the outcome of a decision-making process often depends on the agenda, on the order in which the single issues are taken: thus a consumer-citizen might vote for policy B (an exceptionally high national budget) if it is put to him *after* the approval of policy A (a costly programme of repatriation of all coloured immigrants) but not *before*. Both through words and through deeds, in short, opinions can be altered by forces operative on the side of supply. The Downs model abstracts from such malleability – and from the role played by the chairman who selects and orders the speakers and the issues. It would probably be correct to identify the

Prime Minister as at least the principal chairman of the national debate; and as being able in that capacity, in conjunction with other participants in the political drama, to exercise an active influence on the distribution of attitudes along the Downsian spectrum.

The *third* and final comment that must be made about convergence and divergence in the sense of Downs refers to the voting rules within the framework of which political choices are made and elections are won or lost. These rules themselves can exercise a causative impact on the distribution of attitudes. The adoption of the first-past-the-post/winner-take-all system, for example, is likely to cause me to abandon the Temperance Party in favour of the Labour or the Conservative Party (to convert, in other words, a poly-modal into a bi-modal or even a normal distribution as a limping second-best); while the choice of a system of proportional representation is likely, other things being equal, to stimulate voter heterogeneity such as parallels social heterogeneity. The latter system is more likely to encourage the Parliamentary microcosm to be a representative cross-section of the national macrocosm and to allow the multiple humps associated with minority opinions to reveal themselves than is the former which is its principal alternative. This is not to say that it is the preferable option, only to stress that convergence and divergence in the sense of Downs cannot realistically be considered without explicit reference to the decision-making rules in operation.

2.2.2 The multi-party system

In a multi-party system such as might (but, of course, need not) result from the adoption of proportional representation, government is often by coalition where no one party has a clear mandate in the sense of a viable majority of seats. It is by no means easy to predict the policies that will be supplied in such circumstances.

From the point of view of the voter, even the most rational citizen cannot know in advance precisely what coalition and/or mix of policies his ballot is supporting. Nor can he be certain of the range of compromises which his favoured party will be willing to make in order to win office in a range of potential coalitions: such information is not so much secret in advance of the election as non-existent, depending as it does on the outcome of the contest and thus on how other men cast their vote. In such a situation of radical uncertainty, elections become games as each voter tries to outguess the other's moves; while, of course, given radical ignorance of future coalitions and hypothetical manifestoes, each voter also experiences considerable difficulty even in identifying his favourite party. Choice is easiest where the number of potential coalitions is small, the most likely policy-combinations are known, the distribution of voters along the Downsian scale is as predictable as evidence based on public opinion surveys can ever be. But even then the future is unknown and unknowable where policies supplied are concerned, and elections can hardly be regarded – neither by the players in the game nor by the amused spectator on the sidelines – as deliberately and consciously concerned with the selection of a precise and predictable package.

From the point of view of the coalition itself, once formed, policies are likely to be less consistent and less well integrated one with another than would be the case in the government-and-opposition world of, say, the two-party system: the whole point about coalition government is that an *ad hoc* mix of philosophies and measures is needed to please the majority, (albeit, in the case of each component minority, imperfectly), and that there need be nothing particularly logical about the precise nature of that mix apart from the incontestable fact that it represents the winning combination in the Parliamentary lottery. It would therefore be reasonable to suppose that the coalition takes less decisive action to deal with social problems than would have been the case had a single party formed the government.

From the point of view of each party in the coalition, pressures exist to defend the alliance *both* via ideological convergence (the desire on the part of the coalition-partners to be – and to be seen to be – a united team) *and* via ideological divergence (the desire to win maximum support for the coalition as a whole by appealing through differentiation to as wide a spectrum of public opinion as possible). Ideological divergence will in addition reflect the fact that each party in a coalition is in competition with its allies as well as its opponents: thus it will want to maximise its own share in the total vote for the coalition so as to strengthen thereby not the whole but rather its own position *within* the whole (as measured by number of posts and influence over policies). Yet such planned divergence will take place within a penumbra of planned ambiguity – partly so as to avoid alienating the party's traditional power-base (a particularly important consideration where that base is the principal source of campaign contributions and voluntary labour); partly so as to retain sufficient bargaining counters *vis-à-vis* the party's coalition-partners (present and future). Hence, and looking specifically at policies supplied, the participants in a multi-party system may be expected rationally to combine clarity with obscurity and to recognise the not inconsiderable political capital which is to be derived from selling known personalities in preference to vague policies.

2.2.3 The two distributions

There are in the modern occidental society two sets of distributions which influence the allocation of resources. The first, arising in the market economy, is the distribution of money incomes; and that by its very nature is unequal. The second, associated with the democratic polity, is the distribution of electoral power, and this typically takes the form of that strict equality captured by the concept of one adult/one vote. The modern occidental society, in this as in many another sense, is clearly an asymmetrical society. Social philosophers enamoured of the image of a consumer who 'votes' in the market place for the goods and services of his choice should perhaps be reminded of the differences as well as the similarities between the two distributions. They should also be reminded that a society with two distributions may well not be able to reach that position of social optimality popularly identified with the name of Pareto in which it is impossible to make some persons better off without making other persons worse off. At least in the modern mixed society, they should in no uncertain terms be informed, the social philosopher's lot is not a happy one.

Consider, with Downs, a society with only three citizen/consumers – A, B and C. A and B are unprepared (perhaps unable) to spend money on collective consumption and public goods. C is different: exceptionally distressed by the darkness in his front garden that is caused by the battery of trees in the public space opposite his house, he so greatly values sunlight that he is prepared to pay up to £2000 for the marginal utility or extra satisfaction that the removal of the trees would bring to him. C in the circumstances puts his problem before A and B, who tell him that they like shade but not very much and are prepared to do without it in exchange for the moderate sum of £100 each – provided, needless to say, that A not only pays them their compensation but also covers the full cost (£1000) of having the trees cut down. In such a case A and B neither gain nor lose in satisfaction while C is clearly better off: not only does he acquire a benefit for which he would have been willing to pay £2000, but he acquires it at the very reasonable price of £1200. And he learns to make interpersonal comparisons of utility by what would seem to be a remarkably tolerant method – by listening to the preferences that are revealed by the actors themselves, and adopting the view that they themselves (and not the empathetic spectator) are in the best position to supply information on cardinal utility through the valuations which they themselves propose in monetary units.

Let us suppose now that the same decision is politicised; that A, B and C are not merely citizen/consumers but also voters; that the public space is a public park; and that the question on the agenda is extra taxation to support the extra cost of an extra woodcutter. C detests the trees while A and B merely enjoy the occasional bit of shade. C in addition is willing to pay the entire cost of removing the trees while A and B are not keen to make any contribution at all. Because A and B are more numerous than C, however, the system of political democracy would cause the trees to remain; while the very logic of public goods supported by public finance renders it impossible for C to offer to take over from A and B the burden of the extra taxation. Once the decision is politicised, in other words, the outcome alters: the objective of the rational governing party being to maximise votes rather than to maximise utility, it has no choice but to please A and B (despite the fact that they are not far removed from indifference) and in consequence to displease C (despite the fact that he feels so strongly on the trees question that he would put a large sum of money where his mouth is – if only he could).

The government, in short, does not aim at equalisation of utility-returns as between different projects, and concentrates instead, by the very logic of its position, on the maximisation of vote pay-offs. If one businessman had an investment yielding 2 per cent and another were involved in a project worth 2000 per cent, the latter would seek to borrow the funds controlled by the former and would no doubt offer a premium in excess of 2 per cent for the privilege of the transfer. If, however, A and B are not far removed from indifference in the celebrated case of the umbrageous foliage towards which C apparently entertains such strong feelings of antipathy, yet C does not have a similar option to rent out A's vote and B's in an election focused on this single issue. I have an inalienable right to the pile of acorns currently accumulating dust in my ashtray; but I also have an inalienable right to alienate those acorns in your direction provided that our exchange is voluntary and that you offer me a proper consideration. The position with respect to my vote is somewhat different. I have an inalienable right to one vote. I have no inalienable right to swap my vote with you for an agreed sum of money. Both the acorns and the vote are my property. The former commodity you may buy or rent. The latter you may not have at any price. I retain the right to make no use whatsoever of my vote: save in that minority of countries where the duty of the citizen not to abstain has the force of law, there is no doubt that the voter has the freedom to opt out of voting. I do not retain the right to trade with you something which I hardly value at all (one vote) in exchange for something which, subjectively speaking, I value more highly (a sum of money): were I able to do this, then I, Mr A or Mr B, could offer to sell you, Mr C, my vote on the trees question in exchange for £100 (compensation for my loss of utility), plus £333 (my share in the extra taxation – £1000 divided by 3 – which you generously agreed to refund), plus, let us say, a surplus of £67 (a bribe or inducement which you offer me out of the money you save as a result of settling for less than the full £2000 that you were originally prepared to spend to rid yourself of the arboreal inconvenience). An outside observer who criticises Mr A or Mr B for spending one vote on £500 will be met with the reply that such a decision is of the same nature as C's decision to spend his money on the destruction of the trees, D's decision to buy gin rather than food, or E's decision to budget resources for something too unspeakable to mention. Property is property, A or B will say, and the individual is the best judge of his own interest. Yet the fact remains that while I normally retain the right to spend *less* than my one vote, you can never acquire the right legally to spend *more* votes than the one which is your own.

And it is here that our discussion of the two markets returns us to the discussion of the two distributions with which this sub-section began. In examining the second or politicised case we made the not unrealistic assumption that A, B and C are absolute equals in political power, the proprietors of a single vote each. In examining the first or arbitrage-through-compensation case, however, we carefully avoided the making of any assumption at all about the degree of equality or inequality which obtains when A, B and C go to market. Yet the principle of one adult/one (non-transferable) vote in the political market has no precise counterpart in the market economy, where the rule instead is different actors/different (transferable) incomes. If A, B and C were equal in incomes and merely differed in their taste for trees, some readers would no doubt be very much in sympathy with that market automaticity which allows all three individuals sensitively to equate subjective marginal cost and subjective marginal benefit – so much in sympathy, in fact, that those readers might even wish to see its extension to the political arena as well through an end to what they might describe as the obsolete prohibition on vote-selling. If A and B are very poor and C is very rich, however, then even the friend of the market mechanism might come to have reservations about the purchase and sale of consent, and might wish to argue that the principle of one adult/one (non-transferable) vote is functionally necessary if representative democracy is indeed to remain genuinely representative.

Vote-selling in a mixed society could well mean that the two distributions increasingly march in step, with the distribution of electoral power increasingly coming to parallel the distribution of money incomes. Each reasonably unconcerned citizen, aware how little one vote can influence national politics and how costly information can be, is likely to set a low reservation price on his vote, and the way would then be open for a few rich men, aware how valuable concentrated power can be to the seeker after privilege, to acquire large blocs and disproportionate influence. Such unequal command over commodities may be observed most days of the week at the caviar and emerald sections of Harrods. Vote-selling could well mean that such unequal command extended to commodities such as depreciation policy and capital gains tax as well. An unrealistic solution would be to compel the distribution of money incomes to parallel the distribution of electoral power, i.e. to institute uniform national remuneration: in such a case, if C still wanted to buy the votes of others on the trees question, the moral legitimacy of his action could at least be related to the fact that both A and B have the same income as C and thus the same potential power. A less unrealistic solution would be to allow selling but to encourage pooling of votes among members of the lower-income groups such as to give them countervailing power and therewith the opportunity to press for policies in their own favour. Since some low-income individuals are politically indifferent, however, while those who are rational will sell their vote and then try to free-ride on the less-than-rational who pool, perhaps the most desirable expedient is to retain the present system and the non-transferable vote.

Vote-selling in any case need not ensure equalisation for all persons of subjective costs and subjective benefits at the margin. In the original example of arbitrage-through-compensation, C had to bribe both A and B. In the second or politicised case he would need only to bribe one of them to secure a simple majority – and the other suffers both from loss of shade and from higher taxation without any offsets. Yet it is clearly irrational for C to bribe both A and B when it is unnecessary to do so. The net result is that the non-seller loses utility; that C pockets the difference; and that this is not what is understood by optimality in the sense of Pareto. There is much to be said for individually-negotiated compensation schemes. There is less to be said in defence of a free market in votes. Whether there is anything at all to be said for a free market in political services – the privatised situation in which the rational consumer attends an auction at the Shop of Commons and competes there to purchase the policies of his choice – must remain an open question. Downs and others would no doubt regard such fully entrepreneurial actions as unpatriotic and corrupt, mean and sordid. They should perhaps be reminded that it is not from the benevolence of the butcher, the brewer and the baker that we expect our dinner; that the butcher, the brewer and the baker expect to be paid not in power but in money; and that the very logic of the economic approach to political democracy would seem to suggest that every politician not only has but ought to have his price.

2.2.4 Competition and strategy

A government, in the Downs model, tries to maximise popular support. It therefore concentrates its efforts on supplying those policies which earn it the maximum number of votes and seeks to finance that spending by measures which will lose it the minimum. It may well be mistaken as to the precise location of the maxima and the minima; and those mistakes may well cost it the election. Apart from error and ignorance, however, there are cases in which even a well-informed and rational government can be defeated by the opposition – provided that the opposition has the Machiavellian common *nous* to utilise one of the following three competitive strategies to which Anthony Downs draws attention.

The *first* strategy involves 100 per cent matching of the present government's policies – if these are genuinely majority-pleasing, a well-informed and rational opposition really has no alternative but to follow suit – accompanied by an appeal to its own record when last in office. Assuming that its performance in the past appears attractive now when compared with that of the present government, it is then in a good position to argue that if it were once again in power it would do the same as the incumbent but do so better. Thus does consensus devour its children.

The *second* strategy involves a coalition of minorities. The opposition, if and only if the government must declare itself on each issue before its competitors reveal their stand, can in certain circumstances mobilise a majority of voters capable of defeating a majority-pleasing incumbent simply by adopting a minority-position on each key issue. Here the preconditions for success are, first, that more than half the citizens who vote are in a minority on some issue (i.e. that the government does not always please the same set of people when it takes the majority position on different matters because there is not perfect consensus within the electorate); second, that a voter holding a minority view has a stronger preference for those policies which he favours when in the minority than for those which he favours when in the majority (i.e. that voters feel more passionately when deviating from the normal view than when conforming to it); and, third, that the opposition is exceptionally well-informed as to the nature and strength of the voters' preferences (i.e. that it is able to an enviable extent to escape from that uncertainty which enshrouds most of human action in the real world). In such circumstances, if the government employs the majority principle consistently, the opposition can defeat it by supporting the minority position on every issue; while if the government takes a minority position on even one issue, the opposition can win the next election by matching it on every other issue but taking the majority position on that one. The result is that, theoretically speaking, government and opposition may be expected to alternate in power, each surviving no longer than a single election period at a time.

The *third* strategy involves the paradox of voting, the impossibility case most widely associated with Arrow's book of 1951 but which has in fact a long history that extends back, via E.J. Nanson (1850-1936) (especially his *Methods of Election* of 1907) and even Condorcet (1743–94) (especially his *Essai sur l'application de l'analyse à la probabilité des décisions rendues à la pluralité des voix* of 1785) to Jean-Charles de Borda (1733–99)) (especially his '*Mémoire sur les élections au scrutin*' of 1781). The impossibility case was known to Lewis Carroll when, at Christ Church, Oxford, he wrestled, his theory being much influenced by college practice, with the problems of voting, committees and decisions under his real name of the Reverend Charles Lutwidge Dodgson (1832–98) (especially in *A Discussion of the Various Methods of Procedure in Conducting Elections* of 1873 and in 'The Principles of Parliamentary Representation' of 1885).[15] The impossibility case is clearly somewhat older than *Social Choice and Individual Values*; but it is almost certainly in Arrow's important book that Downs, in common with many other economists and political scientists, first made its acquaintance.

The problem is this: if the number of mutually-exclusive alternatives is greater than two (so that some issues can be resolved by either *f* or *g* or *h*) and if the preferences of voters are disparate and diverse (so that there is no overall consensus among voters A, B and C), then no one of the three alternatives can get a simple majority over each of the others – and a government in power (however well-informed and politically adept it may be) will not be able to pursue a majority-pleasing strategy for the simple reason that no such strategy exists. Suppose the ranking scheme to be as follows:

Choice/Voter	A	B	C
First	*f*	*g*	*h*
Second	*g*	*h*	*f*
Third	*h*	*f*	*g*

In such a situation, no alternative enjoys majority support and the government party, whichever option it selects, is vulnerable to electoral defeat. The strategy of the opposition party should, in such a situation, therefore be to match the government on all other issues (i.e. to wait for the government first to commit itself and then promise an identical policy if elected), narrow the election to the one issue to which the paradox of voting relates, and then defeat the government by moving as follows: if the government picks *f*, the opposition picks *h* (which B and C prefer to *f*), if the government picks *g*, the opposition picks *f* (which A and C prefer to *g*), if the government picks *h*, the opposition picks *g* (which A and B prefer to *h*). Given such a game, there is no majority-pleasing policy whatsoever that the government could employ in a bid to win the election. Thus does lack of consensus devour its children. Only, however, if a number of rather restrictive assumptions are made.

We must assume, for one thing, that there exists some significant social problem with respect to which there obtain at least three mutually-exclusive solutions – as would be the case, let us say, were the issue to be unemployment and the options downward revision of expectations, fiscal stimulus to total demand and emigration of surplus population. Were the third alternative to be deleted, A, B and C would have to make a choice from a restricted range of only two possibilities and a majority-decision would be reached. Were, of course, a fourth alternative as well to be on offer (early retirement, for example), then a new ranking scheme could easily result in which it remained impossible for the incumbent to persuade any two of the three voters to prefer the same one of the four options to its three counterparts.

Then we must assume that the differences between the options are clearly specified and free of ambiguity – as would be the case, for instance, where voters took their decision to float or not to float on the basis of a single plank in an electoral platform, a single promise in a whole manifesto.

Yet the fact is that the normal election is not a referendum on the policy-alternatives that might reasonably be adopted to resolve a single problem (the problem, say, of unemployment, where the policy-alternatives are those, considered in the previous paragraph, of downward revision of expectations, fiscal stimulus to total demand and emigration of surplus population). Rather, the normal election is a multi-problem contest in which the voter is asked not so much to make decisions relevant only to single issues as to make choices among what Arrow calls 'social states', where a 'social state' is to be conceptualised as embracing 'a whole bundle of issues' and where in consequence 'the significant question is not the existence of a majority on each issue but the existence of a majority on the bundle of issues represented by the candidate over any other attainable bundle.'[16] Downs is enough of a social realist to appreciate the normal election is concerned with the bundle rather than with the singleton. Parliaments, he concedes, do indeed proceed *seriatim*, voting the first bill before the second and the second before the third. Not so electorates, however; and any argument would therefore be badly in error that rested, say, 'upon the voters considering each road-repair bill as an isolated act, separate from other such bills, rather than considering all repairs at once as part of a unified program.'[17] Not just road-repair bills, moreover, but all bills, since what most interests rational voters evaluating the record at discrete intervals is not the balance of net costs and net benefits with respect to a single measure but rather the balance with respect to the whole package – and this every politicians knows: 'He knows the voters will consider his performance as a whole . . . His survival in office is at stake, and politicians place a high value upon survival in office.'[18] The difference between Downs' broader approach to 'performance as a whole' and the narrower approach that he adopts when explaining how a rational opposition might make use of the paradox of voting in such a way as to defeat a rational incumbent is not, as it happens, great so long as the political parties offer similar packages on all issues (the environment, law and order, support to opera and ballet, race relations) save one (perhaps unemployment, the illustration given above). The real

difference arises where the parties differ on many issues; since there is
then no clear and unambiguous competitive strategy that the
opposition can employ in order, Arrow-like, to vanquish the
incumbent. This is not to say that the opposition has no chance of
defeating the incumbent by means of well-worn strategems such as the
remixed package and the redifferentiated product, only to say that in
such circumstances the paradox of voting cannot figure significantly in
any strategy that it might choose to adopt.

Another assumption that underlies the Downsian usage of the
Arrovian paradox is that of majority voting – obviously so, since there
is no point in employing a majority-pleasing electoral strategy if the
voting rule is to be unanimity of consent. The counterpart of every
pleased majority is, however, the displeased minority, and it is felt
concern for the position of the minority that has caused the political
economists of the Virginia School such as Tullock (who gives the
instance of the compulsory deportation of all Jews to Israel) to express
serious reservations about the employment of the majority rule.
Downs for his own part is a strong defender not only of the majority but
of the simple majority (of a voting-rule, in other words, that selects as
its cut-off point nothing more ambitious than the nearest whole
number above 50 per cent). His defence is based on his belief (which
the Jews compulsorily deported to Israel would probably not share)
that the tail ought not to wag the dog nor the minority be in a position
to tell the rest of us what to do. He defends his conviction that simple
majority is more in keeping with the ideal of equal citizenship than is
augmented majority in the following manner: 'Any rule requiring
more than a simple majority for passage of an act allows a minority to
prevent action by the majority, thus giving the vote of each member of
the minority more weight than the vote of each member of the
majority. For example, if a majority of two-thirds is required for
passage, then opposition by 34 per cent of the voters can prevent the
other 66 per cent from carrying out their desires. In effect, the opinion
of each member of the 34 per cent minority is weighted the same as the
opinion of 1.94 members of the 66 per cent majority. All rules of voting
other than the majority rule have this same defect.'[19] Downs is
therefore personally very much in favour of that kind of voting-rule
which is also the precondition for the instabilities of the Arrovian
paradox to manifest themselves in the political arena, and with respect
to which Tullock has issued a not unexpected warning: 'It may be that
the problems posed by Arrow and Black will eventually be solved, but,
until they are, arguments for simple majority voting rest on a perilous

foundation.'[20] Tullock's fears are, as it happens, far easier to share in the *seriatim* case of sequential single issues than in the package-deal case of bundled pluses and minuses. In the former case it is clear that if A and B are supplied with the policy which they demand then C is not, but condemned instead to the embittered minority-status of the cat that got the dog-food *and* had to pay for it. In the latter case, however, the position is more complex: alliances are revolving (A and B on one issue, B and C on the next), logrolling swaps are arranged (A's vote for B's on one bill, B's vote for A's on another), and political compensation may help in that way to minimise the extent to which a single minority bears the whole of the utility-loss associated with a negotiated parcel of policies. Nor should it be forgotten just how frequently it happens that the legal system takes upon itself the task of arranging for pecuniary compensation to be paid *ex post facto* to aggrieved minorities who are the innocent victims of the diswelfares imposed by majority rule: in the pure Arrow case if A and B decide to build a road where C's house now stands, then C must sleep in the park, but in the real world C is more likely to receive remuneration such as sugars the pill. All of which is to say that Tullock's fears with respect to majority voting may be exaggerated. Be that as it may, majority voting is quite clearly one of the assumptions that underlies the Downsian usage of the Arrovian paradox in the context of competitive strategies.

A further assumption is that the opposition party is able accurately to identify those issues which involve a paradox of voting and is able precisely to specify the preference-rankings of the voting public – a heroic postulation of perfect (or even adequate) knowledge of the As, the Bs and the Cs, the *f*s, the *g*s and the *h*s such as is far more common in the world of high theory than in that of practical politics. Of course opinion polls generate valuable information; but a sample is nonetheless not a population, nor an interview an election, nor yesterday's intent always a good indicator of tomorrow's action. Even if the opposition party should, therefore, succeed in plotting a map of today's preferences, it should never lose sight of the fact that that map is static while reality is dynamic. Free discussion within the community is likely to cause some voters to re-think their wants and opinions; and both the government and the opposition party will themselves no doubt be active in the attempt to alter the ranking scheme in their own favour, either by means of information (as where a party, to take a simple example, teaches the voter who simultaneously prefers health to illness and alcohol to tea that his orderings are inconsistent) or by means of manipulation (as where each party demonstrates a low level of self-denial and self-restraint by indulging irresponsibly in promise-inflation in the hope that myopic voter will fail to perceive that the price of short-run gain is long-run instability) or, indeed, by means of a change in the rule by which individual utilities are aggregated (either in the electorate at large or among its representatives in Parliament).

Arrow conspicuously neglects the ongoing nature of learning from experience and he excludes by assumption the restriction of citizen sovereignty by producer power ('The social welfare function is not to be imposed', let alone 'dictatorial',[21] he states), and it is for his underestimation of mutability over time which is absolutely continuous that thinkers such as Abram Bergson have rightly taken him to task. Thus Bergson writes: 'Arrow assumes that the individual values in social states are a datum. In the real world, of course, they are variable, at least, in the long run, and among other things are affected by the rule of collective decision-making itself.[22] Where reality is dynamic, uncertainty is endemic; and parties on the point of employing the impossibility theorem as part of their competitive strategy would in the circumstances be well-advised to proceed with care.

Yet another assumption is that of ideological flexibility – that an opposition party, in its pursuit of power, is fully prepared to do whatever is necessary in order to outmanoeuvre the competition, to checkmate the reigning champion. If, therefore, to return to our example of measures to combat unemployment, the government opts for expectations-policy the opposition counters with a call for emigration, whereas if the government goes for fiscal stimulus the opposition opts for expectations-policy. While not wishing to deny that such entrepreneurial alertness is as important in politics as it is in other areas of social and economic life, it must nonetheless be pointed out that persons or team of persons who continually change their mind on important issues are, in contrast to the small greengrocer who converts his shop to an off-licence or the Chinese restaurant which goes macrobiotic, less likely to be praised for their adaptability and flexibility than criticised for their instability and indecisiveness. Few voters will have much respect for a party which seems not to know its own mind – and this observation holds true whether voters make decisions on the basis of issues or on the basis of personalities. There is also an important point to be made about precommitment and the keeping of promises (even where the contract is not, as is the case with the political, legally enforceable), since few voters will have much respect for a party which seems not to have much respect for its own manifesto: if I voted for you because you told me in the course of your campaign that your bigotry matched if not exceeded my racialism, I will feel shocked and cheated if you subsequently redifferentiate your product in favour of unregulated immigration purely in order to make electoral capital out of an Arrow problem which you have correctly identified. While you, the producer, may well intend, once elected, to re-rat (and so repatriate the aforementioned immigrants, as you originally undertook to do), I, the consumer, may well lose confidence in your conviction and expect you to re-re-rat, should a new Arrow problem appear on the horizon. The conclusion that must be reached is that brand-loyalty in oligopolistic political competition may be significant but it is not infinite; and that tinkering redefinition on an ongoing basis may indeed win the support of marginal floaters, but perhaps only at the expense of alienating existing purchasers of a commodity now signally altered in its specifications. This constraint is regrettably absent from most models of changing horses in midstream in an attempt to capture the rent to opportunism. It is neglected, for example, by William Nordhaus, in his theory of the political business cycle and his assertion that the incumbent is likely to alter his economic policies halfway through a Parliament: 'Immediately after an election the victor will raise unemployment to some relatively high level in order to combat inflation. As elections approach, the unemployment rate will be lowered.'[23] It is neglected, similarly, by Anthony Downs, who in his account of the paradox of voting chooses to assume that there is no Phillips-like trade-off between plasticity and conviction. Should, however, it be the case that the would-be voter-pleaser stands to lose at least as much on the swings as he gains on the roundabouts, then he would have no rational choice but to consider carefully if it is indeed worth his while to win the battle but lose the war.

The final assumption that underlies the Downsian approach to the paradox of voting is that of heterogeneity of voter preferences. We must assume, in other words, that voters (or, more realistically, groups of voters) A, B and C genuinely differ radically in their attitudes and opinions. The possibility that this could happen cannot, of course, be ruled out altogether, and a society could presumably exist in which the population was splintered into three camps of more or less equal size on an important issue such as unemployment. Intuitively, however, one would expect there normally to obtain a relatively high degree of overlap of attitudes and bunching of opinions in a relatively homogeneous society with a single central value system and a single system of socialisation – and the greater the degree of consensus, the smaller the likelihood that an authentic impossibility case will arise. It is perhaps worth reflecting in addition that a society in which the disparate orientations that generate the paradox of voting were common might not merely be a society in which government and opposition succeed one another with revolving-door frequency but, more significantly, a society so chaotic as to render governance by the democratic system all but impossible.

What is in fact remarkable in the light of the Arrow paradox, is not how unstable and violent but rather how peaceful and conciliatory real-world democratic systems in fact turn out to be. The views of no less distinguished a theorist of collective action than Mancur Olson would seem to be particularly close to the mark: 'Since it is clear from Arrow's work that in certain circumstances social choices will not be stable and transitive, it might be supposed that government behavior would be too erratic and unstable to be efficient. Yet behavior of democratic governments does not often appear to be nearly as erratic or unpredictable as a naive application of Arrow's analysis might suggest. The conditions that give rise to the Arrow paradox often don't exist, and even when they do, the complex network of institutions and checks and balances in democratic governments may keep policy from changing rapidly enough to be erratic or unstable.'[24] Rapid policy-reversals are by no means common in the real world, Olson states (and where they occur it might be, he reflects, 'because the left hand of a bureaucracy has worked against the right hand for reasons that have nothing to do with the Arrow paradox');[25] and observations such as this lead him to the conclusion that, 'without denying the extraordinary theoretical and normative importance of the Arrow paradox',[26] still its practical significance would seem to be somewhat less than its analytical rigour. Olson's conclusion on the Arrow case of inconsistency and instability is that of John Plamenatz as well, who observes simply that 'such problems are of purely theoretical interest and politicians have not heard of them.'[27] It is also the conclusion of this sub-section on Competition and Strategy which, with its account of six restrictive assumptions that underlie Downs' use of the paradox of voting, brings this section on Policies Supplied to a close.

2.3 POLICIES DEMANDED

The discussion in the previous section on policies supplied in the democratic polity embraced four sets of observations – those grouped, respectively, under the headings of Convergence and Divergence, the Multi-party System, the Two Distributions and Competition and Strategy. Looking now at the act of vote-spending from the perspective of the sovereign consumer-citizen, we shall group our points concerning policies demanded under a similar number of headings.

2.3.1 The voting decision

Democracy in the sense of Downs involves voting and presumes rationality. Thence an intellectual problem and perhaps a central contradiction. Downs says that a citizen who values living in a democracy 'will actually get his reward even if he himself does not vote as long as a sufficient number of other citizens do.'[1] Downs does not say why any economising citizen should therefore vote at all.

What Downs does say is that voting matters since without it there would be no democracy: 'The advantage of voting *per se* is that it makes democracy possible. If no one votes, then the system collapses because no government is chosen. We assume that the citizens of a democracy subscribe to its principles and therefore derive benefits from its continuance.'[2] No absolute value is involved, and citizens desire to see democracy survive exclusively because of the private benefits which they expect to reap from it. The reader should in the circumstances take great care not to misinterpret passages such as the following: 'Rational men in a democracy are motivated to some extent by a sense of social responsibility relatively independent of their own short-run gains and losses.'[3] The focus here is not on 'social responsibility' but on 'rational men' and 'gains and losses', and long-run interest, not social duty, as rapidly becomes apparent, remains paramount: 'Each individual knows he can gain at some moments by violating the rules of the game, but he also knows that consistent violation by many citizens will destroy the game and introduce social chaos. Since he himself would be a loser if chaos prevailed, he resists the momentary temptation to let short-run individual rationality triumph over long-run individual rationality. Surely, such resistance is rational.'[4]

The Downsian point is clear enough, that voting *per se* is rational (even for a citizen who is totally indifferent as to the outcome of the election) since the very act of voting is low-cost insurance against the destruction of the democratic system itself. The Downsian logic is, however, less clear: if my fellow-citizens invest in the survival of the system, it is obviously irrational for me to waste time and effort in doing so as well, while if my fellow-citizens decide not to collaborate and insure, then the democratic system is hardly likely to be saved by my vote alone. It is in the circumstances something of a mystery as to why Downs is so strongly convinced that the rational citizen 'is willing to bear certain short-run costs he could avoid in order to do his share in providing long-run benefits'[5]: the rational citizen in the sense of Downs is surely not the man who is willing to 'do his share' at all but rather his mirror-image, the free rider who consciously abstains from contributing to the costs of a public good on the assumption that others will not do likewise and that the indivisible benefit will therefore continue to be provided. What each can do in the area of abstention, naturally enough, all cannot; and, given that 'each citizen is thus trapped in a maze of conjectural variation',[6] one would have expected Downsian man to be an advocate of constraint, either moral (a sense of collective commitment) or social (the case of informal sanctions such as ostracism being applied against the self-interested and calculatively rational volunteer fire-fighter who fiddles while Rome burns) or legal (as where voting *per se* is compulsory). What Downs himself says is rather different, that individual uncertainty has the same *de facto* impact as constrained certainty: given that not all voters are likely to think alike, dispersion itself ensures that while some will be confident enough to abstain, others will be anxious enough to vote – thereby rescuing the whole democratic enterprise from the status of a party which no one bothered to attend. Tullock has come up with yet another explanation of the voting decision, also rooted in individual rationality but focusing in this case on the entertainment value of the theory of – quite literally – *games*: 'The basic reason for the flourishing nature of our democracy is the fact that politics is our most popular hobby.'[7] Selective incentives evidently cast giant shadows.

Whatever the 'basic reason' (and while the purchase of entertainment is in some measure compatible with Downsian perspectives on calculative rationality, the internalised norms of a Kantian gentleman driven to 'do his share' because of a strong sense of civic duty can only by means of a virtually tautologous definition of the calculative and the rational be made such), the fact remains that people do vote. Downs notes, however, that those who vote and those who do not are unlikely to be a random cross-section of the community. The percentage of low-income citizens who abstain in elections is, he argues, likely to be higher than the percentage of higher-income citizens who abstain, *ceteris paribus*. The explanation which he gives for this phenomenon involves both the direct cost of voting (purchase of information, polling charges where levied, transport to and from polling stations) plus the opportunity cost of voting (where elections are not held on evenings or at weekends and voters lose income when they take time off work – a problem more for the voter on piecework than for the citizen on a salary); and it also involves expected benefit (as where a poor and uneducated man, because of lack of information and/or general knowledge, incorrectly believes his party-differential to be small and for that reason decides not to vote). Whatever the explanation, the implication is clear, that the electorate is likely to have a class-bias because of differential participation-rates and that this bias is likely to have some impact on the nature of policies demanded.

2.3.2 Investment in information

Each individual is assumed, in the Downsian model, rationally to maximise his utility-income (including that portion of his utility-income which is derived from government activity), rationally therefore to cast his vote for the party which will yield him the highest stream of expected benefits. But to behave in so rational a manner the individual must acquire information. He must study the present performance of the party in power (possibly weighting the data by a trend factor to pick up improvement or deterioration in competence), the past performance of the opposition when in government (such historical evidence being particularly valuable where the policies proposed by the parties appear very similar and the election must be decided on technical expertise alone), and the electoral promises of the parties (although no rational voter will rank words as highly as deeds when trying to work out his expected party differentials). Clearly, voting is not a free good but one which necessitates costs if it is maximally to afford benefits; and the real question then becomes whether the return on a marginal investment of scarce resources is an adequate one. In making his decision the rational citizen will take some or all of the following considerations into account.

First, vote-value. The probability that one man's vote will sway the election is very small (but not zero), and it is highly unlikely that the wrong party will be elected should one man vote without having collected sufficient information. Just as it is irrational to vote at all, so it is irrational, where one vote has little chance of influencing outcomes, to waste scarce resources on overcoming uncertainty.

Second, party differential. If the voter believes the parties will yield him approximately the same utility-income, the expected benefits from his voting correctly (as compared with the expected benefits should he make a mistake) are low – and the incentive to incur information-costs correspondingly small.

Third, initial prejudice. The more strongly a rational voter initially favours one party, the less likely he is *ceteris paribus* to buy information: new facts are less likely to cause him to change his mind and are therefore a less valuable acquisition. The more strongly, of course, a *non*-rational voter initially favours one party, the more likely he is *ceteris paribus* to buy information (in order to follow the fortunes of his favourite team) and even to cast his vote without a thought as to vote-value (in order to express his deeply-felt emotive affiliation with the lads in the trenches) – all of this being well and good but also irrelevant to a discussion of the behaviour-patterns of the *rational* voter.

Fourth, free riders. Political democracy operates most sensitively when citizens are well-informed. Yet it is fully rational for the individual citizen not to invest in information at all (in the limiting case, to vote at random) so long as the others do not also shirk their share of the costs. Even, therefore, where a democracy compels its citizens not to abstain (and such compulsion is itself costly in terms of economic resources and of individual freedom), still it cannot force them to make themselves wise (not least because of the fact that there is no reliable, objective, inexpensive and unambiguous way of measuring how much relevant political information a voter actually possesses when he comes to vote). The most a democracy can do is to ensure that background knowledge on socio-political issues is provided in the schools. This, however, does not resolve the Citizen's Dilemma of the adult who rationally underinvests, gambling that others will not do likewise. If rational, they will; and the outcome will be rather like the situation which results when each of two clinging vines decides to utilise the other for support.

Fifth, strategic voting. It is sometimes said that there is no analogue in the political market to the economist's notions of saving rather than spending, investing rather than consuming. It is, of course, obvious that a vote not used in the election of 1851 cannot be married to its successor in the election of 1852 in such a way as to grant its proprietor two votes, nor invested at compound interest in such a way as to yield him nine votes in 1911: a society which forbids vote-selling is unlikely to treat with any greater sympathy practices such as vote-hoarding and vote-lending. One suspects nonetheless that a less literal approach to the definition of saving and investing is capable of generating quite useful predictions. In certain circumstances, for example, voters are known rationally to support a party other than the one they would most like to see in office not merely because they are convinced that their favourite party stands no chance of being elected (a reason for moving to the second-choice so as not to waste the vote) but – the crucial point in the present context – because they wish to register the information that they now regard their favourite party as being too moderate or too extreme. Such voters are clearly treating their vote not as short-run consumer spending but as an investment project with a long-run payoff, and the same may be said of those activists who conspicuously abstain from voting at all: such behaviour is entirely rational where they recognise that their party is not a homogeneous team and are confident that an electoral defeat will alter the balance of power in favour of the alternative wing. Similarly, some voters rationally protect a hopeless party with their vote on the basis of logic such as is employed when their nation protects an infant industry with a tariff – as where those voters are future-orientated and believe that the party (possibly a new one occupying the centre-ground between two existings peaks) will not remain a hopeless cause given time. In the case of that saving and investing of votes which takes the form of strategic voting, however, action is particularly risky in view of the extent to which the results expected are not expected for a considerable period of time; and that suggests in turn that such action will not take place without a considerable prior investment in information. I can afford not to become informed at all should I regard my current vote-value or my party differential as zero. I cannot afford the luxury of such ignorance should I regard my vote, following Downs, as part of a long-term strategy to alter the *status quo*.

2.3.3 Information without investment

Information is never completely free in view of the fact that the time needed to absorb it is without any doubt a cost. Much information is nonetheless free in the sense that no pecuniary marginal cost must be incurred in order to acquire it.

Which is not to say that free information is free of class-bias or that all members of the community enjoy equality of opportunity with respect to information without investment. Downs seems if anything himself to believe the opposite, citing as he does two instances of probable imbalance accompanied by two cases of possible imbalance. The *first* case of probable imbalance involves access to high-quality informal contacts. Thus the chief executive of a giant corporation receives better free information from colleagues and friends (many of them experts, specialists, professionals and analysts in their own right) than does, say, a typical manual labourer on the typical shop floor. The chief executive is also more likely than is the manual labourer to lunch with politicians and bureaucrats, and to obtain information of a specifically *political* nature in that way – perhaps in exchange for important intelligence concerning the business sector of the economy to which the manual labourer (or even his union) simply does not have access.

The *second* case of probable imbalance involves type of entertainment. Clearly, a man who reads history as a hobby is more likely to absorb free information with socio-political relevance than is one who reads crime novels and the same line of reasoning may be extended to the choice of radio and television programmes (since different programmes convey different doses of the unintended by-product of informal education). Rich and poor do not enjoy identical amounts of formal education; they do not have the same sub-cultural norms with respect to leisure-time interests; and there is accordingly some reason to expect some difference in quantity and quality of reliable, socially-significant information which they unexpectedly acquire by virtue of the type of entertainment which they consume.

Turning now from probable imbalance to possible imbalance, the *first* case here involves time and the *second* involves status. With respect to time, it is certainly possible that high income is correlated with abundant leisure in which to acquire information – except that many rich men are such precisely because they are overworked, while many within the leisured classes demonstrate no abnormal concern with intellectual values. With respect to status, it may well be that persons in well-off *milieux* are able to obtain prestige by appearing knowledgeable about politics – except that inquisitiveness, gregariousness and the status derived from information are found to some extent in all income groups (it is not just in the Senior Common Room but in the works canteen as well, after all, that newspapers are read and sociable conversations on political issues take place). When speaking of time and status, therefore, Downs is only able to identify a possible inequality in access to free information, in contrast to the probable imbalance which he is prepared to diagnose in the case of informal contacts and type of entertainment. All talk of inequality and imbalance, however, reminds us of the fundamental point that is being made – that equality of voting rights should not be assumed automatically to be accompanied by equality of *informed* participation. To the extent that an informed citizen is better able to make a rational choice than is a less informed citizen, moreover, to that extent his vote is likely to be a more high-powered, more finely-tuned vote. Certain periods and societies have seen fit to give educated persons *de jure* superior voting rights. Downs' analysis suggests that perhaps – *de facto* – we do the same.

2.3.4 Democracy and economic policy

One of the most interesting tasks which an economic theory of democracy can undertake is to seek to formulate predictions concerning the specifically *economic* policies that are likely to be demanded in a society which enjoys the benefits of democratic institutions. Downs suggest three such predictions. Not one of them is likely to inspire the reader with any real confidence in the optimality of the outcomes thrown up by the political democracy.

The *first* prediction is that economic policy will be biased towards producers and away from consumers – and this despite the obvious fact that the consumers of almost every good are far more numerous than the producers and governments must gain the support of the majority, not the minority, if they are to retain their power. Downs' argument, however, is that each of us is a member of a (producing) minority as well as of the (consuming) majority; that each of us is, in the language of ordinal utility, likely consistently to rank the former affiliation above the latter; and that all of us are, cardinally speaking, likely to feel so passionately about our minority interest that we are susceptible of putting it far above our felt interest when in the majority.

Our reasons for doing this are entirely logical. On the side of benefits, we spend in many areas but normally earn in only one; and we therefore come to believe that what matters most to us is the disproportionate gain which we make from the introduction of an income-boosting measure such as a licence restricting entry into our trade – not the tiny loss which we experience as consumers from, let us say, the adoption of a 10 per cent tariff on the importation of potatoes.

On the side of costs, moreover, and precisely because we spend in many areas but normally earn in only one, the extra expense incurred to procure the extra information is perceived by us to be relatively low: information-gathering correlated with specialised economic function in a world of division of labour is very likely indeed to be widely regarded as a far cheaper activity than is the acquisition of data concerning areas with which we are less intimately acquainted. The benefits, in short, are widely regarded as being disproportionately high, the costs as being relatively low; and both causes together help to account for a bias in national decision-making in favour of those who produce, not those who consume, in a given field.

Nor do rational producers stop there. They pool information and obtain economies of scale in the collection and dissemination of data; they present, as a lobby, sophisticated arguments to government (and typically the cost is tax-deductible); and – a further point – they make available free but slanted information to the general public in an attempt to convince the majority that the vested interest of a minority is in fact the national interest of the collectivity as a whole. Much of this free information is, ironically enough, not free at all; as where it takes the form of commercial advertising ultimately paid for by the consumer of the product. The present point, however, is not one about cost so much as about manipulation; and it reinforces the other reservations which Downs clearly entertains concerning the role of the producer interest in the formulation of the economic policy of a democratic society.

The *second* prediction is that democratic governments have an in-built tendency to redistribute income from the rich to the poor. The reason is obvious: the distribution of income being pyramid-shaped, the have-nots towards the bottom are far more numerous than the haves towards the top, and it is therefore worth the while of a rational government to sacrifice the support of the minority in order to acquire that of the majority. Thus does others' envy make cowards of parties all.

It is well-known, of course, that equality of voting rights does not produce equality of after-tax incomes; and this means that limiting factors to envy, given political democracy, must exist and must be identified. Downs for his own part draws attention to what he regards as three such limiting factors. The first is economic – that governments do what is necessary to ensure proper incentives to effort (even, apparently – the reason for such a decision is not given – where it costs them votes in an attempt to stimulate a sound rate of economic growth for which their successors in office will then be able to claim the credit). The second is societal – that today's poor hope to be tomorrow's rich and are thus marginally less intolerant of inequality than they would have been in the absence of so optimistic a bias to their uncertainty (the rags-to-riches image of the open society clearly benefiting the relatively privileged at least as much as it does the relatively deprived). The third is political – that wealthy individuals are able to harness pecuniary motivation to the chariot of fiscal moderation (in forms ranging from campaign contributions to offers of future employment by way of the occasional packet of notes or gratuitous trip to Bermuda) in order in this way, following the exemplary precedent of the butcher, the brewer and the baker, not to beg but rather to *buy* the requisite political influence for themselves.

The Downsian possibles of (economic) growth through (political) suicide, unquenchable optimism breeding unrealistic aspirations and the putting of the money where the mouth is are by no means the only reasons why redistribution stops when it does (the most obvious factor, that most of us if situated behind a thick Rawlsian veil would probably regard total levelling as simply *unfair*, is not mentioned), and no account may in addition reasonably be regarded as complete which ignores countervailing forces such as left-wing political ideas or the power of militants in parties and unions. Nor is it entirely satisfying to identify redistribution of income with the progressive income tax *per se*: the State supplies benefits as well as imposing costs, after all, and it is not the council-house tenant or the addict in receipt of social work who is mostly likely to have three children at university, to be the recipient of a grant to new industry in a development area, or to require the services of the State-supplied export credit guarantee in order to boost his income. It is, one is compelled to say, far from obvious that democratic governments do in fact have an in-built tendency to redistribute income from rich to poor.

Even if that prediction were indeed to constitute a testable hypothesis subsequently proven true, moreover, the same can hardly be said of Downs' explanation of the root causes of the phenomenon: he attributes moderate levelling to majority pressures from below, another thinker would explain it in terms of a rational investment made by rich risk-averters in the survival of the capitalist system, and it is all but impossible in practice to discriminate between the alternative hypotheses. The same observation must be made about Downs' first prediction: he says that economic policy will be biased towards producers and away from consumers, but not only are the roles of the

majority and the minority there unexpectedly inverted as compared
with the second prediction (in that way undermining confidence in the
theory), not only is no conclusive evidence in fact presented to show
that the interests of real-world consumers are *on balance* frustrated by
the interests of real-world producers (selective anecdotes do not make
up a complete picture where representativeness is essential), but the
Downsian hypothesis (which focuses on differential awareness of gains
and losses) is in most cases indistinguishable on the basis of results
from its Marxian competitor (which focuses on bourgeois policies
favouring the class-interest of the bourgeois minority). Nor is Downs'
third prediction any more obviously testable: a theorist who takes as
his ideal and his bench-mark the perceptions that would arise if
information were perfect, but who then immediately concedes that
'even if the world's most brilliant man spent twenty-four hours a day
reading newspapers and journals, he would be unable to keep himself
well-informed about all aspects of [public] policies',[8] is unlikely to be
taken seriously when he says that phenomenon A in the real world is
too large, phenomenon B too small. In the case of Downs' first
prediction and of his third, in short, the same observation would seem
to be called for as in the case of the second – that non-testable
propositions deduced from non-empirical assumptions can hardly be
said to satisfy the strict and scientific standards which are captured by
Downs in his declaration that his theory can indeed by employed 'to
reach significant, non-obvious conclusions applicable to the real
world'.[9]

The *third* prediction – a late addition by Downs to his theory but an
important one – is that the government budget is too small in a
democracy. Buchanan, Tullock and other Virginia authors have, as is
well known, tended to argue the opposite, that political democracy
leads to an over-expansion of the State sector.[10] Downs does not
answer all of their contentions (some of which, notably vote-buying via
the expansion of public services, are easily deduced using his own
logic), but he does take issue with them on the question of whether it
might not be the case, given majority voting, that government
spending swells to super-optimal size precisely because majority and
minority alike are compelled to pay via taxation for public goods from
which the majority alone derives the utility. His *critique* alludes to the
implicit Wicksellianism of the package deal (a point considered in the
previous section) but otherwise appears, contrary to Downs' avowed
intentions, to lend a certain measured support to the Virginia view:
'Clearly', he writes, 'no voter will support a program which requires

him to pay more in taxes than he receives in benefits if a better alternative is available. Hence, no party will formulate a program which requires a majority to do this. It is true that a majority bloc might form and vote roads only for itself, paid for both by itself and by the minority who get no roads. . . . Thus, a minority might find itself sustaining net losses through government action. But this conclusion is vastly different from [the] argument that all citizens (or at least a substantial majority) would be net losers. Since the majority would be net gainers, we could not conclude that the government budget was too large.'[11] Downs' *critique* of Virginia on over-supply does not entirely convince, but neither, to be honest, does his own defence of the opposite position, his own assertion that, because of division of labour and specialisation of knowledge, the State sector is likely actually to be under-expanded and sub-optimal in size: 'Society's complexity demands more government action, but it also makes each field of action more remote from the ken of the average man . . . Thus, as remote benefits become more important, they become less likely to be attained.'[12] Less likely to be attained, one hastens to say, not because less desirable: on society's needs (as opposed to individuals' wants), on the functional requirements of an interdependent collectivity, on the proper position within that social organism of the State, Downs writes with all the conviction of the beneficent ruler who has acquired perfect knowledge at zero cost rather than as a cautious thinker who has studied with profit *An Economic Theory of Democracy*. Less likely to be attained, one is compelled to stress, because less visible. A little evolution is a dangerous thing, it would appear, where one hand becomes less and less aware of what the other is doing and actors reveal in consequence of such ignorance preferences different from those which they would have revealed had they only been better informed.

Given increasing social complexity, Downs argues, taxes are bound to become relatively more visible (and therefore more resented) as compared with the benefits which they help to finance (particularly where those benefits are by their nature remote, uncertain and difficult to publicise). Consider the case of economic aid given by a superpower to a small and distant country. That economic aid would be fully in the economic self-interest of the rational citizen of that superpower were he aware of the high probability that without such aid there would be a revolution in the distant country that would then involve his own country, at even greater cost, in the provision of military aid. Yet that rational citizen will probably be unaware of the strong case to be made in favour of such economic aid – and this precisely because he is rational. Increasing social complexity may, after all, be compared to an increasingly well-stocked supermarket. Resources being scarce, the rational shopper must make a choice, and in the market for information what this is likely to mean is that the rational citizen will rationally choose marginally to economise on knowledge where issues which he somehow regards as marginal are concerned. His choice may prove a bad one – he may later come to experience the disappointment and the regret which will instantly be recognised by all rational shoppers whose *ex posts* have ever failed to live up to their *ex antes*. What he cannot avoid, however, is the need to make a choice *per se*. Thence the prediction – that 'rational ignorance among the citizenry leads governments to omit certain specific types of expenditures from their budgets which would be there if citizens were not ignorant.'[13]

Hence the problem – that the representative citizen's perceived welfare would actually be increased by the State expenditures and that it would nonetheless be irrational for a majority-pleasing government to give him benefits of which he is either completely unaware or at least less aware than he is of the well-advertised private sector satisfactions which he must sacrifice in order to support the burden of his taxes: 'Hidden benefits cannot influence votes',[14] evolution brings complexity and hiddenness, and that is why the government budget is too small in a democracy.

Downs' assertion that the complexities of social evolution necessitate increased collective intervention is, naturally, a highly controversial one. If, however, his analysis were to be correct, then a solution to the problem would have to be sought, and sought within the framework of the model which spawned the dilemma.

One obvious solution is the expanded provision of free information on the costs and benefits of State activities. Hidden benefits cannot influence votes. This solution would have the merit of making clear precisely what benefits were indeed on offer, and at precisely what cost. Many of us, for example, know nothing of the free eye-testing in schools which helps to identify an uncorrected squint before it comes to put a far greater financial strain on the National Health Service; and few of us have ever stopped to think just how many crimes in the West End of London are never actually committed because the potential pickpocket knows something that you and I do not – that there are on duty a large number of policemen in plain clothes. One obvious solution to the Downsian problem of under-provision of services is, accordingly, the expanded provision of information about services provided: given that 'ability to pay and desire to pay are not identical',[15] it is clearly desire to pay that must be manipulated – and manipulated, perhaps, in no more sinister a manner than by producing the previously unitemised bill. Gordon Tullock, speaking of the ethical sensibilities of the member of an interest-group, points out just how high the return can be to a deliberately *low* level of investment in information: 'It may, indeed, be better for the pressure group voter not to know much about particular issues. Surely, the more the Iowa farmer had learned about the farm program, the more likely he would have been to have felt that there was a potential conflict between his ideas of right and wrong and his material interests. By not thinking much about the issue, he was able to follow his self-interest with a clear conscience.'[16] Anthony Downs, speaking of why the government budget is too small in a democracy, could have made a similar point concerning the potentially high payoff to a *high* level of information-diffusion. In order to be fully in keeping with the spirit of his own model, however, Downs would have had then to state that diffusion must not be confused with absorption, in view of the fact, previously mentioned, that even free information is never completely free because time is itself a cost. So great a cost, one would have thought, that expanded provision of free information on an increasingly complex future can never be a complete solution to the Downsian problem of improper outcomes where ignorance is rational.

An alternative solution, the standard Galbraithian solution, is paternalism and discretion – the situation where voters delegate decision-making powers on all but general guidelines to trustworthy leaders and expert advisers, subject to the clear requirement that the leaders and the advisers continue to retain their confidence. For such a system to operate smoothly it is not necessary for the agent to regard office-holding as a means rather than an end or to see himself as a philosopher-ruler forcing through policies which are in the interests of all but not of each. On the contrary: for such a system to operate smoothly it is only necessary for the principal to renew the contract of the agent at regular intervals and to signify in that way that the exchange relationship remains intact. There is, it must be said, at least one very important reason for thinking that such democratic paternalism, such contractual discretion, might not after all be the solution to the problem of under-provision caused by the ignorance of the voters, and that reason is the ignorance of the leaders and the experts themselves. It is, after all, not just the citizen and the party in the Downsian model that suffer from radical uncertainty – that find it difficult to predict uncertain turnouts of the voters and the extremists or to anticipate the market strategies of oligopolistic competitors – but the government itself. Thus Downs points out that the State, in the example previously considered of the trees and the shade, *could* levy a tax on C in order to subsidise and thereby compensate A and B; but he quickly introduces a note of realism by adding that 'lack of knowledge about the preferences of individual citizens makes it technically impossible for the government to discriminate either accurately or inexpensively.'[17] Downs for similar reasons give short shrift to the no doubt very clever construct of a tax on potential earnings (as opposed to the present-day tax on income actually earned) in order to discourage that tax-avoidance which takes the form of substitution of leisure for work: such a tax, he comments, would be a great success, provided only that the government had the ability 'to read minds or to judge income-earning potentials infallibly'.[18] The government, it is obvious, does not have that ability; and the question then becomes the open one of whether its undeniable ignorance (with respect, say, to the unique individual's perceived marginal utility schedule or felt marginal cost) is so great as to invalidate the wise leaders/regular elections solution to the problem – always assuming it is a real problem – of a government budget that is, regrettably, too small in a democracy.

Always assuming it is a real problem. Downs and Galbraith assert that it is a real problem, Buchanan and Tullock assert that it is not a real problem, and Harry Johnson, characteristically cautious about any real problem that is not his own, asserts that the real problem associated with the government budget in a democracy is not one of size at all but rather one of composition: 'My own view . . . is that neither general proposition is correct, but that instead the governmental process tends to under-allocate resources in some directions and over-allocate them in others.'[19] The social services and the relief of poverty are under-funded, Johnson says, and the reason is quite simply the interested individual's calculus of private costs and private benefits – because, in other words, 'for such items of public expenditure the social return is nebulous and problematical to the average citizen while the private cost to the taxpayer, and especially the fact that the cost is incurred largely for the benefit of others, is all too clear.'[20] National defence and the subsidisation of long-established industries, on the other hand, are over-funded – a phenonmenon, Johnson reflects, which hardly comes as a complete surprise to any observer familiar with the disproportionate political influence exercised by the concentrated as compared with the diffuse, the producer as compared with the consumer, the old as compared with the new, the senescent as compared with the burgeoning: 'The political process is inherently conservative, in the sense that it is strongly biased towards the preservation of what currently exists rather than the promotion of change and development.'[21] Johnson's logic and method of analysis will be more than familiar to the reader of the three sections of the present chapter, and so too will be his debt to the deductions of Downs on democracy – with a select number of other innovative contributions such as that of Becker to the theory of human capital and of Stigler to the economics of information, Johnson maintained, one of the 'new developments and insights of analytical economics that have made it a more useful and illuminating guide to the understanding of contemporary society.'[22] The fact that Downs and Johnson diverged in their reactions to the size of the budget is thus of considerably less significance than the fact that they both took the view that the market paradigm was an extremely valuable analytical tool for the purposes of providing an accurate picture of collective action in modern society.

For it is the provision of an accurate picture that in the last analysis most powerfully legitimates the enterprise of both authors. As Harry Johnson puts it, expressing his regret that professional economists are more and more retreating from relevance and reality into the abstruse abstractions of 'set theory, mathematical models and regression results', what economists most need now is new tools that will enable them to make a useful contribution to the wider society: after all, he says, 'economics is essentially a *social* science, concerned to further understanding of society by the application of scientific methods of analysis and research to the economic aspects of society's activities.'[23] Anthony Downs, one feels sure, would agree most sincerely with the nature of Harry Johnson's aspirations. Whether *An Economic Theory of Democracy* actually satisfies Johnson's twin criteria of relevance and reality is a matter, however, about which it is somewhat more difficult to be certain.

3 Organisations and Interests

Much of traditional economic theory is predicated on the proposition that scarce social resources are normally allocated by the price mechanism and that the inner workings of organisational structures are of little relevance to the student of production, consumption and distribution. The traditional economist tends therefore to formulate his arguments in terms of market exchanges, while leaving to the social psychologist and the sociologist of bureaucratic behaviour the study of the institutional black box: his concern being with individuals making choices, he reasons, there is simply no need for him to look in any detail at the manner in which obedient servants and faceless automatons passively administer endowments which are not their own. The good steward has no personal impact on the decisions made, the goals adopted: his role is exclusively to execute the commands passed down to him that originate with his employer. The bad steward does have a personal impact on the direction taken by the whole (much as a runaway horse can influence the itinerary of a coach journey) but only until his employer learns of the commands that were not executed and opts to execute the bad steward in their place. Either way, the traditional economist concludes, there is no need for him to treat internal organisation as if it were a significant mode of resource allocation in its own right: stewards do as they are told or discover the true meaning of the Visible Boot.[1]

Much of traditional economic theory adopts the constructs of self-interest and calculative rationality; and Anthony Downs, as we saw in the previous chapter, applies those very constructs to the non-economic allocative processes of the political market. Downs' view of politicians and voters as egoists, not altruists, has been called cynical and selfish; and in a sense it undeniably is. Such is the cost, however, of a homogeneous and unified theory of human action, since Downs has done no more than to extend to the political market a framework of discourse long accepted without question in the case of the economic. Having satisfied himself that the exercise could usefully be performed for politicians and voters, Downs not surprisingly turned his attention to the behaviour-patterns of the stewards that they employ. His framework of discourse was that of traditional economic

60

theory. His conclusions were not. It is with those conclusions – and with the non-neutrality of bureaucracy in the specification of the public interest – that we shall be concerned in this chapter. If much of welfare economics is concerned with market failure and much of the previous chapter was devoted to government failure, then it would be true to say that the *leitmotiv* of the present discussion is organisational failure, so much is this chapter the story not of pre-programmed robots responding without thinking to the will of others but of self-conscious utility-maximisers with a unique will of their own and perhaps even the power to impose that will on the rest of their community. The ideological implications of a situation wherein the voter hires a politician who then hires a bureaucrat who then inverts the master-servant relationship by proclaiming himself the best judge of the citizen's genuine interests (as opposed to revealed preferences) are not without ambiguity. The reader would do well to remember, however, that organisational success may well offset organisational failure; and that no one but a charlatan or a fool allows himself to become so obsessed with the liabilities that he forgets to blend in the assets.

3.1 METHODOLOGY

The approach which Downs adopts in *Inside Bureaucracy* is that of methodological individualism. His unit of analysis is the goal-orientated individual bureaucrat (not the inanimate bureaucratic structure), his point of departure the irrefutable fact that even civil servants have tastes and preferences, his general conclusion that bargaining and exchanging *within* organisations can play an important part in the specification of collective ends. His assertion that only persons can have attitudes and make decisions would seem to be self-evident, however much it would also seem to be at variance with those theories of bureaucratic behaviour which assign pride of place to the immutable organisational chart and the clearly-prespecified role of the cog in the wheel. It is also an assertion which Downs is hardly alone in making. William Niskanen was to say as much four years later in his *Bureaucracy and Representative Government* of 1971 while Gordon Tullock had applied methodological individualism to organisational theory two years before Downs in his *The Politics of Bureaucracy* of 1965. Downs frequently pays tribute to Tullock's insights ('The basic idea for this section has been taken from the work of Gordon

Tullock',[1] he states in one place; 'This usage is taken from Gordon Tullock',[2] he announces in another), as indeed does Niskanen: 'Tullock is always provocative and stimulating. I and many others owe him a great debt for stimulating our own thinking.'[3] All three authors in turn cannot but have been much stimulated by Mises' *Bureaucracy* of 1944, the first attempt at a subjectivist theory of structured hierarchy. But none of this must be taken as detracting in any way from the originality and significance of Downs' *Inside Bureaucracy* of 1967: more systematic than Mises' and Tullock's, more guarded about unwarranted precision than Niskanen's, Downs' formulation is in many ways the most satisfying from among the quartet of classics.

The approach being that of methodological individualism, it is bound to be in large measure deductive – deductive precisely because no one as yet can inspect under a microscope the motives that dwell in other men's minds (or, for that matter, in his own). Downs makes clear that he regards his work not as an intellectual game but as a positive investigation with a practical purpose, namely 'to enable analysts to make accurate predictions about how real-world bureaus will behave'.[4] Since to the methodological individualist the behaviour of real-world bureaus emanates from nothing more nor less than the behaviour of real-world bureaucrats, accurate predictions clearly presuppose sound psychological axioms from which logically to derive the requisite body of theory. Any axioms will do provided that they generate *ex ante* expectations that turn out to be broadly consonant with *ex post* experience; but Downs, for his own part, is convinced that it is the two standard *a prioris* of the othodox microeconomics which at the end of the day will yield the best practicable picture of external reality.

3.1.1   Self-interest

Bureaucrats, Downs maintains, are correctly to be conceptualised as active maximisers of personal utility: 'The fundamental premise of the theory is that bureaucratic officials, like all other agents in society, are significantly though not solely motivated by their own self-interests. Therefore, this theory follows the tradition of economic thought from Adam Smith forward.'[5] That tradition lays great stress on purposive behaviour: 'Utility maximisation really means the rational pursuit of one's goals.'[6] More specifically, that tradition assigns a very high weighting indeed to the pecuniary incentive as compared with alternatives such as internalised social norms or Kantian absolutes or the conditioned reflexes of the well-trained pigeon – and so does Downs when seeking to explain the motivation of an individual charged with the administration of an entity which he does not own: 'This is not to say that non-economic incentives are unimportant in such organizations; in some case they are vital. Moreover, a few individuals can be relied upon to do their best merely because they enjoy their work, have a strong sense of duty, or get a feeling of power from their activities. But most large organizations responsible for a wide variety of jobs, from low-level labor to high-level policy planning, cannot depend upon personal inclinations as the main motives for getting these jobs done continuously, and under all conditions. Such reliability is most likely to be exhibited by people who must work because they need the money.'[7] Money matters, and any theory is likely to be seriously at fault which underestimates the extent to which the predictable behaviour of the representative bureaucrat is a direct function of the pecuniary incentive which he is offered.

Money matters, and so too do the other goals which, together with money income, 'can be considered "pure" manifestations of self-interest'[8] – power (within the bureau or outside it), prestige (frequently correlated, as are income and power, with internal promotion), convenience (in the sense of a desire to minimise personal effort, presumably per unit of output) and security ('this is defined as a low probability of future losses in power, income, prestige, or inconvenience').[9] Self-interested motivation, it would appear, is quite a mixed bag; and the most one can say is that the five goals which Downs subsumes under the general rubric of egoistic all seem to point towards broadly the same modes of superior-pleasing conduct.

Egoism matters, but Downs does not say that it is all that matters. What he does say is that the five egoistic objectives are more likely than not to be found in combination with a further motive, and one that is 'almost purely altruistic'.[10] That motive is a commitment to the 'public interest'. Looking at the society as a whole, Downs makes absolutely clear that he believes in the existence of a moral consensus which provides the members of the community with constraints and guidelines that inhibit the freedom of choice of the player who wishes to abide by the rules: 'Under normal conditions, men accept certain constraints on their pursuit of self-interest imposed by the widely shared ethical values of their own cultures. For example, an official interested in increasing his wealth may still indignantly refuse to accept monetary bribes. Thus the prevalence of self-interest in our theory does not entirely exclude other types of behavior, or imply that people will pursue their own interests without any ethical or other restraints.'[11]

Downs does, of course, acknowledge the possibility that the espousal of 'widely shared ethical values' might be no more that the deliberate (and self-interested) purchase of an unspoiled image and a good conscience – a possibility which is clearly not neglected by Tullock when he writes that 'a man who gives all of his food to the poor does so because the hunger of the poor disturbs him more than his own hunger.'[12] No less interesting than Downs' reluctant acceptance of the possibility that egoistic man might cleave to the path of consensus exclusively out of fear lest the Impartial Spectator chide him for spending too much time in the society of the Invisible Hand is, however, Downs' warning that it might not always be feasible to extend the notion of consensus to the perceived charter of the bureau itself. Looking at society as a whole, Downs indicates that he has reasonable confidence in the convergence of subjective perceptions. Looking at that microcosm of society that is the bureau, meanwhile, Downs points to a 'public interest' that is rooted in Ego and not in Alter: 'The "public interest" is here defined as what each official believes the bureau ought to do to best carry out its social function. Thus we are not positing the existence of any single objective version of the public interest, but only many diverse public opinions concerning it.'[13] Given that diversity, officials then bargain with one another and the precise specification of the 'public interest' which is ultimately ground out by painstaking negotiations is unlikely to correspond in every detail to any single individual's personal ideal. A compromise and a package-deal though it may be, Downs is adamant about one thing: a commitment to the 'public interest' is 'almost purely altruistic', and thus not to be confused with the five ' "pure" manifestations of self interest' which were examined in the previous paragraph.

Nor, for that matter, with the two borderline cases in which motivation is mixed. One of these is pride in proficiency of performance as an end in its own right: what shifts this mode of activity from pure egoism to the border region is presumably the fact that the motive is non-instrumental, any consequent success an unintended outcome. The second is personal loyalty, where this loyalty is to be defined in an alarmingly open-ended manner as 'personal allegiance to either the official's own work-group, his bureau as a whole, a larger organization containing the bureau (the government if he is in a government bureau), or the nation.'[14] Such allegiance undeniably yields utility, but it is emotive and affectual in nature and not in its essence linked to the five specific goals which Downs explicitly defines as egoistic. Downs' definition of egoistic may thus justly be regarded as embracing only a sub-set of those purposive activities which the average person would treat as self-interested. The advantage of such a limitation of scope is that the theory does not degenerate into a tautology of the form of 'I do what I like because I like what I do'. The disadvantage is that the demarcations made are frequently arbitrary and often also ambiguous.

Ideological commitment is a case in point. Downs says that the attachment of an official to a particular programme or policy (the attachment of the nuclear physicist in the Atomic Energy Commission to rearmament or disarmament, for example) 'could be caused solely by personal identification (self-interest), or solely by conviction concerning the objective importance of the program (altruism), or by both'[15]. The word 'conviction' betrays the ambiguity. A bureaucrat who did not believe that his personal activity was in some way in line with the public interest would find it difficult to develop any real attachment to his work: there cannot be many classroom teachers who are also committed de-schoolers sharing fully Ivan Illich's belief that 'learning is the human activity which least needs manipulation by others',[16] or who are willing to take into account Illich's warning that 'people who have been schooled down to size let unmeasured experience slip out of their hands'.[17] A bureaucrat who did not rapidly come to identify with the purposes of his bureau would not only find himself compelled to lunch alone but would also reveal himself as being remarkably insensitive to new ideas: a bureaucracy develops what Galbraith has called 'bureaucratic truth' (he gives the instance of the American superpower mystique, founded 'on official convenience and belief . . . rather than on the underlying reality')[18] and many have expressed their concern at the ideational capture which is so often the fate of the new indoctrinee. That indoctrinee comes to identify personally with the function of his bureau as he perceives it to be – that is self-interest in the sense of Downs. He also comes to believe in the objective importance of the activities performed by his bureau to the wider society beyond the time-clock and the tea-trolley – that is altruism. Yet both his self-interest and his altruism are in truth emanations of one and the same cause, namely his ideological commitment. The advantage of the demarcations which Downs seeks to make is that they are bulwarks against the tautologisation of theory. That they are frequently arbitrary and often also ambiguous is a disadvantage, however, the importance of which simply cannot be denied. Borderline cases are clearly troublesome cases, but their presence, Downs insists, should not be neglected: 'The prevalence of self-interest in our theory does not entirely exclude other types of behavior, or imply that people will pursue their own interests without any ethical or other restraints.'[19] Prevalence nonetheless means prevalence; and that at least reduces the significance of troublesome cases not immediately reducible to self-interest, narrowly defined.

The Downsian approach is one of methodological individualism, a conceptualisation of the human condition which focuses not on the moulding of the atom by the structure so much as on the shaping of the whole by the parts: 'Individuals are the basic decision-units in our theory.'[20] That being the case, Downs has no choice but to take on board the myriad complexities to which his basic units are heir. One of these is the internal mix of motives, since the same individual might pursue different goals in different situations – pay and prestige here, the charitable interests there. Another is the heterogeneity of human types and the fundamental fact that different kinds of personalities are attracted to different kinds of goals. Leaving to the individual and his trusty psychiatrist the question of why a physicist with a degree from a reputable establishment would seek to win promotion by developing a bomb and then perversely tender his resignation when that explosive device is dropped on unknown foreigners with hardly a degree between them, Downs devotes considerable attention to a classificatory schema of character types which he believes to be needed if predictions concerning bureaucratic behaviour are indeed to be formulated with confidence. That schema disaggregates the totality of officials into five categories reflecting five Weberian ideal types. Prevalence means prevalence in the Downsian model. That having been said, the first two types are to be defined as being purely self-interested, the third, the fourth and the fifth as being in the grip of mixed motivation. None of the ideal types refers to the monk or the martyr whose incentive is solely service: so few present-day bureaucrats are altruists and nothing else, Downs evidently believes, that the category if included would prove nothing but an empty box that ought therefore to be excised by means of Occam's famous razor. Five ideal types remain.

The *first* personality-type is that of the *climber*, a self-interested actor who, obsessed with the five egotistical goals, seeks to attain his objectives by means of strategies including those involving promotion (based on objective monitoring and testing of performance and/or a quasi-feudal relationship with a patron who is studiously pleased), aggrandisement (expanding the power and other privileges associated with an existing job or rank, both as an end in its own right and as an investment in a future promotion pyramided upon a good reputation carefully built up), and job-hopping (shifting to a new and more satisfactory position outside the original bureau or hierarchy, assuming the skills are transferable – the difference between the computer programmer and the customs inspector – and the specialist therefore is not 'locked in'). The climber is fully aware that all change involves cost: 'The depth of the individual's commitment to a given goal depends upon the total cost to him of adapting his behavior to a change in that goal. If such a change requires a drastic rearrangement of his behavior, this represents a very large psychic and economic cost to him.'[21] He weighs the cost against the benefit, evaluates the trade-off as between the respective utilities – and *ceteris paribus* goes for risk when the alternative is stagnation.

The climber is obviously more amenable to change than is the exemplar of the *second* class of personality-type, namely the *conserver*. If the climber wants more and more, then it would be true to say that the conserver fears less and less. Thus it is that he too is a self-interested actor, albeit one so lacking in the self-confident optimism that is the *sine qua non* for gambling on the uncertainties of upheaval that he clings desperately to the security and convenience that are afforded by the *status quo*. Individuals of the conserver bent clearly have 'an asymmetrical attitude towards change', seeing as they strongly oppose losses in their existing privileges but do not actively solicit new ones: 'In part, this relative indifference to gain occurs because they are not basically as ambitious or avaricious as climbers. In part, it occurs because they do not believe they have much chance of receiving significant gains in power, income and prestige. Hence both their underlying values and their expectations contribute to the net belief that negative change would be very bad, but positive change would not be very good.'[22] Whether conservers are born change-avoiders or whether a growing apperception of their own limitations renders them change-avoiders, the fact remains that cautious and anxious persons falling into the category of conservers genuinely believe that they lose more often from change than they gain; and tend therefore to develop an attachment to their job so close as to be reminiscent of the right of an owner to his property. The climber, after all, will move on, while the conserver expects to devote the whole of his career future to his present post. What this means in turn is that a bureau dominated by the intrinsically trepidatious and the excessively timorous (to say nothing of the genuinely inferior – 'people of mediocre abilities whose past failures have erased any optimism they may once have had about future prospects')[23] will generate behaviour-patterns quite different from those produced by a bureau dominated by the climber.

The *third* personality-type is that of the *zealot*; and here motivation is mixed, perhaps even verging on the altruistic, so much is the inner-directed actor imbued with a passionate commitment to the pursuit of the public interest as he perceives it to be. The zealot is not insensitive to personal rewards such as promotion; but he is strongly tempted to strive to secure an implementation of his own pet projects (his 'sacred policies'). The zealot is obviously not a man to be discouraged by the opposition of colleagues and superiors (who, to be honest, he is likely frequently to offend through callously ignoring their attitudes and interests): undaunted by conflict and ostracism, he continues, agressively, energetically and enthusiastically, to fight for his favoured cause (the development of a sophisticated submarine fleet, for example, or the reafforestation of over-grazed hillsides in Wales). Nothing would please him more than to turn out to be the Weberian charismatic leader who is able to create a bureau of his own in order thereby to put his own ideas into practice.

The *fourth* type is the *advocate*. Optimistic, innovative and expansionary, advocates like zealots experience mixed motivation in that they seek to expand and shape the functions of their bureau both because office-holding is satisfying in itself and because it enables them to serve what they see as being the public interest. Advocates definitely resemble zealots. With, however, one major difference: advocates are 'strongly subject to influence by their superiors, equals, and subordinates. Nevertheless, they are often quite aggressive in pressing for what they believe best suits their organizations. Thus they are willing to engage in conflict if they are supported by their colleagues, but are not likely to be "loners" like many zealots.'[24] They are thus more moderate in their demands than are the most strident of their co-workers precisely because of the high value they assign to integration and the group: 'They are more conservative because their loyalty leads them to oppose changes that might benefit them personally but injure their organizations.'[25] Sociability, cooperativeness and a sense of belonging are evidently arguments in their utility function alongside the dual desire to better their own condition and that of the wider society of which they are a part; and it is in effect in their openness to others that they most decisively part company with their narrower cousins, the zealots.

Fifth and last is the *statesman*, the bureaucratic type which more than any other resembles the textbook image of detached service to externally-imposed guidelines not of the actor's own inspiration. Here as always, of course, the pursuit of accurate predictions dictates that allowance be made for individual idiosyncracies; and while many statesmen are known to be lazy (in the sense that they 'espouse very broad views but undertake little action' and 'make good critics but poor achievers'),[26] many others are known to be active (in the sense that they deliberately lobby on behalf of personal and public interest, albeit not to the extent of actually entering into conflictual situations not compatible with compromise). Exceptions can be cited but the rule is the rule, and it is none other than the Weberian criterion of conditioned impersonality and 'obedient compliance'. As Weber puts it: 'The professional bureaucrat is chained to his activity by his entire material and ideal existence. In the great majority of cases, he is only a single cog in an ever-moving mechanism, which prescribes to him an essentially fixed route of march. The official is entrusted with specialized tasks and normally the mechanism cannot be put into motion or arrested by him. . . . Once established and having fulfilled its task, an office tends to continue in existence and be held by another incumbent.'[27] The 'professional bureaucrat' in the theory of Max Weber is the 'statesman' in the theory of Anthony Downs – the standard and the normal character-type in the work of the former authority, only one possibility among five, however, in the work of the latter. Nor indeed even the most significant; and Downs comments on how frequently it is the case that 'statesmen are found at the lowest levels because men who enter bureaus and consistently evidence statesmanlike behavior are rarely promoted. . . . It is our ironic conclusion that bureaucracies have few places for officials who are loyal to society as a whole.'[28] However ironical this result may appear to the Downsian, it is bound to appear even more ironical to the Weberian. This latter will hardly be pleased with the suggestion that the selfless servant of the national interest as communicated to him by the supra-bureaucratic leadership is less likely to win promotion and exercise influence than is, say, the irresponsible opportunist or the persistent obsessive – and will respond, acknowledging that we are here dealing with motivational and subjectively-based hypotheses which are virtually impossible to test, by citing the impassioned defence of *Verstehen* which Gordon Tullock himself enters in introducing his own work on officials and their attitudes: 'For a number of the assertions that will be made in this book, the supporting evidence must be found in the mind of the reader. That is to say, instead of presenting concrete evidence, I shall simply try to convince the skeptical reader by appealing to his own intuition and experience.'[29] Thus is honour to be saved on all sides.

Drawing together the disparate strands in Downs' theory of bureaucratic self-interest, what emerges is that he presents three categories of incentives (egoistic, altruistic and mixed) and five categories of personality types (the climber, the conserver, the zealot, the advocate and the statesman). So sophisticated is this theory that no clear prediction can be made from it without first introducing any number of sociological *caveats* and psychological qualifying clauses such as are conspicuous by their absence from certain of the alternative models of bureaucratic behaviour.

Niskanen's theory is such an alternative and a useful case in point, containing as it does the celebrated contention that 'bureaucrats act so as to maximize their bureau's budget': 'Among the several variables that may enter the bureaucrat's utility-function are the following: salary, perquisites of the office, public reputation, power, patronage, output of the bureau, ease of making changes, and ease of managing the bureau. All of these variables except the last two, I contend, are a positive monotonic function of the total *budget* of the bureau during the bureaucrat's tenure in office.'[30] Niskanen's fascination with the size of the bureau's budget is not easy to understand, even if one takes into account the fact that the pay of the American civil servant (unlike that of his British counterpart) is influenced in some measure by the quantitative significance of his Department. A bureaucrat driven by lust for power can slake his thirst through personal promotion within his Ministry or through internal transfer to a more dominant one (from the Ministry of Agriculture to the Treasury, let us say) – neither course of action correlated in any particular way with the size of the bureau's budget. Some promotions, moreover, are rewards for cutting budgets (the ultimate antidote to maximising them); while it is not in any case the size of budgets that maximises the quantity supplied of promotions so much as the rate of growth of budgets (and Niskanen tends illegitimately to confound the magnitude with its rate of expansion). Most of all, Niskanen fails to incorporate the multiplicity of bureaucratic character-types to which Downs draws attention by means of his five-part schema. Yet it is in truth far easier to show that the personal goals of the climber can be attained through budget-maximisation than it is to produce an analogous demonstration in the case of the conserver (who genuinely fears the traumas of change), the zealot and the advocate (who could well be satisfied with a small budget if skewed towards their favourite schemes), or the statesman (whose interest in ease of administration, leisure enjoyed at place of work and a quiet life is fully consonant with zero growth in a backwater allocation). Niskanen does not take into account the personal welfare-functions of this confusing complex of characters. Downs does. Niskanen is thus the more confident of the two authors, Downs the more tentative and open.

The Downsian approach to bureaucratic self-interest is not always capable of generating unambiguous predictions. What the Downsian approach does generate is a framework for bargaining and negotiating as between a number of unique individuals – each with a unique bundle of affects (love, anger, charity, patriotism, anxiety or whatever), each with a unique combination of ascriptive traits (race, gender, marital status and age, to cite but four), each with a unique structure of motivation (egoistic, altruistic or mixed) – who may usefully be categorised in five main classes of personality-types for the purposes of analysing the behaviour-patterns of bureaucrats. Downs' approach is thus fully political in that it is centred round the jockeying and manoeuvring for control on the part of self-interested individuals and coalitions (perhaps shifting coalitions) of self-interested individuals. The same is true of the behavioural theories of the firm with which the approach has, it must be conceded, something more than a superficial affinity.[31]

Neo-classical theories of the firm, treating the organisation as a black box, the inner workings of which need neither to be specified nor to be examined, tend to take the maximisation of long-term profit as the sole objective of the representative firm. Behavioural theories, on the other hand, refusing to treat as a reasonable assumption that which can never be more than a loose hypothesis, tend to open the black box and to proceed then, insisting strongly on the empirical or inductive approach in preference to the abstract systems of the logico-deductive method, to argue that the goals of a particular firm can only be established *a postiori* by means of a careful inspection of all relevant evidence. Owner-capitalists, as every behavioural theorist who has ever purchased a share would be the first to concede, may confidently be expected to lick their lips at the prospect of good profits. So too, however, may salaried managers when confronted with the spectacle of good lunches at the company's expense – to say nothing of expensive office furnishings and luxurious motor-vehicles, a high salary and the opportunity to exercise dominance, social status purchased by a high-profile but cost-ineffective advertising strategy aimed at maximising growth of sales irrespective of returns to investment, the minimisation of uncertainty through the absorption of a competitor whose entrepreneurial flair has become a nuisance and the maximisation of self-perceived social service through the conspicuous donation of the shareholders' money to worthy causes involving musicians, animals, children and the unemployed. Just as salaried managers want whatever it is that salaried managers want, moreover, so too do the technocrats who advise them from a lower level in the organisation want whatever it is that graduates, experts and skilled specialists want – security, independence, job-satisfaction, an outlet for professional excellence, an opportunity for a moderate amount of overseas travel, all the other potential payoffs (including the attractive pay-cheque) which make the middle-class life-style so deeply rewarding. In the background are the unions (who want better wages, fewer redundancies, and greater consultation), the creditors (who regard risky innovation and a creative exercise of discretion with the same enthusiasm as Little Red Riding Hood did the Wolf) and the representatives of political authority (who exhort profit-seekers and empire-builders not to lose sight of good citizenship and the public interest). Neo-classical theories of the firm, treating the organisation as they do as a black box, cannot incorporate the incessant jockeying and manoeuvring which render the innards of that black box red in tooth and claw. Behavioural theories, on the other hand, are well-equipped to embrace the multiplicity of incentives and instincts which make their home within the organisation and which, via intra-firm conflicts, grind out a unique bundle of objectives quite unlike any other. Behavioural theories of the firm are able to explain what the neo-classical theories cannot, namely the precise manner in which the discrete goals of unique individuals are reconciled and coordinated within the bosom of a single organisation. They do so by means of an approach which is fully political in nature, an approach which assigns pride of place to bargaining and negotiating of advantages as a mode of conflict resolution. The resultant mix of objectives is *a priori* unknown and unknowable; and it is no exaggeration but a statement of the obvious to declare, with Cyert and March, that, ultimately, 'it makes only slightly more sense to say that the goal of a business organization is to maximize profit than to say that its goal is to maximize the salary of Sam Smith, Assistant to the Janitor'.[32]

Bargaining and negotiating within the business organisation is, in the behavioural theory of the firm that is developed by Cyert and March, the *fons et origo* of the goals which it pursues. Bargaining and negotiating within the civil service as between discrete individuals and coalitions of individuals has a similar role to play in the behavioural theory of bureaucracy that is developed by Anthony Downs. In the one case as in the other, it would evidently be fair to conclude, any discussion which includes the formulation and articulation of self-*interest* as an argument must also account for the combination and co-ordination of a multiplicity of separate self-*interests* if it is genuinely to explain the actual bundle of objectives that is actually selected by the whole – and to do so in terms of the swaps and trades, the compromises and side-payments, with which the calculus of consent is inevitably saddled, given the wide range of disparate demands and pet projects in a community comprised of differentiated personalities. All things considered, Herbert Simon reflects, it cannot reasonably be expected that organisation man 'turns off the switch of his own desires from nine to five',[33] and the inescapable inference is that bureaucrats, as Downs maintains, are correctly to be conceptualised as active maximisers of personal utility. How far they will in practice *succeed* in attaining the self-interested objectives which they set themselves is, of course, another matter.

3.1.2 Calculative rationality

Downs, like all theorists of public choice, has considerable confidence in the real-world relevance and predictive power of his image of man as a maximising being with an aversion to waste: 'Bureaucratic officials (and all other social agents) seek to attain their goals rationally. In other words, they act in the most efficient manner possible given their limited capabilities and the cost of information. Hence all the agents in our theory are utility maximizers. In practical terms, this implies that whenever the cost of attaining any given goal rises in terms of time, effort, or money, they seek to attain less of that goal, other things being equal. Conversely, whenever the cost of attaining a goal falls, they seek to attain more of it.'[34] As the relative prices of attaining alternative goals vary, in other words, the rational individual is assumed cost-effectively to substitute the cheaper target for the more expensive one. To the extent, needless to say, that it is in his personal make-up to make the adjustment. A conserver might be prepared at the margin to substitute the easily-won promotion for the quiet enjoyment of the *status quo*. Not so a zealot, however, invited to substitute the saving of trees for the saving of whales. The flexible response presupposes the continuous indifference curve; and the actor with the kink is the actor least likely to produce the adaptive reaction to the change in stimuli.

Calculative rationality in the sense of Downs involves both the economical use of scarce means and the consistent ranking of alternative ends. Even so, however, and as is the case in the economics of politics, the bureaucrat might rationally elect to be less than perfectly informed about the external environment to which he seeks rationally to adapt. The reason is cost. Information, as previously noted, is not a free good (in the sense that 'it takes time, effort, and sometimes money to obtain data and comprehend their meaning'); and there is the further constraint on the flowering of the knowledge-based society that 'decision-makers have only limited capabilities regarding the amount of time they can spend making decisions, the number of issues they can consider simultaneously, and the amount of data they can absorb regarding any one problem'.[35] Nor should the intrinsic unknowability of outcomes ever be neglected: 'Although some uncertainty can be eliminated by acquiring information, an important degree of ineradicable uncertainty is usually involved in making decisions.'[36] Where the consequences of action are unpredictable at the best of times, there is *ceteris paribus* a definite disincentive to the sinking of scarce resources in the collection of intelligence to which the future rate of return is so speculative.

Rationality in such a situation is clearly something other than merely selecting the 'correct' solution and thereupon relapsing into the sleepy passivity of the stationary-state equilibrium. That the selection of the 'correct' solution remains the ideal is not, of course, in question. It is an ideal which has been well described by many students of rational decision-making, and not least by Herbert Simon himself: 'It is not enough, in selecting a cantilever design for a bridge across a particular river, to know that this design will serve the purpose of bridging the river. The wisdom of the choice depends on whether the cantilever design will bridge the river more effectively and more economically than a suspension bridge, or a viaduct, or some other design.'[37] Simply, the comparison of alternatives and the selection of optima being activities involving costs as well as benefits, the 'correct' solution is likely very frequently to prove intolerably expensive and the solution ultimately adopted therefore to be adopted on the basis of the second-best of incomplete information that Simon entitles 'bounded rationality' and that he describes as follows: 'The central concern of administrative theory is with the boundary between the rational and the non-rational aspects of human social behavior. Administrative theory is peculiarly the theory of intended and bounded rationality – of the behavior of human beings who *satisfice* because they have not the wits to *maximize*.'[38]

The textbook abstraction of 'economic man' is assumed to be clever enough to go for gold in the sense that he has it in his power to identify and select 'the best alternative from among all those available to him'.[39] The rest of us, sadly, are condemned by our lack of knowledge to settle for something more modest, namely 'a course of action that is satisfactory or "good enough".'[40] Something better might be just around the corner, The problem lies in deciding whether or not it is worthwhile devoting scarce resources to actually having a look. It is a problem of choosing to choose which is central to the organisational thought of Herbert Simon. It is a problem initially of inaugurating and subsequently of terminating search which is central as well to the theory of rational action within bureaucratic structures that is developed by Anthony Downs. It is also a problem, it would be fair to add, to which mainstream economics has devoted somewhat less attention than it has, let us say, to the mathematical specification of some unique matrix of market-clearing prices such as serves to ensure partial equilibrium in each individual market and general equilibrium in all. The standard quote in the decentralised system of mainstream economics is taken to be the free gift of the Walrasian auctioneer *ex machina*. The standard quote in the decentralised system of real-world economics is conspicuous by its absence, and the Walrasian auctioneer as well: 'Price dispersion is a manifestation – and, indeed, it is the measure – of ignorance in the market.'[41] The words are those of George Stigler, who has laid particular stress on the extent to which Fallen Man, driven from the paradise of omniscience, is compelled to toil for his survival in the vineyards of searching and sampling, and who has strongly criticised mainstream economics for treating information-gathering as a thing apart: 'Information is a valuable resource: knowledge *is* power. And yet it occupies a slum dwelling in the town of economics. Mostly it is ignored.'[42] Mainstream economics is in the circumstances able to specify the 'correct' solution to virtually any problem involving choosing and pricing. The remarkable thing about that 'correct' solution is that it is also profoundly 'incorrect'. Young people basically value nothing so highly as they do a result which is both right and wrong at the same time. The consequence is that courses in mainstream economics are hopelessly oversubscribed.

Mainstream economics may neglect the symbiotic linkages between

information-gathering and decision-making, but not so George
Stigler. Taking as his point of departure the fact that even the *absence*
of price-heterogenity can only be established by investing time and
other economic resources (all with an opportunity cost) in the process
of searching and sampling, he argues that the resources expended in
this way are no more to be regarded as waste than are the resources
expended in any other tributary of the mighty stream of buying and
selling. Naturally enough, 'the expected saving from given search will
be greater, the greater the dispersion of prices. The saving will also
obviously be greater, the greater the expenditure on the commodity'.[43]
The underlying rule is a simple one: search involving expense as well as
conveying benefit, the rational actor will proceed to that optimum and
equilibrium where the marginal cost of continuing to shop around is
just equal to the marginal revenue he expects will be his reward for so
doing.

   Professor Stigler's rational actor adopts an optimising posture. That
posture, it must be said, differentiates his conduct sharply from the
satisficing that is practised, more modestly, by the rational actor as
conceptualised by Professor Simon. Thus Simon writes: 'In an
optimizing model, the correct point of termination is found by
equating the marginal cost of search with the (expected) marginal
improvement in the set of alternatives. In a satisficing model, search
terminates when the best offer exceeds an aspiration level that itself
adjusts gradually to the value of the offers received so far.'[44] Time and
energy entailing cost, clearly, the satisfactory alternative that arrives
early on in the sequence has a distinct advantage over the
no-less-satisfactory (perhaps the even-more-satisfactory) alternative
that ballots the lower place on the agenda: 'In most global models of
rational choice, all alternatives are evaluated before a choice is made.
In actual human decision-making, alternatives are often examined
sequentially. We may, or may not, know the mechanism that
determines the order of procedure. When alternatives are examined
sequentially, we may regard the first satisfactory alternative that is
evaluated as such as the one actually selected.'[45] There is, Simon adds
with all the resignation of the realist, no body of theory that is capable
of predicting the precise ordering of the alternatives that present
themselves to the attention of the rational actor: 'In general, an action
will be chosen before the search has revealed all possible alternatives.
One example of this kind of problem is the sale of a house, or some
other asset, when offers are received sequentially and remain open for
only a limited time.'[46] Something better might be just around the

corner. On the other hand, it might not be. All things considered, there is much to be said in favour of settling for Mildred.

Downs shares the concerns of both Stigler and Simon with the difficulties of applying the norm of calculative rationality to decision-making procedures characterised by incomplete information. *An Economic Theory of Democracy*, as we have seen, does not hesitate to introduce Stigler-type marginal calculations such as would almost certainly account for Simon's hardly enthusiastic reception of that work, were it not for the fact that Simon explicitly states that he does not rate very highly Downs' use even of the maximizing framework: 'While it employs the language of economics', Simon observes of Downs' book, 'it limits itself to verbal, nonrigorous reasoning which certainly does not make any essential use of maximizing assumptions . . . and which largely translates into the economic vocabulary generalizations that were already part of the science and folklore of politics.'[47] *Inside Bureaucracy* adopts a more cautious, more guarded, more Simon-like approach to the dynamics of collective choice in conditions of considerable ignorance about present-day conditions, radical uncertainty with respect to future outcomes. That which is 'supremely rational' is thereby transmuted, in the language of Simon, into that which is merely 'reasonable' – but searching and sampling, even without the ambitious standards of optimising and maximising, remain behavioural constructs that are absolutely central to the theories advanced by Downs concerning the operations of institutions.

Thus, in the *Bureaucracy* as in the *Democracy* case, it is made clear, some information is less costly than other kinds of intelligence (conversation with friends or watching television, for example) and some data is accumulated as a by-product of other modes of activity (such as reading newspapers and journals in connection with one's work). Given that time is never costless, nonetheless it would be fair to say that 'all men are continuously engaged in scanning their immediate environment to some degree' and that 'this combination of unprogrammed free information streams and habitually programmed scanning provides a minimum degree of constant, "automatic" search. Every official in every bureau undertakes such search regardless of how well satisfied he is with his own current behavior or that of his bureau.'[48] Dissatisfaction with the *status quo*, it may confidently be predicted, is likely to cause such officials rationally to choose to invest still more intensively in the search for scarce information. Nor is the collection of data the end of the story; for the decision then remains to be made of how best to act upon the information that has been collected. And there is more. Since it is in the nature of information appertaining to the human condition to alter 'continually', the bureaucrat must face up to the fact that no decision made can be regarded as anything other than provisional, and that he is compelled by the logic of his situation perpetually to redefine 'the locus of his equilibrium position' in order thereby to reflect 'his recent experience regarding what is really possible'.[49] Rationality, one is tempted to observe, is to Downs a flow and not a stock.

A concluding word by way of summary is now required. The approach which Downs adopts in *Inside Bureaucracy* is that of methodological individualism, in that the principal focus of his investigations remains the acting individual's conscious pursuit of his self-prescribed objectives, not the passive adaptation of the fully-flexible lump of clay to the externally-imposed constraints of a structure regarding which no atom ever expressed a reaction. The approach is essentially a deductive one, relying for the generation of robust predictions with real-world relevance upon the methodology of logical inference from sound axioms. The behavioural *a prioris* which Downs employs are those of self-interest and calculative rationality. They are as familiar to every student of exchange as they are likely to be regarded with suspicion by virtually every student of authority. The former will search for and find abundant evidence in the political market of the interested and rational trading of the *quid* for the *quo* that Adam Smith encapsulated for all time in the *dictum* 'Give me that which I want, and you shall have this which you want. . . . Nobody but a beggar chuses to depend chiefly upon the benevolence of his fellow-citizens.'[50] The latter will not deny that there is much in the behaviour of bureaucrats which reminds him far more of the Fall (in the sense of Adam) than it does of *Pflicht* (in the sense of Kant), but he will assign primary predictive power nonetheless to the concepts of duty, obedience, commitment and, above all, loyalty, about which Max Weber wrote as follows: 'Entrance into an office, including one in the private economy, is considered an acceptance of a specific obligation of faithful management in return for a secure existence. It is decisive for the specific nature of modern loyalty to an office that, in the pure type, it does not establish a relationship to a *person* . . . Modern loyalty is devoted to impersonal and functional purposes. Behind functional purposes, of course, 'ideas of culture-values' usually stand.'[51] The ongoing debate between Smith and Max, between the principle of exchange and that of authority, is unlikely to be resolved before tea-time, let alone before lunch. The most that can be said is that it seems to be relatively clear in which camp the impartial spectator ought to situate Anthony Downs.

3.2 THE BUREAU: RESPONSIBILITY AND RESPONSIVE-NESS

An organisation may be defined as 'a system of consciously co-ordinated activities or forces of two or more persons explicitly created to achieve specific ends.'[1] It is thus a system of specialised functions, mutual adaptation and division of labour. The Ministry of Agriculture is an organisation. So is the family. Every bureau is an organisation but not every organisation is a bureau. A bureau is a specific type of organisation, and one which, in the perspective of Anthony Downs, is to be recognised by virtue of the fact that it exhibits four characteristics.

First, it is large – and Downs has the courtesy to define what he means by this: 'Generally, any organization in which the highest-ranking members know less than half of all the other members can be considered large.'[2] A large organisation, it must be added, is normally also a complex organisation, and one beset with administrative problems somewhat different from those that would obtain in the case of a smaller, less impersonal, less formal organisation. Somewhat different, but also, in the view of Anthony Downs, somewhat more acute.

Second, it is constituted in such a way that the majority of its members are employed full-time and dependent upon their service in the bureau for the bulk of their earned income. Such dependence focuses the mind on a single line of activity and breeds rule-governed conduct. A bomber pilot must be reliable, but he is rendered reliable (were he not so beforehand) by the logic of his situation: a man without significant outside earnings (to say nothing of an important private fortune) has no alternative but loyally and carefully to obey orders lest the price of his playing the dilettante should turn out to be the loss of his job.

Third, it hires and promotes employees, continues and terminates employment, principally upon the basis of merit and performance (both realised and expected) and least of all with regard to characteristics not directly linked to achievement (race, religion, class background, political ideology, family connections and age are illustrations of such traits). Of course it happens in a bureau that a superior refuses advancement to a well-qualified candidate exclusively because that candidate is a woman or of foreign origin. The point is that that superior cannot afford to show such prejudice too often: his own advancement is a function of the success of his group, and it is therefore very much in his own self-interest to concentrate on ability and little else.

Fourth, and this is an extremely important feature of a bureau in spite of Max Weber's conspicuous reticence in this connection, 'the major portion of its output is not directly or indirectly evaluated in any markets external to the organization by means of voluntary *quid pro quo* transactions':[3] 'Thus, General Motors as whole is not a bureau because its outputs are evaluated in the outside markets for automobiles, diesel engines, refrigerators, and so on. However, the Public Relations Department of Chevrolet may be a bureau, because there is no accurate way to evaluate its output in dollar terms.'[4] Naturally, even if a bureau does not directly sell its output in the market economy, the shadow of the market may well fall upon it nonetheless and influence its patterns of conduct. Thus the Public Relations Department of Chevrolet would rightly expect to be called to account should its activities be perceived to add nothing to the ultimate profitability of Chevrolet cars; while only a bureau with an exceptionally high degree of non-transferability in the specialised inputs it employs (labour being the obvious example) can afford to price its purchases without due regard being paid to the outside competition of alternative sources of demand. The shadow of the market is not, however, the substance of the market, and Downs' point is clear enough: it is an intrinsic characteristic of a bureau that its output is not traded in outside markets and that valuation is in consequence internal to the organisation, administered, and occa-sionally even arbitrary. As Niskanen succinctly summarises the situation, 'in a single sentence: Bureaus are nonprofit organizations which are financed, at least in part, by a periodic appropriation or grant'.[5] Whether the bureau *is* the organisation (the case of the charity, the church or the political party) or whether it is merely *a part* of the organisation (the aforementioned Public Relations Department of Chevrolet, for example) is not, to Niskanen as to Downs, a matter of primary significance; and Niskanen, like Downs, is quick to concede that 'some competent units in profit-seeking organizations . . . may be bureaus . . . The more difficult it is to identify a component's contribution to corporate profits, the more likely that the component will behave like a bureau.'[6] What is of primary significance is the non-tradeability of outputs and therewith the absence of standard success-indicators such as are represented by market-determined prices. This at any rate is the fourth of the four characteristics with reference to which Anthony Downs chooses to specify the precise nature of a bureau: 'Thus, there is no direct relationship between the services a bureau provides and the income it receives for providing them. Instead, it either receives an allocation of resources from the central budgeting agency of a larger institution of which it is a part (as does a public university), or it obtains resources from nonmarket donors (as does a private university).'[7] A non-bureaucratic organisation is able to relate marginal revenue to marginal cost and to assess the economic contribution of input to output. Not so the bureau: private sector or public sector, the bureau is isolated and insulated from supply and demand.

The bureau permits of extensive division of labour and specialisation of function – no small advantage, in Downs' view, given the multiplied complexities associated with trained expertise and specialist information. The bureau not only enjoys economies of size over time but also finds itself in an abnormally strong position to undertake abnormally difficult tasks – since 'the mere size of the tasks involved requires large organizations to perform them',[8] and the bureau by definition is large. Looking exclusively at the bureau as it manifests itself in the public sector, the list of such tasks is long indeed, and ranges from the regulation of externalities such as pollution through the provision of collective goods yielding indivisible benefits to the control of monopoly, the redistribution of income, the protection of the consumer interest and the maintenance of law and order. So lengthy a list is an open invitation to the sceptical critic to observe that a photograph of the *status quo* simply cannot be taken, as in the work of Downs, to be indicative of the optimal allocation of social duties as between the market sector and the State. Niskanen in particular has admitted that he frequently finds no clear *raison d'être* for the lines of demarcation between public sector and private that obtain in present-day conditions: 'In the contemporary environment, when most goods and services that are augmented by collective action are supplied by bureaus, it is often difficult to understand the functional and historical bases for choosing bureaus, rather than profit-seeking organizations, to supply these services.'[9]

Niskanen also points out that the same absence of logical argumentation, the same tyranny of the *status quo*, the same triumph of convention over questioning, is well illustrated, in discussions *within* the State sector, by the tendency to blur the distinction between government *finance* and bureaucratic *provision*: 'The development of the modern state has been characterized by the parallel growth of government expenditures and the size and number of bureaucratic organizations. Although there are functional reasons for this parallel growth, one should not assume that public services necessarily need be supplied by bureaus. Some bureaus supply private goods and services, and some public services are supplied by other forms of organization. One should be particularly careful to distinguish between the well-developed arguments for government financing of public services and the rather casual arguments for the bureaucratic supply of public services. Much of the debate about government expenditures derives from a failure to distinguish these arguments.'[10] Niskanen is genuinely concerned about the *raison d'être* for situating areas of activity such as tax-collection or the post office in the State rather than the profit-seeking sector, as he is about the logic behind the bureaucratised supplying of goods and services that can adequately be supplied by private enterprise, provided only that private enterprise is adequately armed with public subsidy – and that the community is able successfully to overcome the 'surprisingly pervasive ethical attitude (usually reinforced by the bureaucracy) that it is somehow wrong for the individual to profit by the supply of educational services, hospital services, and military forces'.[11]

Niskanen, in other words, views the bureau and its functioning as eminently controversial in no small measure because he regards the agenda for political intervention as eminently problematic. Downs, as he correctly points out, is more sanguine: 'Downs . . . accepts Mises's assertion that bureaucracy is the essential form of public administration. This leads him to temper his criticism of the methods and performance of bureaus because of a larger concern for the supply of public services.'[12] The list of public sector functions is long, Downs argues; great tasks require great bureaus; great bureaus reap economies of large scale and permit of extensive division of labour and specialisation of function; and thus does the State bureaucracy reveal itself, in Downs' view, to have the capacity to satisfy the criteria both of responsiveness to need and of efficiency of response. Reforms can be made, needless to say, such as will boost responsiveness and efficiency alike, but Downs' fundamental point nonetheless remains this, that governmental responsibilities are significantly greater than those of the minimal State and that the responsible execution of those tasks which are properly its own would simply be impossible without the support of that administrative staff which is known as a bureaucracy.

Responsibility and responsiveness are not, in Downs' perspective, in any way intrinsically incompatible with the essence of the bureau; but he also shares the popular apprehension concerning the extent to which the benefits might be accompanied by costs. Downs does not believe that the monster is about to enslave its maker and treats as a gross exaggeration the idea that bureaucrats consistently repress the choices of individuals (including individuals who, as citizens and voters, hold property-rights in some at least of the bureaus, namely those bureaus which are situated in the public sector). What Downs does believe is that the bureaucratic mode of organisation is encumbered by certain disadvantages which, while not constituting insuperable barriers to responsibility and responsiveness, impose definite impediments nonetheless. Those disadvantages form the subject-matter of the three sub-sections which now follow, dealing, respectively, with distortion of information-flows, bureaucratic inertia, and lack of co-ordination.

3.2.1 Distortion of information-flows

The bureau involves division of labour – a benefit. It also involves noise on the line – a cost. One reason for the cost is vested interest, intellectual (as in the case of the blinkered ideologist who fails to see both sides of the argument) or occupational (as in the case of the opportunistic careerist whose answers serve his ambitions). Thus a zealot will wish to see particular causes given disproportionate weighting, a climber will press for policies which favour promotions, a conserver will warn against destabilising upheavals; and the superiors who read the reports of such subordinates may simply not recognise that selective intelligence is being passed upwards as part of an attempt (conscious or subconscious) at behaviour-modification based upon bias.

Besides which, of course, 'all types of official tend to exaggerate data that reflect favorably on themselves and to minimize those that reveal their own shortcomings'.[13] Such manipulative exaggeration is reinforced in its effects by genuine cheating and intentional mendacity – additional aberrations which exist in bureaucracies as they exist in other areas of social life: 'Like most human beings, officials will readily make false reports if the rewards for doing so are high and the probability of being caught or severely punished is low.'[14] Looking bottom-up at partisan advice, one thinks inevitably of yes-men who match their messages to the biases of the boss – climbers, let us say: 'They tend to tell their superiors what would please them most, so that the climbers themselves can win fast promotions.'[15] The well-known phenomenon of the yes-man is precisely paralleled by the lesser-known phenomenon of the no-man – the conserver, for example, who (deliberately or otherwise) misunderstands the instructions passed top-down by a boss misguidedly committed to expansion and change. Both the yes-man and the no-man screen and filter their memoranda, doing so in the light of their own self-interested objectives and with a view to securing the introduction of proposals by and large in keeping with their own ideals and insights. Their partiality is only to be expected, given the axioms which are at the source of the deductions; and it well illustrates the general proposition that vested interest can be a not-insignificant cause of distorted information-flows.

Vested interest is one cause of noise on the line. Overloading at the top is another – since in a tall hierarchy with a number of layers (and *a fortiori* if the organisation happens to be expanding and changing as well as big), the decision-makers at the top may receive significantly more data than they are able rapidly and accurately to digest. The greater the interdependence of a bureau's activities, the greater the volume of paper that they generate; and message-frequency is likely also to be the higher, the more complex are the problems to be analysed, the more in addition those problems must be approached with qualitative and not with quantitative tools. The greater the volume of material to be absorbed, other things being equal, the greater the likelihood of distorted communication. Downs writes: 'It is usually impossible for a large organization to maintain the same quality of messages whenever the total volume of messages per period rises significantly. The topmost member of the organization has a limited message-handling capacity, and only he can perform the ultimate function of co-ordinating all the activities in the bureau. Yet he must degrade some aspect of his communications behavior whenever the total message volume rises (assuming he is initially at his saturation point). He must either receive a lower proportion of all the information transmitted, take longer to process the same proportion, or raise his saturation-point – which reduces his ability to perform noncommunications functions.'[16] The topmost member's lot is not a happy one.

The limited message-handling capacity of the topmost member

means that he is compelled by the infelicitous conjunction of his professional responsibilities and his personal limitations to allocate funds and make other important choices as between a range of alternative activities on the basis of only a fraction of the total information available to him and relevant to his decision. The topmost member, deeply exercised by considerations of responsibility and responsiveness, might, of course, strive to boost that fraction by means of a greater investment of time, effort and money devoted to searching and processing. Precisely because costly resources are involved, however, in the preparing, the sending and the reading of messages, he might judge that the marginal cost of being better informed exceeds the marginal benefit that the extra information would yield; and he might therefore opt, as it would be entirely rational for him to do, for the economically-advisable second-best of the lower fraction of information. Absorbing and using messages is expensive, the cost-conscious decision-maker will reflect; and there is, in the circumstances, much to be said for pre-selection and condensation even if such screening does build in multiplied distortions stage by stage as edited reports (repeatedly excised and amended) make their way upwards. Even if there were not leakages and insertions brought about by the vested interest of the subordinates, there would evidently still be distortion of information-flows – a distortion in this case deliberately purchased by the superiors, who rationally perceive that too much information can prove as wasteful as too little, who recognise that future conditions and outcomes are not easy to predict at the best of times, and who appreciate, in sum, that communication has its costs as well as its benefits.

3.2.2 Bureaucratic inertia

The world is complex, events are in flux, the future is unknowable. What is required in such circumstances is the flexible response, the quick change, the openness to novelty. What is supplied by the administrative structure is all-too-frequently something significantly less functional, namely the standard operating procedure, the habitual adaptive process, the traditional guideline. The advantages of organisational memory, conditioned reflex and semi-permanent institutions *as if* guided by an invisible constitution are undeniable. Those advantages are much stressed, both by the economist with an appreciation of transactions costs (who points out that deliberation and bargaining consume time and other resources and may therefore not be cost-effective where outcomes are unknowable) and by the social conventionalist with a repugnance to kaleidoscopic innovativeness (who is much reassured by statements such as the following, made by Cyert and March: 'As a result of organizational precedents, objectives exhibit much greater stability than would typify a pure bargaining situation. The 'accidents' of organizational genealogy tend to be perpetuated.')[17] Anthony Downs would be the last to deny that cost-effectiveness and institutional stability are valuable advantages indeed. His point is simply that excessive attachment to past practices can prove as unwholesome for a bureau as it is unhealthy for an individual; and that bureaucratic inertia is accordingly to be regarded as a genuine threat to the responsibility and responsiveness which citizens have a right to expect from their administrators.

One of the main causes of excessive conservatism in a bureau is the natural and normal human propensity for people, complain as they will of the boredom and frustration which they associate with being stuck in a rut, in fact to derive a certain satisfaction from patterned, structured conduct: 'When a person has experienced a certain utility income from some set of variables for a given amount of time, he begins to structure his behavior regarding those variables around that level of utility income. The idea is very similar to Duesenberry's concept of long-run consumption levels, or Friedman's permanent income hypothesis.'[18] Few things are more habit-forming than forming habits – whence Downs' inference that, once a bureaucrat has become accustomed to a particular utility-income derived from a habitual pattern, that bureaucrat will tend (at least initially) to regard any gap between actual and preferred performance, any disparity between the achieved and the aspired-to, as a transitory deviation which can reasonably be ignored rather than as a permanent alteration which requires rational decision-making followed by a revised course of action. Bureaucrats, like other people, Downs argues, experience kinks and discontinuities in their utility-functions; and this psychological predisposition to reason away the need for change is, accordingly, a significant cause of bureaucratic inertia.

Most of all, needless to say, where the key posts in the bureau are dominated by conservers in whom the antipathy to change is particularly marked, the desire to hold on to such security and convenience as they already possess is particularly strong. As noted in the previous section, some of these persons are genuinely mediocre, with good reasons to be less than optimistic about improving their own position in the future; while others may be technically competent but still excluded from advance by factors such as age over which they have no control. This is not to deny that an unexpected promotion may come the way of a conserver, or that the conspicuous failure of a policy with which he is associated might galvanise him into action, only to stress that the conserver normally acts as if he owns his job: 'His attitude closely resembles one of proprietorship.'[19] Proprietorship means territoriality (the inverse of empire-building) and territoriality means wasteful over-investment in resistance to adaptation (the inverse of good husbandry of scarce resources). From the point of view of the individual bureau, 'using resources to defend and expand its own territory is a rational way of reducing the costs of adapting to unforeseen or undesirable changes', but not so from your point of view or mine: 'Bureaus consume a great deal of time and energy in territorial struggles that create no socially useful products.'[20] Thus do conservers manage to combine delay, extravagance and isolation from the dynamic environment in a package which not all citizen-consumers (however greater their personal commitment to *orderly* process) would genuinely regard as attractive.

Inertia is *ceteris paribus* less where the leaders of the bureau are climbers. It is worth remembering, however, that climbing as an activity need not be for all seasons; and that is why it is very often the case among those who sprint out as Hamlet that they crawl home as Polonius. Long service creates a vested interest in routines and habits; failure to win promotion either within the bureau or outside it engenders disillusionment such as tends to snowball into detachment; and the corrosive effect of the petty frustrations of bureaucratic life upon initial enthusiasm is yet another factor operating to convert the climber ultimately to the conserving cause. The position seems to be this, that 'the longer an official has been in a bureau, the more he has been exposed to the difficulties and frustrations of trying to change its behavior; hence the less optimistic he is likely to be about achieving future changes. Also, the longer he has failed to get into the "mainstream" leading to the top, the less expectation he has of getting there in the future.'[21] Besides which, even the successful climber at or near the top has an incentive to become a conserver simply because, his elevated station being what it is, any further change in the *status quo* is more likely to diminish his authority and other rewards than to augment them.

Not only a conserver, but a blocker as well; for there are few things the successful climber at or near the top fears more than he does the

potentially still more successful climber with his powers of imagination, initiative and innovativeness fully intact. To the extent that
successes out of anxiety prefer mediocrities whose excellence lies in
carrying out the orders of their superiors to high fliers whose radical
new ideas cause them to be perceived as a major threat, those
successful climbers cast a vote in favour of bureaucratic inertia in the
next generation. Readers of Max Weber will think inevitably of that
routinisation of charisma which the German sociologist anticipated
would set in once the initial political entrepreneur had retired from the
scene. Friends of Michael Cassio, on the other hand, will reflect how
easy it is for black-hearted villains and green-eyed monsters to come
between a good man and his merited deserts. It is only a matter of time,
they will warn, until the Venetian diplomat, embittered by
queue-jumping and aggravated beyond endurance by office politics,
turns to his hobbies rather than his job for satisfaction; and in that way
becomes *de facto* a conserver himself.

Promotion blocked damps down enthusiasm, but so does promotion
postponed: 'If idealistic young recruits are placed in routinized
positions for a long time before they are given significant responsibilities, they will have little opportunity to act like advocates even if they
are inclined to do so. Their natural enthusiasm for advocacy,
therefore, may be significantly eroded by the time they reach positions
where it might be effective.'[22] Such postponement of advance is
undeniably a force working for inertia – and thus a reason for calling
into question the wisdom of rejecting the aggressive and achievement-
orientated system of promotion by results in favour of the
non-competitive alternative of promotion by seniority. Buggins in the
latter case finally gets his turn, but only at a cost to the organisation
represented by the emigration of the more talented but more junior
Muggins to a more go-ahead employer with a deeper appreciation of
the concept of natural selection. Buggins himself, it must be added,
must have faced the same temptation to ship out when his own
advancement was delayed by the tenure of Juggins; and, while his
ability to resist that temptation might be indicative of a laudable
loyalty to his bureau, it might also mean that the bureau is a
monopsonist with respect to non-transferable skills (as where he is
employed by the Communist Party of the Soviet Union) or, for that
matter, that he is ambitious and hungry to move on but so second-rate
that no one ever calls him for interview. Whatever the reason why
Buggins chose to wait while Muggins chose to go, it is clear that
promotion by seniority can *ceteris paribus* represent a force working
for inertia.

As can, needless to say, the slow growth of the bureau (or, worse still, any contraction in its size), particularly where stagnation follows hard on the heels of a period of rapid recruitment: given that 'the higher the rate of personnel turnover in a bureau, the lower the proportion of conservers therein',[23] the probable attitudes and expectations of a significant 'age lump' that can no longer realistically hope for early promotion such as obtains in the fast-growing organisation and that in addition faces only very limited outside opportunities for advancement and enhancement, are hardly those that foster dynamism and a high valuation of novelty. Put in other terms, the problem is that the amount of inertia in a bureau reflects in no small measure the proportion of climbers to conservers contained within it; and that promotion postponed, like promotion blocked, contributes in no small measure to the rendering of a bureau conserver-dominated.

So does a sound appreciation of the economic costs of change; for the simple fact is that the learning of the bureau's established structures, patterns and practices is not a free good but rather an investment of time and other resources on which the bureaucrat wishes to see a satisfactory rate of return. Clearly, 'this past investment represents a form of "sunk costs" in his life which induces inertia therein. Changing his behavior patterns involves losses in utility now derived from it and costs in setting up a new pattern to replace it.'[24] The greater the investment, the greater the incentive to avoid innovation, the greater the expected reward that will be required to induce the rational official to make major changes in his behaviour-patterns, the greater the time-lag before the self-interested maximiser accepts that it is no longer economic to 'wait to see whether the change is likely to last, and if it is large enough to offset the costs of shifting those patterns':[25] no investor who wishes to survive as such can afford to bear 'the costs of restructuring his larger behavior patterns in response to every change in his utility income',[26] and the bureaucrat is precisely such an investor. The Downsian bureau being nothing other than the sum of its bureaucrats, it is no surprise that the pursuit of value for money renders it no less inflexible: 'The larger the costs of getting an organization to adopt a new behavior pattern, the greater will be the organization's resistance to it, other things being equal.'[27] Small changes may be made in response to pressures, internal or from outside. Profound and far-reaching ones will not be made unless the expected benefits outweigh the sunk costs. Bygones in the Downsian world are, apparently, not forever bygone. A Downsian bureaucrat, apparently, never forgets.

A final cause of bureaucratic inertia, a final source of organisational ossification and rigidity, is the employment by top decision-makers fearing control-loss of monitoring devices and detailed codes such as bind the bureau into 'a virtual straitjacket of rules hardly conducive to flexible behavior'.[28] Their concern lest they experience leakage of authority is a well-founded one, and one which is bound to be magnified by such factors as growth in a bureau already large, diversification of function, multiplication of levels in a multi-layered hierarchy. Whether red tape and a strict adherence to schemata are the optimal solutions to the very real problem of complexity is more debatable: initiative and risk-taking fall victim to the tyranny of the *status quo*, while replication of the done thing, however deficient it may be perceived to be, at least fits easily into the existing network of controls. The outcome is inertia; and inertia is not always and everywhere that which is demanded.

Nor, to be honest, is it always and everywhere that which is supplied – as Downs himself indicates: 'All organizations have inherent tendencies to expand. What sets bureaus apart is that they do not have as many restraints upon expansion, nor do their restraints function as automatically.'[29] Despite the undeniable operation of forces such as breed and form inertial conservatism, in other words, there would appear to exist other factors within the bureau that are friendly to size and most of all to expansion. It is in the circumstances not entirely fair to suggest, as Niskanen does, that Downs is unaware of those countervailing factors and of their implications for the bureau's budget: 'Downs develops a comprehensive theory of management processes within bureaus but stops short of developing the consequences of maximizing behavior on the budget and output performance of bureaus.'[30] Not quite so; for the truth is that the Downsian bureau can indeed expand – and frequently does so.

The Downsian deductions proceed from the axioms of self interest and calculative rationality; and where those axioms point to success, success to performance, and performance to growth, there an organisation obsessed with productivity (associated, let us say, with economies of scale, the spreading of the fixed cost of specialised research and development, the elimination of excess capacity) will also be an organisation obsessed with the expansion which is the precondition for high output per unit of input. Expansion contributes further to quality of performance by enabling the bureau to attract and retain the most capable personnel, as opposed to the second-raters who would stay with it *faute de mieux* if it were stagnating or even contracting. *Morale* too is boosted by expansion: 'There is a nearly universal tendency to impute an inflated degree of social significance to one's job as a subtle means of massaging one's ego',[31] and an organisation with a growing budget is better placed than is a stationary one to resolve potential conflicts of interest by offering pecuniary recognition to the importance of all (and not just some) of its parts. Here as elsewhere, it would appear, the function of growth as a safety-valve and a solvent of tensions should not be underestimated.

Nor should the fact that the playing of the positive-sum game of expansion has this attraction to organisation men on a salary, that the money with which they play is not their own and that the opportunity costs accordingly are borne exclusively by others. Organisation men are in such circumstances all too willing to make common cause with their clients in pressing for an expansion in provision of services which their self-interest might well have led them to cut if only they had been cast in the funding role: 'Most officials are responsible for spending money but not for raising it. They usually produce goods or services eventually consumed by a specific clientele outside the bureau. These goods are either subsidized or amount to outright gifts to the recipients, who, together with a bureau's suppliers, pressure for expansion of its activities. On the other hand, the people upon whom the costs fall – taxpayers in general in the case of government bureaus – are usually uninformed about most expenditure programs. Even if they believe taxes are too high, they have no incentive to seek out any particular program and pressure its operators to spend less. The bureaus are therefore under more pressure to expand their spending than to contract it.'[32] Thus does the marriage of vested interest with rational ignorance breed unwarranted expansion – a prediction, it must be said, which is precisely the opposite of the Downsian contention that the national budget is too small in a democracy that was examined in the previous chapter. Officials in receipt of promotions and consumers in receipt of free gifts will disagree, but the impartial spectator is bound to observe that expansion brought about in this way can hardly be taken to be expansion that is fully in the public interest.

Personality-types are a further influence on expansion. Conservers, and they figure prominently in the Downsian explanation of bureaucratic inertia, do not seek to expand their bureau's budget unless and until the gap between satisfactory performance and realised performance is so great as effectively to rule out inaction as an option. Zealots are different: while not directly concerned with a growth in the bureau's budget *per se* (merely with an augmentation in the resources devoted to their 'sacred policies'), they are likely as realists to appreciate that expansion in the resources at their disposal is easier to bring about, in terms of internal politics, if the whole bureau is expanding than if the rational zealot has no alternative but to capture the funding of his colleagues. Climbers, again, and advocates, also press for expansion, the former because of their conviction that it subserves power, prestige and others of their personal career-objectives, the latter because of a narrowness of outlook combined with a single-mindedness of purpose which causes them to pursue their goal with so much determination that Downs is forced to conclude that 'the most aggressive and persistent "bureaucratic imperialism" usually comes from advocates rather than climbers'.[33] Precisely because they fight with arguments, moreover, and because those arguments will inevitably exaggerate both the shortcomings of the *status quo* and the unique value of their own bureau in putting things right, advocates are a particular source of embarrassment to political leaders: 'The leaders wish to present the public with the impression that everything is under control, whereas advocates seek to magnify the problems facing their bureaus so they can procure more resources.'[34] Nothing succeeds like complaint; the squeaky hinge gets the oil; and statesmen are bound to share the admiration of the reader for the successful aggrandisement of his bureau that is brought about by the advocate, to say nothing of the zealot and the climber.

Aggrandisement is not, however, the same as novelty – all too often it means nothing more than merely more of the same – and that is why the presence of bureaucratic expansion in the analysis modifies but need not negate the prediction of bureaucratic inertia. More of the same is, indeed, more than implicit in all five of the personality-types which Downs presents. Thus the zealot and the advocate are fundamentally conservers with respect to their beliefs and convictions, the climber with respect to the structure which he wishes to turn to his own advantage, the statesman with respect to the identity of the organisation in which he has invested so much of his own. Not one of the personality-types which Downs presents is that of the charismatic mould-breaker whose study it is, entrepreneur-like, to take risks, to think imaginatively, to pioneer something new. Each of the personality-types, on the contrary, is fully compatible with a cautious temperament, a closed mind and a multi-period utility-function. All of the personality-types, in short, are fully compatible with the phenomenon of bureaucratic inertia which Downs clearly regards as a not-insignificant obstacle to responsibility and responsiveness on the part of officials and the structure which their self-interest and calculative rationality cause them to construct.

3.2.3 Lack of coordination

As a bureau (let alone a network of bureaus) grows in size, so do distortion of information-flows and bureacratic inertia become ever more pressing problems. The same is the case with degeneration in overview on the part of the man at the top, who finds it increasingly difficult responsibly and responsively to rule his empire: 'No one can fully control the behavior of a large organization. . . . The larger any organization becomes, the weaker is the control over its actions exercized by those at the top. . . . The larger any organization becomes, the poorer is the co-ordination among its actions. These rather obvious laws are inescapable results of the fact that each person's mental capacity is limited.'[35]

A tall hierarchy honeycombed with complex, detailed and interdependent relationships is a labyrinth of mysteries that must be mapped, a multiplicity of possibilities that must be planned. The perceived demand is normally satisfied: 'The need for detailed co-ordination of myriad specialized activities normally generates a high ratio of co-ordinators to direct producers.'[36] Satisfied, therefore, at a price, since with the growth of the bureau and with growing specialisation within it there would appear to go a growth in the proportion of non-productive to productive activity on the part of its personnel. Often, indeed, 'the best talent in the bureau will be diverted away from action into administration';[37] and many friends of the bureau will no doubt regard such a transfer as a waste.

A waste perhaps; but arguably also a necessary waste in view of the breakdown in articulation that would almost certainly result in the absence of time-consuming activities such as the writing and reading of extensive reports, risk-repressing devices such as the drafting and enforcing of detailed regulations. The benefit from the activities and the devices is perspective and predictability. The cost is delayed projects and limited horizons.

The cost is modest relative to the benefit where the alternative is to allow overspecialised agents a free hand to introduce new policies irrespective of the consequences for others – and 'such grandiose but impractical policy formation is actually a very common phenomenon, particularly among officials entrusted with long-run planning. For example, city planners are notorious for designing master plans that call for absurdly unrealistic behavior on the part of other agents (such as massive expenditure on parks and nearly perfect law enforcement). We will refer to this too broad approach as the *superman syndrome*.'[38] Grandiose and impractical policy formation of the kind exemplified by town planning that takes no account of wider ramifications illustrates nothing so much as the potential for conflicts, contradictions and inconsistencies that exists within the loose federation that is a single bureau (let alone a beehive of bureaus). Such conflicts, contradictions and inconsistencies, such collective confusion and organisational irrationality, are endemic to the structure: given the self-interest and the calculative rationality of the individuals who make up the system, it is only to be expected that 'officials will tend to consider those alternatives that benefit their own interests before those adverse to their interests'.[39] The fact is, in the real-world bureau, that 'officials *always* use some of whatever discretionary powers they have to benefit themselves and the bureau sections to which they are loyal rather than the bureau as a whole';[40] and that it is precisely this *always*, this ever-present threat that the actions of the parts may diverge significantly from the goals of the whole, that renders indispensable the policing and planning function of the coordinators and the administrators.

Their task is not an easy one in a world where the official upon whom the supervisors are dependent for raw data and expert opinion tends to search for and evaluate information in the first instance in the light of his own bias and temperament: 'His perception apparatus will partially screen out data adverse to his interests, and magnify those favoring his interests.'[41] A slippery animal who applies the theory of rational choice to the preparation of the agenda, who exaggerates the importance of information that is to his taste while entirely concealing the existence of intelligence incompatible with his objectives, who drags his feet when asked to execute an order with which he disagrees but enthusiastically throws himself body and soul into those programmes which appeal to him, the most one can say of the official is that his power cries out to be countervailed; and that it is the difficult task of the coordinators and the administrators to do the countervailing.

In view of the divisions and conflicts within the bureau, there is clearly a premium on selecting those policy-measures with respect to which consensus is most easily won and on setting to one side any course of action that is likely to prove contentious. One characteristic of such second-best policies is likely to be simplicity: 'Since relatively simple proposals are much easier to discuss and obtain consensus about than complicated ones, officials will tend to consider such proposals first. This implies that over any given period, a bureau will tend to choose policies that are simpler than those it would choose if its members had perfect information about all possible proposals.'[42] A further characteristic is risk-aversion where possible, risk-concealment where not: 'Officials will tend to propose alternatives involving as little uncertainty as possible in order to avoid complicated and conflict-engendering negotiations. Thus, over any given period, a bureau will tend to adopt actions that do not take sufficient account of future uncertainties.'[43] A third characteristic is the emergence of the illogical policy-mix by virtue of bureaucratic bargaining and a series of institutionalised swaps strongly reminiscent of political logrolling: 'The evaluation process in bureaus is fragmentalized; so officials proposing policies often need to obtain support from a number of others only marginally concerned. These officials usually bargain for a *quid pro quo* in return for their support. A common *quid pro quo* is including something in the alternatives that benefits them, even though it does not directly affect the performance gap concerned. Another is omitting from these alternatives anything damaging to their interests, even though it would benefit the bureau as a whole.'[44] The illogical policy-mix, the careful and cautious strategy, the intentional simplifications of a 'shrinking violet syndrome' that tends unduly to 'narrow the impact of the actions taken by the bureau'[45] – these characteristics of the second-best course of action orientated first and foremost towards consensual decision-making well illustrate the proposition that lack of coordination, alongside distortion of information-flows and bureaucratic inertia, represents a significant threat to the responsibility and responsiveness which citizens have a right to expect from the officials whom they employ in the interests of collective action.

3.3 THE BUREAU: ACCOUNTABILITY AND ACTION

The bureau in the Downsian world is an employee with a will of its own, the bureaucrat a servant whose study it is to restrict the freedom of choice of his master. That being the case, a Downsian might reasonably be expected to draw the inference that, the greater the percentage of national income accruing in the bureaucratised sector of

the economy, the smaller the realm of liberty of the individual citizen.
A Downsian might reasonably be expected to draw that inference.
What is important to note is that Downs himself does not: 'Unlike
some of the severest critics of bureaucracy, we do not contend that
most bureaus are so ossified they should be abolished.'[1] What Downs
does instead is to indicate ways in which the performance of the bureau
might be significantly improved in order that the costs of the
bureaucratic mode of organisation be reduced without simultaneously
impairing the very genuine benefits with which it is associated.

   Downs' prescriptions and solutions fall into five categories, of which
the first – Political Control – demonstrates the extent to which he is a
political economist and the fifth – The Moral Dimension – bears
witness to the fact that he is in private life a man of strong ethical and
religious conviction. The second category of recommendations for
reform is headed Market Control, the third Internal Reorganisation,
and the fourth Conflict Resolution. Five categories is many categories;
and that is why this section on Accountability and Action – and this
chapter, therefore, on Organisations and Interests – ultimately leave
the reader far more optimistic about the viability of bureaucratic
activity in general, State intervention in particular, than the earlier
discussion of self-interest and calculative rationality, of distortion of
information-flows, bureaucratic inertia and lack of coordination, had
led him to expect he would be.

3.3.1 Political control

In the market sector, the relationship between production and
payment is direct: a good or service is generated in anticipation of
profit and sold at a price indicative of supply and demand. In the
bureaucratised sector, the relationship is more complicated, since the
revenues which the official is able to disburse come to him, by virtue of
the very definition of the bureau, from a sponsor and not from a
clientele. More complicated, certainly, but not necessarily more
arbitrary, and this because of a fundamental truth which it is all too
easy to ignore: 'No bureau can survive unless it is continually able to
demonstrate that its services are worthwhile to some group with
influence over sufficient resources to keep it alive. If it is supported by
voluntary contributions, it must impress potential contributors with
the desirability of sacrificing resources to obtain its services. If it is a
government bureau, it must impress those politicians who control the

budget that its functions generate political support or meet vital social needs.'[2] External funding carries with it external control, and this means that bureaucrats cannot have things entirely their own way.

No rational shopper can afford to spend at random, and the same holds true of the self-interested sovereign in the State sector: 'Politicians at the head of the government . . . are just as responsible for raising money as for spending it. They permit only that total amount of spending that they believe will produce more votes (in a democracy) or support (in a dictatorship) than the corresponding amounts of fund raising will lose. This creates an ultimate check on government spending which is transmitted downward to each bureau.'[3] The existence of this 'ultimate check', this ceiling limit on the fiscal total, then forces each cell in the organism both itself to be economical of scarce resources and to struggle actively with other parts of the same whole for a larger share: 'There is no accurate measure of the comparative benefits of different spending acts, or the willingness of recipients to pay for each act. Therefore, each official thinks that if he fights hard enough for his programs, he may obtain enough funds to improve them, or at least avoid cutbacks.'[4] Officials may well be driven by the logic of their organisational goals to press for an expansion in their budgets, but not so the politicians who are their paymasters: 'Most government bureaus have politicians as their ultimate sovereigns, and politicians (unlike officials) are just as sensitive to the cost side of government activity as to the benefit side. Hence politicians are much more reluctant to expand the total size of the government budget than bureaucrats.'[5]

Politicians are much more reluctant to countenance a rise either in total public spending or in the micro-budgets of individual ministries, but the historical evidence demonstrates clearly the distinction between reluctance and refusal: 'The recent expansion of bureaus in democracies has occurred largely in accordance with the desires of major nonbureaucratic institutions therein. Consequently, we may presume that these institutions do not believe the overall bureaucratization of society has been excessive, or they would not continue to support them.'[6] Those major nonbureaucratic institutions are parliamentary majorities, cabinets and ruling parties, and they, dependent as they are upon the support of rational voter-citizens for the continuance of their mandate, simply cannot afford the luxury of failing to expand where a felt need remains unsatisfied – or, indeed, of expanding in an area where producer-interest is powerful but consumer demand non-existent: 'Every government seeks to establish the legitimacy of its authority in the minds of those it governs. In democracies, the governing party obtains the "right" to govern by winning periodic elections involving a significant and free choice among competing parties.[7] Where, more generally, the appointed are accountable to the elected and the elected to the wider community, there outside pressures are most likely to exercise considerable discipline on organisation men: 'Observers who claim that major portions of any nation's bureaucracy are beset by *rigor mortis* usually overlook the pressures exerted upon most bureaus by their power settings. If a major bureau becomes absolutely rigid in its behavior, its sovereign will soon begin hearing loud feedbacks from clients, suppliers, regulatees, rivals and allies. . . . The rigidity cycle is least likely to occur in bureaus that are under strong and constant pressure from such feedbacks.'[8] In such circumstances the bureaucracy might prove to be not so much 'a monolithic monster that concentrates control over many diverse activities in the hands of sinister manipulators at the top'[9] as the obedient servant of a responsible and a responsive leadership – the passive instrument of collective action and not a serious threat to liberty and democracy.

Political control is a check on bureaucratic abuse. It is a valuable and an important check but, alas, only a partial one; and Downs himself points to three significant shortcomings of the political route to fully representative institutions.

The *first* shortcoming has to do with the economic theory of democracy itself, and therewith the prediction that self-interest and calculative rationality on the part of citizens lead very frequently to deliberate under-investment in political intelligence and to deliberate under-involvement in national affairs. One implication of this prediction is that pressure groups and lobbies come to enjoy disproportionate influence: 'A bureau with strong external support among special-interest groups can operate for a long time against the interests of a preponderant majority, especially if they are unaware of its existence.'[10] A further implication is that citizens will normally fail to formulate and articulate clear preferences on policy issues, thereby giving the politicians (even if not the bureaucrats) *de facto* a *carte blanche* with respect to the specification of the public interest. One individual vote in the nation as a whole being so obviously unlikely to sway an election, Downs argues, politics becomes for most voters a peripheral activity where less-than-complete information is rational: 'Legislators, on the other hand, are aware of their own impact on the decision-making process and have every incentive to become informed. Furthermore, there are so many voters that each knows his vote is unlikely to affect the outcome; thus a rationally calculating attitude leads him to political ignorance. But every legislature is small enough so there is a significant probability that an individual's vote may affect the outcome.'[11] Downs never entirely reassures the friend of democracy with respect to the former implication, that involving the pressure group State. With respect to the latter, that involving rational apathy on the part of the voters and a consequent *carte blanche* on the part of the leadership, he is, however, forthcoming as well as reassuring: 'The constituents of the individual are interested in how he has represented them; hence he has a strong incentive both to vote and to become informed about their desires.'[12] More confident than logical, one fears; for a model that incorporates rational apathy cannot also incorporate rational involvement without leaving itself open to certain very obvious criticisms.

The *second* shortcoming has to do with information-imbalance, both as between the politicians and the bureaucrats (leaving the elected leader in some cases with no choice but to rubber-stamp in total incomprehension the expert advice of his specialist appointees) and as between the ministerial heads of discrete departments (each anxious to feather his own nest, each hoping for a better perch). The net result of such information-imbalance is an imbalance in public spending: 'The more legislators emphasize specialized knowledge, the less they emphasize evaluation of the government budget as a whole. Thus the overall budget tends to emerge as the accidental outcome of a number of specialized decisions. This increases the legislature's ability to control the behavior of the individual bureaus in detail, but decreases its ability to develop a well-coordinated program.'[13] A legislature is, needless to say, under that much more pressure to expand a given sphere of activity where information concerning its recent successes has been widely disseminated and has captured the public imagination: 'A bureau must periodically come up with impressive results if it wishes to sustain its growth. NASA's staging of dramatic events at well-spaced intervals illustrates this concept.'[14] A legislature will, therefore, logically speaking, be under that much less pressure to find money for a sphere of activity which, however worthy in itself, is also boringly technical, or the untried response to a rapidly-changing environment, or surrounded by the impenetrable wall of official secrecy – or, indeed, seldom in direct contact with consumer-citizens able to collect information by means of a personal sampling of the wares: 'Excessive rigidity in such bureaus as the State Department,

AID, and the military services, therefore, may persist for extensive periods.'[15] Faced with the poorly-mixed bundles of policies that eloquently testify to the multiplied injustices of unequal information that is also unequal power, the most the Downsian democrat can offer by way of consolation to his anxious compatriots is the reassuring reminder that information in non-democratic societies is more deficient still: 'The suppression of most open expressions of dissatisfaction tends to isolate the regime from accurate knowledge of what the governed really think or desire.'[16] Dissenting opinions are suppressed, administered prices conceal micro-shortages and micro-gluts, their bureaucrats are at least as secretive, as manipulative and as unresponsive as are our own; and thus it is that the Downsian democrat is able to conclude by way of consolation that the one-eyed man has much to be thankful for when placed side by side with his Ruritanian cousin. Few things can be worse than to be born in Ruritania. That having been said, information-imbalance holds no great attraction either.

The *third* shortcoming has to do with incrementalism and with the tyranny of the *status quo* of which it is cause and effect. The problem is that untried alternatives have uncertain payoffs, any departure from convention breeds conflict by upsetting a way of life, the act of changing is itself beset with costs. The solution known as incrementalism is to base this year's budget on last year's practice, to treat this period's experience not as a unique one-off but as a part of a series which has a logic of its own. As Wildavsky says: 'Once enacted a budget becomes a precedent: the fact that something has been done before vastly increases the chances that it will be done again.'[17] Economically speaking, of course, such a procedure does have the undeniable advantage of prolonging the useful life of a given investment in search and decision-making – an investment which, in Downs' view, represents a sunk cost such as in and of itself would tend rationally to produce inertia. The sheer stability associated with the perpetuation of the traditional 'good enough' will in addition have a strong appeal to all those who believe themselves to be in possession of a vested interest (material or intellectual) in the 'done thing – not least politicians in governments and conservers in bureaus: 'Incumbent politicians, together with conservers, have an interest in preserving the *status quo*, for they wish to sustain those elements of it that put them into office.'[18] Economising and satisficing, habituation and perpetuation, all of these are characteristics of muddling through by means of incrementalism which are not without their attractions. Those undeniable attractions must not be allowed to eclipse the very real shortcomings with which the incrementalist system is beset. One such shortcoming arises because social circumstances do change over time and often require a radical and dynamic response rather than an across-the-board rule: thus the same rate of growth in resourcing for hospitals as for schools might be inappropriate if the percentage of old people in the population were rising at a time when the percentage of young children happened to be falling. Another shortcoming involves the serial or cumulative effect of history-dependence to which Lindblom among others has drawn attention:[19] securing the initial financial commitment to a new long-term project might be difficult, these authors maintain, but thereafter all but the most risible of follies comes under the protective umbrella of waste-avoidance (momentum indeed dictating that incipient failure be rewarded with funding, not scrapping) extended by the visible hand of the voter-pleaser (in the sense that it is more popular to open a school than to close one). A further shortcoming is related to the phenomenon of unexpected knock-ons and snowballing unintendeds that is so much a part of fragmented decision-making as to have occasioned reference to *disjointed* incrementalism[20] (analogous to, perhaps even a cause of *'unbalanced* growth'):[21] thus if one ministry in isolation secures funding for a single project (a new hospital, let us say), it simultaneously imposes upon other ministries a *fait accompli* in the form of a need to respond with complements rather than compliments (access-roads, streetlighting, social workers, to name but three) for which there would have been no call had the agenda or order in which decisions on new projects are taken in fact been different. All things considered, it would appear, incrementalism is not in itself the obvious technique by means of which to render bureaucrats the passive instruments of a socially-sensitive political leadership. The difficulties associated with incrementalism must not, of course, be exaggerated – since much of public spending is non-incremental; since incremental-ism applied to the aggregated budget of an entire ministry does not rule out the possibility of aggressive competition within that ministry and a consequent internal readjustment of relative shares; since decision-making coalitions are in a more or less permanent state of flux, and such shifts of bargaining strength are bound to have an impact on *who*, incrementally, marginally, gets *what*. The difficulties associated with incrementalism must not, therefore, be exaggerated. Nor, however, should they be ignored. Wildavsky is one author who takes great care not to ignore them: 'The budget', he says, 'is like an iceberg. By far the largest part of it is below the surface, outside the control of anyone.'[22] Downs is another.

Political control is a check on bureaucratic abuse, but Downs makes clear that that check is subject to three significant shortcomings – those having to do with the logic of the political market, the absence of adequate intelligence, and the reliance on what a businessman would allege to be suspiciously like cost-plus pricing, respectively. Other observers will point to further shortcomings. The revolving-door syndrome in Cabinet government, for example, whereby a Machiavellian Prime Minister reshuffles his ministers before they become too attached to a single portfolio: his intention is to consolidate his own power but the latent function of such chopping and changing is to boost the effective power of the senior civil servants who have the experience and provide the continuity. Or bureaucratic symbiosis extended forward from the administrative intertwining of organisation men public and private (as in the Galbraithian world, where 'rarely does the private technostructure meet a public bureaucracy without discovering some area in which there can be co-operation to mutual advantage')[23] to embrace the decision-maker at the top as well: no minister can reasonably be expected to exercise countervailing power over two married monoliths if he was in effect the best man at their wedding. Or the absence of unambiguous standards of service and of objective performance-indicators: it is far easier to pontificate in favour of education of optimal quality at minimal average cost than it is to define the product or secure agreement on the nature of the best-possible delivery-system, and policy-areas such as the relief of poverty, the repression of crime and the promotion of good health present challenges at least as great to the politician who wishes to be responsible and responsive but also knows enough to know when he is confused. Above all, the fact that the politician *is* a politician – since a man whose job it is to satisfy constituents, checkmate his opponents, engineer alliances, make speeches, and all of this while setting aside some time for his wife and family (to say nothing of his hobbies, his private practice and his business interests), is only in the most exceptional circumstances the equal, in terms of native intellect and acquired knowledge, of the mandarins whose presumptive function it is passively to assist him in his deliberations. None of these shortcomings – and none of the shortcomings that figure more prominently in the economic theory of bureaucracy of Anthony Downs – in any way invalidates the hypothetical construct that political control is a check on bureaucratic abuse. What they do demonstrate is that the exercise of such control is fraught with difficulties, frictions and imperfections; and that the debate about democracy must centre on the significance of those deficiencies rather than on their existence. That they exist is not in question. Nor, however, is the existence of bureaucratic abuse.

3.3.2 Market control

Once upon a time Jack was, despite extensive advertising in the best Sundays and the intervention of a suspicious gentleman calling himself a 'headhunter', the sole applicant for the post of water-carrier. He fell down on the job, broke expensive equipment, frightened the office cat, demanded the payment of a vastly-inflated fee in cash – and carried insufficient water. Nothing could be done, a bad water-carrier being infinitely preferable to the unthinkable alternative. Things changed, however, when Jill offered to perform Jack's job and to perform it better. Jill entered into competition with Jack. Jack was forced by the logic of his situation to carry more water and/or to carry water more cheaply: he did not want to lose out to Jill. Jill, meanwhile, was forced by the logic of her situation to step up her carrying and step down her charges: in the kingdom of the water-carriers, she reasoned, it is the two-fisted water-carrier who is queen. Jill was aggressive and pushy, Jack was indolent and careless; and no one who is self-interested and calculatively rational is likely to want to leave his life's savings in a plain brown suitcase in the charge of either. That, however, is not the point: just as every skunk knows that beautiful furs can come from foul-smelling beasts, so every economist knows that competition is capable of converting private vices into public virtues. Competition, as in the case of Jack and Jill, raised the productivity of the producer and cut the cost to the consumer. These benefits are worth having in an economy where citizens are not prepared to carry water for themselves.

Anthony Downs is fully aware of the significant benefits that accrue to the competitive system. Thus it is that he welcomes competition among bureaucrats with something approaching the same enthusiasm that the representative social actor would reserve for competition among water-carriers: 'The competitive struggle for power and significance among officials provides one of the major ways in which society discovers and defines its basic policy alternatives. Self-interest leads men to make their search for new ideas, more evidence, and better policies far more intensive than if they were motivated solely by an "unbiased" desire to serve society.'[24] Given the process of higgling and bargaining which, as we have seen, itself and itself alone generates the precise mix of goals adopted by the bureau, one is tempted to add that the unbiased altruist actually enjoys a positive disadvantage in the competitive struggle for influence and resources unless and until he learns to wheel and deal in defence of his principles with at least the same degree of proficiency in the arts of manipulation as is demonstrated by the most amoral of his colleagues. Be that as it may, Anthony Downs uses the construct of competitive struggle not only as an explanatory variable in the account he provides of why bureaus behave as they do but also as a policy variable in the proposals he makes for improved checks on bureaucratic abuse. Downs makes two specific proposals with respect to control via competition. To these we shall add a third. The bulk of the discussion in this section is devoted to the third. These things happen.

(a)   Competition between bureaus

Overlap in the work of agencies is common, and nowhere more so than in the State sector – the forty-plus universities within a reasonably limited geographical area is a British example, municipal poor relief versus Federal poor relief is an American one. Overlap brings hope.

Overlap permits of comparison, and comparison keeps performers on their toes: the discovery that one school gets good results while another is seen to produce unemployables is likely, other things being equal, to cause the less-efficient institution to strive to introduce improvements. A rival may even deliberately publicise the shortcomings of his competitors (in forecasting, say, a major storm, an incipient epidemic or an economic downturn) in order by this means to make his own successes seem that much more impressive. Bareknuckle brutality (the parallel is to the all-out price war in the economic theory of oligopolistic hostility) will probably be avoided – partly because there cannot exist many services with nothing to lose from the extensive political investigation and media revelation to which excessive publicity can easily lead, partly because a forecaster currently in post at the Treasury dare not be too offensive to the Bank lest he might one day be applying there for a job. A moderate amount of gentlemanly comparison is a different matter, however. It is likely to occur and, when it does so, to have a constructive impact.

Overlap involves not only embarrassment but threat as well; and threat too can have an upgrading effect on achievement. The Soviet Army (and, less obviously, the American postal service) is a monopoly which has no known fear of aggrandising bureaus bent on taking over some of its functions. Other agencies, trapped between bureaucratic imperialism on the one hand and a finite State budget on the other, cannot be so confident. The psychiatric social worker can perform some of the duties of the mental hospital. The locked ward can capture some of the responsibilites of the visitor with the file. Competition between the worker and the ward has much of the character of competition between Jack and Jill. This is one of the many instances where the views of the lunatic and the economist are in perfect accord.

(b)   Competition between sources of information

The bureau has a not-incomprehensible propensity to pre-sift the information it supplies in the light of its own perspectives and organisational goals. The senior bureaucrats and their political masters have in the circumstances a not-inconsiderable incentive to circumvent what they will correctly recognise as would-be monopolistic abuse and to multiply the sources of intelligence on which they can rely for a 'second opinion': 'Merely by reading several good newspapers each day, and letting all his subordinates know he does, a top official can produce a marked reduction in the distortion practiced by his own bureau.'[25] The bureau has a natural tendency to conceal its incompetent failures while playing up its glamorous successes. If it is known that the top man is experimenting with alternative signals and additional indicators, the presumption is that the top man will not only be better informed by virtue of his extra-bureaucratic contacts but also that the bureau itself will make more of an effort to supply him with a reasonably representative cross-section of the whole truth: the bureau is uncertain as to what he might have picked up from outside, and the fear of being caught out is undeniably a very real spur to assiduity on the part of his risk-averting subordinates.

The top man can glean intelligence from extra-bureaucratic sources such as a free press, an informal network of friends and acquaintances, the external expert on a short-term contract, the tenured academic outsider with nothing to lose. The top man can make use of official reports prepared in ministries complementary to his own (as where, say, the CIA and the State Department exchange assessments as if to verify one another's results) and can, indeed, commission more than one report on the same or a similar topic from members of his own staff: unless the subordinates collude and pre-reconcile differences, and always assuming that their biases, interests and data-bases are not identical, such competition among bureaucrats to produce accurate reports in exchange for anticipated rewards is likely (apart from breeding enmity in place of collegiality) to foster responsible attitudes with respect to truth-telling.

The top man himself, moreover, should he happen personally to be the product of the system, is in a strong position to make his own contribution to the unscrambling of cumulative noise: 'Every general was once a lieutenant and remembers the type of distortion he used when he forwarded information to his own superiors.'[26] In a strong position, that is, provided that schoolboy games have not altered since he was a lad (where stagnation is the norm, in other words, dynamism the exception); and that the general once a lieutenant is enough of a psychologist to be able to read the personality-types of duplicitous characters who are also devious (to know his climbers from his conservers, in other words, his creepers from his crawlers) – and, obviously, that he himself has acquired enough distance from the distortions of his youth to be in a position to provide countervailing power to bureaucratic bias (as opposed to providing refinement and reinforcement of that bias prior to passing it upwards to his own superiors in a manner eminently likely to boost *morale* and win him the approbation of his staff). Such 'provided thats' are restrictive. Not, however, impossibly so; and for that reason the top man might himself have a personal contribution to make to the generation of dependable intelligence.

Competition between sources of information has undoubted potential. Also, sadly, certain potential deficiences. One of these involves the over-provision of specialist information, leading as a consequence to the employment of wastefully time-consuming screening devices in order to separate the wheat from the chaff. Another involves the under-provision of technical intelligence, as where a knowledge-hoarding bureau, not keen to compete, refuses to divulge non-replicable information because of a strict policy of official secrecy. Over-riding both considerations is the serious problem, previously mentioned, of definition of terms and therewith the establishment of non-problematic success indicators: where competition between sources of information entails the asking of different questions as well as the processing of different answers, the would-be reformer is in danger of becoming as paralysed by the wide range of options on offer as was Buridan's ass when presented with an extensive menu of choices as if by an invisible waiter who expected no tip. Competition between sources of information, one is forced to conclude, is a good thing of which the claims should not, however, be exaggerated.

(c) Privatisation

The bureaucratised system is a politicised one, a system in which clients put pressure on sponsors to allocate funds to bureaucrats. Three groups are involved (as opposed to the traditional two of the market mode), mutually-satisfactory bargains are not struck directly between buyers and sellers, and the lack of any automatic linkage between expenditure and income renders the sensitive evaluation of supply relative to demand very difficult indeed. Given the bureaucratised system, 'the absence of any explicit *quid pro quo* relationship between bureau costs and benefits tends to conceal situations in which the costs of maintaining the bureau outweigh its benefits'[27] and thus to promote an over-expansion and a longevity which would be exceptional and not normal were the services of the bureau to be precisely specified by sovereign consumers and sold to them at prices indicative of marginal cost and marginal revenue.

Besides that, 'the market further provides a guide for evaluating the performance of individuals within the firm. A salesman who brings in twice as many orders as another is obviously more valuable to the firm.'[28] Business provides a monetary yardstick by means of which performance may be appraised and compared. Bureaucracy does not and cannot, and this inability to assess the economic contribution of inputs, together with the lack of information on the subjective valuation of outputs, leads Downs to make the following statement about the relative attractiveness to the student of scarce resources of business versus bureau: 'We can intuitively postulate that the total amount of waste and inefficiency in society is likely to rise as bureaucracy becomes more prominent. This seems probable because true waste is so much harder to define and detect in bureaus than in private firms. Also, there are not automatic mechanisms for limiting it in the former as there are in the latter.'[29] All in all, the market mode would appear to provide a better test of that which it is worthwhile to produce, a set of incentives more conducive to the cutting of costs and the raising of productivity, than does the bureaucratised alternative – and that is why it comes as somewhat of a surprise to discover that

Downs makes no proposal at all for the institution of market freedom where today there is bureaucratic constraint. No doubt he would very much like to be in a position to put forward radical proposals such as would challenge the comfortable conservatism of the *status quo*. He is, however, unable to do so. The reason for his reluctance is his commitment to the functionality of the bureau, his conviction that tasks exist in the complex modern society which nothing short of the complex modern bureau can properly execute.

Downs, looking around him at the form-filling society, sees rising living standards and shorter working weeks at the head of the queue: 'The average individual's overall freedom is actually expanding rapidly. Even though the regulations imposed on him by bureaus continue to multiply, his action alternatives multiply even faster.'[30] Nor is it any accident or chance of fate that they should do so: 'Increased bureaucratic regulations are actually one of the causes of his greater freedom. The forces generating ever wider options are the same ones that generate the need for more bureaucratic rules. Without increased bureaucratic regulation, such forces as technological change, urbanization, and more intensive division of labor would either be impossible, or would lead to greater social disorganization and a narrower range of choice for the individual. Thus, greater bureaucratization is one of the inherent costs of greater freedom.'[31] Richard Henry Tawney said: 'The mother of liberty has, in fact, been law.'[32] The father has been enterprise, Anthony Downs would wish to add; but otherwise the social democrat and the theorist of public choice would find themselves, broadly speaking, in agreement with respect to the value of bureaucratic regulation and the interventionist State.

Downs starts from the premise that bureaucracy is here to stay: 'It is not possible to eliminate bureaus from modern societies. Certain vital social functions must be performed by nonmarket-oriented organizations that possess all the traits defined as characterizing bureaus.'[33] Not just bureaucracy in general but State bureaucracy in particular: 'All governments must perform a great many of these activities because they include the major reasons why governments exist.'[34] The key word is 'these'; and it is at this point that the libertarian observer will declare Downs' list of functions properly governmental to be arbitrary and normative, too long and too controversial, neither the product of natural laws of economic structure nor the single-valued outcome of his own economic theory of democracy. The key word, however, is 'these' and the 'these' to Downs is the this.

First, the creation of a framework of law and order reflecting equal rights and impartial rules: 'Markets respond to money signals given to them by potential buyers and sellers, and money is very unequally distributed in almost every society. Therefore, systems of law and order cannot be based upon markets if they are to treat all citizens as equal before the law.'[35] Equal citizens merit equal treatment, Downs argues; and that to him means the bureaucratised option. Libertarian observers will complain that he neglects the very real benefits that would accrue to a competitive system of private-sector arbitrators, financed where appropriate by a fully compensatory structure of means-tested vouchers; while political radicals will point out that the economic costs of adjudication itself are as nothing compared with the accompanying costs (briefing a solicitor, taking time off work) which render access even to the bureaucratised option difficult if not impossible for large sectors of the population. Downs himself sees things, however, more simply – and is also, one is bound to add, strangely oblivious to the alternatives to, the shortcomings of, the *status quo* mode of delivery of law and order.

Second, the provision of further collective goods analogous to law and order (the *sine qua non* for the viability both of the public and of the private sectors of the Downsian mixed economy) in that they possess the two essential characteristics of indivisible benefits (in the sense that even free riders who have not paid are in a position to consume) and consensual legitimation (in the sense that the majority of citizens favour State intervention in the area of activity in question). Downs gives the examples of defence and education as cases where private markets are bound to fail and the community, recognising that economic fact of life but also keen to see the service supplied, opts in consequence for the coerced conformity of the Whitehall product. Not everyone would wish to disagree with Downs on the desirability of mercenary armies. Education is a different matter; and the fact that it is currently being supplied principally by means of bureaucratised structures must not be taken to mean that, a private sector alternative being unthinkable and unworkable, State bureaucracy in the field of education inevitably enjoys the same longevity as the service itself.

Third, the redistribution of income, where 'the citizenry' takes the view that voluntary provision for states of dependency is insufficient and that coercion ought to take the place of charity – the problem being that 'the persons from whom money is so taken will usually not yield it without being required to do so by law'.[36] The transfer-payments which Downs instances are unemployment compensation, medical care for the poor, and support to young children. Not one of these is non-problematic – the first because of the feedback effect (which is unknown) of the compensation on the unemployment itself, the second because of the complex of difficulties associated with the choice between subsidising the patient and subsidising the institution, the third because child benefits can so easily have perverse consequences (as where a given tax-allowance yields greater 'fiscal welfare'[37] to the richer father paying progressive income tax at the higher marginal rate than it does to the poorer father who pays at the lower). Other transfer-payments may be more problematic still. Support to the arts or to the religious festivals of ethnic minorities, for example, are bound to provoke a degree of controversy about public versus private which is not easy to reconcile with the complacent attitude towards the bureaucratised option which Downs is so eager to adopt.

Fourth, the regulation of monopolies (including allegedly natural monpolies such as telecommunications and electric power) and the defence of the public against its own ignorance with respect to the technical properties of, say, food, drugs, and cigarettes): 'To protect themselves from harmful exploitation by producers in such instances, consumers in a democracy often have the government establish regulatory or inspection agencies which must be insulated from market pressures.'[38] That such agencies are in fact established is not, of course, in dispute. Whether they are genuinely demand-led is, however, another matter; and it is somewhat of a suprise that the theorist of bureaucratic self-interest and calculative rationality does not recognise the possibility of special pleading in the expansion of bodies of the very existence of many of which the vast majority of citizens are totally unaware. Nor is it obvious that such agencies defend the interests of the consumer as well as would a more effective degree of competition. This point is made with some force by Milton Friedman when, comparing the postal services and the railways with television sets and computers, he says: 'The shoddy products are all produced by governments or government-regulated industries. The outstanding products are all produced by private enterprise with little or no government involvement.'[39] Friedman also records that, in the 1970s (a decade in which 'economic growth in the United States slowed drastically'), 'the number of government bureaucrats employed in regulatory activities tripled'.[40] Friedman acknowledges the extent to which his own thinking on State intervention in the mixed economy has been influenced by 'a fresh approach to political science that has come mainly from economists.'[41] Friedman mentions the names of Becker and Buchanan, Stigler and Tullock – and Anthony Downs.

Fifth, the coordination and stabilisation of levels of economic activity. One illustration of this function is American agriculture, where producers are so numerous, so small and so dispersed that research is insufficient and development sporadic: 'As a result, governments may devise nonmarket agencies to carry out research in such fields and to reduce the shock caused thereto by the resulting technical changes in production'.[42] Another illustration is macroeconomic policy, since Downs takes the view that it is the responsibility of the State and its bureaucracy to monitor aggregate performance and to implement corrective strategies in the field of demand-management. With respect to the latter instance, the most that can be said is that a committed monetarist will not share Downs' optimism concerning the necessity for and efficacy of the well-known tool-kit that is employed with the intention of fine-tuning; while with respect to the former the convinced adherent of the economic theory of democracy is likely to observe tersely that this is no more than he would have expected, given that producer-power is normally disproportionate and vested interest always and everywhere a strong incentive to press politicians for privileges.

Sixth, the protection of third parties from the diswelfares of unwelcome externalities. The Downsian world is evidently characterised by a considerable degree of consensus as to which spillovers constitute 'socially undesirable outcomes'[43] – as opposed to a more conflictual and even a more politicised world in which one man's pollution-control is obtained at the price of another man's involuntary unemployment. The Downsian world is in addition one in which agreed-upon correction proceeds by means of legislated expedients such as zoning schemes, traffic restrictions and controls on the emission of effluent such as smoke – as opposed to the more market-centred, more voluntaristic expedient of levying a tax on the creation of the neighbourhood effect and then leaving it to individuals to choose how much of the expensive inconvenience they wish to consume. The Downsian world, in the case of the sixth of the 'vital social functions' properly in the hands of the bureau, as in the case of the previous five, is clearly a non-problematic one in which a government does what a government has to do and the community is fully prepared to see the State play what is in effect a highly interventionist role in economic and social processes. The Downsian world is not, needless to say, one which every monetarist, every anarchist or even every public choice theorist would find instantaneously recognisable.

Downs' list of functions properly governmental is by no means a

short one – and Downs does admit that some at least of the activities
cited could, theoretically speaking, be hived off to the private sector:
'Private firms could undoubtedly carry out through voluntary *quid pro
quo* transactions many of the service functions now entrusted to
government agencies. Provision of electric power or first-class mail
service are examples of such potentially marketable services.'[44] Some
at least of the activities currently being performed by bureaus could,
Downs concedes, at least theoretically speaking, be performed by
firms. His tantalising admission is, sadly, not followed up, but followed
instead by the following: 'Nevertheless, shifting certain marketable
services from government agencies to private firms would not
eliminate the need for a significant number of large nonmarket-
oriented organizations, that is, bureaus.'[45] It is difficult to explain why
Downs moves so rapidly from the 'now entrusted' to the 'would not
eliminate' that he finds no time to dwell upon the intermediate case of
the 'would certainly reduce' that forms the centrepiece of the
argument of every pragmatist who has ever defended the privatisation
of hospital catering while simultaneously opposing the privatisation of
hospital doctoring.

The logic of his omission would seem to lie in the cross-subsidisation
of non-economic by economic benefits: 'For example, the Post Office
Department provides subsidies to several activities (such as Rural Free
Delivery) that are not self-supporting on a voluntary *quid pro quo*
basis, but produce external benefits regarded by Congress as
significant.'[46] A Congress genuinely committed to competition and
genuinely concerned about over-bureaucratisation would, one would
have guessed, have opted unhesitatingly for privatisation accompanied by carefully earmarked supplementation in preference to the
indiscriminate cross-subsidisation to which Downs refers; while his
specific illustration (which is one of so-called natural monopoly) raises
complex questions about how permanent a high-profit position can
ever be, save where it is protected by State and law from the
intervention of ingenious interlopers – complex questions, it must be
recorded, with respect to which Downs never entirely satisfies the
reader interested to learn more about the pros and cons of
privatisation as compared with nationalisation, competition as
compared with State supply.

Even if the cross-subsidisation and the natural monopoly objections
could somehow be countered by the free marketeer, there is a further
warning which Downs would wish to issue to those who say they can
imagine a world without public bureaus. That warning involves

consumer ignorance and the consequent need for regulation of standards. The example which Downs provides involves privatised schooling, voucher schemes and parental choice: 'If no regulations were imposed upon the production of education by private entrepreneurs, then some might succeed in selling shoddy education to irresponsible or ignorant parents. In this case, society would be ignoring certain important indivisible benefits of providing a minimum quality of education to every child.'[47] The Downsian example may involve education but the Downsian principle which it illustrates is of far greater generality – that as societies become more complex, more specialised, technically more sophisticated, the inevitable concomitant of division of labour, urbanisation, the externalities of economic development, the emergence of novel and potentially conflictual situations, the growing size and intricacy of the web of interdependence, is likely to be a greater reliance on government action for regulation and resolution.

Government action means bureaucratic action; and Downs is on balance not at all surprised that the share of the bureau and of its employees has risen so significantly in the twentieth century as a percentage of the gross national product and of the total labour force, respectively. What would surprise him, give his belief in the high income elasticity of demand for the services of bureaus, would be if there were to occur not a rise but a fall. A rise, it must be added, which he confidently expects to accelerate as developed societies increasingly progress through the secondary or manufacturing stage to the post-industrial state built round the tertiary sector of distribution and services – an inevitable shift which 'may include an increased emphasis on certain services that must be (or have traditionally been) furnished by nonmarket-oriented organizations. One example is education; another is public subsidization of non-self-supporting aesthetic or recreational facilities, such as art museums, music centers, sports stadia, and large parks.'[48] More old people in the population means a greater need for day-centres, more crime produces more policemen; and these forces on the demand side that lead to an expansion of bureaucracies are paralleled by developments on the supply side involving productivity-boosting technological change and the exploitation of economies of scale in manufacturing and related areas such as will release labour for employment in the burgeoning bureaus. Thus it is that 'faster mechanisation of nonbureaucratic jobs tends to increase the proportion of bureaucrats in the employed labour force',[49] the proportion of employees, in other words, who generate no directly marketable product. As societies evolve, so too, evidently, do bureaucracies evolve, and at a faster pace – and State bureaucracies most significantly of all: 'In the nature of post-industrial society, the government has become the single largest employer in the society.'[50] The words are those of Daniel Bell. The sentiment is not one with which Anthony Downs would wish to take issue.

Yet bureaucrats entail distortion of information-flows, organisational inertia and lack of coordination, which are, all three, administrative imperfections to the elucidation of which Downs has made a pioneering contribution of such importance that one is struck by the complacency with which he accepts that the bureau is an inescapable fact of modern life. Downs' significant admission, in the specific case of the public sector bureaucracy, that some at least of the functions currently being performed by governments could, theoretically speaking, be performed by firms does indicate some doubt in his own mind as to the extent to which the public sector bureau genuinely is here to stay. Such doubt opens the door to proposals for market control through extensive privatisation – proposals which Downs, as it happens, makes no attempt to explore. Taken in, perhaps, by the rhetoric of organisation men with a pecuniary interest in advertising the efficiencies of large size, he appears to be convinced that a transfer of property-rights would leave bureaucratic structures and their performance unaffected. His neglect of the economies of *small* size is unfortunate: privatisation can well lead to de-bureaucratisation, and therewith to greater variety and diversification of product, as would certainly be a possible scenario in the case of the privatised provision of formal education. Even more unfortunate is, however, Downs' neglect of the manner in which competition (even competition among the few) tends to exert so beneficial an impact on the organisation man as to constitute a strong argument in itself for privatisation and market control.

Consider the Leibenstein problem of labour contracts that are never fully specified, partly because of the prohibitive transactions costs to which detailed description accompanied by intensive supervision would give rise, partly because uncertainty as to the future business environment renders some exercise of individual discretion and judgement indispensable. The Leibenstein world is one in which potential welfare gains to be reaped from improved allocative efficiency are 'of small magnitude', 'trivial', 'exceedingly small'[51] but also one in which, because of acknowledged ambiguity and vagueness at the stage of contracting, because of restricted monitoring and control at the stage of enforcement, internal (or 'x') inefficiency becomes a problem precisely because each employee acquires the power in the organisation to invent at least a part of his own job-description: 'The atomic decision-making units, as it were, are the individuals *in* the firm rather than the firm as such. Each individual decides (1) the *activities* he will carry out, (2) the *pace* at which he will carry out these activities, (3) the *quality* of the activities, and (4) the *time* spent on the activities. Thus each individual chooses an activity-pace-quality-time (APQT) bundle.'[52] The combination of separable components put together by the rational employee in the sense of Leibenstein resembles nothing so closely as the mix of multiple characteristics that is made up by the rational consumer in the sense of Lancaster: 'A meal (treated as a single good) possesses nutrional characteristics but it also possesses aesthetic characteristics, and different meals will possess these characteristics in different relative proportions. Furthermore, a dinner party, a combination of two goods, a meal and a social setting, may possess nutritional, aesthetic, and perhaps intellectual characteristics, different from the combination obtainable from a meal and social gathering consumed separately.'[53] Lancaster's important conclusion is that it is not from the good *per se* that the consumer derives utility but rather from its several properties: 'Even a single good will possess more than one characteristic, so that the simplest consumption activity will be characterized by joint outputs.'[54]

The rational consumer in the sense of Lancaster is, of course, assumed to be backing up his choice-calculus with his own money. Not so the rational employee in the sense of Leibenstein, however, who interprets his role, selects his APQT bundle, maximises his utility, pursues the normal and healthy objectives of the organisation man on a salary, and does all of this while devoting the minimum possible attention he can to the interests of the silent principals who are his nominal masters. The rational employee in the sense of Leibenstein cannot, needless to say, exercise the same neglect with respect to the goals and aspirations of the peers and colleagues who are his team-mates: 'Since most individuals interact with others in their work, the nature of the interactions and job-interpretations set constraints on the APQT bundles each can choose . . . Each person hired brings, in addition to his work potential, a set of desires, attitudes, and sense of responsibility about the activities of others around him, and contributes to the creation of an atmosphere of approval or disapproval which determines in part the nature of the APQT bundles that are chosen.'[55] Each person hired has, it would appear, a marked propensity to rank the mink-lined curtains, supernumerary staff, overpriced meals and other side-payments made to the devil upon whose cooperation he is forced every day to depend, above the high profits and maximal efficiency which the silent devil who holds the equity but cannot command a bribe would himself, if asked, confess he wished to see. Each person hired does not, it must be added, have equal skill in rent-seeking through bluff and feint – nor, indeed, equal opportunity to derive supra-functional benefits from the comfortable cushion of lags and frictions which Cyert and March term 'organizational slack' and of which they write as follows: 'Because of . . . frictions in the mutual adjustment of payments and demands, there is ordinarily a disparity between the resources available to the organization and the payments required to maintain the coalition. This difference between total resources and total necessary payments is what we have called *organizational slack*. Slack consists in payments to members of the coalition in excess of what is required to maintain the organization.'[56]

It is exceptionally difficult to make out a strong case in favour of organisational slack, just as it is difficult to defend with any real sincerity the incidence of x-inefficiency, differential openings to seek excessive renumeration, rewards of agents ranked above objectives of principals. That is an important reason why privatisation of bureaucracies accompanied by competition between purveyors may well prove a far more powerful solvent of organisational abuse than the approach of Anthony Downs to the employment of this expedient would lead the reader to suppose. The point is that an APQT bundle which raises average unit costs by virtue of unnecessary executive travel, or a thick layer of institutional fat such as insulates idleness from the pursuit of competence, is only likely to survive in the long run where the consumer has no reasonable alternative source of supply. Privatisation accompanied by competition is therefore the enemy of bureaucratic self-indulgence and careless indolence, and a step in the right direction of organisational behaviour orientated towards the revealed preferences of sovereign consumers: the logic of natural selection, the pressure of aggressive rivalries, the survival-motive, these forces have a strong tendency to see to that. As Milton Friedman explains it, the position is this: 'Unless the behavior of businessmen in some way or other approximated behavior consistent with the maximization of returns, it seems unlikely that they would remain in business for long. Let the apparent immediate determinant of business behavior be anything at all – habitual reaction, random chance, or whatnot. Whenever this determinant happens to lead to behavior consistent with rational and informed maximization of returns, the business will prosper and acquire resources with which to expand; whenever it does not, the business will tend to lose resources and can be kept in existence only by the addition of resources from outside.'[57] Rational and informed maximisation, needless to say, is all but coterminous with consumer-pleasing conduct save in the awkward situation where the supplier is a monopolist and the shopper has no choice. Which is to say that privatisation of the bureau accompanied by effective competition may well prove a powerful solvent of organisational abuse, and for that reason a strong argument in favour of market control. Whether privatisation not accompanied by effective competition would be as attractive to the concerned citizen anxious to render the activities of organisation men subservient to those of the wider community is more controversial. Much depends on the relative costs and benefits of the various prescriptions and solutions which constitute the reasonable alternatives to market control. The first of these (political control) was examined in the first part of this section. The fifth of these is the moral dimension, the fourth conflict resolution; and it is to the third that we now turn our attention.

3.3.3 Internal reorganisation

Officials in stable agencies tend to get into a rut – the problem of bureaucratic inertia. They tend to filter intelligence and screen advice in the light of standard practice and vested interest – the problem of distortion of information-flows. They tend to formulate plans and develop projects without much attention being paid to the consequences and implications of those plans and projects for other bureaus – the problem of lack of coordination. Inertia, distortion and malarticulation are, all three, abuses associated with bureaucracies – and internal reorganisation is in some measure an antidote.

Reorganisation in itself involves change, and change by definition is a threat to the stability of a stable agency. The shock upsets the network of personal loyalties, lunchtime cliques, informal alliances, patron-client friendships; revamping, restructuring and repositioning have the effect of breaking up what Simon calls 'the patterns of who-talks-to-whom-how-often-about-what';[58] and the climate of uncertainty which accompanies the upheaval stimulates the de-sheltered to look again at schemes involving novelty, experimentation and flexibility that they had in less challenging times been tempted to dismiss as excessively radical. Technological advance in a dynamic society itself has the potential, of course, to impose precisely such instabilities and compel precisely such changes; and the same might reasonably be said about a range of other mutations in the external environment (some forcing the closure of an established bureau due to the conspicuous completion of a finite *ad hoc* task, others leading to the creation of a new bureau in response to a new imperative such as might be thrown into prominence by an unexpected emergency). Reorganisation introduced specifically to combat bureaucratic abuse is a valuable complement to reorganisation with the explicit charter of embracing technological advance and other mutations, but a word of warning is in order: precisely because today's new rule can easily ossify into tomorrow's *status quo*, what is needed to keep the bureau on its toes is more nearly permanent change than once-for-all change, lest the efficiency gained in the short run gradually be obliterated in the long.

In some cases reorganisation will of necessity involve the redesigning of the whole bureau. In other cases, more modestly, it will involve nothing more ambitious than the frequent rotation of staff within the framework of an ongoing structure. Rotation at the very least separates the yes-men from their quasi-feudal master, and in that way helps to reduce, in Downs' view, the harm done by second-rate subordinates who loyally subordinate their own preferences and the wants of their clients to the interests of their leader: 'Since loyalty can be proved only through experience, a leader whose subordinates have demonstrated their loyalty to him over the years will be reluctant to replace them. As a result, the incumbents are to a certain degree insulated from competition, and need not perform their official duties as efficiently as they would if personal loyalty were irrelevant.'[59] Frequent rotation breaks up such relationships and ends the *de facto* subsidisation of incompetence which they entail. It introduces a marked degree of freshness into the debates of committees and sub-committees, thereby making the outcome of those debates that much less predictable.

Climbers will recognise in rotation a means of circumventing an age-lump blocking a particular ladder but not others; and will therefore not be adverse to turnover and the transfer of functions. Conservers, of course, will stress the need for continuity, both as an end in its own right (since tradition in their view is in essence a good thing) and as a means to some other end (as where a knowledge of personalities and the employment of informal systems undeniably economises on the scarce resources of time and energy and in that way contributes to the attainment of economic efficiency). Statesmen are, presumably, statesmenlike when rotated, zealots are difficult at the best of times, and the attitude of advocates is particularly interesting: 'The longer an advocate remains in a given position, the more likely he is to espouse policies based upon a magnified view of the relative importance of that position. Conversely, if advocates are frequently rotated, they develop more detached views of each job.'[60] This lesson would appear not to have been lost upon the Foreign Service, since Downs, writing of diplomats, has this to say about a phenomenon which in a not-dissimilar area of bureaucracy is known as 'regulatory capture': 'If U.S. officials remain in any given nation for long, their increasing attachment to its culture may cause their goals to shift toward those prevalent in that nation. If such a centrifugal shift occurred everywhere, there would be an enormous decline in goal consensus within the State Department as a whole. Fear of this outcome is one reason for the State Department's frequent rotation of its overseas personnel.'[61]

Almost as dangerous as the bureaucratic structure *per se*, it would appear, is the tyranny of the smaller bureaus which comprise the whole. Frequent rotation at least has the advantage of reducing the individual's attachment to the parts and of thereby causing him to look at the larger organisational interest. No one but an organisation man would, of course, assert that that larger organisational interest is the same as the public interest: to say that rotation draws the bureaucrat away from the path of sin is not to say that it returns him to the path of righteousness, only that it helps to minimise the harm that he is capable of doing.

Even without redesigning, even without reorganising, there is quite a simple internal reform that might be introduced by a leadership hostile to abuse, and that entails the adoption of the by-passing strategy – the strategy, in other words, where officials by-pass the normal hierarchical structure and communicate directly with other officials several layers removed from themselves on the organisational chart. Such a device circumvents the distorted communication associated with multiple filtering, allowing a top decision-maker, for example, to 'obtain information directly "from the horse's mouth", or to transmit complex orders directly to those who have to carry them out'.[62] The contact might be once-for-all or recurrent; it might be initiated by an inferior (to speed up a process being delayed by conservers, let us say) or by a superior (keen, for example, to acquire information he suspects is being concealed by intermediates); and it is particularly likely to be made where only the key expert, and not his immediate boss, has the data and skill which the top leadership requires (the reason why, 'the more finely specialized an organization is, the more its leaders will resort to by-passing to discover what is really going on').[63] Obviously, however, immediate superiors do not like to be by-passed, aware as they are that recourse to the device tends to cost them both influence (in the sense of opportunity to advise and distort) and status (since it is bad for the image to be seen to be ignored). By-passing is accordingly an expedient that must be employed with circumspection rather than full publicity. That it must sometimes be employed, however, Downs does not doubt – and one reason for his confidence about by-passing is his sensitivity to change. The more knowledge top officials have about the various distortions their subordinates are likely to introduce, Downs says, the more easily they will be able automatically to make the necessary allowances, and thus the less they will have to fall back upon by-passing strategies for necessary correctives: 'Hence stable organizations will use by-passing less than dynamic ones.'[64] The inverse is true with respect to dynamic organisations, he reasons; and no one but a conserver could fail to notice their presence among us.

By-passing within an existing hierarchy tends *ceteris paribus* to reduce the incidence of bureaucratic abuse. So too, more radically, does the flattening of the hierarchy in the interests of flexibility against the backdrop of an unpredictable environment: 'When uncertainty prevails, potential relationships among the possible components of a task cannot be foreseen accurately. Hence the task cannot be divided into many parts assigned to specialists unless the specialists are in constant communication with each other and can continually redefine their relationships as they gain more knowledge. This requirement is best served by a flat hierarchy, since it provides greater authority to each official and allows greater emphasis upon direct horizontal relationships.'[65] Flatness in addition reduces noise on the line, since there is clearly less room for messages to become exaggerated or garbled where the number of times the story is retold is reduced: 'Having only a few levels in the hierarchy reduces the number of screenings and thus keeps the degree of distortion low.'[66]

Reduced distortion and improved adaptation are undeniable benefits, but flatness has its costs as well – and not least because the breadth which it embodies has the obvious effect of widening the average span of control of the representative decision-maker. With widening, after all, there all too often goes overload, and with overload the loose reign which is the lower level's delight: 'Officials who have wide spans of control cannot spend much time supervising each of their subordinates and these consequently have a great deal of discretion. . . . Thus, paradoxically, many organizations with low vertical message distortion tend to use vertical communications channels less intensively than those with high vertical distortion.'[67] The flatness reduces the loss (a benefit) but also the control (a cost), and the most one can say is that the control-loss will be the less, the more the functions involve routinised activities which can be reported upwards using quantitative measures and objective indicators: in such cases, clearly, 'centralized control can be maintained in spite of wide spans of control because of the relative ease of checking performance through these indexes'.[68]

Not in all cases, however, is there scope for decentralisation and devolution of responsibility, despite the saving of time and other resources which such action brings with it: in some cases paper and decisions must be passed up through a tall hierarchy to the officials at the top rather than being effectively dealt with at the intermediate or the lower levels. Should interdependencies within the bureau be exceptionally complex, for example, then 'the taller its hierarchy is likely to be' – 'if the relationships among these activities are sufficiently predictable to allow intensive specialization'.[69] If, of course, they are not, then a competition develops between tallness (in order to cope with complexity) and flatness (the friend of uncertainty). The outcome of that competition is unknowable *a priori*, but Downs is keen nonetheless to venture a guess, that the bureau 'will normally have a flat hierarchy even though its task involves detailed interdependencies among specialized activities'.[70] Tall or flat, the crucial point is that structure *matters* in any discussion of bureaucracy; and that internal reorganisation represents the third of the five categories of prescriptions and solutions which constitute the Downsian reply to bureaucratic abuse.

3.3.4 Conflict resolution

Conflict exits, both within bureaus (top versus bottom, say, or zealots versus conservers) and between bureaus (scarce resources and differing objectives being the most volatile of all social science combinations); and conflict need not be a bad thing. Within the team, after all, conflict has a unifying impact, the struggle against a common enemy helping to promote an *esprit de corps* and an internal solidarity which might well serve to keep productivity high despite the disruption to inertia of some new departure; while within the society as a whole conflict might be no more divisive and no less beneficial than the standard case of economic rivalry. Not all conflict need be a bad thing and much of conflict is undeniably good and healthy, Where, however, conflict undermining charter and constitution twists organisations and collectivities down by-ways which it was never intended that they should follow, then, clearly, in those circumstances, most reasonable members of the community would accept that the functioning of the social organism had turned malign and that effective social action waited upon the adoption of proper modes of conflict resolution.

One important mode of conflict resolution, in Downs' perspective, is concord based upon preannounced, multi-period regulations such as defuse the conflict before ever it emerges, precisely because they ensure unanimity of consensus on the nature of due process: 'People whose basic philosophic outlooks are completely contradictory can nevertheless cooperate quite successfully in segmental relationships so long as they agree upon the specific rules of procedure required. Thus the sources of goal divergence in bureaus spring mainly from differences of opinion or beliefs about segmental relationships rather than about basic philosophic, religious, ethical, or emotional orientation.'[71] Such specific rules of procedure, promulgated in advance of the game being played and subsequently adhered to by the totality of the contestants, provide a normative structure in the form of good processes rather than uni-valued end states; and therewith a shared framework of guidance and guidelines that may be drawn upon with equal legitimacy by all parties to a dispute, provided only that all genuinely rank peaceful co-existence above the zero-sum nastiness of the *bellum omnium contra omnes*. As the distinguished proceduralist Buchanan has put it: 'We require rules for living together for the simple reason that without them we would surely fight.'[72] Applied to the Downsian bureau, the pre-existence of rules for living together obviously has a valuable contribution to make to the resolution of potentially conflictual matters. Promotion is a case in point, where formal and impersonal mechanisms employing clearly-specified criteria undeniably lend legitimacy to a decision which could otherwise all too easily be disruptive of internal order. Even greater legitimacy would result, one would suspect, were the consensus to specify the precise content of the criteria as well as the specific nature of the decision-making structures which are to employ them and – returning to the case of promotion – this is, arguably, the reason why the principle of demonstrated merit is so often preferred to the next-best criterion of long-serving seniority, let alone the eminently divisive also-rans of sex, race, colour, religion or place of birth. Promotion on the basis of performance is, after all, widely perceived as being not merely equitable in its own right but also an integral part of adaptation and survival of the whole: clearly, 'continued failure by the bureau to perform its functions with at least a minimum degree of technical competence will cause its customers to become dissatisfied with its behavior. As a result, they will either subject the bureau to a drastic purge of leadership or give it much smaller amounts of resources. To avoid both outcomes, every bureau must make actual or potential role performance a major factor in its personnel policies.'[73] Achievement being functional given the external environment, it is likely to win widespread support; so too is the practice of employing formal and impersonal mechanisms; and the conclusion to be drawn is that acceptable procedures are indeed an important mode of conflict resolution.

Impartial assessment based upon preannounced standards presupposes, however, accuracy of evaluation – and yet performance (whether of the indivdual bureaucrat or of the bureau as a whole) is notoriously difficult to measure. Staff appraisal schemes, written reports, superiors' impressions, sponsor's reactions, all have their role to play in monitoring the progress of officials; but too much must not be claimed for any one of these expedients. Success or failure can only be defined with reference to an ideal that is frequently intensely contentious in certain bureaucratised areas such as education or health; a concentration on objective indicators might cause agents and agencies deliberately to neglect discretionary tasks which, where unquantifiable, do not count for purposes of reward; and there is, of course, here as elsewhere, the inequality of information that always and everywhere gives a definite advantage to the special-pleader with the vested interest. Monitoring, it would appear, has its limitations as well as its attractions; and the most the outside observer can reasonably recommend would appear to be the mix of monitoring devices.

A mix, it must be said, which ought, in Downs' view, to make liberal use of the outside agency. The outside agency has a separate hierarchy and promotions structure, after all, with the result that its members have no personal interest in any particular rearrangement of institutions. Detached outsiders, moreover, are often well placed to make impartial judgements precisely because they lack personal links with the bureau being monitored (as where, located behind a thick veil of ignorance such as obscures the minutiae of office politics, they are asked to rank two climbers on criteria other than superior-pleasing flattery). The attempt to supervise one bureau by means of another does mean, of course, that the monitoring agency must itself come under control; but at least the monitors, being rational, do know that their own performance-rating will rise if they manage to detect shortcomings, errors and malpractices in the bureau being scrutinised, and that they therefore have a genuine incentive to ferret out such failings.

Yet the employment of the parallel hierarchy is not without its problems, and Downs never denies that these can be very real problems indeed. For one thing, information-hungry monitors tend to demand more and more documentation, frequently compelling the operators to prepare costly reports and to keep over-detailed records with which they would otherwise have dispensed on the grounds that such knowledge is not needed save by the regulators. Over time, in other words, officials of the monitoring agency 'become advocates of greater control over the operating bureaus they monitor, both because they wish to perform their function better and because this increases their significance. As a result, the officials in separate monitoring agencies tend to agitate for ever more detailed reports from operating bureaus, and ever greater limitations on the discretion of those bureaus.'[74] The extra paperwork generates delay and involves expense; and the nuisance combined with the waste will simply not be worthwhile where the monitors' reports are in the event never read and acted upon by the higher-level officials, or where fear of potential scrutiny has in practice little or no ameliorative impact on the performance of the frontlinesmen liable to review. Moreover, a second difficulty, the monitoring agents may come from the bureau being regulated, they may hope one day to return to it, and they may, in effect, enter into friendly symbiosis via interated contact unless rotation is frequent, fraternisation prohibited, or monitors selected from groups (ethnic, for example) traditionally hostile to the enemies to be regulated: 'However, reduction of prolonged contact is partly incompatible with intense specialization. For example, the Bureau of the Budget would be much less effective if it had not developed specialized monitors who have dealt with the same government agencies for years.'[75]

The trade-off between intellectual capture and information famine is hardly a very attractive one. It is a trade-off, however, with which the member of the monitoring agency in the sense of Downs is bound to be well acquainted – and other potential watchdogs as well. The academic observer up against an Official Secrets Act, for example, dependent for data upon selective leaks which he knows will dry up should his published findings go against his allies' interests; or the media analyst who is fully aware that he cannot do his job without lobby briefings and off-the-record conversations such as convey information that he believes to be good but skewed, accurate but unrepresentative. All of which points to the conclusion that it is easier to call for impartial assessment than to perform it.

Conflict can be resolved by formal procedures and by impartial assessment (including outside assessment), but it can also be resolved – even before it arises – by means of the shared perspective and the common outlook: 'The greater the homogeneity among an organization's members, the flatter its hierarchy can be. Similarities of self-interest, cultural backgrounds, technical training, and moral values among bureau members are likely to reduce the incidence of conflicts among them. This will allow greater delegation of authority to individual officials without loss of effective coordination, thereby encouraging a flat hierarchy.'[76] Organisational consensus evidently does much to promote harmonious personal relationships, to lessen the need for continuous supervision, to ensure that each official becomes his own policeman, to standardise job-images even where (the Leibenstein case) job descriptions cannot be precisely structured: 'Within any organization, greater goal consensus reduces the number and intensity of conflicts among members, thus improving the organization's overall coordination. Moreover, as the goals of lower-level members become more like those of top-level members, the relative amount of authority leakage declines. This enhances the power of top-level officials and makes the organization more efficient in achieving the goals those officials select.'[77] Organisational consensus, after all, by boosting personal involvement and self-monitored conduct, by repressing potential conflicts of objectives such as prevent the decentralisation of discretion to subordinates, cannot but enhance the productivity of the bureau as a whole: 'Top-level officials can retain the same quality and quantity of output as before, but reduce the controls, reports, and other performance checks used to maintain it.'[78] Organisational consensus, in short, is undeniably the enemy of bureaucratic abuse – *ceteris paribus*.

Ceteris paribus – since similarity of outlook has its price as well as its utility. Thus the counterpart of improvements in quantity, quality and cost might well be less variety, experimentation and innovation, precisely because of the bureau's vested interest in defending its organisational ideology, its 'verbal image of that portion of the good society relevant to the functions of the particular bureau concerned, plus the chief means of constructing that portion.'[79] Again, the counterpart of accelerated sharing of scarce information and a reduction in the amount of time spent quarrelling in committees might turn out to be the conserver's reluctance to contemplate novelty, with the associated inability to adapt to an environment in flux. All in all, one is tempted to point out, circumstances exist in which disagreement is positively functional and it is consistency based upon consensus that presents the greater threat to efficiency: rapid change, uncertain outcome, complex interests, differentiated intelligence, all are arguments which militate against the knee-jerk response to the traditional compromise despite the undeniable fact that it serves as a bulwark against the psychological, social and economic costs of radical upheaval in the *status quo*. Control via consensus, one is compelled to state, clearly has its costs as well as its benefits; and the advocate of the expedient should accordingly take great care to include in his defence the explicit warning that the check on bureaucratic abuse is operative only subject to the *caveat* of *ceteris paribus*.

That goal consensus is a valuable means of ensuring consistency conflict or coercion is, however, albeit subject to the *ceteris paribus caveat*, not seriously in question. Goal consensus is functional and useful; and Downs, recognising its potential for reconciling interests and transcending differences, accordingly looks carefully at the devices which the leaders might wish to employ in order to defuse tensions in this way. Three in particular appear to him to be of particular importance.

The first technique is *selective recruitment*, where top-level officials rationally seek to select new members for the bureau whose goals already resemble those of existing staff. Naturally, 'the broader the scope of activities involved in any given position, the more general the talents required, and the harder it is to define them';[80] and to that extent even the specification of skills, traits and characteristics required is fraught with difficulties. Even more difficult, however, is the task of searching for the persons with the desired bundle of attitudes and aptitudes (both current and potential); of identifying the individuals in possession of those attitudes and aptitudes; and of enticing them to join the bureau and remain within it. There is, clearly, much to be said for internal promotion, since this at least ensures that key posts will be occupied by persons who have already been screened by their superiors and found to be committed to continuity. A similar line of reasoning would clearly legitimate the personal approach to a friend or colleague outside the bureau; or appointment reflecting nepotism, tribal loyalty, the common religion (all cases where apparently spurious and non-rational characteristics reveal themselves to be eminently rational for the purpose of selection that reflects consensus); and the family background of the applicant ought also, logically speaking, to be carefully inspected. It is in this connection that left-wing intellectuals such as C. Wright Mills and Ralph Milliband draw attention to the interlocking elites which they believe to be the norm in advanced capitalist societies. They situate the State bureaucracy in a matrix of birth and privilege which advocates of recruitment on grounds of ability, narrowly defined, will hardly find congenial. Congenial or not, Milliband argues, recruitment on the basis of criteria other than merit, narrowly defined, is in practice the order of the day: 'Those who control and determine selection and promotion at the highest level of the state service are themselves most likely to be members of the upper and middle classes, by social origin or by virtue of their own professional success, and are likely to carry in their minds a particular image of how a high-ranking civil servant or military officer ought to think, speak, behave and react; and that image will be drawn in terms of the class to which they belong.'[81]

Selective recruitment on grounds of background and image is, in the sense of Milliband, an integral part of the control-mechanism that is, in the sense of Marx and Engels, the modern State: 'The executive of the modern State is but a committee for managing the common affairs of the whole bourgeoisie',[82] the earlier authors had written, and Milliband would add that this celebrated conclusion could hardly be expected to hold true in a society which appointed its administrators on grounds of technical competence and little else. Downs, it would be fair to say, makes a case for selective recruitment which has little to do with the perpetuation of a ruling class, and far more to do with the stifling at birth of situations which might one day become conflictual. That a more-than-average element of conservatism might produce integration cannot be denied by anyone with an openness to the principle of interchangeable parts. Far more debatable are the implications of conservative replication and the integration of the ongoing whole for the efficient functioning of the administrative structure. That the past might come to precommit the future is recognised not only by Buchanan (speaking of the national constitution) but by Leibenstein (speaking of corporate tradition): 'To some extent, the history of the firm will determine the role interpretation choice set and the transmission of role interpretations between successive generations of workers.'[83] The advantage of standardised expectations is conflict-resolution. The disadvantage is bureaucratic abuse taking the form of inertia, distortion and malarticulation. The mechanism is selective recruitment – the first of the three devices for fostering goal consensus that are considered by Anthony Downs.

The second technique is *indoctrination*, where goal consensus is actively promoted subsequent to appointment and not taken to be the free gift of childhood socialisation buttressed by the right schools, universities, regiments and West End clubs. Acclimatisation and persuasion, propaganda and training, are obviously more costly to employ than is the alternative of buying off the peg – and, less obviously, less efficient as well with respect to the production of the desired concord – and that is why rational leaders of successful bureaus 'try to minimize the need for indoctrination through selective recruitment. Those requiring strong, deep-level consensus will recruit with far greater selectivity than those not requiring such consensus.'[84]

The technique of indoctrination is more costly and less efficient than is the closest substitute. It breeds the inflexibilities of the inertial response (a genuine problem where matter is in motion and ideas become obsolete). It carries the threat, common to all forms of on-the-job training, that the expensive investment is wasted should the human capital move on. Indoctrinated consensus is in addition particularly prone to corrosion when exposed to external reality (the case of Soviet diplomatic missions in the West) – unless, of course, the indoctrinees are cloistered in a form of monastic isolation so extreme that it undermines their ability to perform their assigned tasks (the case of Soviet diplomatic missions in the West). But the option is available should it be needed; and it constitutes the second of the devices on Downs' list.

The third technique is *ideology*, where a verbal image of the 'good society' and the contribution made by a particular bureau to its actualisation serves to unite disparate bureaucrats behind a common banner. All officials, after all, 'want to be able to defend their behavior as serving widely accepted social functions. This is perfectly rational even for an official motivated entirely by self-interest, since society generally awards more prestige to those who perform worthwhile services than to those who do not.'[85] The source of the shared perception that the bureau is good and useful is not of primary importance: it could be background and education (as picked up by selective recruitment); it could be manipulation on the job (as is instanced by indoctrination); it could be the free information streams of radio and television (and, allowing for bias for or against generals and/or social workers, the fact is that not all bureaus receive equal publicity precisely because not all are perceived as having the same entertainment or news value); it could be national debates reflecting specialist advice (to say nothing of taxpayers' opinions as discerned by vote-seeking politicians). Whatever the source of the shared perception, what is of significance in the context of conflict-resolution is for all intents and purposes simply the fact that it exists; and that it, by existing, supplies a *raison d'être* that is in and of itself capable of giving the bureau cohesion and unity.

The organisational ideology in many situations is the *sine qua non* for effective performance – where initiative and risk-taking necessitate discretion that does not lend itself to control via monitoring, for example (and 'every bureau must delegate a certain amount of uncheckable discretion to its members'),[86] or where 'the bureau's function requires its members to act in strong opposition to their own interests' ('For example, police officers are expected to risk their lives and to resist bribes').[87] In the case, say, of soldiers in the changing environment of battle, or of diplomats in distant places, communication is less than ideal, the monitoring and comparison of performance exceptionally difficult – and self-policing by means of internalised normative standards an intellective argument in the national production function for which there exists in effect no close substitute. In such circumstances, in short, the bureau has no alternative but to 'rely heavily upon strong and deep goal consensus'[88] if it is indeed to do what is expected of it. Normative constraint in the form of the organisational ideology evidently has an exceptionally important role to play both in fostering organisational cohesion and in promoting organisational efficiency. That a model which begins with the economist's invisible hand of self-interest rationally pursued should thus end with the sociologist's invisible hand of shared values affectually reinforced will come as somewhat of a surprise to those readers who conceive of the methodological individualism of public choice theory as virtually synonymous with the selfishness and the amorality of Hobbesian man on the trail of wealth and dominance. Those readers must be reminded that methodological individualism is no more than its name suggests, a mode of analysis and not a matrix of conclusions; and that Anthony Downs, at any rate, sees no contradiction between the fragmented individualism that constitutes his methodological framework and the voluntary adoption of the ethical discipline with which the following section on the moral dimension will be directly concerned and with which the present section on conflict resolution comes to an end.

3.3.5 The moral dimension

The Downsian monad makes his own decisions but he does not do so in an ethical vacuum of his own choosing. No doubt many a bureaucrat would optimally attain self-specified goals such as rapid career-advancement by means of self-seeking strategems such as the undetectable assassination of his rivals, the unexpected betrayal of his friends, the unverifiable falsification of his evidence – and yet intuition suggests that the representative individual, egoistic though he may be, would nonetheless hold back from employing strategems such as these because of a voice within that calls out to him to resist temptation lest the price of excessive self-love be a painfully spoiled self-image. To argue thus is not, abandoning the economist's approach to bureaucracy, to retreat into the more traditional constructs of self-sacrificing altruism, public service and the common good, only to say that shared values can and do figure prominently in the bureaucrat's utility-function and that it would be a gross over-simplification to take the office-holder's objectives as being pay, perks and promotions, and little else. The fact is that a social consensus which strongly condemns options such as assassination, betrayal and falsification easily becomes an integral part of the individual's consciousness; and where this is the case, where the sensitive are compelled by conscience to conform, the tension between the social and the individual in some measure disappears. Buchanan, with Tullock, delimits the duality in the following *dictum*: 'It is not from the benevolence of the bureaucrat that we expect our research grant or our welfare check, but out of his regard to his own, not the public interest.'[89] Downs transcends the duality through his appeal to goal-consensus: where both the society as a whole and the sub-section of that society that resides in a given bureau are united, say, in the condemnation of bribery, there is every likelihood that the individual police officer will himself have internalised that condemnation, and will in that way have made the public interest in some measure congruent with his own. To act in response to the dictates of one's own self-interest is in such a case the same as to act in response to the shared values of one's partners in a common culture, the precise distinction between egoism and altruism a matter of semantics and nothing more.

It is significant that Anthony Downs should rely in this way upon ethical self-policing to resolve the prisoner's dilemma that is faced by the bobby on the beat when confronted with a bully with a bribe. Not, however, entirely surprising; since it is, after all, the invisible chains of shared values far more than the visible hand of the fuller trough which account for the paradox, noted in the previous chapter, that the good citizen resolutely donates (rather like his blood) his vote, despite the widely-appreciated fact that the single vote, save in the most marginal of marginal constituencies, is unlikely to have any real influence upon the outcome of an election. The good citizen knows all that there is to know about the importance of being unimportant; but he wishes nonetheless, to the consternation of the cost-counting calculator, to make his own small investment in the public good of the public good. His decision to invest is not, in the sense of traditional economic theory, a rational one; for just as the corrupt policeman who dines with smugglers can still derive the personal benefits of a crime-free community provided only that his colleagues dine with their wives, so the bad citizen who goes to the shop rather than to the polling station is in no way denied the advantages of the democratic system of government where 'a preponderant majority of the system's participants',[90] resisting such temptations most of the time, go instead to the polls and not to the shop. That prepondant majority are the good citizens whose investment in the public good of the public good is, although clearly non-rational in the sense of traditional economic theory, nothing short of indispensable 'if the system is to work': 'Therefore any realistic consideration of politics must take into account the necessity for this non-rational commitment, and indicate that it in fact affects behavior at least some of the time.'[91]

The problem is the ease with which the individual, whether as the bureaucrat or as the voter who is his ultimate master, can fall victim to the attractions of playing the free rider – it being, after all, fully in keeping with the rational pursuit of his personal self-interest both to desire that the collective good should be supplied and to desire that it should be supplied by others: 'Every system of social behavior is based on a set of rules governing the conduct of its participants. If enough participants violate enough of the rules enough of the time, the system ceases to work. Yet every participant sooner or later encounters a situation in which he can make a short-run gain by violating some rule, and the only loss he sees is the contribution of this violation to the general breakdown of the system – which in most cases appears extremely small.'[92] What each can do, needless to say, all cannot; and the inescapable inference is that all, anxious to retain the undeniable benefits of the system in the long run, have no choice but to compromise with respect to the rational pursuit of self-interest in the short.

The mechanism for ensuring that the cooperative compromise is in fact concluded by social actors exposed to strong temptations is the centrepiece of the dilemma faced by a public-choice theorist such as Mueller whose individualism evidently extends beyond the merely methodological to embrace a particular (and a particularly hedonistic) theory of human nature as well: 'The methodology of public choice is that of economics.. . . The basic behavioral postulate of public choice, as for economics, is that man is an egoistic, rational, utility maximizer. This places public choice within the stream of political philosophy extending at least from Thomas Hobbes and Benedict Spinoza.'[93] Mueller does not mention the name of the distinguished economic theoretician, Alfred Marshall, who made a clear distinction in his work between thoughtful purposivenes and self-centred greediness, and who reached with some satisfaction the following conclusion on the state of British mankind as it was at the time when he assumed his Cambridge Chair: 'Whenever we get a glimpse of the economic man he is not selfish.'[94] Marshall would, one suspects, not be entirely happy with Mueller's assertion that egoism and economics go hand in hand – and nor, quite explicitly, would Anthony Downs, who writes as follows in defence of the broad definition of utility income: 'There can be no simple identification of "acting for one's own greatest benefit" with selfishness in the narrow sense because self-denying charity is often a great source of benefits to oneself. Thus our model leaves room for altruism in spite of its basic reliance upon the self-interest axiom.'[95]

Downs' model leaves room for altruism. It also leaves room for the moral dimension; and it is in terms of the mechanism of morality that Downs in the last analysis is able to explain the observed presence of cooperative compromise in loosely-defined relationships where the Hobbesian economist would expect to find nothing but self-centred free riders, obsessed with taking and totally unmotivated to give. That the individual bureaucrat (say, the police officer) and the individual citizen (say, the voter) are exposed to strong temptations is not in question, but neither is the capacity of fallen men not to give in – 'and their resistance must ultimately be supported by an ethical commitment on their part. The necessity of this commitment explains why all societies indoctrinate their members with such non-rational props as internal guilt and reward feelings to buttress the dominant rules.'[96] Downsian man, in short, trapped like the rest of us between anarchy and Leviathan, turns for support to the traditions and the conventions of a self-reproducing society. They do not let him down. It is just as well that they do not, for the fact is, in the Downsian perspective, that a close substitute for some personal morality is simply not to be found.

Downs writes as follows on the functional significance of the central value system: 'A successful democratic society (one capable of passing the test of survival) must continuously indoctrinate its citizens with the values contained in its basic minimal consensus. They must be taught sufficiently similar intermediate values that their behavior, by and large, is consistent with the system. Such behavior must include willingness to make personal sacrifices to keep the system from perishing, adherence to a few basic moral rules, observation of the political constitution, and agreement on a vague set of policy principles. These values must be given enough moral force in the mind of each person that he usually overcomes the temptation always faced by every member of an organization: the desire to break the rules in order to procure some short-run personal advantage at the expense of furthering the long-run purposes of the organization, which are themselves ultimately beneficial to him.'[97] What the Hobbesian economist would make of Downs' use of concepts captured by words such as 'ethical', 'non-rational', 'guilt', 'sacrifices' and 'usually' must remain a matter of intense speculation in view of the fact that the *pukka* article has not as yet openly accused the distinguished pioneer of being too close to the sociologist and the clergyman, too far from the constable and the contract-maker who are the standard stars in the public-choice drama.

More important, perhaps, is Downs' evident conviction that his unexpected account of the role played by social values and moral norms in the democratic process is supported by empirical evidence confirming his hypothesis that real-world decision-makers genuinely regard themselves as being bound by the 'basic minimal consensus'. A case in point is 'President Truman's ordering United States troops to defend Korea, even though he undoubtedly realized that this act would cause heavy losses of political support for his party and himself. Since he believed the survival of the system to be at stake, he based his decision on his view of the public interest rather than on the narrower motives.'[98] President Truman, it would appear, was 'not motivated by the same unadulterated self-interest that spurs profit-maximizing entrepreneurs and utility-maximizing consumers in economic theory'[99] – an unadulterated self-interest, it must be added, that is far from absent in the more simplistic formulations of Downs' own interpretation of the political sphere. President Truman, Downs insists, was indeed inspired by the rational pursuit of personal self-interest (as opposed to the beneficent altruism, the self-sacrificing devotion, the emotive commitment to some non-consensual 'common good' such as hardly figures prominently in the public-choice literature). Simply, Downs argues, President Truman made a clear distinction in his own mind between short-run personal advantage and long-term self-interest (a distinction which the student of the political economy of James Buchanan will immediately recognise as being that between the operational and the constitutional concern); and then, believing as he did that the very survival of the American democratic system was itself at stake, consciously opted to spend some of the former gain in order to purchase more of the latter. He was wise to do so; since the ultimate self-interest of the political democrat is poorly served by the ultimate abrogation of political democracy. Nor would a sensitive man want to have on his conscience the burden of guilt that would be his albatross if he did as short-term self-interest would seem to dictate and, defaulting on the defence of the Asian ally, compounded his offence by murdering the leaders of the opposition party and converting the upper house into a retirement home. Which is to say that the 'basic minimal consensus' is the *sine qua non* of the successful democratic society – and that a close substitute for some personal morality is simply not to be found.

President Truman apparently took the moral dimension in some measure into account in determining how best to attain his private and personal objectives. So, apparently, do the Downsian bureaucrats who patrol the streets and who, to repeat, are driven by a 'strong and deep goal consensus' not unlike the professional ethic of the dentist or the social worker to 'risk their lives' and to 'resist bribes'. That these bureaucrats can be compelled to act in a manner that is responsible and responsive by virtue of their accountability to political masters who are in turn accountable to the electorate is, of course, an important potential action-option; just as expanded market control is a second, internal reorganisation is a third and conflict resolution is a fourth. Downs' point is simply that those four action-options are not always and everywhere sufficient to render public officials genuinely civil, genuinely servants; and that in some cases something more than structure is called for. That something more is social convention and cultural tradition – internalised *ought-to-bes*, in short, exercising such a measure of external authority over the individual atom as to have the force of the moral dimension.

Only the individual officer in the dark alleyway can decide whether to give chase to the known murderer; and the community has, in such circumstances, no alternative but to rely for the execution of the contract upon conscious self-policing and the consistent ranking (following the exemplary Downsian example of President Truman) of social over private survival. A not dissimilar situation arises in the case of truthfulness. Every bureaucrat is paid to collect and process information – and yet every bureaucrat knows that that very information can retard his promotion and perhaps even render him redundant. Every bureaucrat is accordingly impelled by the logic of his situation to embrace that 'self-interest seeking with guile' which Oliver Williamson has termed 'opportunism'. Opportunism in the sense of Williamson is 'scarcely limited to more blatant forms, such as lying, stealing and cheating' and, indeed, 'more often involves subtle forms of deceit' such as the selective and strategic revelation of truth: 'Opportunism refers to the incomplete or distorted disclosure of information, especially to calculated efforts to mislead, distort, disguise, obfuscate, or otherwise confuse.'[100] Calculated efforts, of course, such as the axioms of self-interest and calculative rationality might reasonably cause the concerned citizen to expect will be made by the Downsian bureaucrat, aware as that official must be of the high returns to even a moderate investment of time and energy in exaggeration and concealment. Given that no bureaucrat can tell the *whole* truth (his presentation in such a case would be far too long and too complicated to be of any use), given that each bureaucrat must therefore decide *what part* of the truth is the relevant part to reveal (and what part, by implication, must remain in the obscurity of the files to which the bureau alone has access), opportunism in the sense of Williamson is bound to appear exceptionally attractive to the man on a salary with well-defined objectives of his own – and a proper appreciation of the fact that information is not evenly distributed in a world therefore potentially characterised by what Williamson has termed 'information impactedness': 'Information impactedness . . . exists in circumstances in which one of the parties to an exchange is much better informed than is the other regarding underlying conditions germane to the trade, and the second party cannot achieve information parity except at great cost – because he cannot rely on the first party to disclose the information in a fully candid manner.'[101]

Information impactedness in the sense of Williamson is quite clearly a threat to rational decision-making on the part of the principals. Even so, however, even Williamson does not go so far as to predict that the self-interest of the agents will always and everywhere lead them to embrace 'self-interest seeking with guile', despite the multiple temptations faced by fallen men to do so; and to the manipulative nastiness of opportunism and impactedness even Williamson is prepared to juxtapose the significantly less dismal alternative of 'simple self-interest seeking' – the case where veracity will be valued, 'initial positions will be fully and candidly disclosed upon inquiry, state of the world declarations will be accurate, and execution is oath- or rule-bound'.[102] Simple self-interest seeking is intuitively more agreeable than is self-interest seeking with guile; but it is also the more difficult to reconcile with the unadulterated pursuit of the short-run gain. Something more than gain-maximisation, narrowly defined, would appear to be called for. That something more, in the present case of truth-telling, as in the previous cases of responsible voting, effective policing and President Truman, might well be the taking of the moral dimension in some measure into account.

A little morality is the oil that lubricates the wheels of trade. It is also a dangerous thing. A convention of non-manipulative disclosure represses the deliberate distortion of information-flows on the part of the self-seeking bureaucrat who craves a promotion – but it does nothing to repress the no less damaging distortion that is caused by pre-screening and pre-filtering of the raw data through the multi-period systems of the team's conventional wisdom. A network of group loyalties stimulates via informal sanctions the obedient execution of duties and inculcates self-policing patterns of conduct – but it also discourages innovative nonconformity and thereby contributes to the climate of institutional ossification and bureaucratic inertia to which the advocate of habitual standards and accepted norms is, indeed, explicitly committed., An *esprit de corps* within each individual bureau of the larger bureaucracy may well reinforce the 'strong and deep goal consensus' of the microcosm – but it may also promote a cliquish myopia that frustrates administrative coordination, furthers organisational malarticulation, and causes civil servants to ride roughshod over the 'widely shared ethical values of their own cultures' where those values conflict with the more immediate moral standards of the small group itself. The moral dimension, one is compelled to conclude, is able to resolve some of the problems with which bureaus are afflicted, but it also, undeniably, creates others. It is at any rate the fifth of the five categories of recommendations that are to be found in Anthony Downs' account of accountability and action, responsibility and responsiveness. Not every reader will be equally attracted by every category of proposal. That some constraint must be placed upon the powers of the servants to substitute their own objectives for their masters' interest is, however, as clear as Peter Jackson's warning is vivid: 'If the controllers of an atomic energy plant or a genetic engineering research station are risk lovers, they could be placing the society at a greater risk than the members of society would be willing to accept voluntarily.'[103] It must be the task of any responsible theory of collective action to ensure that it is the members and not the controllers who, at the end of the day, are given the last word.

Part II
Olson

4 Free Riders and Free Markets

Hell is other people. So is economics. Economics, therefore, is Hell. Every voter knows as much when, trapped in the maze of conjectural variation and strategic interaction where so much of the human drama is willy-nilly played out, he attempts to calculate his vote-value in the light of the darkness cast by the simultaneous attempt of each of his fellow-citizens to do likewise. His position, indicative as it is of the dilemmas and difficulties born of radical uncertainty and interdependent outcomes, is an uncomfortable one, but also, sadly, the standard case in a world not of *kamikaze* pilots, blood donors and Good Samaritans but rather of self-interested maximisers of benefit and minimisers of cost. David Hume knew as much when, trapped in the conventionalised conformity of a Calvinist Edinburgh never able fully to integrate the innovativeness of his individuality, he was able nonetheless to pen the following account of the paradox of individual choice. 'Two neighbours may agree to drain a meadow, which they possess in common; because 'tis easy for them to know each others mind; and each must perceive, that the immediate consequence of his failing in his part, is the abandoning of the whole project. But 'tis very difficult, and indeed impossible, that a thousand persons should agree in any such action; it being difficult for them to concert so complicated a design, and still more difficult for them to execute it; while each seeks a pretext to free himself of the trouble and expense, and would lay the whole burden on others.'[1] Each neighbour would like to enjoy the undoubted utility-income that arises from draining without himself having to shoulder his shovel and drain. What one can do, however, all cannot; for it is the central tenet of the economics of shirking that, as Arthur Stinchcombe explains, 'each one is better off if he or she gets a salary without working, but all are worse off in a society of slackers'.[2] The optimal scenario for the would-be slacker involves a society in which all citizens are cooperators save himself, the pessimal scenario a society in which all are as venal as he is – and the most likely scenario the blank sheet of paper on which experience will write once choices have been made but not before.

Hell is other people. So is economics. Economics, therefore, is Hell. Every undergraduate student knows as much. So does Mancur Olson,

141

whose own contribution is first and foremost not to the economics of precision but rather to the economics of doubt – to the economics of conjectural variation and strategic interaction, of radical uncertainty and interdependent outcomes. Olson's contribution will therefore have little appeal to the reader with perfect knowledge both of his own future actions and of the reactions of his fellows to those actions. Other readers, more in sympathy with a perspective which conceives of much of human life along the lines of the game played against one another by two prisoners, each tempted to purchase immunity by implicating the other and neither certain that the other will not similarly default, will find much in Olson's *Logic of Collective Action* that repays careful study with cumulative interest.

It is with Olson's *Logic of Collective Action* that the three parts of this chapter are concerned. The first section, which deals with methodology, demonstrates that Olson, like Downs, proceeds deductively from the twin axioms of self-interest and calculative rationality to derive propositions applicable to market and non-market organisations alike. The second section, focusing (as did Hume) on the size of the group as a relevant theoretical construct, examines the three categories of groups which Olson takes into account, together with the two expedients which he adduces in explanation of the fact that even large alliances self-evidently come into being, namely coercion (as in the case of compulsory taxation, democratically imposed) and selective incentives (as in the case of social opportunities accessible as a by-product to those farmers who participate in a protest-march in support of higher farm-prices). The third section ranges more widely, embracing additional dimensions of the complex problem of which Olson so successfully illuminates one aspect. The fact that Olson's hypotheses can be amplified in this manner in no way detracts from their importance. What it does suggest, however, is that their explanatory power is somewhat more limited than would be the contention of the extreme economystic. Olson himself would be the first to recognise that he tells only a small part of a very complex story. The reader cannot do better than to follow Olson's own example.

4.1 METHODOLOGY

Much of traditional economic theory proceeds on the assumption that an individual, while consciously striving to maximise only his own personal wellbeing or that of his household, simultaneously contributes nonetheless to the wellbeing of the whole community, *as if* guided to do this by an Invisible Hand. Yet traditional economic theory does not, in making that assumption, distinguish sufficiently between private goods (where the pleasures of consumption are confined exclusively to the paying customer) and public goods (where the benefits are generalised even to those members of the group who do not bear the costs). Mancur Olson has argued that a more adequate theory of collective behaviour is needed, and has sought, in *The Logic of Collective Action*, to develop the requisite explanation. His investigation begins with the twin axioms of self-interest and calculative rationality that he shares with Anthony Downs and with other distinguished deductivists who are happy to approach the social and the political market with the tools traditionally employed in the analysis of the economic. It is, in the circumstances, with his axioms that any account of his contribution must inevitably commence.

4.1.1 Self-interest

Olson places a great deal of emphasis on the prevalence of self-seeking behaviour and the pursuit of individual satisfactions. It is that emphasis on personal gain which leads him to predict that, while much of individual action is indeed refracted through organisations set up explicitly to further the interests of their members, yet self-interest, properly understood, may actually tend to cause a self-seeking individual *not* to join. Common interests need not mean collective pursuit of common goals, in other words, where the nature of the organisation and the service is such that no individual can be excluded from enjoying the benefits even though he has opted out of contributing towards the costs. On the contrary: even where there is complete agreement on the common goal, self-interest, properly understood, dictates that the self-seeking individual should allow the other members of the group to provide the public good while himself choosing to travel free. Should all members of the group reason in this way, of course, then the public good will not be provided at all. Be that as it may, the crucial point is that group consensus cannot be expected necessarily to generate spontaneous voluntary collective action. Because of the manner in which self-interest informs individual action, group consensus is, if anything, only a permissive factor: 'A lack of consensus is inimical to the prospects for group action and group cohesion. But it does not follow that perfect consensus, both about the desire for the collective good and the most efficient means of getting it, will always bring about the achievement of the group goal.'[1] Given self-interest, the opposite is, logically speaking, more likely to be the case.

Olson places a great deal of emphasis on self-interest, but he also concedes that a good case should not be pressed too far and that 'economic incentives are not . . . the only incentives'.[2] He is aware, for example, of the motivational force that inheres in belief and belonging: 'Many nations draw . . . strength and unity from some powerful ideology, such as democracy or communism, as well as from a common religion, language, or cultural inheritance.'[3] And elsewhere he seems to suggest that other-regarding attitudes can be inculcated and social pressures harnessed, even in very large ('latent') groups, via the mass media: 'If the members of a latent group are somehow continuously bombarded with propaganda about the worthiness of the attempt to satisfy the common interest in question, they may perhaps in time develop social pressures not entrely unlike those that can be generated in a face-to-face group, and these social pressures may help the latent group to obtain the collective good.'[4] Olson points out that an organisation must first exist (and, presumably, have attained some minimal size) if it is to be able to finance such propaganda; but, given that, his idea both of you watching me and of me watching me does open the door to a somewhat wider perception of self interest than is standard practice among economists, by introducing the case where people act *as if* altruistically, in order thereby to purchase utilities such as social acceptance and self-approbation. In such a case (because of a desire, say, for prestige, respect or friendship) people act in such a way as to be conspicuous contributors to the public good. Their behaviour is fully compatible with the self-interest axiom and Olson clearly says as much, pointing out that the very concept of internalised moral norms has connotations of costs and benefits: 'Even in the case where moral attitudes determine whether or not a person will act in a group-oriented way, the crucial factor is that the moral reaction serves as a "selective incentive". If the sense of guilt, or the destruction of self-esteem, that occurs when a person feels he has forsaken his moral code, affected those who had contributed toward the achievement of a group good, as well as those who had not, the moral code could not help to mobilize a latent group. To repeat: the point is that moral attitudes could mobilize a latent group only to the extent they provided selective incentives.'[5]

Suppose, however, that such attitudes did provide such incentives:

the resultant patterns of conduct would be fully compatible with the self-interest assumption, broadly defined, but they would at the same time call into question the significance and prevalence of free-ridership and the underprovision of public goods. The Downsian bureaucrat called a policeman is a case in point. The Downsian officer who refuses a bribe might be own-gain-maximising in the sense that he sees himself, by means of his refusal, as purchasing non-dismissal or buying promotion – or even (as Downs himself would have it) as making a long-term investment in the atmosphere of law and order that protects his house from being burgled and his friends from being mugged. Alternatively, that officer might supply the public good of honesty because he ranks the warmth of belonging above the stigma of ostracism that would be his fate were he to infringe valued conventions; or because he does not want to look mean in his own eyes, paying for the receipt of the bribe in the currency of a spoiled self-image. In all of these cases the officer may be said to be acting as self-interest would dictate. The sheer variety of the cases makes absolutely clear, however, that self-interest is itself a multi-faceted thing.

Olson is aware of the distinction between the narrow and the broad definitions of self-interest, and of the implications of a wide array of potential selective incentives for the public-good problems which are the centrepiece of his theory. At the same time, he does not feel prepared to assign the same weighting to the broad definition as he would to the narrow one. Were he to do so, he correctly observes, were he to assign the same importance to the pursuit of '*individual, noncollective* satisfaction in the form of a feeling of personal moral worth, or because of a desire for respectability or praise' as he would to the more orthodox incentives of money gained and effort spared, then he would be left with a theory which, approaching a tautology, is therefore 'not . . . especially useful': so broad a theory of self-interested action, he insists, 'becomes correct simply by virtue of its logical consistency, and is no longer capable of empirical refutation'.[6]

Not that empirical refutation is easy to come by, since Olson also reminds the reader that subjective variables are by their very nature non-observable: 'It is not possible to get empirical proof of the motivation behind any person's action.'[7] That being the case, of course, one would have expected him to proceed cautiously and pragmatically, precisely because the mix of motives is likely to vary from one case to the next and the only reasonable test in the circumstances to be the agnostic's rule of reason. One would have expected him in the circumstances to have provided a complex model of human motivation, assigning some place to all of the key constructs in any complete theory of collective action – self-interest and calculative rationality, certainly, but also convention, morality, sentiment, sanctions and the restructuring of property-rights. What Olson provides is something more modest – a theory which may or may not account for litter on the commons but which cannot begin to explain the orientation of an integrated community of devout monks cleaning their church prior to the celebration of the Mass. Clearly, Olson's theory is not a *general* theory of human action, and Olson does not say that it is. An author who recognises that his work explains some non-market phenomena but not all is unlikely (even if he himself never says precisely *which* phenomena are Olson phenomena and *which* phenomena are not) to have much in common with the more enthusiastic of his followers, who seek to make the foundations support a weight far greater than was ever intended for them by their designer. Perhaps what needs to be said is no more than this: Olson's use of the self-interest construct is appropriate where it is appropriate but inappropriate where it is not. Few readers will wish to disagree.

4.1.2 Calculative rationality

Olson defines economics not in terms of scarce goods and finite services but in terms of purposive action and the logic of choice: 'Economic (or more precisely mircroeconomic) theory is in a fundamental sense more nearly a theory of rational behavior than a theory of material goods.'[8] Thus it is, in Olson's view, that *any* end may be regarded as economically relevant (the purchase of status by means of suicide as much as the purchase of apples by means of cash), *any* mode of collective action amenable to economic analysis (prisoners protesting for better meals as much as speculators outbidding exchange-rate fluctuations), provided only that 'behavior is purposive and there are not enough resources to achieve all purposes':[9] 'It is not primarily the *objects* of inquiry, but mainly the method and assumptions, that distinguish economics from the other social sciences.'[10] Olson, choosing to build his theory of collective action upon the firm foundations of traditional economics, thereby precommits his approach to the assumption of calculative rationality. It must be inferred that he does so because he thinks such a normative standard is capable of generating good predictions: otherwise he would not, being rational, deliberately choose to waste the reader's time.

Olson does not, of course, make the naive assertion that all of collective action is governed by the norm of calculative rationality. On the contrary, he scrupulously cites instances – the labour of love, the commitment to lost causes, the fanatical service of a charismatic leader – which demonstrate clearly that he is far from confounding the calculus of advantage with the whole of human life. Such cases are bound to crop up, Olson says, and where they do – where, for example, 'nonrational or irrational behavior is the basis for a lobby' – then 'it would perhaps be better to turn to psychology or social psychology than to economics for a relevant theory'.[11] What Olson is saying is absolutely clear, that the assumption of calculative rationality is appropriate where the assumption of calculative rationality is appropriate but inappropriate where it is not. Few readers will wish to disagree.

Olson does not assert that all of collective action is governed by the norm of calculative rationality, but he is confident nonetheless that calculative rationality matters and matters very much: 'The logical possibility that groups composed of either altruistic individuals or irrational individuals may sometimes act in their common or group interests . . . is usually of no practical importance.'[12] The economist's orientation being of such real-world significance, it is no suprise that Olson takes very seriously indeed the predictions that are deduced from the axiom. Thus Olson writes that unions can survive 'because of emotions so strong that they would lead individuals to behave irrationally, in the sense that they would contribute to a union even though a single individual's contribution would have no perceptible effect on a union's fortunes, and even though they would get the benefits of the union's achievements whether they supported it or not'[13] – and then quickly adds that such a non-calculative, non-rational waste of resources may only be expected in the short run, only 'for brief periods' until reason restores its normal dominance over the emotions. His logic is well illustrated by the case of the nation-state which, able to mobilise the affectual force of patriotism ('probably the strongest non-economic motive to organizational allegiance in modern times'),[14] still opts for compulsory taxation in preference to voluntary donation: the citizen, correctly recognising that the benefits are 'generalized' and 'inseparable'[15], would otherwise abstain from payment and leave the costs for others. The unsympathetic reader will perhaps accuse Olson of biasing the argument in his own favour by describing an individual defined to be *patriotic* as acting in a manner that no one could call other than *rational*: the true patriot, the critic will say, has so powerful an emotive attachment to his nation as to be oblivious to the shopkeeper consideration that one citizen's contribution is unnecessary if the others pull their weight, ineffective if they do not. That Olson biases the argument in favour of 'rational individuals interested in a common goal'[16] and away from generous patriots or compassionate philathropists is not in question. His reason for doing so, however, is clear: the patriots and the philanthropists are 'usually of no practical importance' as compared with the cost-counters and the yield-maximisers, and no responsible theorist takes a minority as the basis for his generalisations.

Olson is able to discount the significance for his theory of the altruistic and the irrational. So too is he able to discount the possibility that the very activities of joining, participating and cooperating are themselves productive of a significant measure of satisfaction in their own right. A theory in which the costs are congruent with the benefits is not difficult to formulate. It would, however, be of little interest to a thinker such as Olson who supports his contention that the representative social actor has little of a gregarious instinct to belong and to get involved by means of an appeal to the empirical evidence: 'The average person does *not* in fact typically belong to large voluntary organizations.'[17] The streets are awash with free riders. The streets are not awash with blood donors. Good or bad, that's the way it is.

Olson's theory of collective action relies heavily on Olson's assumption of calculative rationality. Olson himself, however, would be the first to acknowledge that the normative orientation of the High Street and the Exchange is seldom perfectly congruent with that which is observable in non-market settings: 'There is probably less rationality, at least in the sense in which that word is used in economics, in noneconomic than in economic groups. The easily calculable relationships and the objective standards of success and failure in economic life probably develop the rational faculties to a greater degree than non-economic activities do. The theory developed here would accordingly fit economic groups on the whole better than it would fit non-economic groups.'[18] Better, perhaps; but the theory is self-avowedly intended nonetheless to elucidate collective action in non-market settings, and to produce results which are valid and useful rather than limited and trivial. The norm being the consistent deployment of scarce means in such a way as optimally to attain discrete and ranked ends, the actuary's calculus of costs and benefits is arguably most likely to provide a good guide to the way in which real-world men and women actually think in the case of those non-market groupings of which the functions are most closely related to the activities of buying and selling – trades unions and professional lobbies, for example. Olson's own illustrations extend beyond getting and spending, however, and beyond non-market institutions on the fringes of getting and spending: the nation-state, the North Atlantic Treaty Organisation, the proletarian revolution, the charity – the only criterion for inclusion is the postulation of self-interested behaviour governed by the norm of calculative rationality. Not all of human life is here. Only a part of human life is here. Those instances of collective action which are suitable for inclusion are included. Those which are not suitable for inclusion are excluded. The debate is not about the need to include and exclude but about where to draw the line.

4.2   GROUP SIZE

Olson categorises groups in terms of whether they exist in market or non-market situations (i.e. whether or not they make exchanges at monetary values determined by supply and demand); in terms of whether they are 'exclusive' (i.e. want to keep new members out and perhaps even eliminate some of the existing ones) or 'inclusive' (i.e. want to attract new members in while making sure not to lose old ones); and, most of all, in terms of group size. Here Olson distinguishes three cases.

4.2.1   The group of one

In market situations the smallest group is the group of one – the monopoly or monopsony. In non-market situations the smallest group is 'the single individual outside the market seeking some non-collective good, some good without external economies or diseconomies'.[1] In the case of the group of one the individual is the group, the self-interested individual maximises the group's welfare through rationally maximising his own, and there is no public-good problem. There may, however, be a power problem – which explains why the industry of one is 'exclusive' (since the incumbent's monopoly profits only exist so long as there is no new entrant) while the pressure group of one is 'inclusive' (because in such a case strength increases with size and so does finance).

4.2.2 The small group

In market situations the small group is the oligopolised industry, where prices are supra-competitive, but only as long as no one producer unilaterally decides to flood the shared market. In such an environment the participants are interdependent, aware of their interdependence and confronted with the inescapable reality that individual actions have collective consequences: 'In a market situation the "collective good" – the higher price – is such that if one firm sells more at that price, other firms must sell less, so that the benefit it provides is fixed in supply.'[2] Here what one firm can do all cannot and coordination (explicit or tacit) becomes for that reason indispensable: 'It is paradoxically almost always essential that there be 100 per cent participation of those who remain in the group. In essence this is because even one nonparticipant can usually take all the benefits brought about by the action of the collusive firms for himself. Unless the costs of the nonparticipating firm rise too rapidly with increases in output, it can continually expand its output to take advantage of the higher price brought about by the collusive action until the collusive firms, if they foolishly continue to maintain the higher price, have reduced their output to zero, all for the benefit of the nonparticipating firm.'[3] Because unanimous participation is required, the hold-out has very great bargaining power, and such situations are indeed characterised by considerable bargaining. Rivals in such circumstances are also collaborators, but even so there is no reason to suppose they will hit on precisely that quantity and price which an omniscient observer would regard as optimal. Not least, incidentally, because of the transactions costs which arise in market situations such as these: firms lose money every day that the good is not supplied, and that in itself is a valid reason for cutting short the processes of searching and bargaining before what might well have been an even more lucrative equilibrium has been discovered.

In non-market situations the small group may be either 'privileged' or 'intermediate', and it will be useful to examine each of these two possibilities in turn.

Consider first the 'privileged' group, the group where 'each of its members, or at least some one of them, has an incentive to see that the collective good is provided, even if he has to bear the full burden of providing it himself.'[4] A group of this description is likely to exist where the beneficiaries are unequal in size (an objective concept) and/or interest (a subjective dimension) in the collective good. Put simply, the United States gains disproportionately from NATO (and some small countries can hence afford to be neutral) while a great landowner gains disproportionately from a reduction in the land-tax (so that the numerous lesser landowners might rationally decide not to lobby at all). Put formally, 'there is a systematic tendency for "exploitation" of the great by the small'.[5] The large member is known to suffer more than the small from a reduction in the quantity of the collective good supplied and his bargaining power is strictly limited precisely because the threat to withdraw his support is not credible. In some cases, of course, a group agreement will be made to share the costs of the benefit; but even in the absence of such an agreement the large beneficiary (or subset of such beneficiaries) will supply some quantity of the good unilaterally. Some quantity – but not necessarily the optimal quantity. Indeed, if the good is reasonably divisible, that quantity is in fact *likely* to prove sub-optimal: 'This tendency towards suboptimality is due to the fact that a collective good is, by definition, such that other individuals in the group cannot be kept from consuming it once any individual in the group has provided it for himself. . . . In addition, the amounts of the collective good that a member of the group receives free from other members will further reduce his incentive to provide more of that good at his own expense.'[6] The small member wants the good but has no incentive to use scarce resources in order himself to contribute to its being supplied: the large member, after all, also wants the good, and wants so large a quantity of it that the small member can reasonably expect to obtain free of charge as much of the good as he wishes. Because the small member opts to ride free on the provision made by the large, the conclusion is inevitably that all members (large and small) taken together will have to make do with a smaller quantity of the public good than they would ideally have wished to see supplied, while each taken in isolation is tolerably satisfied (the large member) or more than satisfied (the small). Sub-optimal it may be, but some supply is indeed forthcoming without coordinated action in the case of the 'privileged' group.

Consider now the 'intermediate' group, the group 'in which no single member gets a share of the benefit sufficient to give him an incentive to provide the good himself, but which does not have so many members that no one member will notice whether any other member is or is not helping to provide the collective good'.[7] The situation here is one of radical uncertainty as to the reactions of others, strategic interaction becomes the rule of the day, the theory of games becomes paramount, and there is no way of predicting how much (if any) of the public good will be supplied: 'If, in a reasonably small organization, a particular person stops paying for the collective good he enjoys, the costs will rise noticeably for each of the others in the group; accordingly, they may then refuse to continue making their contributions, and the collective good may no longer be provided. However, the first person could realize that this might be the result of his refusal to pay anything for the collective good, and that he would be worse off when the collective good is not provided than when it was provided and he met part of the cost. Accordingly he might continue making a contribution toward the purchase of the collective good. He might; or he might not. As in oligopoly in a market situation, the result is indeterminate.'[8]

4.2.3 The large group

In market situations the large-group case may be taken to mean the perfectly competitive market, where the going price is a public good available to all if available to any. Each producer, should the demand curve for his supply happen to be infinitely elastic, will wish to maximise his profits by expanding his output, taking the price as a constant. What one can do, however, all cannot – since the unintended effect of a collective increase in quantity supplied is a depression in the price of the good. No producer in such a situation will be happy to see the price of the commodity fall. Yet it would simply not be rational for a single perfect competitor to restrict rather than to increase his own tiny proportion of total output supplied: 'A man who tried to hold back a flood with a pail would probably be considered more of a crank than a saint',[9] and his sacrifice would in any case represent a cost with which no visible benefit is associated. The perfect competitor who unilaterally reduces his output reduces his profits (which goes against his own self-interest) and will have no perceptible impact on the price of the product (which means that his decision is irrational because his efforts are futile). The perfect competitor who unilaterally expands his output should all others contract theirs increases his profits (since he sells more at a higher price), and does not spoil the market for himself or the others (since his own share in quantity supplied of the product is so insignificant as to render him by definition a price-taker). Unilateral action in the collective interest, it is clear, cannot meaningfully be expected from a group of perfect competitors who are self-interested and calculatively rational as well as numerous. Nor is there much likelihood of such producers spontaneously clubbing together in order to resolve in common the problem of their common welfare; for 'the larger the group, the smaller the fraction of the total group benefit any person acting in the group interest receives, and the less adequate the reward for any group-oriented action'.[10] The larger the group, the smaller the probability that it will *ceteris paribus* supply the optimal quantity of the collective good. Perhaps it will provide none at all.

In non-market situations four instances may be cited which illustrate the dynamics and dilemmas of large ('latent') groups – groups where, as in the market case of perfect competition, 'if one member does or does not help provide the collective good, no other one member will be significantly affected and therefore none has any reason to react'.[11]

First a corporation with many shareholders. Each individual shareholder in such a corporation correctly perceives that his own personal power *vis-à-vis* management is small, his own vote-value in the sense of Downs is low: this means that it would be irrational for him to become involved precisely because no one would notice him in the crowd. The shareholder is aware in addition that even if one individual were to be successful in altering company policy, the payoff (in the currency of higher dividends and increased share-prices) would have to be shared with other holders rather than reserved for the active and the involved alone: this means that it would not be in his self-interest to participate in decision-making unless his private extra remuneration were at least equal to his private extra burden (a state of affairs which is certainly possible but not, especially where share-ownership is widely spread and individual holdings are small, likely to be a frequent occurrence). The result is that, in a corporation with many shareholders, the power of the owners tends to be *de jure* but not *de facto* and management typically enjoys unchallenged autonomy.

Second, demand-pull inflation: 'The rational individual in the economic system does not curtail his spending to prevent inflation . . . because he knows, first, that his own efforts would not have a noticeable effect, and second, that he would get the benefits of any price stability that others achieved in any case.'[12] If there were only one spender in the economy he could cut prices at a stroke through rational action in his own self-interest. There being a very large number of spenders, however, all 'free to further their individual interests'[13] and no one with any logical incentive to reduce his own demands upon limited supplies, the outcome in an uncoordinated *laissez-faire* environment is that no action is taken at all.

Third, class-solidarity and class-consciousness. Karl Marx makes great play of collective action emanating from class interests – most of all, the economic interests of the bourgeoisie with respect to the ownership of capital and of the proletariat with respect to labour-power. Olson's reply is that such action cannot reasonably be expected given the nature of latent groups such as these: 'Just as the class is selfish', he says, 'so too is the individual',[14] and the inference is that each individual capitalist will be motivated by 'cold and egotistical calculation'[15] to look after his shop (gambling that the others will look after the executive committee of the capitalist class and similar matters of collective concern) while each individual worker will tend to opt out of making the revolution (reasoning that he can have the benefits of any upheaval without personally paying the costs and that one revolutionary more or less will in any case make little difference to the course of events). The absence of class-conflict today, Olson concludes, need therefore not be taken as demonstrating underlying social harmony: it might only prove to what extent apathy is the rational response where groups are large. Admittedly there is more to Marx than self-interest and calculative rationality; but the emotive element in Marxism – the rhetoric of love and hatred, fraternal commitment and the resentment of injustice – Olson deliberately chooses to treat as *obiter dictum* and to set to one side. Such non-rational motivation, Olson maintains, goes against the main thrust of Marx's argument, which is economic, interested and practical – in effect, that it is not easy to conceptualise an individual capitalist who is selfishly exploitative in the factory but altruistically non-calculative with respect to the class. Besides which, Olson says, 'even if Marx really had irrational emotional behavior in mind, his theory still suffers, for it is hard to believe that irrational behavior could provide the motive power for *all* social change throughout human history.'[16] What does provide the motive power in the Marxian model is thus left unexplained – one of the most fundamental of the cultural contradictions of capitalism being, apparently, the rational reluctance of individuals within classes (however antagonistic) to become actively involved in the historical dialectic.

Fourth, collective provision at the national level. Olson, looking to the future, has, like Anthony Downs, no doubt that urbanisation, congestion and the increasing nuisance of externalities all necessitate greater governmental intervention: 'The farmer in a sparsely settled area who is careless about disposing of his garbage, or who has a noisy household, or who decides to go off to work just when everyone else does, creates no problems for anyone else, whereas the same behavior in a crowded city imposes costs on others.'[17] What some can have, in the modern urban environment, all cannot, but that does not mean, Olson reflects, that the governmental expedients of regulation and especially of provision will necessarily produce social cohesion. Sharing tends all too often to be a focus for divisiveness in its own right: 'Diverse wants or values with respect to a collective good are a basis for conflict, whereas different wants with respect to individual or private goods are not. Everyone in the domain of a collective good must put up with about the same level and type of collective good, whereas with different tastes for private goods each individual can consume whatever mix of good he prefers.'[18] To predict a greater proportion of public goods is thus probably to predict greater resentment (of uniformity and inflexibility), not greater harmony and greater integration (based upon a shared infrastructure and a common culture); and such discontent is likely to be heightened by the precise nature of the public goods provided. An important reason here is that, while latent groups such as ordinary citizens, small farmers or day labourers tend *ceteris paribus* to be weak, yet 'business interests generally can voluntarily and directly organize and act to further their common interests'.[19] The business community has political influence disproportionate to its size, and this is due, paradoxically perhaps, not so much to its unity as to its heterogeneity: businesses, after all, divide up into industries, and these, where oligopolised, produced privileged or intermediate groups small enough to organise into lobbies. Hence the unsettling observation already encountered in the work of Anthony Downs, that the special interests of the few are likely (despite the rule of one adult/one vote) to triumph, in political democracies, over the general interests of the many. But this does not mean that the business community *per se* has disproportionate influence in the shaping of broad questions of national policy. On the contrary, it explicitly does not have such influence, precisely because it too as an aggregate is a large and unwieldy latent group – as is illustrated, to take a single instance, by the fact that 'the business community as a whole has been unsuccessful in its attempts to stop the trend toward social-welfare legislation and progressive taxation'.[20] The actual example is a controversial one – much of the welfare complex is in fact complementary to the interests of the business community (as in the case of a healthy and well-educated labour force) and, besides that, pro-welfare pressure groups themselves represent latent constituencies (causing the reader to ask why, given the assumptions of the model and the obvious temptation to be a free rider, they were ever formed at all) – but Olson's main point is clear, that collective provision at the national level is likely to mean a supply of collective goods in the determination of which self-interested and powerful corporate bodies exercise influence disproportionate to their size and membership. There is accordingly no reason for the parts to add up to a coherent whole, or for national plan to reflect national interest, given that not all citizens, in the modern state, are equally well-placed to win the concessions which they believe they require.

Self-interest and calculative rationality point, in the case of the latent group, to individual abstention from collective action – in its most literal form, to individual abstention from the act of voting: 'Though most people feel they would be better off if their party were in power, they recognize that if their party is going to win, it will as likely win without them, and they will get the benefits in any case.'[21] Yet collective goods *are* provided, even in non-market situations where groups are large; and Olson, without departing from the fundamental axioms of his model, is able to account for this phenomenon in terms of two explanatory variables.

The *first* is coercion. In this case, and recognising that an economising man 'has no incentive to sacrifice any more than he is forced to sacrifice',[22] each is compelled by authority to do his share. Thus it is that some democracies make voting obligatory and that all nations (democratic or not) deny members of the community individual freedom of choice where payment of taxes is involved. Olson extends his theory of coercion from the very large latent group represented by the nation to smaller (but still latent) groups such as the professional association in law or medicine, where membership in the association is often a *sine qua non* for practising the profession. Whether he would be prepared to extend his theory of authoritarian compulsion from laws and entry-restrictions to embrace informal social sanctions and the tyranny of the raised eyebrow is, as we have seen, a possibility which he would indeed entertain, albeit with considerably greater reluctance. Logically speaking, however, coercion is coercion, however it is institutionalised, and that is the significant point with respect to the predictive power of his model.

The *second* is the provision of 'selective incentives'. Here what happens is that an organisation supplying a collective good (say, political lobbying on behalf of an industry or an occupation taken as a whole) *also* provides a stream of private goods which are separable from the collective good and made available exclusively to members of the group who have taken an initiative to become members of the club (paying, presumably, the requisite subscription as well). The selective incentives in a question might be access to statistics and technical publications, legal advice and malpractice insurance, strike benefits and social clubs, educational conferences and other gatherings where valuable contacts can be made, assistance in gaining and retaining employment. The member of the latent group has no reason to join a formal association should he be able to share in the benefits as a free rider. He does have a reason to join should non-shared selective incentives such as these also be involved.

The evolution of trades unionism in the United States provides, in Olson's view, a useful illustration of these two explanatory variables at work. Since many of the benefits provided are indivisible and free, accessible to all who happen to exercise the trade or occupation (agreements negotiated with employers on hours, pay and conditions, for example), it is not easy to see why employees ever decided actually to join the unions, let alone why the unions acquired the size, the economic power, the political influence which in their hey-day they came to enjoy. The reason is selective incentives, non-general benefits, both negative (e.g. threatened or actual violence against would-be strike-breakers seeking to cross a picket-line) and positive (e.g. seniority rights granted to union members and union representation of the member-employee in disputes with the employer). Selective incentives seem to have come first; but then, as soon as a large enough number of workers had been attracted to the union by the temptation of non-collective benefits denied to outsiders, the union was in a strong position to press for compulsory membership as the precondition for employment in the trade, the stick was joined to the carrot and the closed shop was invented.

Which is why, in Olson's view, the closed shop need not be indicative of any greater violation of individual liberty than is obligatory payment of tax. Legitimacy depends, needless to say, on the degree of consensus; but Olson notes that evidence from opinion polls does suggest that a majority of workers (albeit, naturally enough, not all workers) would seem to favour the institutionalised compulsion of each by all in the form of obligatory union membership aimed at discouraging free riding – a preference which is entirely compatible with the fact that most of those very workers do not, quite rationally, themselves turn up at large meetings on which they cannot hope to exercise any influence. The 'right to work' (i.e. not to join a union) is thus logically on a par with the 'right to spend' (i.e. not to pay taxes for public services) in that neither right is an absolute one and both depend on the attitudes and preferences of the relevant constituency. It is, Olson says, one thing to argue that we as a nation have democratically decided that unions are harmful and that we do not want them: *de gustibus non est disputandum*, and this argument is a perfectly valid one. It is, he stresses, quite another thing to argue that we as a nation, because of our belief in individual liberty, ought democratically to deny unions the privilege of the closed shop: this argument involves a fundamental *non sequitur* where coercion of each is necessary, at least within the context of the latent group, for the attainment of goals desired by all. Such is the internal logic of the rational self-interest model.

It is not, of course, obvious that the rational self-interest model always yields good predictions – even when applied *exclusively* to those groupings for which such treatment is appropriate and *not at all* to those for which it is inappropriate. Thus, speaking of union membership, Brian Barry notes the importance of national character and culture (as he puts it: 'Can we hope to explain the generally higher levels of unionism in Britain than in the USA by saying that there are more selective incentives?[23]); he emphasises the explanatory power of peer-group pressure (admittedly a non-economic selective incentive in the sense of the model, but one which Olson himself tends deliberately to play down lest the theory become open-ended and tautologous); and he draws attention to the historical correlation in Britain between changes in union membership and the expected payoff from collective action (a result reinforcing the belief that 'whatever the reason why a person may attach himself to a cause, more enthusiasm for its pursuit is likely to be elicited if it looks as if it has a chance of succeeding than if it appears to be a forlorn hope').[24] Such calculation of expected benefit (analogous to the voter's estimation of party differential in the Downs model) is ruled out by Olson, who chooses instead, in his discussion of union membership, to focus exclusively on what Downs would call the expected vote value. Again, speaking of membership in pressure groups, David Marsh reports as follows on the interviews he conducted with British businessmen to discover their reason for joining the influential employers' association known as the CBI: 'The CBI seems to be valued by its members largely for its influence on government and as a counter-balance to the trade union movement.'[25] Marsh does not seek to deny that firms through joining gain access to certain private goods (selective incentives such as contacts, sociability, exchange of information and ideas) from the enjoyment of which they would otherwise have been excluded, only to stress that most members told him (and they may not have told him the truth) that they joined primarily in order to ensure continued provision of the public good: the contributions of others, they seem to have reasoned, are undeniably unpredictable, but the subscription to the CBI is low and the gamble cost-effective nonetheless.[26] Marsh then has this to say about what he regards as Olson's exaggerated instrumentalism: 'One might ask why any interest group continues to attempt to supply the collective good if potential members only join to obtain selective benefits. Why don't interest groups merely supply selective incentives?'[27]

The criticisms both of Barry and of Marsh are directed in essence at Olson's picture of man as a self-interested and a purposive being seeking rationally to deploy scarce means in order optimally to satisfy determinate wants (whatever these wants may in practice be). Neither author would wish to deny that the individual does get involved in the activities of prediction, calculation, rank-ordering and what Becker, defining rationality, describes as the 'consistent maximization of a well-ordered function, such as a utility or profit function'.[28] What both authors would want to suggest, simply, is that there is much in Fred Hirsch's contention that any model which 'neglects individual objectives that are associated with group values or group processes' must by virtue of its very narrowness prove 'an inadequate explanation of collective action'.[29] Mancur Olson, as we have seen, would be prepared to accept that such objectives can and do exist – objectives, to name but three, not unconnected with identification (with a class, a party or a nation as with a family or a church), attachment (where commitment is the polar opposite to instrumentality), and a sense of interconnected fate (as opposed to a balance-sheet of interlocking interests). What he would add, however, is that a theory which explains too much is no better than one which explains too little; and that, to be specific, the incorporation of any driving force but rationality of choice based upon personal self-interest tends to make the theory of collective action tautologous, non-testable, and useless for practical purposes. Motivation cannot be inferred from action and is desperately difficult to discover at the best of times. Olson's contention is, in view of the intense complexity of such motivation, essentially a very modest one – that free riding is a real-world phenomenon for the occurrence of which his theory is able to account. Those critics who propose an alternative picture of man may be right or they may be wrong, he would argue, but the fact remains that they provide no alternative explanation of why in large groups a single

individual so frequently abstains from voluntarily making a contribution where the cost to himself is positive and benefit to the collectivity
is imperceptible. The phenomenon exists and must be explained.
Olson maintains that he has explained it and explained it correctly. He
has also, one might add, made a valuable contribution to the
legitimation of the more-than-minimal State through his emphasis on
collective coercion, democratically institutionalised – since without
such coercion, the sad fact remains that, alongside market failure,
government failure, or organisational failure, our world is characterised by a further kind of failure as well. Social failure; since 'however
important a function may be, there is no presumption that a latent
group will be able to organize and act to perform this function'.[30] What
all can have, one cannot – without leadership and without compulsion.

4.3   THE PRISONER'S DILEMMA

Consider the arresting case of two suspects, Jack and Jill, who are
guilty of a serious crime and known to be guilty. Being self-interested
and calculatively rational in their work, Jack and Jill took care to leave
behind no fingerprints, footprints, bits of clothing or other shreds of
evidence which could be used against them to secure a conviction. The
police have no option but to hope that one or both of the prisoners will
confess.

Jack and Jill are self-interested and calculatively rational, but so are
the police. That is why they put the two prisoners in separate cells,
interrogate them separately about the crime, deny them any
opportunity of communicating with one another – and offer each the
incentive of going completely free if he (or she) agrees to break ranks
and confess. The police do not need two confessions to convict two
criminals of a single crime and so they make clear that the concession is
open to one and only one defector. If both confess, neither goes
completely or even partially free and both serve the full sentence. If
neither confesses, neither is convicted – of the serious crime. But Jack
and Jill, as luck would have it, are also guilty of a less serious crime; and
for this second crime the police do have evidence sufficient to convict.
That being the case, the possibility of going completely free becomes
particularly attractive: even the shorter sentence for the less serious
crime, it is clear, is unlikely to be ranked by either Jack or Jill as
anything but inferior to no sentence at all.

Having presented each prisoner with the menu of choices, the police then opt to play a waiting game and to give both Jack and Jill adequate time to reflect on alternative scenarios and strategies such as might be appropriate to a situation characterised by radical uncertainty and interdependent outcomes. For Jack, the ideal payoff to his gamble would be for him to confess while Jill refused to defect. For Jill the position is essentially the same save that she would like the roles to be reversed. Each has a private incentive to deceive the other, since in the game which they are playing the prize goes to the nasty partner while the virtuous partner receives the penalty. The police, meanwhile, aware that Jack and Jill are both experiencing a strong temptation to behave as individual self-interest would normally dictate, hope that each will confess, which is to say that both will confess, which is to say that neither will go free, which is to say that both will serve the full sentence that is the proper punishment for the serious crime which they committed. The police, most of whom would probably like to believe that cheaters never prosper, will no doubt find it grimly appropriate that both prisoners make an equal contribution to the generation of what each would unquestionably recognise as his or her own worst possible payoff. In some cases at least, it would appear, the policeman's lot *is* a happy one. Not so that of the political economist who said that 'It is not from the benevolence of the butcher, the brewer, or the baker that we expect our dinner, but from their regard to their own interest': his well-known eulogy of self-seeking conduct is bound to have as hollow a ring to it for Jack and Jill as the echo of their footsteps along the corridors of Pentonville and Holloway. After all, they will reason, had they only ignored the advice of the Scotsman and decided instead to act from benevolence – or *as if* from benevolence – their situation would be vastly improved. Each would still be in prison, but serving the shorter sentence for the less serious crime. Each would prefer going free to serving the shorter sentence but would rank the shorter sentence above the longer one. Each was driven by individual self-interest to try for the first-best outcome and the direct result of such selfishness is that both ended up with the third-best pay-off instead. Each should therefore have refused to confess to the more serious crime, served the shorter sentence for the less serious crime, and accepted that second-best is preferable to third-best where first-best is unattainable. *If* first-best is unattainable, of course – and each knows that in certain circumstances the prize is there to be won. Jack and Jill cannot both enjoy first-best. Either Jack or Jill, however, can win the prize that both covet, imposing on the other the penalty of third-best. Both prisoners have strong incentive to cooperate. Both prisoners also have a strong incentive to defect. The prisoner's lot is not a happy one.

Problems like that faced by Jack and Jill are endemic to situations characterised by radical uncertainty and interdependent outcomes, situations in which each actor correctly recognises the behaviour of all other actors to be an important part of the external environment to the constraints of which he must adapt himself but in which each actor knows how little he knows where the future moves and reactions of his fellows are concerned. One illustration is the oligopolised industry boasting a kinked demand curve, where if Punch raises his prices, Judy might not raise hers (thereby competing away Punch's customers) while if Judy reduces her prices Punch might immediately follow suit (thereby leaving relativities unchanged but at a depressingly lower absolute level). A second illustration is Olson's latent group, where each self-interested and calculatively rational individual has an incentive to abstain from making any voluntary contribution towards the provision of a collective good (say, the services of a trades union or an employers' association), no matter how strongly he himself believes that the collective good ought to be supplied: if all others pay their fares, such an individual will reason, *minimus inter pares* can afford to ride free, while if no others stand up to be ticketed, one person's donation will have the same impact upon the provision of the collective good as does a single snowflake upon the provision of a ski-slope in Scotland. Whether in the small-group market situation or in the large-group non-market case, it would appear, radical uncertainty and interdependent outcomes severely circumscribe the potentiality of even the most aware and purposive of actors to make themselves the masters of their own fate.

The large-group case is in a very real sense the sadder of the two. Punch and Judy, able as they are to manoeuvre and scheme, block and circumvent, bluff and trick, are at least in a position where each can maintain that individual actions have significant consequences – and that even third-best is preferable to being swept along by the tide of events without any opportunity to shape and influence, contribute and advise. History stands up when Punch and Judy enter the room. Not so when you restrain your dog from fouling the footpath or when I shut my shop for an hour in order to cast my vote. One vote more, one nuisance less – there is nothing in it. The individual is never more alone than when part of a crowd. History does not stand up when you and I enter the room precisely because history neither notices nor cares. The lonely crowd's lot is not a happy one.

And yet the fact is that people do exist who restrain their dog from fouling the footpath, who take the trouble to cast one vote among many, who volunteer for military service in time of war and shop for housebound invalids in a blizzard or a flood, who donate blood to benefit unknown strangers and leave tips in restaurants they are never likely to revisit, who tell the truth when selling a used car that the vendor knows to be intrinsically as appealing as a rotten lemon, who are prepared to assist a confused old lady to cross the road or to jump into an icy canal to rescue a drowning child, who respond to public appeals by saving water in a drought and energy in a balance-of-payments crisis, who join a boycott by refusing to buy the agricultural produce of a country with whose policies on racial issues there is widespread discontent, who work diligently even when shirkers cannot be indentified, who voluntarily declare all their sources of earnings for purposes of income-tax even when contributors to the cash-in-hand economy cannot be traced, who make gifts to churches and charities, do not use public swimming pools while receiving treatment for a possibly contagious disease, and never drop litter even when they are absolutely certain that no one is watching. Such persons do exist, however difficult it is to explain their behaviour-patterns in terms of theories derived from the assumptions of self-interest and calculative rationality. He who tells the truth is acting against his own self-interest – since he could leave it to others to produce the public goods of truth-telling and promise-keeping while, acting as a free rider on the general atmosphere of trust and honesty, himself proceeding to dispose of his own brakeless wreck at a vastly inflated price. He who saves water in a drought is acting irrationally – since his wheat may wither, his cattle may cease to give milk, his children may go hungry, and still the net value of his sacrifice be no more than a drop in the bucket. Yet such persons do exist, and if Jack and Jill are both among them, then the prisoner's dilemma ceases to exist: neither confesses, neither expects the other to confess, neither goes completely free, both serve the shorter rather than the longer sentence, and students of the Scotsman, rendered speechless by the apparent triumph of coopera-tion over egoism, resolve in future to draw upon their Socrates exclusively in connection with topics such as the theory of value on which his opinions are crystal-clear.

Political economists such as Olson are able to derive their observations and predictions concerning the probable direction of collective action with a certain degree of confidence. That confidence is not, as it happens, shared by all political economists. Doubters will accept that free riders enjoy nothing so much as the anonymity of a large group but will insist that this is not the same thing as saying that all large groups are comprised essentially of free riders – and will stress that the collective dilemma even of a whole nation need not be any more acute than was that of the two prisoners once they had learned when and how to cooperate. Doubters will agree that radical uncertainty and interdependent outcomes *could mean* third-best solutions and empty polling-stations, but they will point to the fact that people demonstrably do sign petitions or hand in money found in the street as evidence that they *need not mean* that the dismal scenario is in practice the typical one. Doubters will therefore suggest that the work of political economists such as Olson tells only a part of a very complex story; that a more general theory of collective action is needed if a proper account is indeed to be provided of important real-world interactions within small groups as well as large; and that such a general theory, beginning nowhere better than with the assumptions and conclusions of political economists such as Olson, should seek to incorporate no less than five dimensions of the dilemma. These five dimensions are in truth overlapping and interdependent, not mutually exclusive; and not one of the five is entirely incompatible with Olson's theory of rational choice which each, however, is able to broaden and enrich. The five dimensions are, respectively, Convention, Morality, Sentiment, Sanctions and Formalisation. Each constitutes in turn the subject of one of the five sub-sections which follow.

4.3.1 Convention

In some cases of radical uncertainty and interdependent outcomes, a one-shot game is played. In other cases the precise game in question is only one game in an ongoing series of similar games involving the same or similar participants. In the one-shot game Jack and Jill have no incentive to regard today's cooperation as an investment in tomorrow's acknowledged trustworthiness (there is by definition no tomorrow) and have no opportunity to learn over time the habitual and traditional ways of doing things which, serving as institutionalised norms and recognisable signposts, demonstrate just how valuable for today is the learning by past doing that is carried over from yesterday (there is by definition no yesterday). In the replicated, iterated, repeated game, by contrast, in the game which has a future and a past as well as a present, there is a tendency for patterns and customs to emerge, and for Jack and Jill to orientate their behaviour towards one another with reference to established rules, ongoing processes, and stable conventions. Such conformity to precedent undeniably restricts their individual freedom spontaneously to take new initiatives. No one but the most unaccountable of bookkeepers would, however, wish to focus exclusively on the costs of convention without mentioned the benefits.

The *first* and most significant of these benefits is coordination of expectations and actions. Thus it is the convention to shop with pounds in Britain, with dollars in the United States: both currencies are legally available in both countries but merchants in each country have clearly got into a rut which it is in the self-interest of would-be trading-partners to respect. Similarly with market-days (each chooses Friday because of the convention that all choose Friday). Similarly with syntax, slang, spelling, jargon and accent (where he who wishes to communicate and be comprehensible would be well-advised to opt for the normal in preference to the idiosyncratic). Similarly with dress (since the 'done thing' provides valuable assistance in selecting the uniform proper for a military parade, a cocktail party, or a meeting of the university convocation). Similarly with the right-of-way at an intersection and the practice of driving on the left-hand side of the road in a country such as Britain (where, as Sugden puts it, 'the rule that we should drive on the left is self-enforcing': 'To drive on the right in a country in which people normally drive on the left is to choose a quick route to the hospital or the cemetery').[1] In all of these cases the adoption of a common convention (and, by implication, the rejection of all alternatives and rivals to it) has the valuable property of serving as a basis for legitimate expectations and reasonable predictions.

For the purpose of such standardisation, such convergence, such imaginative anticipation, moreover, the medium is the message and, in terms of actual content, one rule is as good as another. It is the rule and not the content, after all, that ensures the requisite coordination of expectations and actions. Thus it is, as Thomas Schelling explains, that 'any key that is mutually recognized as the key becomes *the* key': 'People *can* often concert their intentions or expectations with others if each knows that the other is trying to do the same. Most situations – perhaps every situation for people who are practiced at this kind of game – provide some clue for coordinating behavior, some focal point for each person's expectation of what the other expects him to expect to be expected to do.'[2] What is important for purposes of social orderliness is not the precise content of the convention that causes us to measure distance by the foot and not the centimetre, or to rely on an alphabetical order that goes from A to Z, or to put our clocks one hour ahead in spring and one hour back in autumn, or to treat nine-to-five as the standard working day for purposes of doing business. What is important is that *whatever* the precise content of the convention, it is accepted by all members of the relevant group as the unique convention to be adopted in the sequential replays of a patterned game.

The *second* of the benefits that arise from the collective choice of a shared convention bears a strong resemblance to the purchase of insurance in that it has much of the character of an inter-temporal trading relationship. Thus a convention of full disclosure in business dealings would mean that I in effect exchange my truthfulness today (with respect to my exhausted four-wheeler) for your truthfulness tomorrow (with respect to your basketful of ailing citrus fruit); while a convention of proper reciprocation would permit me to buy the first round of drinks in a pub or refrain unilaterally from practising the trombone at anti-social hours with a reasonable degree of confidence that you will not subsequently reveal yourself to be a free-drinker or a free-practiser who consumes collective goods without contributing to their production. A shared convention is likely to prove particularly valuable from the perspective of insurance where the repeated game is not extended and anonymous but continues to involve the same small pool of participants – as where Jack and Jill commit not one serious crime but a whole series of serious crimes, secure in the knowledge that there is convention among thieves and that the other may be relied upon to resolve the potentially conflictual situation through recourse to the cooperative strategy. To do otherwise would be to destroy his or her reputation as a trustworthy rogue and to put at risk his or her future earnings from collaborative villainy, a desperate state of affairs which neither Jack nor Jill would want to bring about save in the very last round of their game.

Even in a crowd situation, however, where personal standing counts for little and general experience is the only basis of knowledge, a shared convention can retain much of the character of insurance. It does this most strikingly in the case of positive-sum games where all players are awarded prizes (as happens where all members of the group adopt the same rules of the road or the same practices with respect to linguistic symbols) but it does this, albeit perhaps less effectively, in the case of zero-sum games as well: thus complete strangers in crowded theatres with unnumbered seats are seen, in the real world, to resist the undeniable temptation to relocate in the interval to seats temporarily abandoned by their established inhabitants. One man's restraint today is another man's restraint tomorrow; and thus does the adoption of a shared convention provide the insurance necessary to guarantee that an evening at the theatre will not inevitably feel not only nasty and brutish but also very, very long.

The *third* of the benefits conferred by convention relates to the saving of scarce resources that would otherwise have been expended on the collection of information and the making of decisions. The very stability of habits and traditions has a demonstration or an educational effect which involves the inculcation of common attitudes and the reproduction of standard responses. Thus a child newly arrived in an ongoing society picks up through personal experience (and even before money has been invested in the formation of human capital through formal instruction) a very great deal indeed of what he needs to know in order meaningfully to participate in an ongoing social game: 'The dictionary may eventually tell me what a seven-year-old means by "dynamite"', Schelling reminds his reader, 'but that's not where the seven-year-old learned to say it.'[3] Where, more generally, the citizen has benefited from childhood conditioning and internalisation of norms, where he has observed customs and roles at work in the culture of which he forms a part, his need for additional information and overt leadership will be less than would be that, say, of an economist from Mars who does not know when to applaud in a theatre or why it is improper to offer a samba to the signal of a rock-'n-roll tune. Were that economist to escape sudden death at the hands of the actors, the audience, or his rather surprised dancing-partner, however, were he then to live among us for some time, that economist from Mars would almost certainly come eventually to live as we do – relying, that is to say, on the instrumental rationality embodied in shared conventions and collective rules of thumb such as enable us significantly to economise on information costs and of which Schotter says: 'Their major benefit is that by solving unimportant problems quickly, they allow the agents in the economy to allocate their effort elsewhere to solve more important problems.'[4]

Besides that, and in a sense precisely *because* they provide information on socially-acceptable modes of conduct, established institutions economise not only on search-costs but on decision-making costs as well. Conventions and rules represent a normative standard, a set of pre-existent general principles in terms of which concrete contemporary cases may then be evaluated by means of logic and reasoning from analogy. The fact that they are pre-existent to the present and handed down from the past has the additional attraction to authors such as Rawls and Buchanan, Harsanyi and Schelling, that a particular decision made under their good guidance will have an aura of fairness about it.[5] Aura or no aura, however, the availability of pre-existent conventions undeniably reduces the *quantum* of time and effort that must be invested in making a concrete decision on a particular issue – on which plane to save in an airport-emergency where one must crash, for example, or on when to call off an expensive search for a small craft lost at sea. Such procedural precommitment permits of a saving of scarce resources and is in that way a valuable benefit conferred by convention.

Convention is conservative, and that is its advantage. It permits Jack and Jill, detained in separate cells without any opportunity for personal communication, nonetheless to orientate their strategies towards one another through reference to background knowledge and practice; while it allows Romeo and Juliet, lost in New York City without any prearranged meeting place, each to form the expectation of most probably meeting the other at the place most frequently associated in the surrounding society with the conception of people meeting – namely, Grand Central Station.[6] Convention also serves as the star that guides the sailor in the case of Firm A and Firm B who, aware that oligopolistic collusion via private dinner-parties is strictly prohibited by law, rely instead on an established system of price leadership and implicit territoriality which has performed tolerably well, time out of mind. Their reliance on the tried-and-tested norms of the *status quo* is fully rational: the prisoners cooperate, the lovers meet, the competitors connive and all are demonstrably able to manage their own respective interactions with success precisely because of the conservative nature of convention which enables them to extrapolate future practices from past.

Such extrapolation, needless to say, would become impossible in a rapidly-changing environment; and it would for that reason be correct to say that, just as the conservatism of convention imposes blinkers on the kaleidoscope of infinite possibilities, so the dynamism of change itself significantly restricts the efficacy of traditionalised practices. It is in the rapidly-changing environment that the farmer nearest the source is most likely to seize disproportionate amounts of irrigation water for himself; the self-interested myopic to graze whole herds upon the commons irrespective of the long-run consequences for himself and others; the too-clever-by-half schoolmaster to question our spelling of 'enough', our pronunciation of Leominster, our fidelity to a calendar with non-standard months and an extra day shunted in once every four years; the *parvenu* entrepreneur to cut his price and improve his product without so much as a by-your-leave from those of us who had made a positive commitment to the mutually-beneficial institution of cartelised backscratching long before he was born. It is in the rapidly-changing environment that convention most comes under strain – and is least likely to generate an equilibrium solution to the dilemmas and difficulties born of radical uncertainty and interdependent outcomes.

4.3.2 Morality

The shared convention, like the rules of hygiene, derives its legitimacy from its efficacy – from the fact that, once established, it is in the personal interest of each and every member of the group to adhere to it. The appeal is to individual utility, the content is ethically indifferent, and the unique action-clause is the rational perception of self-interested man that the shared convention *per se* is infinitely preferable to the normative confusion and combative beastliness which, in the view of thinkers such as Buchanan, is bound to reign in its absence. Given the fearful storm which is the alternative, any port is welcome haven – in the view of thinkers who eulogise the shared convention *per se*.

The approach of the moralist is somewhat different. No moralist would deny that the *ought-to-be* can coincide with the *is* – or conceal the fact that he himself would very much like to live in a society in which this supremely desirable congruence had come to hold sway. What the moralist would say, however, is that the concept of *is-ness* is fundamentally different from the concept of *ought-ness*; and that the latter is qualitatively superior to the former in every respect. The moralist would accordingly wish to see his society's dilemma of collective action resolved not simply through reliance on the shared convention *per se* but on the shared *moral* convention in particular. He would seek therefore to distinguish carefully in his own mind the *is* from the *ought-to-be* and to search assiduously for potential sources of ethical legitimation.

One such source is *adaptation* to environment *as if* guided by an Invisible Hand. It is in a sense less bruising to man's self-respect and pride in achievement if illustrations of spontaneous development and automatic adjustment are drawn from fields of study other than the human sciences. From biology, for example, where unintended outcomes are for obvious reasons far more common than the results of conscious action. As Garret Hardin says: 'In nature the criterion is survival. Is it better for a species to be small and hideable, or large and powerful? Natural selection commensurates the incommensurables.'[7]

Less bruising examples from fields like biology may be, but that does not impede authors such as Hayek from arguing that evolution is a cultural phenomenon as well – or from stressing just how much of man's history is not man-made: 'We have never designed our economic system. We were not intelligent enough for that. We have tumbled into it and it has carried us to unforeseen heights'.[8] Thus Hayek, echoing in this respect Herbert Spencer's organicist *credo* that society is a growth and not a manufacture,[9] loses no opportunity to play down the significance of thinking and intending, managing and planning, for the evolution of culture: 'To understand this development we must completely discard the conception that man was able to develop culture because he was endowed with reason. What apparently distinguished him was the capacity to imitate and to pass on what he had learned.'[10] Hayek's view is evidently that man best exercises his intelligence not so much by selecting proper rules of conduct as by submitting unquestioningly to the authority of those rules of conduct which have demonstrably come to flourish in the specific conditions of a specific environment: 'In other words: man has certainly more often learnt to do the right thing without comprehending why it was the right thing, and he still is often served better by custom than understanding. Other objects were primarily defined for him by the appropriate way of conduct towards them. It was a repertoire of learnt rules which told him what was the right and what was the wrong way of acting in different circumstances that gave him his increased capacity to adapt to changing conditions – and particularly to cooperate with the other members of his group.'[11] If adaptation to changing conditions is a good thing, if evolutionary up-grading over time is a good thing, then so too is voluntary acceptance of shared conventions a good thing – not because they are shared conventions *per se* but they are a particular set of shared conventions, one uniquely appropriate to the unique imperatives of a particular time and place and prone to thrive for precisely that reason: 'Culture is neither natural nor artifical, neither genetically transmitted nor rationally designed. It is a tradition of learnt rules of conduct which have never been "invented" and whose functions the acting individuals usually do not understand.'[12]

Acting individuals no more need to understand the concrete functions of specific traditions than the Sunday gardener needs to know why the rose and the apple are better suited to the soil and the climate of his country than are the jacaranda and the orchid. What acting individuals do need to understand, Hayek maintains, is the unique appropriateness for the job to be done of the customs and conventions that are observed to take root and gain widespread acceptance. Evolutionary functionalists such as Hayek cannot therefore reasonably be accused of merely *deriving ought-ness* from *is-ness* when what they are actually doing is in fact far more ambitious: they are *attributing ought-ness* to *is-ness* with all the confidence in the logic of the momentum inherent in matter that was shown by Fred Hirsch when he asserted that 'the functional need for a change in the social ethic can be expected, over time, to promote it'.[13] While Hirsch in other moods does reveal himself as the last person on Earth one would have wanted to cast in the role of the optimistic adaptationalist, the point he is making in the present context is unambiguously evolutionary and functionalist insofar as he is contending that cultural *norms* are bound ultimately to develop such as satisfy cultural *needs*. Alfred Marshall took a similar stand, as when he drew attention to 'strong proof of the marvellous growth in recent times of a spirit of honesty and uprightness in commercial matters'[14] and then insisted that our modern modes of doing business (as in the case of the separation of ownership from control in the joint-stock company[15] or the institution of verbal contracts in the Stock and Cotton Exchanges)[16] would actually be all but *impossible* in the absence of character traits such as truthfulness and trustworthiness: 'Even the most purely business relations of life assume honesty and good faith; while many of them take for granted, if not generosity, yet at least the absence of meanness, and the pride which every honest man takes in acquitting himself well.'[17] The character traits that are evolving, Marshall is saying, are precisely those cultural norms that are uniquely appropriate for the purpose of collective adaptation to common environment – and that such unique appropriateness is valid grounds for according to them the status not simply of *shared* but of *moral* conventions as well.

One potential source of ethical legitimation is adaptation to environment. A second is the *deus ex machina* of a revealed religion (or of a secular ideology invested in a similar manner with significant non-ego authority). Thus, whereas Adam Smith was able to account for at least some of what later generations have come to call the

Victorian virtues in terms of adaptation and environment (as in his reference to 'The habits . . . of order, oeconomy and attention, to which mercantile business naturally forms a merchant'),[18] Max Weber sought to explain the emergence of the capitalist ethos – the valuation of diligent labour, individual self-reliance, personal responsibility, deferred gratification, calculative rationality, in particular – by treating it as the unintended by-product of religious reformation in the sixteenth century. The Calvinist doctrinal system, Weber said, quite fortuitously supplied the missing *ought-to-bes* that then released the genie of economic change; for the effect of the new Protestant Ethic was such that the bourgeois businessman could for the first time 'follow his pecuniary interests as he would and feel that he was fulfilling a duty in doing so. The power of religious asceticism provided him in addition with sober, conscientious, and unusually industrious workmen, who clung to their work as to a life purpose willed by God.'[19]

The new mercantile and industrial middle classes, one must assume, took their Calvinism straight and without any admixture of Jesus – since otherwise they would have come into contact with a promulgator of *ought-to-bes* who drove from the Temple all those who were buying and selling there, who stated that no man can be the slave both of God and of money, who made the point that it is easier for a camel to pass through the eye of a needle than for a rich man to enter the Kingdom of Heaven, and who, through these and other utterances, caused no less a Chicago economist than James Buchanan's greatest mentor, Frank Knight, to declare: 'If there is anything on which divergent interpretations would have to agree, it would be the admission that the Christian conception of goodness is the antithesis of competitive.'[20] Such was also, less unexpectedly, the view of R. H. Tawney, Labour Party stalwart and High Church Anglican, whose writings are imbued with the conviction that market capitalism is 'not so much un-Christian as anti-Christian',[21] with the insistence that to resign so much of the conduct of man in society 'to the forces of self-interest and greed is to de-Christianise both it and the individual souls whose attitude and outlook are necessarily in large measure determined by the nature of their social environment'.[22] Both Knight and Tawney, it would be fair to add, appear to have based their respective interpretations of Christ's moral doctrines exclusively on passages from the Gospels such as the following: 'Love your enemies, do good to those who hate you, bless those who curse you, pray for those who treat you badly. To the man who slaps you on one cheek, present the other cheek too; to the man who takes your cloak from you, do not refuse your tunic.'[23]

Merchants and industrialists who happen also to be Christians will no doubt wish to point instead to those passages in which Jesus (perhaps because of a belief in the debasement of human nature consequent upon the Fall of Man) couches his appeal in terms not of love but of interest. Witness the case of Jesus on tolerance: 'Do not judge, and you will not be judged; because the judgements you give are the judgements you will get, and the amount you measure out is the amount you will be given.'[24] Or on compassion: 'Be compassionate as your Father is compassionate . . . Give, and there will be gifts for you.'[25] Or on the fig tree which sought to act the free rider: 'As he was returning to the city in the early morning, he felt hungry. Seeing a fig tree by the road, he went up to it and found nothing on it but leaves. And he said to it, "May you never bear fruit again"; and at that instant the fig tree withered.'[26]

Whether Christ's moral doctrines are genuinely rooted in the Hobbesian *bellum* and the contractarian *quid pro quo* (as the Calvinist capitalist in the sense of Max Weber would rationally wish them to be) or whether, alternatively, their essence is better captured by the concept of benevolence of intent (the view of Knight and Tawney), the principal point for our present purposes is simply that they exist and that they are backed up by significant non-ego authority. As with the teachings of the revealed religion such as Christianity, so with the precepts of the secular ideology such as Marxism – and thus does confidence in the sagacity of truly-enlightened intellectual leadership confer upon the normative standards propounded and promulgated the status not simply of *shared* but of *moral* conventions as well.

A second potential source of ethical legitimation is the *deus ex machina* of the revealed religion or the secular ideology. A third is the authority of all over each that comes about when men and women live together in society – and this precisely because the very nature of the shared experience is such as to magnify the moral force of the shared conventions that unite the group. Social solidarity, in this perspective is therefore to be regarded as something more than merely the *product* of common *ought-to-bes*: it is also, and this is more controversial, to be regarded as the unique legitimising agent which alone confers upon those *ought-to-bes* whatever degree of *ought-ness* they happen to possess. In the words of Emile Durkheim: 'Society is not a simple aggregate of individuals who, when they enter it, bring their own intrinsic morality with them; rather, man is a moral being only because he lives in society, since morality consists in being solidary with a group and varies with this solidarity. Let all social life disappear, and moral life would disappear with it, since it would no longer have any objective.'[27]

Durkheim would not hesitate to accept that isolated man is perfectly capable of formulating conventions (the case, say, of Robinson Crusoe choosing to lie on the beach in such a spot as to make the incoming tide his alarm-clock). What Durkheim would deny is that isolated man is in and of himself capable of converting those conventions, once formulated, into specifically *moral* conventions, or of investing his possibly very sensible rules of conduct with any genuinely *ethical* legitimation. That task, Durkheim argues, can only be performed by the authority of all over each – by society *sui generis*, an entity as different qualitively from the individual persons and personalities who make it up as a cake is different from a cupboard full of ingredients. Thus Robinson Crusoe, Durkheim reasons, can as an individual decide that drinking alcohol or smoking cannabis is not for him, but cannot as an individual convert those actions into contraventions of the moral code. The reason is simple: Crusoe is alone and without the indispensable sounding-board of that shared approbation or shared outrage which magnify the strength of the individual's perceptions for no other reason than the fact that those sentiments are held in common. The model is the football crowd or the political demonstration (each whole capable of engendering in the discrete parts feelings far more powerful than the single individual would have rationally expected the matter at issue to produce); and, in Durkheim's perspective, the crowd and the demonstration have a great deal in common with the modern society where questions of morality are concerned. Consider the case of a crime committed in a closed community: 'Crime brings together honest men and concentrates them. We have only to notice what happens, particularly in a small town, when some moral scandal has just occurred. Men stop each other on the street, they visit each other, they seek to come together to talk of the event and to wax indignant in common.'[28] Their individual reason, in such a case, may provide sound arguments against cannibalism by consent or the allocation by auction-sale of High Court judgements, but it is nonetheless their social solidarity which alone has the power to transform the casual conversation into the collectively-binding *ought-to-be*.

As in the small group, so in the large; and it is therefore Durkheim's advice to the student of ethical legitimation that he should 'denounce as a shallow ideal that narrow commercialism which reduces society to nothing more than a vast apparatus of production and exchange',[29] that he should assign pride of place in any theory of normative constraint to collective representations, the collective consciousness, the collective conscience, that he should, in sum, at all times remember that 'morality, in all its forms, is never met with except in society'.[30] Durkheim does not say that adaptation to environment is unimportant (a convinced functionalist, he indeed says the opposite: 'No fact relating to life – and this applies to moral facts – can endure if it is not of some use, if it does not answer some need')[31] – only that scientific evidence by itself represents nothing more than a sleeping *is*, able only to be transformed into a lively *ought-to-be* by means of strongly held societal valuations. Nor does Durkheim deny the existence and significance of religious feelings: so intense are the pressures of all upon each when two or more are gathered together, he argues, that no one should be surprised to learn that 'it is inter-social factors which have given birth to the religious sentiment'[32] – since it is, after all, 'a universal fact that, when a conviction of any strength is held by the same community of men, it inevitably takes on a religious character'.[33] What Durkheim does conclude is that all roads in any discussion of ethical legitimation must and do lead back to the authority of all over each that comes about when men and women live together in society – the sole source, in his view, not simply of *shared* but of *moral* conventions as well.

Whatever may be the source of their legitimation, there is no disputing the fact that shared moral conventions by their very nature provide externally-imposed discipline such as circumscribes and restricts an acting individual's freedom of choice. The conventions are regarded as legitimate and the constraints therefore as tolerable, but the externality of the discipline is, of course, no less real for being seen as right and proper. T. H. Green describes the impact of moral discipline upon individual inclination in the following way: 'The institutions by which man is moralised, by which he comes to do what he sees that he must, as distinct from what he would like, express a conception of the common good. . . . Through them that conception takes form and reality; and . . . it is in turn through its presence in the individual that they have a constraining power over him, a power which is not that of mere fear, still less a physical compulsion, but which leads him to do what he is not inclined to because there is a law that he should.'[34] In that sense the notion of the specifically *moral* convention is fundamentally human; for while most species are endowed with the ability to develop regularities and patterns, to man alone is granted the faculty to formulate a conception of the common

good such as causes him voluntarily to call for and welcome
externally-imposed discipline that represses individual appetites in the
interests of some non-ego standard of *ought-ness* which he regards as
just.

Human societies, both less developed and less traditional, are
characterised by a high incidence of actions emanating from
ought-to-bes. Thus peasants are observed who lend their plough and
oxen to other peasants simply because it is the right thing to do so;
holidaymakers exist who bag their litter rather than depositing in on
the beach; secretaries are known who continue performing well at
work even after they have handed in their notice and unionists who call
for job-sharing (and, but less commonly, the voluntary pay-freeze) in
preference to dismissals when demand falls. Some of these
observations, admittedly, might be explicable in terms of the
inter-temporal investment (as where you enthusiastically pay taxes
today that fund the pensions of current claimants on the basis of the
conservative expectation that the as-yet unborn will show similar
enthusiasm tomorrow when it is your turn to cash in your chips) –
except for the fact that many if not all inter-temporal transactions
(however much motivated by interest) would in effect be inconceivable in the absence of background moral values such as honesty and
trustworthiness. In the case of the currently-funded pensions, your
enthusiasm is contingent on your belief that future generations will
play fair by present-day standards (their principled refusal to default
being reinforced, you will hope, by the specificity of the Biblical
Commandment to 'honour your father and your mother'). As with
time, so with space, in Sugden's instance of two stamp-collectors
dwelling at a distance from one another. You as seller wish to receive
the payment before you part with your property, he as buyer wishes to
see your stamp before he posts on his cash, and in the absence of
background moral values there is every likelihood that the mutually-
beneficial exchange between you and your would-be trading partner
will never ultimately be effectuated: 'It is clear that your position and
his are symmetrical with one another: you cannot both be safe. So you
agree to a symmetrical solution. You promise to put the stamp in the
post straight away and he promises to do the same with the money.
Will he keep his promise? Will you?'[35] Of course he will, and so will
you – provided that each party regards his individual interests as fully
subordinate to some non-ego standard of *ought-ness* which he regards
as just, and of which the Biblical Commandment that 'you shall not

steal' would appear in the present case to be a uniquely apposite illustration.

Schelling says: 'Some personal morality is an enormous social asset.'[36] The pension-payers and the stamp-collectors would not wish to dissent. Nor would Jack and Jill if imprisoned in a one-shot game but aware that each is constrained by moral values such as discourage the practice of letting the side down. Nor would Olson's latent group, where persons whose self-interest and calculative rationality would *ceteris paribus* have inspired them to play the free rider decide instead to join neighbourhood-watch schemes, attend PTA meetings, canvass door-to-door in local council elections, limit the size of their own families to the average that their nation can afford, and express their commitment to the perpetuation of their race by refusing to pre-select the gender of their children. Whatever may be the source of ethical legitimation, one is compelled to conclude, there can be no doubt that a little morality goes a very long way.

4.3.3 Sentiment

Consider the case of Romeo and Juliet, two young Mantuans who become involved in collective action. Each was, no doubt, an eminently attractive property on the marriage-market. Their families, however, were not on good terms because of some long-forgotten slight from which they, like the rest of us, derived great pleasure from remembering. Romeo should, in the circumstances, rationally speaking, have ranked collective action with Rosaline over collective action with Juliet; while Juliet ought, upon mature reflection and in the clear light of logic and calculation, to have opted to indulge in collective action not with Romeo (who was Montague and thus the bearer of a bad name) but with the Count Paris (who was not a Montague, although the bearer of a name which to an impartial auditor does not sound significantly better). Neither party in the event behaved in a manner likely to recommend itself to the attention of the personnel officer of a large departmental store in need of a chief buyer, and both are obviously much to blame for ultimately provoking unprecedented woe that could have been prevented had they only paid more attention to marginal cost and marginal benefit at the initial planning stage, but their conduct (however naughty it may appear to the certified economist) is nonetheless comprehensible and explicable: Romeo and Juliet were in love. Being in love, Romeo and Juliet acted on the basis of unthinking impulses and emotive stimuli such as would cause Romeo to donate a kidney to save Juliet's life, such as would cause Juliet never to invite the nurse to dinner out of respect for Romeo's aversion to what he calls 'that nattering old woman' – such as would cause both Romeo and Juliet, should they happen to rob Friar Lawrence and subsequently be imprisoned in the same cells as had previously been assigned to Jack and Jill, never to betray the other because of sympathy, commitment and concern.

It could, of course, be argued that their failure to follow the selfish strategy when faced with the prisoner's dilemma is in itself a selfish strategy – since once each has internalised the feelings of the other and conflated the pleasure and pain of Alter with the welfare and disutility of Ego, Romeo by imposing unhappiness on Juliet also imposes unhappiness on himself, while Juliet by remaining silent experiences the same joy as does a parent when observing a favourite child's delight in a birthday present. It could in addition be argued that such sentiments are themselves not incompatible with rational maximisation but merely additional arguments in the utility function – as where, to take Gary Becker's example, a man 'would read in bed at night only if the value of reading exceeded the value (to him) of the loss in sleep suffered by his wife, or he would eat with his fingers only if its value exceeded the value (to him) of the disgust experienced by his family. The development of manners and other personal behavior "rules" between family members well illustrates how apparent "external" effects can be internalized by social interaction between members.'[37] Egostic or altruistic, spontaneous or calculative, the fact remains – unless the historical record has been deplorably falsified – that Romeo and Juliet were in love; and that the collective action of these two young Mantuans is significantly to be explained in terms of sentiment.

Consider now the case of Othello and Iago. The former was a coloured gentleman able not only to enunciate but to defeat the Anthropophagi and who had married a white woman some years younger than himself. The latter was a Venetian giving as his profession 'Othello's Ancient' (a job description tailor-made to delay immigration proceedings at London-Heathrow by at least half an hour). Othello had a military background and (perhaps because of the team spirit, the *esprit de corps*, the feelings of solidarity and fraternity which such cooperative activity directed against a common enemy tends to breed and form) would appear to have developed a propensity to trust his closest associate without appreciating just how strong are the temptations experienced by laggard subordinates. Iago's background is less well documented, but we do know that he was envious of

Cassio (whose promotion he deeply resented), and that he hated the Moor (partly, one suspects, because of that non-rational scapegoating which outsiders frequently experience at the hands of an established tribe wishing thereby to express its Us-ness). Iago's orientation with respect to collective action was thus the antithesis of that of Romeo and Juliet: cunning and competitive where they were cooperative, aggressive and malevolent where they were self-sacrificing, Iago was hardly the sort of person one would wish to meet on a dark night in a prisoner's dilemma. The reason is not reason but sentiment: Iago seems to have had severe personal problems (ranging from a compulsive lust for power to an obsessive lust for lust) and these drove him, as if guided by an invisible neurosis, to manifest his emotions and impulses not through construction but through destruction, not through compromise but through conflict, not through peace but through war. Confronted with a rhapsodising Romeo or a streaming Juliet one pops into The Cheese Hamlet or the Chinese greengrocers' until they have gone by. Confronted with an Iago one changes one's job.

Romeo and Juliet were a dyad. So were Othello and Iago. Interaction within couples or pairs is very likely indeed to be characterised by a strongly personal element. On the one hand, knowing the other person, one is able to develop sentiments of one's own towards that unique individual which are totally non-generic: the sentiments may be those involving friendship, gratitiude and obligation or they may embrace jealousy, bitterness and anger, but at least they are targeted and fine-tuned. On the other hand, and because direct acquaintance is the quintessential university of the human passions, one is able to put oneself to some extent in the shoes of one's partner and to feel at first foot where they pinch: interpersonal comparisons of sentiments are by definition impossible, but it is nonetheless easier for an Iago to put himself inside the mind of an Othello whom he knows than of a king, a professor, a monk or a pauper with whom he has never had any personal contact at all. A strict constructionist might even wish to interpret the Biblical instruction to 'love your neighbour as yourself' along these lines. Pointing out how difficult it is to *love* someone that one has never actually met (as opposed to feeling tolerant towards unknown strangers and prepared to respect their idiosyncratic individuality), arguing furthermore that authentic empathy presupposes one-to-one knowledge (since different people experience different intensity of reaction even where the same circumstance stimulates what appears to be a broadly similar sentiment), such a strict constructionist would wish to seize upon the word 'neighbour' and interpret it literally. Sentiment is not sentiment, such a strict constructionist will maintain, save where it is orientated not towards representatives and categories but towards singletons and one-offs: just as charity begins at home, so sentiment begins – and ends – with one's own circle of family, friends and close associates, and no one would think very highly of a Romeo whose sentiments were such that he sent a Valentine to *every* girl in Mantua.

It is undeniable that dyadic interaction affords unique opportunities both to react to the behaviour-patterns and to enter into the mental states of discrete others. Given that I can say how happy or unhappy I would be if in your position but that I cannot possibly know how happy or unhappy you in fact happen to be, personal acquaintance at least reduces the extent to which recourse must be made to fantasy and imagination, if only because it allows thoughts and emotions to be conveyed by means of words, gestures, facial expressions and other recognisable symbols. Personal acquaintance, in other words, is a great aid to the development of that empathetic identification which Adam Smith calls 'sympathy' – and which he for his own part unambiguously saw as other-regarding in nature: 'Sympathy . . . cannot, in any sense, be regarded as a selfish principle. When I sympathise with your sorrow or your indignation, it may be pretended, indeed, that my emotion is founded in self-love, because it arises from bringing your case home to myself, from putting myself in your situation, and thence conceiving what I should feel in the like circumstances. But though sympathy is very properly said to arise from an imaginary change of situations with the person principally concerned, yet this imaginary change is not supposed to happen to me in my own person and character. When I condole with you for the loss of your only son, in order to enter into your grief, I do not consider what I, a person of such a character and profession, should suffer, if I had a son, and if that son was unfortunately to die; but I consider what I would suffer if I was really you; and I not only change circumstances with you, but I change persons and characters. My grief, therefore, is entirely upon your account, and not in the least upon my own.'[38] After all, 'a man may sympathize with a woman in child-bed, though it is impossible that he should conceive himself as suffering her pains in his own proper person and character.'[39]

Sympathy and the consequent action based upon sentiment are, in the view of Adam Smith, closely bound up with the concept of dyadic interaction and personal acquaintance – the reason why, in his theory, an individual feels the greatest sympathy with respect to himself (logically so, since his introspection yields him an intimacy of access to his own thoughts and emotions such as not even the most sensitive psychoanalyst can hope to approximate) and then, after himself, with respect to those friends and relations with whom his ties are constant, close and continuous. Thus the parent with whom an individual is best able to sympathise for the loss of an only son turns out to be a colleague at work of such long association as to merit the name of 'brother';[40] while the woman giving birth is not just any woman but Mrs O'Leary who canvasses for the Socialists and lives in Festival Court. Again, a father reserves his 'warmest affections'[41] for his family – provided, however, that they 'usually live in the same house with himself':[42] 'The force of blood . . . exists nowhere but in tragedies and romances.'[43] Beyond self, friends and family, Smith conceded, we are in fact able to sympathise with our fellow-countryman, so in that sense affectual identification is possible – albeit weaker than in the more nuclear of the concentric circles – even where we have no personal experience of each and every one of our partners in the common culture: thus is born, from contiguity, assimilation and perceived group identity, the undeniable and often very strong sentiment of patriotism. But at the boundaries of the nation, Smith stated, an individual's involvement with others finally grinds to a halt; and it would in practice be astonishing if an individual were not more upset by the loss of a finger then he would be if 'the great empire of China, with all its myriads of inhabitants, was suddenly swallowed up by an earthquake.'[44] The idea is clear enough: you and I might be willing to pay an allowance to a favourite child, or to give Mrs O'Leary some blankets and a pink pram, or even to vote in favour of improved poor-relief at the cost of higher taxation, but our affectual ties and brotherly sentiments can hardly be said to extend to the victims of famine in Africa, civil war in South-East Asia or climatic disturbance in the Carribbean. As Schelling puts it: 'John Donne was partly right: the bell tolls for thee, usually, if thou didst send to know for whom it tolls, but most of us get used to the noise, and go about our business.'[45]

And yet many people, overcoming their indifference and simultaneously resisting the temptation to act as free riders, do in fact become involved, because of sentiment, in the affairs of unknown others. At home they give blood, and this to Richard Titmuss was a sensitive social indicator pointing to a high degree of social responsibility: 'Altruism in giving to a stranger does not begin and end with blood donations. It may touch every aspect of life and affect the whole fabric of values.'[46] Internationally they make contributions to assist lepers in tropical countries and imprisoned intellectuals under totalitarian regimes. Inter-temporally they not only put money aside for their own children but also become involved in modes of collective action aimed at reducing the rate of depletion of non-replaceable natural resources or at preventing the storage of toxic waste on the seabed in containers which are entirely safe for no more than three generations.

People even become involved, because of sentiment, in the affairs of animals. Attending a demonstration to protest against the repression of religious freedom in 'the great empire of China' might be explicable in terms of common humanity (the well-known anxiety that there but for the grace of God go any of us), or in terms of empathetic identification (as where an English Baptist feels able to imagine what must be happening in the mind and soul of a devout Chinese), or even, if one so wishes, in terms of the Rawlsian veil of ignorance (behind which a white man might wonder if he is really a black woman and a Spanish atheist entertain the possibility of a lifetime in a Shanghai jail for the crime of being a Tibetan Presbyterian). Joining in a similar demonstration on behalf of seals clubbed to death for their pelts, pigs slaughtered without first being stunned, dogs and cats employed for purposes of vivisection, gibbons injected with germs, is a different matter entirely – since none of us can put his hand on his heart and swear that he is able to think as a seal thinks, to feel as a gibbon feels. But many people do nonetheless become involved in the affairs of animals; and this reminds us that, whatever may be the subjective ranking in one's own mind of emotion and passion as compared with reason and calculation, it simply cannot be denied that much of real-world collective action is the product of sentiment and little else. Whatever the attractions of being a free rider, occasionally it is the heart and not the mind that must ultimately be held to account.

Nor should it be forgotten to what an extent collective action *per se* is capable of appealing to sentiment. Yet just as people can derive pleasure from drinking a cup of tea, so they can obtain satisfaction from community service and participatory involvement, from following the crowd and belonging to a tribe, from integration, cohesion, cooperation, collaboration and the intense togetherness of the spirit of Dunkirk. Thus Buchanan, speaking of clubs and groupings such as constitute the centrepiece of Olson's logic of collective action, makes the point that sometimes membership is its own reward: 'Note that an economic theory of clubs can strictly apply only to the extent that the motivation for joining in sharing arrangements is itself economic; that is, only if choices are made on the basis of costs and benefits of particular goods and services as these are confronted by the individual. In so far as individuals join clubs for camaraderie, as such, the theory does not apply.'[47] And Hirschman, stressing that in his view individual is not the antithesis of collective where the very process of sharing effort yields greater utility than does the shirking of joint activity, reaches the conclusion that very often it is the free rider who misses out: 'There is much fulfillment associated with the citizen's exertions for the public happiness. . . . To elect a free ride under the circumstances would be equivalent to declining a delicious meal and to swallow instead a satiation-producing pill that is not even particularly effective!'[48]

Thus it is that the members of a football supporters' club enjoy not merely the Olson-type selective incentives of priority booking and cheap travel to away-games but also the opportunity for a shared experience with other human beings; while the participant in a riot or march may lose his job and perhaps even his life but it would nonetheless be wrong to underestimate the psychic gains which he undeniably derives from the constructive processes of collective striving. It is the transformation of self which occurs in *Gemeinschaft*-type situations that accounts for a wide range of solidaristic manifestations – canvassing on behalf of a political party, activity within an interest group, attendance at meetings of the local council – such as would be all but inexplicable within the confines of the Olson model. Action in such cases is not a cost but a benefit; and to that extent the frontiers between producing and consuming, between public and private, become correspondingly blurred.

Collective action emanating from sentiment can, of course, be malign – as where the team-spirit of the barracks breeds rather than combats inertia, stagnation, passivity and conformity; or where a nation of Iagos builds its common identity and perception of patriotic dedication not upon civic virtues involving the unpaid recording of books for the blind or membership in a voluntary newspaper-recycling scheme but upon rallies, revolutions and wars orientated towards the Final Solution of the Romeo and Juliet Problem; or where a colony of exceptionally sociable oligopolists maintains price-stability despite differences in cost-curves because of long association and the feeling on the part of even the most vigorous tree in the Marshallian forest that it would somehow be unseemly for a gentleman to fell an old friend. The crucial point, however, is that collective action emanating from

sentiment *need not* be malign – no more malign, at least, than the
investment made by loving parents in the upward social mobility of
their children, or the decision made by concerned workers to 'pass the
hat' and 'carry' a disabled colleague who had served diligently time out
of mind before an accident, or the commitment made by sensitive
citizens to the physical survival of unborn children under threat of
abortion or of whales in need of saving. Not everyone, reflecting on the
less attractive aspects of collective action emanating from sentiment,
will be entirely happy with David Collard's diagnosis that, 'of the
famous trio, liberty, equality and fraternity, it is the last and most
neglected that make the other two simultaneously possible';[49] for not
everyone will be prepared enthusiastically to embrace the idea that the
precondition for individual self-determination and generic (as
opposed to *ad hominem*) citizenship-rights is a dimension which is
unambiguously emotive and non-rational in nature. Happy or not, no
one would wish to deny the relevance of such a dimension to any
positive theory of collective action. As Sen puts it : 'The *purely*
economic man is indeed close to being an economic moron. . . . To run
an organisation *entirely* on incentives to personal gain is pretty much a
hopeless task.'[50]

   As an example of personal involvement Sen instances the Downsian
case of elections: even where the probable payoff to a single voter is
negligible, he reflects, nonetheless citizens do tend to turn out, and the
reason in such circumstances is that they are 'guided not so much by
maximisation of expected utility, but something much simpler, viz.
just a desire to record one's true preference'.[51] The opportunity for
personal involvement of this kind may not, of course, provide an
adequate outlet for the collective sentiments; and it is precisely
because of his conviction that they do not that Hirschman identifies
apathy and disillusionment in the modern polity. The problem,
Hirschman argues, is not over-commitment (although that in itself can
be a potent cause of disappointment with results). The problem is
under-involvement: 'Under modern conditions citizens are subject to
strict limits with regard to their involvement in public affairs as certain
public institutions keep them from expressing the full intensity of their
feelings on these matters.'[52] The idea is that alienation is bound to
result where consultation is discrete rather than continuous – and
where each citizen is given an identical vote irrespective of the
intensity of the particular preference that each wishes to record: 'The
fact that the enthusiastic partisans of a certain cause or candidate are
restricted to one vote each, in just the same way as their most

lukewarm supporters, cannot possibly be construed by the former as a benefit or a free ride. On the contrary, they would like nothing better than to be able to express a stronger preference and are prevented from doing so by the "one man, one vote" rule. Consumers' surplus turns here into voters' frustration.'[53] People denied outlets for their sentiments, Hirschman argues, are prone to relapse embittered into the second-best solution of neglecting collective in favour of private affairs, but the institutional failure arises not on the side of demand but on that of supply. You and I desperately covet the opportunity to register our convictions and opinions within the broad framework of the political market. He and she, however, make absolutely clear that, beyond the election held once every four or five years on the basis of the intensity-free voting-rule, we are to do as we are told and not aspire to a more active personal involvement in politics. Hirschman concludes that such other-directedness is regrettable insofar as it wastes some of the good juice of sentiment which could otherwise make an even more important contribution than it does today to collective action in our society, our economy and our nation as a whole. That sentiment does even now make a highly significant contribution to collective action – and to the theory of collective action – cannot, however, be denied.

4.3.4 Sanctions

The shared convention, the shared moral convention and the impulsion of sentiment, all three provide normative guidelines to Jack and Jill in their respective prison cells. Behind those guidelines, moreover, there are sanctions, and it is the existence of the sanctions which accounts for the fact that the rules are not merely noted but respected as well. Any fool can promulgate. Enforcement is more ambitious. The three parts of this sub-section deal with three modes of enforcement.

(a)   The self-policing strategy

The non-conflictual guideline is normally self-enforcing in the sense that each of us conforms to it precisely because he expects the others to do likewise: there is simply nothing to be gained from talking Dutch in a Spanish-speaking environment, and much to be lost from driving on the right where the natives perversely prefer the left. The origin of the guideline does not require explanation – it may be as natural as the law of gravity or as manufactured as the rules of commensalism. All that is of significance is that the guideline results from a bandwagon effect and then snowballs via further imitation into a self-fulfilling prophecy. Of course mistakes are made and regrets experienced in the course of learning the code. The point is merely that there is no premium on novelty, no incentive to deviate or defect from the acknowledged standard, and every reason to do the done thing in an attempt to play the ongoing game. He who wishes to drive another day will rationally refrain from driving each time that he encounters a traffic-light just turned red; and thus does the non-conflictual guideline normally become self-enforcing.

Even in situations of conflicting interests, moreover, a self-policing strategy may still develop spontaneously and operate successfully without any central direction being necessary. Axelrod gives the example of the mutual restraint which evolved among egoists in the First World War: 'The live-and-let-live system that emerged in the bitter trench warfare of World War I demonstrates that friendship is hardly necessary for cooperation based upon reciprocity to get started. Under suitable circumstances, cooperation can develop even between antagonists.'[54] Specifically, soldiers on both sides came to honour the tacit convention (despite the fact that the practice was, of course, both illegal in itself and refractory to the very *raison d'être* of trench warfare) of minimising the extent to which they shot to kill. Battalions in the trenches were dug in and immobile for long periods, and were thus uniquely well suited to the implementation of such a tit-for-tat strategy: since the probability that the same players would meet again in future rounds was extremely high (and the probability that significant numbers of men on either side were keen to die was extremely low), each side had a strong incentive to develop a combination of practices which can best be described as 'nice, retaliatory, forgiving, and clear'.[55] Nice – because, given continuity and iterated contact (as opposed to the one-shot interaction), a cooperative action is more likely to provoke a cooperative response than is an initial defection. Retaliatory – because he who consistently turns the other cheek (as opposed to threatening a gunboat and practising the balance of terror) is in effect as much to blame for the ultimate collapse of reciprocated niceness as is the unscrupulous bully who seeks to play the free rider on the coat-tails of the local softie. Forgiving – because once the would-be predator has been taught that his partner is not so nice that he can be exploited without limit, tit-for-tat must not be allowed to degenerate into echoing acts of nastiness but returned, as if guided by the forgetfulness of the damped spiral, from the permanent feud to the path of mutual cooperativeness. Clear – because long-term cooperation presupposes for its success that the strategy is intelligible to the other player, and a complex rule is by its very nature difficult for others to follow. Given that combination of practices, Axelrod asserts, even a random disturbance or an occasional defection (an attempt, say, to test the other's reaction, to ascertain whether it will be hard or conciliatory) will not put an end to cooperative reciprocity – a strategy which is both self-enforcing and entirely unplanned: 'The individuals do not have to be rational : the evolutionary process allows the successful strategies to thrive, even if the players do not know why or how. Nor do the players have to exchange messages or commitments: they do not need words, because their deeds speak for them. Likewise, there is no need to assume trust between the players: the use of reciprocity can be enough to make defection unproductive. Altruism is not needed: successful strategies can elicit cooperation even from an egoist. Finally, no central authority is needed: cooperation based on reciprocity can be self-policing.'[56]

Always assuming a high probability that the same players will meet again in subsequent rounds – and that each genuinely ranks the cooperative ideal above the gladiatorial thrill – and that each is able, despite overall uncertainty, to imagine future states and to attach some utility (perhaps highly discounted as compared with the present) to such outcomes – and that each unambiguously possesses valued counters which can serve as a basis for trade. The contiguity condition would seem to point to decentralisation and the closed community, although the cause of recognition, recollection and reputation, would naturally also be advanced by improved publicity and the institutionalised sharing of reliable information. With respect to the cooperative ideal, the family and the school, should they wish to inculcate at an early age the values which will in later life prove most functional, could lay particular stress on team-centred sports, on subjects such as history which demonstrate the continuity of collective conventions – and on never permanently playing dove to the cheater's hawk lest he thereby develop bad habits which will ultimately harm not only the initial Good Samaritan but later cohorts of bystanders as well.

Then, concerning the conceptualisation and attractiveness of future interactions, there is much to be said for dividing up large packages into small pieces (since step-by-step negotiation is living proof that

time is absolutely continuous), for replacing long-term by short-term
contracts (since the imminence of a review keeps everyone on his toes
and anxious to build up confidence in the value of reciprocal benefits),
for substituting progress-payments for lump sums (since here again, as
Axelrod explains, 'decomposing the interaction promotes the stability
of cooperation by making the gains from cheating on the current move
that much less important relative to the gains from potential mutual
cooperation on later moves').[57] Finally, there is the condition
involving valued counters and the exchange paradigm. Jack and Jill in
their respective prison cells were fortunate each to possess a tradeable
commodity with a market value – his cooperation for her non-
defection, his silence for her silence. A divorced wife whose
ex-husband falls behind in discretionary maintenance payments might
also be said to possess a tradeable commodity – where she has the
option of withdrawing access to the child of the marriage in the course
of bargaining for a return to the agreed-upon contract. An ageing
politician who has rolled his last log, however, or a moribund
corporation about to go bankrupt, is not in so advantegeous a position
with respect to the inter-temporal exchange of favours and the
mutually-beneficial tit-for-tat relationship. This is not to say that the
politician or the corporation will have no access to any sanctions at all –
only to say that they cannot reasonably expect those sanctions to
develop within the framework of the self-policing strategy.

(b)   Social sanctions

Adam Smith stated that it is not from the benevolence of the butcher,
the brewer or the baker that we expect our dinner. While one is
tempted to point out that one's butcher happens also to be the local
secretary of the Save the Children Fund, one's brewer organises trips
to the seaside for old-age pensioners, and one's baker doubles as a
sidesman in the village church where his son sings treble in the choir,
the lesson is clear enough – that it is self-love and not altruism which is
the prime mover in the economic market.

   Life in the marketplace is not, however, the whole of human life, nor
self-love the sum total of the human sentiments; and few authors have
in fact done more to broaden the conception of human nature insofar
as it relates to collective action than did the Scottish eclectic himself.
Smith's point of departure is man's attachment to society itself: 'Man
. . . has a natural love for society, and desires that the union of
mankind should be preserved for its own sake, and though he himself

was to derive no benefit from it. The orderly and flourishing state of society is agreeable to him, and he takes delight in contemplating it.'[58] Man is sentimentally attached to society itself, he is keen to play his own small part in it with the utmost propriety, and he is therefore exceptionally sensitive to the reasoned judgements made of him by well-informed others: 'Nature, when she formed man for society, endowed him with an original desire to please, and an original aversion to offend his brethren. She taught him to feel pleasure in their favourable, and pain in their unfavourable regard. She rendered their approbation most flattering and most agreeable to him for its own sake; and their disapprobation most mortifying and most offensive.'[59] It is evidently to nature herself that we are indebted for the fact that the butcher does not jump the queue in order to bag the tenderest lamb, that the brewer turns down his radio so as not to disturb his sleeping neighbours, and that the baker goes to Weight-Watchers in an attempt to harness laughter and praise to the plough of calorie-control. It is just as well that nature makes no charge for the service which she renders to collective action. We as a collectivity could never afford to pay her what she is worth.

Social sanctions relate to shared conventions which they reinforce. They are specific to a particular reference-group, whether large (the nation, the race, the world) or small (the couple, the partnership, the family). Where standards are undisputed and peers are sensitive, there such sanctions are likely to be particularly effective. We condemn the thoughtless man who carelessly drops litter in a public park for polluting a common amenity which is not his private property. We ostracise the intelligent woman who inexplicably refuses to marry an intelligent man for reducing our country's potential stock of gifted children through her irresponsible love-affair with an oaf. Doctors refuse to share a table at a conference-dinner with a surgeon suspected of prescribing dangerous drugs or of carrying out unnecessary operations purely for pecuniary profit. Workers in a factory dispatch to Coventry or some equally dreadful place an associate who only returns to his bench when the foreman is actually supervising – but reward with respect and the warmth of fellowship a team-mate who is known not to be so diligent that he carries on working when the rest of us go on strike; whose craftsmanship is qualitatively of so high a standard as to reflect credit upon his brothers in the trade or mystery; who always buys his round of drinks in a pub and who enjoys a phenomenally healthy position in the blood-donation chart which we have publicly posted on the notice-board in the canteen. We tax or punish him with our disapprobation whenever he sins against our shared *done thing*; we subsidise or reward him with our praise and sympathy whenever he conducts himself in harmony with our collective expectations; and thus is social man integrated into a network of informal pressures which is every bit as much a set of backscratching relationships as is the tit-for-tat strategy of cooperative reciprocity that is played by a rational businessman bent on investing in durable links founded upon a reputation for trustworthiness.

The businessman's fear is that conspicuous unfairness will be stigmatised in such a way as to cost him profits. The social actor's fear is that deviance and defection will meet its comeuppance in the pub or at the chapel get-together. The cases are symmetrical. The butcher whose mutton is known not to be gristly will be rewarded with money. The brewer who enthusiastically involves himself in national concerns will be rewarded with a beerage. The baker who refuses to drive because he is drunk will be rewarded with congratulations. Jack and Jill, should they forget that there is honour among thieves and opt to tell the truth about one another, will live to learn what it means to be cut dead by one's acquaintances in the Mile End Road. Jack and Jill, should they remember how powerful a force is the opinion of others and opt instead to dissemble, will be paid with praise, which they may well regard as payment enough. It is all very well to say that economic man adapts to his environment. What cannot be emphasised too strongly is that economic man is also social man, and that other people's attitudes are part of the environment to which all but the most self-reliant loner must inevitably adapt.

Social man wants applause, but he also wants to *deserve* applause. He wants, in other words (those, in this case, of Adam Smith), 'not only praise, but praise-worthiness; or to be that thing which, though it should be praised by nobody, is, however, the natural and proper object of praise'.[60] Social woman is no different: 'A woman who paints could derive, one should imagine, but little vanity from the compliments that are paid to her complexion.'[61] Both social man and social woman, it would appear, do not so extensively trade in the marketplace for silly show that they are deaf to the judgements passed by an 'impartial and well-informed spectator'[62] who, dwelling within each of us and completely up to date both with collective standards and individual actions, does his best to make us conform to shared conventions even when no real spectator is there to see us.

Thus Mr A gives a tip to a taxi-driver whom he is never likely to see again (i.e. where there is no tit-for-tat element) and who will probably not invest in future tips beng paid to other drivers by means of a rude word now (i.e. where there are no informal social sanctions), and does so because he has internalised the social norm that such a tip is a legitimate entitlement – and because, in the circumstances, he does not want to see himself as the driver undeniably will, namely as a man who has shown abnormal and unjustifiable meanness. Similarly, Mrs B tells the *whole* truth in applying for life-insurance despite the fact that the company only asks explicitly about her debt position (never more than a few thousand on a single credit-card), her involvement in dangerous sports (nothing but whist with the exception of hang-gliding and parachuting), and her medical history (basically just the near fatal accident two years ago when the *Flying Scotsman* suddenly presented itself on a railway-line where she had chosen to have a lie-down): the company knows nothing about the drink and the drugs, the carelessness and the risk-addiction, but Mrs B knows and, voluntarily declaring that she is accident-prone, she demands that a surcharge be levied by the company lest the average premium ultimately be raised by her reticence and the cost of her secrecy then have to be paid by the healthy and the safe – a burden of guilt which no sensitive conscience would wish to support.

Mr A is Jack, Mrs B is Jill. Each, within the confines of his or her prison cell, will evidently experience a strong temptation to cooperate rather than to defect. Each clearly wants to enjoy a good self-image and to evade the discommodity of a spoiled identity. Both Jack and Jill are model prisoners and a genuine credit to the corporate standards of the shoplifters' guild; for both demonstrably manifest through their behaviour-patterns the extent to which they are subject to social sanctions operating both in the Mile End Road and within the confines of his or her own mind. Their real dilemma, one is tempted to point out, is that they will to that extent remain prisoners even after the Yard has set them free. Too much socialisation is arguably as bad as too little; and perhaps Jack and Jill might delicately be advised to take their repressions and their guilts to a psychoanalyst (assuming one could be found who did not deliberately exaggerate their neuroses in order, being self-interested and calculatively rational, to keep them longer as his patients). Looking on the brighter side, however, at least Jack and Jill are likely to vote.

(c) Legal sanctions

The model is the commons, where it is fully rational for each gain-maximising herdsman to pasture as many cattle as he possibly can: the extra cost per beast to him is zero and the extra revenue therefore rather like manna from Heaven which the individual is understandably keen to gather up. What one can do, however, all cannot, since as more and more herdsmen add more and more cattle to a fixed endowment of the commons the land becomes over-grazed and the cattle become lean and hungry. A half-starved cow is worth less on the market than is a fat, contented, healthy one, and it is in the circumtances fully rational for each gain-maximising herdsman to seek to rebuild his income by crowding still further the public good. One cow more, one cow less, he will reason, the impact is clearly analogous to that made on the price of a good by a perfect competitor who varies the quantity he supplies, i.e. no impact at all.

Thus it is, as Garrett Hardin explains, that 'each man is locked into a system that compels him to increase his herd without limit – in a world that is limited. Ruin is the destination toward which all men rush, each pursing his own best interest, in a society that believes in the freedom of the commons. Freedom in a commons brings ruin to all.'[63] No one, not even the staunchest advocate of *laissez-faire* liberalism, can regard a system of pastoral anarchy such as brings ruin to all with any real warmth – or deny that in such a case law might be the friend, not the enemy, of liberty.

The introduction of legal sanctions to enforce shared conventions represents, admittedly, some infringement of individual freedom: 'But what does "freedom" mean? When men mutually agreed to pass laws against robbing, mankind became more free, not less so. Individuals locked into the logic of the commons are free only to bring on universal ruin; once they see the necessity of mutual coercion, they become free to pursue other goals.'[64] Hardin's solution to the tragedy of the commons is evidently that of Olson, his legitimation of overall compulsion that of Buchanan: 'The only kind of coercion I recommend is mutual coercion, mutually agreed upon by the majority of the people affected.'[65] Hardin is evidently unconvinced that self-policing strategies, peer-group pressures and/or an appeal to conscience will prove adequate to prevent 'independent, rational, free enterprisers' from fouling their own nest. Being rational, those independent free-enterprisers will not want a fouled nest, and will accordingly opt, Hardin evidently believes, for coordination via coercion and compulsion.

All or almost all of the herdsmen recognise the need for limitations to be imposed on the numbers of cattle that can legitimately be pastured by each. The cowmen therefore hire a governor and instruct him (given that what all can do, each cannot) to promulgate and enforce on their behalf the restrictive quotas which they have come to regard as far superior to the chaos and the ruin which is the alternative. Nor are the cowmen alone in this practice, as Schelling has so frequently pointed out: 'The barber shops, for example, appreciate mandatory closing on Wednesday in Massachusetts, since it precludes competitors from staying open. No agency short of the federal government, to take another example, could possibly institute cotton acreage controls on a workable scale.'[66] Then there are the protective helmets which not one of the hulking outdoor types who play hockey would wish to be the first to don but which all – taking the view that no sportsman wants to look foolish but neither does he want to look dead – would very much like to wear: coercion in such a case generates an outcome which is eminently Pareto-efficient in that the vain at least look equally silly while the fit in fact become more consistently fit.[67]

As with hockey helmets, so with motorcycle helmets or the general usage of seat-belts or the general abstention from atmospheric pollutants that threaten the ozone layer: A will conform if he is certain that B will conform, but no one likes to be ridiculed as a sucker by a free rider who in the absence of legal sanctions makes it absolutely clear that he has not the least intention of practising self-restraint. That is why Jack and Jill, in their respective prison-cells, trapped as they are in a spiderweb of radical uncertainty and interdependent outcomes, will declare themselves strongly in favour of an enforceable rule which proscribes defection and prescribes cooperation. Such disciplined regulation, they will reflect, gives them a reciprocity and an optimality which are conspicuously absent in the world of spontaneous interaction.

Jack and Jill opt voluntarily for the arrangements that bind them – which is to say that it would be a mistake to treat those binding arrangements as indicative of paternalism and other-directedness when the truth is that they merely represent coercion by consent and precommitment of collective action, democratically imposed. Most of us are familiar enough with the precommitment of individual action as few of us would get through the day without a considerable amount of strategic self-management. Most of us, as Schelling so accurately says, 'have little tricks we play on ourselves to make us do the things we ought to do or to keep us from the things we have foresworn. We place the alarm clock across the room so we cannot turn it off without getting out of bed. We put things out of sight or out of reach for the moment of temptation.'⁶⁸ We hide the chocolates and the alcohol in order to prevent backsliding; we avoid purchasing a television lest we impose too great a strain on our self-control; we register for keep-fit classes in the knowledge that we could but would not do the same exercises at home; we are careful not to do the week's shopping when we are hungry or to carry a credit-card when we think we might over-spend on impulse. In these and other ways we hire our own internal Dr Jekyll and instruct him (given that, as Schelling explains, some if not most of us are 'not a *single* rational individual': 'Some of us, for some decisions, are more like a small collectivity than like the textbook consumer.')⁶⁹ to regulate and police on behalf of our 'authentic' wants and our 'real' self the occasional excrescences of our own internal Mr Hyde.

Sometimes, moreover, we hire an external Dr Jekyll as well and ask him to do things which an internal Dr Jekyll is not capable of doing – as where a man compels his wife to swear an oath on the Bible that she will never prepare him his favourite sweet until he gives up smoking; or where an invalid who wishes to die but is terrified of dying hires the service of cold-blooded assassin willing to do anything for money; or where a callow youth of unprecedented immaturity volunteers for military service in hope that military discipline will make a man of him; or where Ulysses, ranking himself *ex ante facto* as the rational Ulysses above himself as the deluded Ulysses which he imaginatively anticipated he would become under the influence of the Sirens' song, entered with the members of his crew into (quite literally) a binding contract. Such advance planning based on calculative expectations is quintessentially human (in the sense that the capacity of, let us say, a dog for empathising with his own future feelings and then designing the appropriate problem-solving mechanisms is believed to be rather limited). It is also extremely common: as Elster says, binding oneself in advance is not only 'a privileged way of resolving the problem of weakness of will' but it is 'the main technique for achieving rationality by indirect means'.⁷⁰

It is also exceptionally beneficial, where the coerced self-restraint does in the event serve successfully to ward off the undesired consequences of some anticipated future self-betrayal. The bound Ulysses was obviously not the free Ulysses. The free Ulysses, however, would inevitably have become the drowned Ulysses. The rational Ulysses, ranking the bound Ulysses above the drowned Ulysses, therefore hired a band of external Dr Jekylls and issued the instruction: 'Rather bound than drowned'. The rational Ulysses recognised that some people pay an arm and a leg for a ticket but that a whole life is too much to spend on a single song. The rational Ulysses survived – a state of affairs which must have bred within Penelope the same gratitude towards the members of Ulysses' crew that any representative wife would feel today towards a group of friends who pocketed the car-keys of an inebriated spouse to prevent him prematurely from meeting his siren. Penelope was right to feel gratitude, but wrong to direct it towards the agents when it was in this case so clearly the principal himself who deserved the praise. It was Ulysses himself who consciously re-designed the parameters of his environment in such a way as to make it subserve his authentic desires and not his fleeting whims – as did Penelope herself, it must be said, when she deliberately burnt the combination to the safe in which were stored the chocolates and the alcohol. A few seconds on the lips, a few years on the hips, she reasoned; and a woman cannot be too careful when married to a man with more than a passing interest in sirens.

Most of us are familiar enough with the precommitment of individual action that is exemplified by the hiding of the chocolates and the alcohol, the contracting for binding in preference to drowning. Few of us will in the circumstances have any difficulty in grasping the nature of precommitment of collective action, democratically imposed – the Olson case of coercion – so close is the latter case in its essentials to the former. In the individual case, each of us, operating in isolation, either acts as his own or opts personally to employ his own Dr Jekyll. In the collective case, all of us, operating in unison, decide collaboratively to hire a shared Dr Jekyll (the State, for example) and equip him with all the legal sanctions he will require if he is effectively to carry out our will. The two cases are in all but scale the same. Both reflect the same rational aspiration to enter into binding commitments in advance lest one subsequently becomes Hyde-bound by default. Most of us will probably prefer the made-to-measure tailoring of the former case to the mass-produced alternative of the latter one. Few of us, however, would wish to assign to the collective case no legitimacy at all.

One mode of collective precommitment is typified by the democratic imposition of licensing hours – a prudential move by all to block off outlets for the undeniable temptations experienced by each to spend more of his time and money in public houses than he would in a sober moment rationally have chosen to do. Where licensing hours are imposed in a non-democratic manner what they reflect most often are the crusading attitudes of a ruling élite with respect to the preferences and behaviour-patterns of the rank-and-file. Where licensing hours are imposed by a law the content of which is prescribed by consensus, however, the position is quite different, being that not of paternalism but of self-paternalism, not of coercion by others but of coercion by oneself. Ulysses hired a crew to assist him in the furtherance of what he saw as his genuine objectives. His fellow citizens hired a government in an effort to overcome what they themselves regarded as their own personal weakness of will. The principle is the same for the collectivity as for the individual and is well captured by Elster in the following account of the pre-emptive strike of self against self: 'If I have designed a new type of fishing net that will enable me to catch twice as much as the old one, and if I know that while I make the new net I shall get so hungry that I will prefer to go fishing with the old and as a consequence never get enough time for uninterrupted work on the new, then *destruction of the old net* could be a rational choice: an indirect strategy compelling me to use the indirect strategy of investing in a new net.'[71] Fully comparable to the fisherman's recognition that necessity is the mother of investment is the citizen's recognition that restraint is the antidote to temptation. From the rationality of this recognition then follow compulsory saving towards old-age pensions, punitive taxation of nicotine, salt and sugar, the de-legalisation of gambling, the prohibition of all shops selling cigarettes within a radius of 100 miles from the town-centre, the introduction of a television-free day in a bid to encourage intelligent conversation accompanied by the reading of books – and the democratic imposition of licensing hours.

An alternative mode of collective precommitment relates not to the game played against the self but to the game played against the non-ego opponent whose next move is as unknowable to A as is A's next move to B. It is this mode of precommitment which not only returns us to Jack and Jill in their respective prison-cells but also provides a solution to their dilemma in the form of an external Dr Jekyll whom both agree to appoint as their coordinator and their enforcer in an environment of radical uncertainty and interdependent outcomes to which neither Jack nor Jill derives any real pleasure from adapting. Dr Jekyll introduces a law threatening with imprisonment any prisoner who implicates another – as before, a source of support to the resolve of those suffering from what he calls *akrasia* (and what you and I call weakness of will); but now a source of coordinated expectations as well with respect to the probable next move of the non-ego opponent in the game of life. His success with Jack and Jill leads to an invitation to pilot and guide the commons. Before long he is the national chairman of our collective democracy and charged with implementing our will by means of rules. Thus he introduces laws prohibiting those practices which all of us regard as undersirable but which no single individual can do much to stop – littering, queue-jumping, smoking in a non-smoking compartment, crossing the road when the light is red. Simultaneously he introduces laws rendering compulsory those activities which all of us would like to see universalised but which no isolated actor can make general – the donation of blood, the payment of tax, the recycling of glass bottles. He replaces the optional tip with the automatic service charge (both to ensure that no waiter should starve to death where all his diners decided on the same day to play the free rider on the generosity of others and to prevent the great evil of tip-inflation that sweeps through the land when all try to give tips above the average and the average tip in consequence rises). He makes attendance in the polling-booths optional only for those furnished with a properly-signed medical certificate (reminding citizens how ill the strategic abstention of those expecting a landslide win in fact accords with the spirit of democracy where the outcome is that a well-organised party representative only of a minority-interest forms the government instead). He expands total demand via public spending in an attempt to reduce unemployment, and in so doing he quotes Schelling on the Keynesian paradox of thrift: 'An output of one part of the system is an input to another part. We cannot all get rich by not spending our money, any more than at Christmastime we can all receive more value than we give by spending less on each other's presents.'[72] All of us want to see an increase in total demand. Each of us wants to save. All of us are grateful to Dr Jekyll for helping us to escape from the tyranny of small decisions as it presents itself in the case of the level of demand.

And in the case of an excessively large population, yet another instance where the decentralised mechanism is not up to the job. All of us in our democracy share the view of Garrett Hardin that this is yet another of those sad cases where market failure is inevitable precisely because, in effect, what each can do, all cannot: 'We can make little progress in working towards optimum population size until we explicitly exorcize the spirt of Adam Smith in the field of practical demography.'[73] Adam Smith goes out. Dr Jekyll comes in. Dr Jekyll recognises the limitations of automaticity and cannot Hyde from himself the fact that, as Michael Lipton points out, 'the more children couples produce, the more workers will compete for jobs *14–55 years hence*; therefore, the lower will be the proportion of their time spent in

employment, their wage-rate, the proportion of such workers who
remit to support their aged parents, and the average remittance by
each remitting worker' – but that, despite this depressing prospect, the
isolated couples have no open-market option of concluding with other
couples binding and beneficial contracts to restrict family size, and
therefore opt quite rationally to over-graze still further the already
exhausted commons: 'If all other families are conceiving as many
human tickets to the job queue as they can, then so must you and your
wife, even if each decision lengthens the queue.'[74] Dr Jekyll believes
that quality of population matters as well as quantity, and chooses
therefore not to rely too heavily on peer-group pressures accompanied
by an appeal to conscience: such policies clearly discriminate in favour
of insensitive free riders and irresponsible Bad Samaritans, and this
means that the percentage of children born of selfish parents rises
steadily over time, causing sensitivity and responsibility then gradually
to wither away as character traits within our nation. Dr Jekyll in the
circumstances opts for limitation of births through recourse to laws and
sanctions, and decrees that every couple must go to prison that breeds
more than two children. Draconian though it may seem at the time, the
pill is sugared by progress: unemployment and the cost of rearing
children tend to fall, average health, pay and savings tend to rise, and
the reduction in family size need not cut into the pensions paid by adult
children to aged parents in countries without a formal welfare state
where more children in consequence of smaller families ultimately
survive to remit. In the absence of such laws and sanctions, isolated
couples, ignorant as to whether or not others are procreating sensibly
and having sound incentives themselves to cheat, will in the
impoverished conditions of the less-developed countries in which the
strategic breeding of offspring is so frequently set tend to flood their
nation with a greater population than its economy can support. Legal
sanctions, however, stem the tide, arrest the flow, and thereby release
that nation from the prisoner's dilemma of its population expansion.
What all can do (operating in unison), each (operating in isolation)
cannot; and thus does collective precommitment, democratically
imposed, ultimately raise the level of perceived welfare in the nation as
a whole. This is coercion in the sense of Olson. It is also coercion in the
sense of sense.

Laws and sanctions undeniably yield considerable benefits to a
collectivity confronted with a prisoner's dilemma. They also, however,
entail costs. The costs might in certain cases actually exceed the
benefits. Dr Jekyll might not be the passive servant of the social

consensus but might have ideological beliefs and career objectives of his own; and he might be aided and abetted in the imposition of conventions that are not yours and mine by a staff of bureaucrats and officials who have better things to do than to scan the horizon in the hope of sighting a social welfare function in the middle distance. Then there are the transactions costs of collecting information on the subjective valuation of individual utility and of marrying up data on revealed preferences of different kinds and intensities in such a way as to guarantee Wicksellian unanimity of consent – or, alternatively, the psychic costs that arise where divergent interests and attitudes are not universally reconciled and where the counterpart of the majority's electoral victory is the minority's bitter sensation of alienation, frustration and exclusion. As Buchanan says: 'The selection of a set of enforcement-punishment institutions which makes the median man happy must leave others on both sides of the choice spectrum unhappy. There will be some persons who consider the median choice to be overly restrictive and others who consider the median choice to be unduly permissive in its operation and effects.'[75]

Buchanan also says that 'one of the most disturbing characteristics of modern society is the nongenerality of preference changes',[76] and the very presence within the community of such non-generality (in sharp contrast to the 'all of us want to see' of the full consensus model) points to the emergence of yet more paid-out costs in the form of expenditures on policemen and law-courts, coupled with yet more psychic costs where the rules in the event are evaded (and government itself thereby discredited) precisely because they are prohibitively expensive or even impossible to enforce. The enforcement of the code occasions both paid-out costs (in order, say to repress the ingestion of prohibited hallucinogens) and psychic costs (due, say, to the ubiquitous nature of conspicuous flouting through recourse to black markets), but these are entirely to be expected in view of the fact that collective precommitment, being by definition *future*-orientated, is by virtue of that orientation in no small measure *non*-consultative: as Elster states, the 'Ulysses strategy is to precommit later generations by laying down a constitution including clauses that prevent its being easily changed. . . . The *paradox of democracy* can be thus expressed: each generation wants to be free to bind its successors, while not being bound by its predecessors. This contradiction has a structure similar to what has been called the central contradiction of capitalism: each capitalist wants low wages for his own workers (this makes for high profits) and high wages for all other workers (this makes for high demand). In both cases it is possible for any given generation (or any given capitalist) to eat its cake and have it, but all generations (or all capitalists) cannot simultaneously achieve this goal.'[77] Such inter-temporal inflexibilities are a cause of expense in enforcement as well as of resentment of injustice. They are an important reminder of the undeniable fact that the considerable benefits potentially conferred upon the collectivity by the good Dr Jekyll do not come cheap. Social sanctions and the self-policing strategy are less expensive. They may, however, be less effective. Or more effective. To establish the truth we have no alternative but to question Jack and Jill. Jack and Jill joke that they are not articulate because they have never enjoyed the benefits of what Alfred Marshall called 'life in a residentiary university of the Anglo-Saxon type'.[78] Then, keeping their own counsels, they return to watching television.

4.3.5 Formalisation

A pure public good in economic theory has, strictly defined, four intrinsic characteristics. The first is indivisibility or jointness: on the side of demand additional consumers can be added at zero marginal cost to existing users while on the side of supply, in Samuelson's words, 'increasing a public good for society simultaneously increases it for each and every man'.[79] The second is non-excludability: the commodity not lending itself to being parcelled out, there is no technical means (or, from another perspective, no way short of incurring a prohibitive economic cost) of denying access to free riders without at the same time starving contributors of the provision for which they have paid. The third is non-exhaustibility: if Iago eats this particular loaf of bread it thereupon disappears for all time from Othello's particular opportunity-set but we can all enjoy in common the services of an unpolluted atmosphere or of national defence without one individual's consumption of such a good representing a 'subtraction from any other individual's consumption of that good'.[80] The fourth and final characteristic of a public good is acknowledge-ment: whether the requisite interpretation and aggregation of individuals' judgements is done via the voting mechanism or whether, alternatively, it is performed on behalf of the collectivity by sagacious leaders with a hotline direct to that 'consistent set of ethical preferences among all the possible states of the system'[81] which is the social welfare function, the crucial point is that a public good is not a public good if it is not seen to be a public good. Non-desiredness is a possibility (in which case the public good should perhaps be called a public bad). Invisibility or latency is not.

Many public goods are in the State sector – State-supplied roads, parks and lighthouses, to name but three. Some public goods are in the private sector – trustworthiness and reliability, literacy and numeracy, for example, or (to choose an illustration befriended by a minus-sign) the contagious disease. Most public goods in real-world conditions deviate in some small way from the strict definition given above, either in terms of its letter (the addition of further cattle to an already-overstocked commons clearly violates the third criterion of *as much* and *as good*) or in terms of its spirit (I may vote for a lighthouse as part of a package deal which includes improved conditions for prisoners but am unlikely personally to make much use of it, having no ship). Few public goods in real-world conditions deviate so greatly from that definition as to negate the proposition that, while publicness is clearly a matter of degree, there is nonetheless a great deal of it about. Thence the Olson problem of free riders on buses and trains of which others have borne the cost. Thence the Jack and Jill problem of radical uncertainty and interdependent outcomes amongst isolated prisoners in their respective prison-cells. Thence the recourse to the expedient of formalisation.

Let us suppose that shared conventions fail to keep down noise-levels on a crowded beach; and shared moral conventions do nothing to reduce the incidence of dangerous driving; and that sentiment has not the least impact on the hoarding of food in a period of famine; and that sanctions arouse mirth rather than fear (because, say, the group is too large and too variant to play the self-policing tit-for-tat strategy; or because social sanctions are battered to death by a pathological hardness of heart; or because the law is so costly that the community cannot expect from it more than a minimum of order). In such circumstances the student of society may be exhausted – but the list of possibilites is not. Formalisation remains. The theory, paraphrasing the celebrated insights of an unknown intellectual with a strong line in poor syntax, is 'if you can't join 'em, lick 'em'. The practice is to terminate altogether the publicness of the public good. Where the public good is situated in the State sector, this process of termination is normally known as 'privatisation'. Where the public good is already situated in the private sector, the free rider will turn to drink and Jack and Jill will go on tranquillisers if not reassured that the correct description of termination of publicness in this case is not 'privatisation' but rather 'individualisation'. Formalisation is equal to the sum of privatisation plus individualisation. Perhaps it is also equal to the challenge presented by a society in which rivers are polluted and roads congested not least because that which *de jure* is owned by all is all too often *de facto* owned by none.

Return now to the commons. The cattle are lean. The peasants are mean. All else having failed, the government approaches each of the interested parties (as identified, say, by long usage and active involvement time-out-of-mind) and presents him with the property-rights to a *pro rata* share in the estate. Each grazier is advised that it is in his own best interest to build good fences, but with respect to numbers of cattle or quantity of organic fertilisers is left to collect his own information and make his own decisions in the light of his own objectives (objectives which, unless he for some reason wishes to go bankrupt and lose his land, are likely to feature the profit-motive in a reasonably prominent role). The commons are no longer a problem. The commons *are* no longer.

Encouraged by the success of formalisation on the commons, the government turns to the roads and encourages motorists to purchase a ticket to ride. The roads might be operated by private-sector proprietors (either as owners or as franchise-holders) or by the State, but they would cease to be public goods in that a user-charge would be levied on direct consumers. Toll-booths would be opened and fences constructed to exclude free-drivers from access to the turnpikes. A black box would be placed under the bonnet of each vehicle to monitor employment of street-miles in town-centres where toll-booths would be expensively impracticable but where the ticket-to-ride principle of contribution proportioned to consumption is nonetheless deemed desirable. Parking-spaces would be metered and rented out at values determined by supply and demand. Perhaps the expedient of auctioning off the right of way at each intersection to the highest bidder would have to be rejected because of the delays and transaction-costs involved in conducting the sale and issuing priced tickets. The fact that in *that case* the public good of the shared convention triumphs over the decentralisation of signals and actions that is represented by formalisation does not, however, mean that the costs of implementation, administration and enforcement are in *every case* so high as to militate unambiguously in favour of collective provision. In some cases they are – it is not easy to see how a citizen who resolutely refused to pay his taxes might without prohibitive cost to his fellow citizens be excluded from the benefits of national defence against foreign aggressors. In some cases they are not – the coin-in-the-slot mode of finance for television viewing (in contrast to the more familar system whereby the stream of public goods known as programmes is paid for either through advertising revenues or flat-rate licence fees) is not only a sensitive indicator of what the public wants to see but is not burdened with the prohibitive adminstrative costs that identify the auctioneer at the crossroads as the *reductio ad absurdam*. The toll-booth on the one hand, the auctioneer at the crossroads on the other, both underline the value and importance of Demsetz's cautious pragmatism in refusing to specify *a priori* which goods are 'public' and which 'private', and in opting simply to 'classify economic goods according to whether marketing costs are too high relative to the benefits of using markets and to the costs of substitute non-market allocation devices'.[82] Where it is economic to formalise, it is feasible to formalise – it is possible, in other words, without an unacceptably high level of economic cost being incurred, to terminate the publicness and the open accessibility of the public good in question.

As with the commons and the roads, so with protection against *akrasia*. The private-good approach was adopted by Penelope (who successfully operated a blocking strategy against herself with respect to the chocolates and the alcohol) and by Ulysses (who made a binding contract with his business associates and paid them a mutually-acceptable *quid pro quo* for their services). The public-good approach was adopted by the decision-making group which went in for the democratic imposition of licensing hours (collective precommitment such as ensures that not one of us will be in a position to allow his weaker nature to yield to temptation in a manner which his stronger self would regard as exceptionally naughty) and of coordinative guidelines (collective precommitment such as ensures that each of us will make the expected moves in life's game and thereby contribute to a climate of certainty within the environment that is shared by all). The advocate of formalisation will argue that the private-good approach is the superior one, representing a made-to-measure mode of compulsion and one which imposes binding exclusively upon those persons who personally request that binding be imposed. He will therefore press a government which has already shown itself responsive to the concept of privatisation in the case of the commons and of the roads to show a similar openness towards the termination of publicness with respect to the transfer from the sphere of collective precommitment to that of individual precommitment of as many measures aimed at combatting weakness of will as may feasibly be formalised.

With respect to the game of self against self, what this means is that the weak-willed smoker, no longer able to shelter under the reassuring blanket of State prohibition of all shops selling cigarettes within a radius of 100 miles of the town centre, will have to purchase his own protection by means of relocating his place of residence in such a way as never to pass within 100 miles of the nearest emporium vending the demon weed. Personal protection will be purchased in a similar manner by the weak-willed but rational executive who ensures (despite the inevitable delays and wastage of staff-time) that each of the company's cheques bears several signatures besides his own; or by the employee who asks that he be assisted to live up to his own highest ideals via the substitution for the fixed salary (a system which he says he finds an inducement to idleness) of payment by results in the form of piece-rates, bonuses and commissions (a system which he says he finds a trigger to that conscientious assiduity which was in him all along) – or by the policeman who, inspired by the example of Ulysses bound (not drowned) and of Penelope slimmed (not ginned), personally requests frequent rotation and reassignment in a conscious attempt to insulate himself from the temptations of the bribes to which the bobbie in the rut is more likely to exposed. All of these instances refer to the game of self against self and illustrate in what way individual precommitment could be purchased by those individuals who individually demand such precommitment – and (in contrast to the public good of collective precommitment) by *those* individuals exclusively and by *no others*.

With respect to the game played against the non-ego opponent, the position insofar as the purchase of protection against *akrasia* is concerned is in its essentials no different. Thus weak-willed oligopolists may sincerely lament the abolition of State-sponsored price-controls (the privatisation, in other words, of the public good of administered values) but nonetheless prove inventive enough to think up a private sector expedient capable of delivering an equivalent dosage of precommitment – as where each firm redesigns its product in such a way as to make it unattractive to the other firms' principal customers; or where the competitors buy large blocs of shares in one another's equity in order to generate the countervailing power requisite to return the industry to the inertia which it had previously enjoyed. The free rider, due to privatisation, might actually cease to ride free – as where donors know that one pint more or one pint less makes little difference to the national pool of blood for transfusion (and therefore vote with their feet to keep their vein firmly at work), but where merchants see that private quantity supplied is directly remunerated with private cash demanded (and therefore sell to a blood bank at a fee that which they would not have found it in their heart to donate so long as blood for transfusion continued to have the status of a public good).

Even Jack and Jill in their respective prison-cells might confess that formalisation could provide them with a way out of their shared dilemma. Formalisation in their particular case could take the form of privatisation – as where the repeal of the good Dr Jekyll's no doubt very fine law threatening with imprisonment any prisoner who implicates another is accompanied by the conclusion between Jack and Jill of a binding contact such as specifies that the defector is to remain subject to precisely the same sanctions. Formalisation in their particular case (given their unique relationship to the courts and the police) is more likely to take the form of innovative individualisation – not the *replacement* of collective by individual precommitment but, more likely, the *creation* of precommitment where antecedent to the private good being created there had not been in existence any public good capable of fulfilling the function in question. To be specific, it is a little-known fact of indisputable historical accuracy that Jack and Jill in advance of embarking on a life of crime of such criminality as to make Bonnie and Clyde look like Romeo and Juliet opted to take a precaution which is not uncommon when two persons of the opposite sex find they cannot control their weakness of will. They got married. Jack hating all women and Jill liking all men with the single exception of Jack, it cannot have been love that caused them to enter into this binding commitment. Nor was it benevolence that caused them to seal their contract, but rather self-interest; for it is a little-known fact of indisputable historical accuracy that Jack and Jill happened to live in a country in which the evidence of husbands and wives against one another was inadmissible in court. Reflecting that *akrasia* and crime were virtually the only things they had in common, Jack and Jill chose rationally to embrace the following proposition: 'Better wed than dead'. In so doing, Jack and Jill also demonstrated that private-sector expedients can and do arise, here as in other cases, such as are able unaided to supply the coordinative precommitment that then represents a viable solution to what they obviously imagined would one day become the prisoners' dilemma.

Formalisation is evidently capable, conceptually speaking, of generating a viable solution to the Olson problem of free riders who have not paid, to the Jack and Jill problem of radical uncertainty and interdependent outcomes, in the specific cases which we have cited of the commons, road-transport and protection against *akrasia*. Formalisation is in addition capable, conceptually speaking, of delivering private-sector surrogates and alternatives of a quantity and a quality such as would be able successfully to fill the social vacuum left behind should shared moral conventions turn out, as some thinkers are prone to suggest, genuinely to have been superseded by the state of *anomie*. Thus, while honesty may be the best policy, it is not the only policy, and that is why we buy good advice from an expert mechanic before committing ourselves to the purchase of a second-hand car, why we pay for a second medical opinion as a routine check on the balance of the first before agreeing to part with what may in truth be a robust and healthy appendix, why we hire an experienced solicitor to examine the lease even if the vendor is our own eldest son and the dwelling in question the very property which we gifted him at the time of his first marriage. It is not from the benevolence of the expert mechanic, the external examiner or the experienced solicitor that we expect the fulfilment of a function which might well be unnecessary if absolute honesty were the operative norm; and that it is why it is to their self-interest and their concern with advancement that we address our appeal. Properly addressed or poorly addressed, however, the crucial point is that the appeal arrives at its destination and that mutual gains from trade are in consequence thereof appointed to a position rendered vacant through the natural wastage of the previous incumbent, normative constraint.

As with honesty and truthfulness, so with compassion and thoughtfulness – and Ronald Coase in particular has actually expressed the view that the suppression of caring at the level of motivation might, surprisingly, lead to an expansion in the quantity of care supplied at the level of outcome. Coase's argument turns on his fundamental conviction that there is typically more than one side to a question, more than one party to a dispute; and that action emanating from compassion with respect to Jill is unlikely to be perceived as action emanating from thoughtfulness when contemplated by Jack. Consider a public house which wanted to locate a ventilating shaft near a cluster of cottages: 'The economic problem was to decide which to choose: a lower cost of beer and worsened amenities in adjoining houses or a higher cost of beer and improved amenities.'[83] Consider a factory manufacturing a wonder-drug which dumps the effluent and dishes the trout: 'If we assume that the harmful effect of the pollution is that it kills the fish, the question to be decided is: is the value of the fish lost greater or less than the value of the product which contamination of the stream makes possible.'[84] Consider an airport which, at the cost of noise-nuisance to its neighbours, facilitates the transport of foreign tourists to that pub and of that drug to foreign markets, and in that way assists home consumers to purchase imported commodities in quantities not limited by exchange controls: 'It is all a question of weighing up the gains that would accrue from eliminating [the] harmful effects against the gains that accrue from allowing them to continue.'[85] It is in the circumstances, Coase says, by no means an easy task to identify guilty parties and innocent victims, or to decide towards whom to to direct one's compassion. Of course the doctor is wronged where the confectioner's machinery, operating on the other side of the party wall from his surgery, causes so much noise and vibration as to render consultations difficult if not impossible. But so too is the confectioner wronged if made subject to an injunction compelling him to donate tranquillity at the expense of his profits and perhaps of his business (and thus of his nation, should we then 'secure more doctoring at the cost of a reduced supply of confectionery products').[86] To avoid harming the confectioner would inflict harm on the doctor. To avoid harming the doctor would inflict harm on the confectioner. The doctor would not have been disturbed by the noise if the confectioner had not worked his machinery. The machinery would have disturbed no one if the doctor had employed the room in question as a laundry-room rather than as a consulting room. Clearly, therefore, 'if we are to discuss the problem in terms of causation, both parties cause the damage'.[87]

The case is one of 'a problem of a reciprocal nature'.[88] The solution, in Coase's view, is in two parts. The first part is proper specification, the precise definition of property rights; and that task is the responsibility of Parliament and the law courts. The second part is the opportunity to trade and bargain, to exchange a proportion or the whole of those rights for a *quid pro quo* enjoying a higher subjective valuation; and the function of arranging such mutually-satisfactory swaps is normally delegated, in the non-planned market economy, to the decentralised pricing system. The two-part mechanism means that each player has two opportunities to win the prize, each opportunity involving a different arena of social life. Thus, even if the judge were to rule in favour of the doctor, the confectioner might then offer to purchase from the doctor the right to continue to operate his machinery – and the doctor might be happy to sell this waiver if the bribe being paid by the confectioner were 'greater than the loss of income which he would suffer from having to move to a more costly or less convenient location or from having to curtail his activities at this location or . . . from having to build a separate wall which would deaden the noise and vibration. The confectioner would have been willing to do this if the amount he would have to pay the doctor was less than the fall in income he would suffer if he had to change his mode of operation at this location, abandon his operation, or move his confectionery business to some other location. The solution of the problem depends essentially on whether the continued use of the machinery adds more to the confectioner's income than it subtracts from the doctor's.'[89] Obviously, if the judge had ruled in favour of the confectioner, then the inconvenience would have continued without any compensation being payable to the doctor. But 'if the doctor's income would have fallen more through continuance of the use of this machinery than it added to the income of the confectioner, there would clearly be room for a bargain whereby the doctor paid the confectioner to stop using the machinery.'[90] And this without any role being assigned to moral sentiments such as compassion and thoughtfulness. Of course the moral sentiments are nice, just as treacle is nice and whist is nice. Luxuries are not necessities, however, and the doctor and the confectioner evidently succeeded in establishing a business relationship that was entirely formalised, purified of moral values having the character of public goods.

What the doctor and the confectioner can do, so, in the perspective of the property-rights economist such as Ronald Coase, can Jack and Jill, by appointing an auctioneer and coming to a mutually-satisfactory agreement on the economic value of their silence. Jack and Jill in such a case opt decisively to render their public good non-public in nature, to allocate on the shopkeeper principle of the *quid pro quo* that which previously had been available for consumption without the intervention of the gatekeeper that is the metering device and the user-charge. Today Jack and Jill, tomorrow the nation and the world, the radical formaliser will conclude. His logic is absolutely clear. Schelling, who believes that 'trust and honesty are of great social worth', says that 'we don't expect the motorist with a disabled car to have to pay $10 to get a passing motorist to phone for help'.[91] The radical formaliser, unconvinced that social morality is the functional equivalent of those instinctual commandments that prevent the adult wolf from terminating the species by devouring its offspring, replies that expectations are a variable, not a constant, and that even the adult motorist cannot reasonably expect to be insulated forever from the challenge of the new.

The differences between the social moderate and the radical formaliser, indicative as they are of fundamental values as well as of technical possibilities, are not easy to resolve. Nor is there any need to resolve them. Jack Spratt could eat no fat. Jill Spratt could eat no lean. Jack's choice was the right choice for Jack. Jill's choice was the right choice for Jill. In prison each Spratt had to make do with the standard diet. In a free society the fare is more varied and the menu more extensive. That is why such a society is called free.

Formalisation is the fifth of the five interconnected solutions to the problem of radical uncertainty and interdependent outcomes that is known as the prisoner's dilemma. The other dimensions are convention, morality, sentiment and sanctions. These five dimensions have constituted the subject matter of this section, which has sought to broaden and enrich the deductions that constitute the substance of Olson's logic of collective action. Nothing that has been said in this section is incompatible with the essence of Olson's theory of rational choice. What this section has sought to show, however, is that there is a whole kaleidoscope of combinations and permutations that is situated just out of reach of the two axioms and the three groups; that Olson's model is quite deliberately limited in its coverage; and that even the sympathetic scholar will inevitably want to make common cause with the sceptic and the doubter in amplifying the partial and the abstract lest the foundations erroneously be confused with the structure that they are intended to support.

5 Collective Action and Economic Growth

Mancur Olson has applied his theory of collective action to the problem of national advance: *The Rise and Decline of Nations* is an ambitious attempt to synthesise the topics of growth and development, efficiency and flexibility, free trade and involuntary unemployment, and to correlate them with the size and power of the special-interest groups which comprise the corporate society. Olson's empirical evidence is taken from a wide range of countries – Germany and Japan in the aftermath of the Second World War, the newly-industrialised countries of Eastern Asia in the 1970s, France reeling from the double shock of the Revolution in 1789 and the Treaty of Rome less than two centuries later, the old cultures and rigid social structures of the north-eastern United States and what would appear to be the whole of the United Kingdom. His interest being comparative, it is no surprise that he harbours doubts about the value of any methodological orientation save the interdisciplinary: 'Why, then, have so many economists failed to anticipate the emergence of new economic realities in the 1970s and the 1980s? Perhaps it is because, wearing professional blinkers, they have looked only straight ahead at phenomena economists have habitually examined. This book attempts to show that if we take the trouble to look to the side, at the domains of other disciplines, we shall gain a different conception of the entire landscape.'[1] Nor is it any surprise, given his interest in comparison and his commitment to interdisciplinarity, that he shows a deep awareness of contingency, relativity, differentiation and the essential uniqueness of each individual social setting such as distinguishes his work clearly from the sweeping over-confidence of the neo-classical theorist: 'The generality and lack of distinctions among societies of various types no doubt reflects the depressingly unhistorical, unevolutionary, comparative-static, and institution-free character of much of modern economics.'[2] To be too general, Olson maintains, is to be deeply unfair to the specific characteristics of discrete societies and time-periods; and for that reason economists must take great care not automatically to equate the multicausal complexities of The Many with the serene simplicity of The One. It would be foolishly unrealistic, Olson stresses, to neglect the multiplicity of social, political and economic variables that impact upon each observable phenomenon. The contribution of

210

special-interest groups to variations in national growth-rates is no exception. Hence the warning, that 'it would be preposterous to offer the present argument as a monocausal explanation'.[3]

Olson's theory is not a monocausal explanation, but it is all the same intended to be a *general* statement, just as Keynes' *General Theory* is intended to be general and Friedman's explanation of inflation ('always and everywhere a monetary phenomenon') is intended to be general. Olson's frequent warnings that there is seldom if ever only *one* independent variable in any intelligent social theory put Brian Barry in mind of MacIntyre on holes: 'In this context, it is salutary to recall Alasdair MacIntyre's parable of the man who sought to come up with a General Theory of Holes. . . . The point here, which I shall not belabor, is that we may be quite sure that a particular hole is where it is for some particular reason without supposing for a moment that we need or could have a general theory for the explanation of holes.'[4] Barry quite correctly perceives, however, that Olson on groups has, the disclaimers and the warnings aside, little or nothing in common with MacIntyre on holes: 'I may have missed something but as far as I can recall there is no point at which Mancur Olson concedes complete failure for his kind of explanation, and few cases in which factors falling outside it are even acknowledged as significant.'[5] The disclaimers and the warnings aside, Olson's bias is undeniably towards 'the scientific principle that the theory that explains the most with the least is most likely to be true'[6] – and that that theory for present purposes is none other than his theory of collective action: 'It is . . . remarkable how well the theory fits that pattern of growth across different nations as well as the pattern of growth within countries.'[7] A criterion of 'the most with the least' is not without its ambiguities (it embraces a single most important cause that explains 5 per cent of variance as easily as one that accounts for 80 per cent), and the same must be said of Olson's 'how well'. Olson's theory is not without its ambiguities. Logic and evidence lead him to rank it, however, not only over the *ad hoc* but also above any single alternative explanation of disparate growth performance known to him.

The precise relationship between groups and growth is considered in the first section of this chapter, some illustrations of the hypotheses in the second, the connection between the *Logic* and the *Rise and Decline* in the third. The reader, having noted with Olson that 'there are many examples of insignificant tribes and peripheral peoples rising to greatness',[8] may well emerge from the tunnel of those three sections with the distinct feeling that he has missed something of importance in

the manicured obscurity of imaginative speculations supported
selectively by anecdotal evidence. Such a reader should be reminded
of the exceptional value in itself of Olson's journey. As Charles
Kindleberger has put it, 'this is big-picture political economy and
economic-cum-social history, of the order of the interpretations of
Marx on class struggle. . . . This is an important addition to the
literature of that growing field along the boundaries of economics,
political science, sociology, and economic history.'[9] Indeed it is; and it
is, arguably, from Olson's ambitions at least as much as from Olson's
conclusions that the contemporary political economist has most to
learn.

5.1 GROUPS AND GROWTH

Olson propounds no growth-model as such. What he does is to
advance nine testable hypotheses. These hypotheses form the
subject-matter of this section and are the following.

5.1.1 Asymmetry

'There will be no countries that attain symmetrical organization of all
groups with a common interest and thereby attain optimal outcomes
through comprehensive bargaining.'[1]
   The decision-making process in the corporate society involves
negotiations and swaps made not between individuals but between
groups of individuals. The Galbraithian doctrine of countervailing
power, the Galbraithian prediction that each potential bully normally
generates his own personal policeman, leads reassuringly to the
optimistic expectation that that process will operate *as if* rational and
efficient: 'Power on one side of a market creates both the need for, and
the prospect of reward to, the exercise of countervailing power from
the other side. This means that, as a common rule, we can rely on
countervailing power to appear as a curb on economic power.'[2]
Olson's logic of collective action, on the other hand, points
pessimistically to a sub-optimal society in which some groups are
over-represented and some, sadly, all but invisible: 'Some groups such
as consumers, taxpayers, the unemployed and the poor do not have
either the selective incentives or the small numbers needed to
organize, so they would be left out of the bargaining.'[3] Such groups,

and this despite the undeniable strength of their common interests, are simply not able to band together effectively in order to pursue mutually-advantageous objectives or to block the machinations of the powerful – who, for their own part, would all the while be involved self-interestedly in 'choosing policies that, though inefficient for the society as a whole, were advantageous for the organized groups because the costs of the policies fell disproportionately on the unorganized.'[4] This unbalanced outcome can hardly be regarded as Pareto-optimal in the sense of economics, or as just in the sense of an ethical theory which associates fairness with impartiality. No other outcome can, however, reasonably be anticipated in the asymmetrical society where some individuals are fortunate enough to be in groups and others unlucky enough to be on their own.

5.1.2 Stability

'Stable societies with unchanged boundaries tend to accumulate more collusions and organizations for collective action over time.'[5]

The transactions costs involved in setting up an interest-group are high; there is resistance to the unfamiliar and fear of the unknown; selective incentives must be arranged (notably where the group is large), coercion bargained into being; social pressures (and 'the censure or even ostracism of those who fail to bear a share of the burdens of collective action can sometimes be an important selective incentive')[6] change but slowly; it is not easy to attract individuals away from older networks of interdependence in advance of demonstrated success on the part of newer ones. For these and other reasons there is typically a time-lag in the development of organisations, irrespective of whether or not common interests are perceived to exist.

Once in place, however, the organisations tend to survive for long periods, and even after the original need that first led to the provision of the collective good has actually disappeared. Social upheaval, violence and instability will threaten them (as will, for that matter, constitutional prohibitions and restrictive practices legislation). Little else will do so. A stable society will hence experience a considerable accretion of special-interest groups and will develop a 'dense network of distributional coalitions'.[7] Some stability is, of course, the *sine qua non* for productive economic activity, if only for the obvious reason that instability provokes a flight from real domestic investment into hoards of metallic wealth and/or overseas holdings of scarce resources.

Too much stability would appear, however, to be somewhat less congenial to national growth and prosperity, breeding as it does the accretion and the network that are the mother and father of struggle and misallocation. Thence the conclusion, that, 'other things being equal, the most rapid growth will occur in societies that have lately experienced upheaval but are expected nonetheless to be stable for the foreseeable future'.[8]

All of which is well and good, except for one thing: there is no known empirical indicator of stable conditions, and in its absence Olson falls back on the proxy variable of length of calendar-time without cataclysmic shocks such as wars and revolutions. Yet a negative proxy which takes as its central focus the *without* rather than the *with* can hardly be expected to satisfy the rigorous thinker at the best of times: the very fact that societies as similar in their stability as Sweden, Switzerland and Britain demonstrate such divergence in the incidence and power of their interest-groups, he will say, indicates clearly that a more detailed model of stability must be provided if a useful explanation of the relationship between groups and growth is to be generated.

Nor is it obvious that Olson's specific candidate for the negative proxy, being political and not economic in nature, is in fact the appropriate one. Olson says little about oil price shocks, about epoch-making changes in tastes and technology, about the revolutionary impact upon a nation of the discovery within its boundaries of new stocks of valuable raw materials, about the manner in which inflation both undermines the power of old coalitions (coalitions severely weakened by the associated redistribution of real income) and stimulates the formation of new ones (coalitions urgently requiring defence against a new enemy with which the constituency previously saw no need to contend). Apparently convinced that major shocks are synonymous with political shocks (and apparently unaware of the frequency with which distributional coalitions are left unaffected by the extra-economic upheavals which to him are coterminous with instability), Olson stresses the importance of non-economic disturbances to an extent that is bound to disturb many an economic historian. One such historian is Jan de Vries who, recognising with Olson that France has experienced 'at least three separate constitutions and military occupation within living memory', also contends that this example, like so many others, only demonstrates that Olson's perception of instability is that of the constitutional lawyer, not that of the entrepreneur: 'I would argue that since World War II the environment for business decision-making has been far less stable in Britain, where nationalization and privatization of enterprise follow each other in irregular cycles and the desirability of EEC membership still remains at issue even after 25 years of debate. Conversely, in France certain technocratic and planning ideals have long inspired public policy, making for a more predictable, and hence more stable, business environment.'[9] Critics such as de Vries, it is clear, would have been more convinced by the validity of the conclusions had Olson proposed some more relevant indicator of stable conditions than is undisrupted time alone. In Olson's defence, however, one is bound to point out how very difficult it in fact is to think up a more appropriate proxy – or, indeed, any proxy at all that will be entirely convincing to all groups of critics.

5.1.3 Size and power

'Members of "small" groups have disproportionate organizational power for collective action, and this disproportion diminishes but does not disappear over time in stable societies.'[10]

Small groups, as the *Logic* considered in Chapter 4 clearly seeks to show, have a greater likelihood of being able to organise for collective action than do large ones: the costs and delays that are inevitably associated with the calculus of consent are *ceteris paribus* that much less. Small groups thus end up with political and social power disproportionate to the numbers of their members and to the aggregate of their incomes – and most of all in societies which have been stable only for short periods of time: the small are small but they are also quick to seize a new opportunity. The wealthy are a small group; and it is no surprise therefore to find that newly-industrialising countries often experience an unequal distribution of incomes, mass poverty co-existing with great fortunes not least because of the influence of the political lobbies and the oligopolistic cartels which small groups find it easier than do large to bring into being.

5.1.4 Inefficiency and ungovernability

'On balance, special-interest organizations and collusions reduce efficiency and aggregate income in the societies in which they operate and make political life more divisive.'[11]

The result appears paradoxical: sales rise as the nation grows more prosperous (save in the case of an inferior good), and it would seem logical to assert that the group best serves its members' interests by helping to boost national efficiency so as thereby to increase the size of the national pie. The crucial point is, however, the importance of being unimportant: each organisation normally representing only a small percentage of national growth-producers, it must, if rational, be aware of the extent to which free riders can fiddle while others work. The rational organisation will in the circumstances, recognising that it comprises less than 100 per cent of the nation and thus enjoys less than 100 per cent of the benefits accruing to its costs, deliberately eschew the growth-producing scenario in favour of the redistribution-of-shares strategy from which it promises itself the greater advantage. A union representing, say, 1 per cent of the workers in a given industry knows that it would have to make that industry at least 100 times more efficient if its members (allowing for the 99 per cent of non-members who reap where they never sowed) are to get back at least as much of the productivity-gains as they contributed. The order is tall where the group is small, and it should come as no surprise that such a union therefore goes for the protective tariff or the make-work policy in preference to the conscious contribution to the public good of economic growth. Such a union reasons that it has no incentive to make sacrifices for the whole industry (to say nothing of the whole nation) but a considerable incentive to sacrifice the interests of the whole to the interests of the part (the social costs imposed by the small being small in any case). Such a union, in short, well illustrates Olson's depressing conclusion that 'the great majority of special-interest organizations redistribute income rather than create it, and in ways that reduce social efficiency and output'.[12]

Inefficiency and slower growth result from the activities of interest-groups that are so overtly 'distributional coalitions' in purpose. So too do the ungovernability and social divisiveness which a popular obsession with reallocating instead of with producing is bound to breed and foster. Conflict over shares and the struggle to skew are thus properly to be blamed not only for the waste of resources that purely reallocative competitiveness invariably embodies but also for a zero-sum nastiness that is in itself a public bad: 'The familiar image of the slicing of the social pie does not really capture the essence of the situation; it is perhaps better to think of wrestlers struggling over the contents of a china shop.'[13] One coalition lobbies government for tax-concessions and subsidies, another erects entry-barriers that limit access to a profession, a third cartellises in order to restrict output and raise price *as if* a single-firm monopoly, and none pursues nor is seen to pursue any interest beyond that of the specific. Social resentments increase where one group's gain is so clearly another group's loss (the down-side of the doctrine of countervailing power), politics becomes divisive rather than neutrally orientated towards the 'common good', cyclical choices creep in as one alliance of vested interests is rapidly superseded by another; and all of this in the limit makes society once again into the well-worn battlefield of the *bellum omnium contra omnes* which no rational tourist can genuinely wish to revisit.

5.1.5 The encompassing organisation

'Encompassing organizations have some incentive to make the society in which they operate more prosperous, and an incentive to redistribute income to their members with as little excess burden as possible, and to cease such redistribution unless the amount redistributed is substantial in relation to the social cost of the redistribution.'[14]

The encompassing organisation is defined as a group which represents a large percentage of the individuals or firms in a productive constituency – a single union in a given industry, for example, or a national pressure-group such as the CBI in Britain which speaks authoritatively for a significant number of the nation's employers. The encompassing organisation is percentagewise large. It is also favourable to efficiency and growth. The reason is simple: a union representing, say, 100 per cent of the wage-earners in a given industry knows that its members enjoy 100 per cent of the benefits resulting from an improvement in productivity (due, for example, to the abandonment of a restrictive practice) and suffer 100 per cent of the losses induced by the adoption of a sub-optimal strategy (support in a process of logrolling for a tariff that, going against the principle of comparative advantage, makes the industry's raw materials more expensive is an obvious illustration). A small craft union of which the membership is only a minuscule part of the total labour-force in the industry might well be prepared to sacrifice some profits to ensure the survival of traditional lines of demarcation and jurisdiction, but the choice before the encompassing organisation will be significantly more tricky: the former union has a minute influence on profitability whereas the latter has a direct incentive to help the employer boost his returns. The more encompassing the organisation, in sum, the smaller the leakage of beneficial externalities to non-members, the greater the burden of inefficiencies internalised by the tort-feasors, and thus the higher the probability *ceteris paribus* that the self-interest of the club will be coincident with the social where the social is to be equated with growth.

The logic extends to the political as well as to the economic market, as is exemplified by the propensity of elected representatives in many if not most democracies to show greater sensitivity to the interests of their own constituents (including special-interest groups with specifically *local* appeal) than they do to the more broadly-based national interest. Perhaps more coherent, more efficiency-orientated policies would be the outcome in countries like the United States, Olson reflects, if party discipline were made stronger in order to make interests less parochial. As it stands, however, the position, in his view, is this: 'A congressional district that contains about 1/435th of the United States will tend to gain from any project for the district financed with federal taxes, so long as the costs are not 435 or more times greater than the benefits. Obviously, congressmen are aware of this.'[15] Voters presumably are not (information about collective goods is itself a collective good and therefore prone to underprovision), but the constitutionalist would no doubt wish to point out that the President does in theory exercise checks and balances on their behalf: he, after all, is elected by the national constituency, and his re-election is therefore a function of how well he has satisfied not some of the parts but the sum that is the whole. Be that as it may, the position of the 435 congressmen is, in the Olson model of the political market, essentially the same as that of the numerous small competitors in the Olson model of the economic market: each there wants the public good of growth while simultaneously enjoying the private good of redistribution, just as each representative wants simultaneously to serve both the national and the constituency interest. In the one case as in the other, sadly, the enterprise cannot succeed.

5.1.6   Delay and overload

'Distributional coalitions make decisions more slowly than the individuals and firms of which they are comprised, tend to have crowded agendas and bargaining tables, and more often fix prices than quantities.'[16]

The hypothesis concerning delay and overload follows directly from the logic of committee-meetings and the need to bargain consensus on the course and costs of collective action to be undertaken. If the decision is to be optimal for the group as a whole, after all, there must be unanimity or near-unanimity of consent: the depressing alternative of resentful instability is all-too-well illustrated by the disgruntled oligopolist who, expanding output instead of contracting it, compels the other members of his cartel to follow suit in self-defence and in that way brings about the collapse of the joint agreement. Where, however, consent must be on a basis of unanimity or near-unanimity, each party has a strong incentive to hold out for the best possible terms (which each secretly defines as the disproportionate share of the gains); and the process of negotiation will inevitably be extremely expensive in terms of the scarce resources that are therein embodied.

Small groups might wish to economise on decision-making costs via the adoption of multi-period rules, while groups too large for voluntary provision ever to be bartered directly have no option but to choose the prearranged expedient. Constitutional procedures in themselves, however, are costly of time; and there is in addition no reason to identify constitutionalism *per se* with a general absence of political and social instability (as witness the Arrow case of shifting coalitions and voting cycles). More optimistically, of course, it is important to note Olson's conviction that instability is not in practice likely to prove a particular problem. One reason is the innate conservatism of groups, participants being very reluctant indeed to affect an alteration in the *status quo* in an uncertain world. A second is the sheer cost of making new decisions and implementing new arrangements, even where circumstances have quite clearly themselves altered significantly. A third is the presence of safeguards that are also hurdles, intended to protect the interests of the minority from the majority (the unanimity rule, perhaps) or, for that matter, the interests of the majority from the arbitrary decisions of the leadership (strike-ballots to defend the rank-and-file is a case in point). A fourth is the two-party system, forcing each party as a unit to focus on national (not specific) interests: in countries with proportional representation and a less encompassing party structure, the undeniable benefits (a wider range of opinions represented and policies advocated, a real chance that checks on error are in operation) are counterbalanced by the considerable costs of the regime where small parties do not speak for the nation, evanescent coalitions do not represent the parties, and instability is more common than in the *de facto* two-party system of present-day Britain or the United States. Instability, evidently, is, in Mancur Olson's perspective, a possible but not an inevitable concomitant of democratic constitutionalism. The costs of the procedures are, however, a different matter: instability may not inevitability ride piggy-back on decision-making arrangements, but the same simply cannot be said of the expenditure of time and money that is so integral a component of the calculus of consent.

Time and money must be spent; and to slowness and costliness must be added further sources of inconvenience such as the multiplication of committees and sub-committees that are the common outcome of the crowded agenda. There are, needless to say, ways of expediting decisions (the employment of impartial outside arbitrators is one; conflict-resolution by means of traditions and conventions – rules, say, of seniority – is another); but their adoption, here as elsewhere, very much depends on how worthwhile each member of the group believes collective action will prove relative to the undoubted burdens involved. Thus it is that the cost-conscious cartel or union so frequently retreats to the inertial position of fixing nominal values (prices or wages) for long periods of time, irrespective of changes in conditions, while leaving the determination of real values (quantities demanded and supplied) to the market-mechanism. Exceptions can be found such as medicine, where the *de facto* monopoly power of the professional association is exercised not to fix fees but (typically disguised in the language of qualifications and standards) to limit entry. In general, however, it is prices and wages that special interests render sticky and inflexible, and quantities that bear the burden of adjustment.

5.1.7   Slower growth

'Distributional coalitions slow down a society's capacity to adopt the new technologies and to reallocate resources in response to changing conditions, and thereby reduce the rate of economic growth.'[17]

The economic situation in modern societies is characterised by continuous change. An important source of such change is scientific and technological progress, invention and innovation, pushed on by the discovery of new resources and pulled in new directions by an alteration in consumers' tastes. In markets without distributional coalitions, the Darwinian struggle is a great stimulus to efficiency, profit-seeking competitiveness a major incentive to change with the times. Such markets may accordingly be expected *ceteris paribus* to experience a faster rate of economic growth than do markets dominated by special-interest groups – by organisations, that is to say, which distort market signals by fixing charges, which delay adaptation because of the costs of consultation, which lobby for governmental subsidies such as then artificially boost the retention of scarce resources in low-productivity declining industries, which (as unions) defend wasteful over-manning and resist economically labour-shedding new technologies, which (as cartels) impose entry-barriers that impede shifts in productive inputs in pursuit of super-normal profits. Such organisations impose a considerable tax on their community in the form of economic growth foregone; for the sad fact is that 'the slower adoption of new technologies and barriers to entry can subtract many times more from the society's output than the special-interest group obtains, particularly over the long run'.[18]

Olson is convinced that distributional coalitions tend to reduce the rate of economic growth. Other observers, pointing to the positive contribution which groups can make to national productiveness, will be less prepared to generalise. Even if associations do happen to promote x-inefficiency, do have the effect of discouraging competitive mutation, do exercise a delaying restraint on the reallocation of resources, such agnostics will say, nonetheless the dampening impact of the groups on experimentation and evolution must be set within a broader context that includes countervailing and growth-furthering influences as well.

One of these is *esprit de corps* and the sense of belonging, the self-perception of being the unique Henry Dubb and not merely the easily-replaceable interchangeable cog in some ongoing exogeneity. Few of us, as James Coleman has explained, adapt well to the notion of personal irrelevance, however valuable it may be 'for the smooth functioning of the organization': 'It takes away something of central importance to each of us: the sense of being *needed*. It is this which makes the family – which is an anachronism from another age in the modern social structure we have created – an important element in our lives. A family member is part of that family as a person, not as an occupant of a position.'[19] The corporate entity to some extent restores that sense of being needed, to some extent returns the concept of *Gemeinschaft* to its traditional position of importance – and the unintended outcome of heightened integration may well be improved morale and thus improved productivity.

Then there is collective discipline which, alongside *esprit de corps*, can make precisely that significant contribution to occupational efficiency which was stressed by the famous Frenchman mentioned in the previous chapter who, starting from the premise that 'human passions stop only before a moral power they respect', assigned a significant role to occupational groups in buttressing the moral power associated with mechanical solidarity from which shirking and dishonesty would recoil in horror and slovenly workmanship seek to escape by the service staircase: 'An occupational activity', Durkheim wrote, 'can be effectively regulated only by a group close enough to it to know how it operates, what its needs are and how it is likely to change. The only one that meets all these conditions is the one which might be formed by all the agents of the same industry united and organised into a single body. This is what we call the "corporation" or "occupational group".'[20] Efficacious regulation in the sense of Durkheim, as the example of the medieval guilds in many respects well illustrates, can undoubtedly prove a synonym for the tyranny of the *status quo* and to that extent a growth-retarding change-depressant. Looking at the advantages, however, there can be no disputing the fact that professional associations play a valuable role in keeping the venal and the vulnerable among their laggard members up to the mark; and that that contribution, productive as it may well be of lagged adaptation, may nonetheless be a significant cause in itself of good husbandry in the use of scarce resources.

Much is dependent, naturally, on the precise balance between the 'lagged' (which tends *ceteris paribus* to reduce the rate of growth) and the 'good' (which tends *ceteris paribus* to feed it). The outcome is an empirical one, and Olson is in no doubt that his theory is very much the prisoner of his evidence – his intention and purpose being, after all, no more than 'to put forth hypotheses that can be tested against the existing statistics on economic growth'.[21] That having been said, hidden causes of economic prosperity such as the two (*esprit de corps* and collective discipline) considered above hardly seem to have proven so strikingly significant in the data as to cause Olson to reverse his basically negative verdict on the economic contribution of special-interest groups. Looking backward to the critical comments already made on time as a proxy for stability and forward to the observations about to be made concerning productivity, the reader will perhaps reflect that different statisticians, employing different tests, may one day come up with different conclusions.

Olson is convinced that distributional coalitions tend to reduce the rate of economic growth, but he takes pains to make the point that the coalitions can play a socially-desirable role nonetheless and that it is not therefore his wish 'to argue for the abolition of common-interest organizations': 'The hypothesis that most common-interest organizations will have an adverse effect on rates of growth of national product does not mean that such organizations are undesirable. They may perform services that are not properly counted in the national income statistics. For example, they ensure a more pluralistic political life and thereby protect democratic freedoms. Labor unions make employees feel less subject to arbitrary actions of particular supervisors.'[22] Olson's illustrations do not, one is bound to say, entirely support the distinction between economic and non-economic that he is drawing. Unions, by reducing alienation at work and providing an outlet for participative altruism, may well make precisely the productive contribution suggested above; while democratic pluralism is as much an economic as a political construct – literally so, as in the clearest Galbraithian case of the monopsonist retailing chain facing a monopolist manufacturer across the bargaining table; less directly so, as where the Consumers' Association, the National Union of Mineworkers, the National Farmers Union, the Association of University Teachers, the Claimants' Union and the Royal College of Physicians each strives to convince non-market rent-dispensers such as elected politicians and appointed bureaucrats that its worthy members and not its pleading rivals are in truth the most special of the special cases.

Olson the economist tends to regard lobbying itself as a deadweight element in the use of resources, its legislative outcomes more likely than not to be reflected in slower economic growth; and draws attention with conspicuous reservations to 'the fact that in the provision of collective goods in democracies, the owners of inputs have a say in determining how much is produced and in what way. Through their political power, teachers, military men, contractors, construction companies and others have an influence on the process of production that probably reduces efficiency.'[23] Olson the *political* economist, however, tends to accept that it is in the very nature of democratic pluralism for group to vie with group for non-market advantage and administered privilege; and to focus his reservations not on the system of bloc bargaining *per se* but simply on the imbalance in the chorus of complaint, on the sad fact 'that some interests are well organized (unionized laborers, doctors, farmers, the military-industrial complex) whereas others (consumers, peaceniks, pollution victims, and non-unionized white collar workers) are not', and that this inequality of power 'leads to an inefficient mix of public outputs'.[24] Meanwhile, there is a third Olson, Olson the concerned citizen who believes that problems of externalities and public goods become ever more important 'as population grows and the economy expands', as 'urbanization and congestion increase': 'In the crowded urban environment, there is a new type of interdependence that rarely existed in the rural environment. If a frontier farmer should leave his garbage in his yard, it would be nobody's business but his own. But if the urban resident does this, there is a problem for the whole neighborhood. The frontier community did not need to worry about pollution, but the modern megalopolis does. Zoning laws are relatively unimportant in the country, very significant in the city.'[25] As we grow, this third Olson is arguing, so we grow more interdependent, so therefore does coordinated collective action increase in importance relative to spontaneous individual action, so therefore do public policy and State intervention come rationally to be demanded by enlightened voters only too aware that without compulsion few of us would be prepared to shoulder burdens from which it is others who derive the benefits: 'We have no incentive to curtail those activities that bring losses to others, but no cost to ourselves; and no incentive to undertake activities that bring a gain to society, but no reward in the marketplace. These activities must therefore be carried on by governments.'[26] Always assuming that Olson the concerned citizen is correct in predicting an increasing involvement of the State as economic growth progresses, the onus must then shift to Olson the *political* economist to propose improvements in the consultative mechanisms such that all interests and interest-groupings are given a voice in the pluralist democracy which is their own – the environmental lobby, certainly, which speaks for beauty, but also the consumers who want cheap coal and the miners who fear redundancies. Olson the economist never denies that the outcome of these debates between coalitions *can* prove to be a faster rate of economic growth (as where, say, pensioners demanding minimum-cost eggs and cheaper chickens successfully rout sentimental feather-bedders for whom battery farming and the associated economies of scale are, strangely, not good enough): his point is simply that mutual-benefit groups do not *normally* have this beneficial impact. Olson the concerned citizen alters the fabric of the discussion by reversing the line of argumentation: his point is not that more groups mean less growth but that more growth means more State. Since more State to the democratic pluralist normally means more groups – 'they ensure a more pluralistic political life and thereby protect democratic freedoms', as an exceptionally eminent pluralist and democrat has so succinctly put it – the task assigned to Olson the *political* economist (that of reconciling the interests of discrete coalitions and promoting the representation of the invisible and the inarticulate) is, clearly, as valuable as it is daunting.

Should growth slip in the interests of consultation, of course, then the theorist of organisations can always console himself with the thought that the groups may in fact be performing 'services that are not properly counted in the national income statistics', that we as a community are in effect buying the services of democratic pluralism and paying for them out of wealth we would have accumulated had we selected some other political regime instead. Statistics, here as elsewhere, present real problems.

The standard example in the literature of under-reporting and imputing is the voluntary substitution of leisure for work. The case of 'income earned by not earning income' is not, however, the only instance of a situation where national income statistics 'don't tell us what we need to know': 'They leave out the learning of our children, the quality of our culture, the advance of science, the compatibility of our families, the liberties and democratic processes we cherish.'[27] What is needed for a proper estimation of national wellbeing are socio-economic indicators that pick up the success of policies adopted, and not merely the cost of inputs employed: 'We need information about the condition of our society; about how much children have learned, not about the time and money used for schooling; about health, not about the number of licensed doctors; about crime, not about the number of policemen; about pollution, not about the agencies that deal with it.'[28] The national income statistics in that way too let us down, by relying too heavily on the measuring rod of money. And there is more: 'They even misconstrue or neglect many values that can readily be measured in monetary terms. When the criminal buys a gun, or the honest citizen buys a lock, the national income rises. When a smoke-spewing factory is constructed near a residential area, the expenditures on that factory add to the national income, but so do the expenses of additional house painting and cleaning forced on the nearby householders by the soot from the factory.'[29] The national income statistics, in short, are, by Olson's own admission, a not-entirely satisfactory index of national welfare or perceived prosperity; and for that reason Olson's correlation of the growth in groups with the growth of the GNP leaves the reader intrigued by what he has been shown but also curious as to how he ought to react. The null hypothesis is that the non-measured is so very important relative to the measured as to render Olson's correlation merely a statistical *was there* – an interesting number, perhaps, but one from which it would be dangerously misleading to draw any significant inference whatsoever. The alternative hypothesis is that the correlation is a serviceable second-best, less than ideal, admittedly, but a reasonable basis for generalisation nonetheless. Olson himself obviously adopts the latter position. Whether he convincingly demonstrates that the former position ought not to be adopted is, as it happens, somewhat less obvious.

Even if it were possible accurately to translate GNP statistics into indices of quality of life, however, even if it were possible meaningfully to legitimate economic growth through reference to felt 'better-offness', still there remains the not inconsiderable difficulty that the empirical evidence validating past progress is no indicator of consensus about the relationship between (objective) growth and (subjective) betterment at some time in the future. Olson, who unlike the Galbraithians believes that advance is authentically demand-led and unlike the ecological Jeremiahs is not a prophet of doom, is, while not anti-growth himself, remarkably open to the arguments of those many for whom 'a growth of national or per capita income has become an ambiguous blessing', to say nothing of 'a noisome evil':[30] 'As growing incomes bring increasingly ambiguous luxuries associated with an imperilled environment, strident social protest, and unabated examples of personal despair', Olson concedes, 'it is time to do some new thinking'.[31] Economic growth, it would appear, has its down-side as well as its charm, and this the socially-responsible student of future developments simply cannot afford to eliminate from his equation: 'Kenneth Boulding has said that anyone who believes exponential growth can go on forever in a finite world is either a madman or an economist. Even if one does not accept this view, it is clear that no sensible person can deny the seriousness of the possibility that current rates of economic growth cannot be sustained indefinitely because of the environmental constraint.'[32]

In view of the value of convention in the regulation of the prisoner's dilemma of strategic interaction (a topic examined in the previous chapter which happens also to figure prominently in the next), it is somewhat surprising that Olson does not extend his discussion of the environmental constraint from physical to include social resources as well. Cultural conservatives such as Mishan and Buchanan have been less cautious in the drawing of the parallel. Thus Mishan, distressed by the 'disintegration of communities' and the 'dissolution of a common frame of ethical reference' that he believes to be the price inevitably paid by a collectivity which kicks over its 'moral props' in the race for rapid change, is capable both of predicting and deploring the 'near-hysterical attempts of the young to divest themselves of responsibility' such as he asserts he increasingly sees around him in the anomic culture: 'In such a milieu, no one need wonder that crime, in particular robbery with violence is one of our fastest growing industries.'[33] And Buchanan, no less concerned about a culture in which 'larger and larger numbers of persons seem to become moral anarchists', about a society in which 'for several decades . . . our moral order has been in the process of erosion',[34] is even more explicit in his approach to the problem of resource-depletion: 'We are living during a period of erosion of the "social capital" that provides the basic framework for our culture, our economy, and our polity.'[35] Olson does not appear to share the pessimism of the cultural conservatives, any more than he would appear to share that of the more alarmist among the environmentalists and the ecologists. If their view of the future were to be accepted, however, then Olson's general antipathy to growth-retarding coalitions would itself become difficult to share: even if the groups do repress growth, one would then have to observe, perhaps what is lost was not worth having in the first place.

5.1.8 Exclusivity

'Distributional coalitions, once big enough to succeed, are exclusive, and seek to limit the diversity of incomes and values of their membership.'[36]

A coalition as it develops is likely to be inclusive, as where a new cartel seeks to enlist all existing operators and a new lobby welcomes aboard anyone and everyone with pressure to contribute. Once some crucial size or membership optimum has been attained, however, the tables are turned and the coalition is likely to become exclusive: arguing along the traditional Malthusian lines that every extra pair of hands also means an extra mouth to feed, the coalition will then seek to keep out new entrants with their sights set on a share of existing spoils. Thus a professional body will have an incentive to keep down the numbers of, say, lawyers or doctors: such a restrictive strategy raises the payoff going to existing participants in the collusive arrangement, who would in its absence be faced with either a lower price for their services or a reduced quantity supplied by each individual entrepreneur. A ruling class, similarly, will rationally strive to practice endogamy in an attempt to prevent the dilution by interlopers of group entitlements and privileges: rules reinforced by social pressures among the socially interactive are employed to compel the sons and the daughters of the propertied and the powerful to intermarry, thereby excluding burdensome outsiders who expect to take but have nothing to give. Instances such as these support the general proposition, that groups once large enough are prone to closing the door.

5.1.9 Complexity

'The accumulation of distributional coalitions increases the complexity of regulation, the role of government, and the complexity of understandings, and changes the direction of social evolution.'[37]

Coalitions use their collusive power to influence market outcomes and/or their lobbying power to influence government policies. The former is a case of complex understandings (and decreased responsiveness of supply to demand), the latter a case of complex regulations (and expanded scope for State involvement). In both cases resources are (perhaps wastefully) diverted away from productive activity and into non-productive outlets such as organising and persuading. In both cases complexity is the outcome – and popular ignorance (as is well illustrated by regulatory arrangements such as specific provisions and exemptions, special tax-codes and non-uniform tariffs) a not-insignificant cause and effect: 'The limited incentive the typical citizen has to monitor public policy also implies that lobbies for special interests can sometime succeed where matters are detailed or complex but not where they are general and simple, and this increases complexity still further.'[38] The reader of Downs will inevitably be reminded of that author's prediction that economic policy in a democracy will be biased towards producers and away from consumers. So, arguably, will a guild of lawyers which obtains a restrictive convention limiting out-of-court settlements, a union of farmers which secures special recognition in the form of soil-banks, intervention-prices and tomato mountains, an association of physicians which is rewarded with regulations that effectively exclude less skilled para-medics from less skilled para-medical employments. The lawyer, the farmer or the physician, after all, each earns his income preponderantly from the production of a single good or service but spends on the consumption of many.

Coalitions lead to complexity and complexity leads to cost – direct cost, in the form of investment in lawyers and litigation, specialist accountants who advise on loopholes and powerful lobbyists who know their way around the minefield of *political* competition; opportunity cost, in the sense of extended delays and extensive bargaining, together with a built-in bias for the *status quo* (however out-of-date the rules and customs may be perceived to be) brought about by the time-costs of renegotiation. The effect of costs such as these upon the direction of activity and the pace of change is profoundly depressing: 'The incentive to produce is diminished; the incentive to seek a larger share of what is produced increases. The reward for pleasing those to whom we sell our goods or labor declines, while the reward for evading or exploiting regulations, politics, and bureaucracy and for asserting our rights through bargaining or the complex understandings becomes greater.'[39] A society which rewards pleasing, evading and asserting is bound to breed and form the personality-traits that are appropriate for the turning of complexity to one's own advantage, just as a society which values productive activity and freedom of exchange is likely to generate somewhat different capabilities and character-patterns. The rule in the one case as in the other is the adaptational imperative of the survival of the fittest and for that reason 'there is evolution in the zoo as there is in the jungle'.[40]

Evolution there will be, in the one case as in the other. Evolution, however, along different lines; since each unique situation imposes a different constraint upon the process of surviving and thriving. Olson leaves the reader in no doubt as to the evolutionary trajectory and the situational constraint which he, Olson, would find most to his taste. Complexity – the centrepiece of the ninth of the nine testable hypotheses which have formed the subject-matter of this section – is not, it would be fair to say, the centrepiece of the specific socio-economic arrangements that Olson himself would find most in keeping with his private and personal preferences.

5.2 ILLUSTRATIONS AND IMPLICATIONS

Olson propounds nine testable hypotheses that link changes in groups to changes in growth. What is testable in principle is not, however, always testable in practice; and Olson, when he comes to present the evidence for his assertions, is compelled in the event to fall back upon instances and inferences that will hardly satisfy the rigorous standards of the sceptical critic. That sceptical critic should be reminded that it is by no means easy to compare economies or to explain developments over time. Olson makes the most that can be made of such proof as can be found. It will be the task of this section to examine, under five headings, the principal illustrations that Olson cites in support of his argument.

5.2.1 Organisations and rapid growth

The theory suggests that countries without distributional coalitions will grow at a faster rate than will countries encumbered by such interest-groups. Olson searches accordingly for historical instances where some major shock such as wartime devastation or violent revolution, occupation by outsiders or a spell of totalitarianism at home, might reasonably be expected to have threatened the coalitions: when peace and freedom were subsequently restored, he argues, it would be a logical inference from his theory that those countries or areas which had benefited from the elimination of the institutional brake should then have experienced a particularly rapid rate of economic growth. Olson, it is clear, is no great friend of the tried and tested merely because *it is*: 'The contention of *some* conservatives that if social institutions have survived a long time, they must necessarily be useful to the society, is wrong.'[1] Those conservatives will presumably reply that Olson is here using 'society' to mean 'economy', and that such shortsightedness is hardly what one would have expected from an interdisciplinary thinker who has characteristically maintained that 'the area of collective goods is to a great extent the area where economics inevitably joins hands with the other social sciences':[2] 'Someone must, in short, take account of the politics in large organizations and the sociology behind changing values. Perhaps, if there is a paradigm change in economics, it will be in the form of a unified approach to social science.'[3] Particularly in the context of the rise and decline of nations, those conservatives will no doubt suggest, it is somewhat unfair to identify growth with *economic* growth, evolution with adaptation to *economic* imperatives. Be that as it may, the fact remains that Olson's principal concern is with economic advance, his principal thesis that interest-groups retard specifically economic progress, and his principal illustrations of the relationship between organisations and rapid economic growth the following:

First, Germany and Japan. Totalitarian Germany under Hitler decimated intermediate corporations such as trades unions; the victorious Allies subsequently did away with Nazi-type organisations and cartels; and the new special-interest groups that emerged in the postwar period (the unions, the employers' associations) turned out to be large and encompassing rather than small and exclusive. Similar institutional developments took place in Japan in approximately the same period. The two countries enjoyed an abnormally rapid rate of economic growth. Olson takes the view that the changes in groups were causally connected with the changes in growth, and that the selective example supports his controversial generalisation. Olson consistently argues that the search for primary significance must never proceed other than with the greatest caution: 'Only the British have Big Ben and only the Germans eat a lot of sauerkraut, but it would of course be absurd to suggest that one is responsible for the slow British growth and the other for the fast German growth.'[4] Olson's warning is apposite but it clearly does not prevent him from expressing – cautiously – his conviction that differences in groups provide a better explanation of differences in growth than does either of the also-rans of culture and catch-up.

Consider first the case of cultural variation. Whether anyone would wish to suggest that this is the most significant connecting link between the heterogenous observations in question is doubtful. What is of particular significance in the present connection is that Olson finds the explanatory variable all but irrelevant. One argument he employs is that traits such as class-consciousness, barriers to social mobility, traditionalist attitudes, prejudices against commerce cannot be used to explain slower growth in modern Britain than in Germany or Japan for the simple reason that such cultural characteristics were even more pronounced at the time of the Industrial Revolution than they are now, and yet were insufficient then to prevent Britain enjoying the fastest growth-rate in the world.[5] A second reason which he advances for the irrelevance of culture is that the abnormal valuation of industriousness and assiduity in Germany and Japan, the frequently-cited taste for leisure in Britain, cannot, logically speaking, explain any significant part of differences not in *levels* of prosperity but in *rates of change*: 'Taken literally, this type of explanation is unquestionably wrong, though related arguments may have value. The rate of economic growth is the rate of *increase* of national income, and though this could logically be due to an *increase* in the industriousness of a people, it could not, in the direct way implied in the familiar argument, be explained by their normal level of effort, which is relevant instead to their *absolute* level of income.'[6] The Germans eat sauerkraut and work hard. Neither variable is picked up, however, by data on differentials in rates of advance.

Consider now the case of catch-up economic growth. Germany and Japan having experienced massive destruction of plant, they had no choice in the postwar period but to invest heavily in new capacity embodying up-to-the-minute technology. Olson is fully aware that such catch-ups must be netted out of totals for the purposes of testing his hypotheses. He would appear to be less aware, however, of the extent to which his proxy for power renders it exceptionally difficult to perform in practice that act of netting upon which an adequate test must inevitably depend. As Abramowitz explains it, the problem is this: 'The operational form in which Olson has cast his ideas makes it hard to distinguish clearly between the behavior predicted by his theory and by the catch-up hypothesis. This is because, in a first application of his theory, Olson proposes that we may treat the number of years preceding a given date, during which a country has been free from serious political or military turmoil, as a proxy for the strength of common-interest groups. Since it is likely that a country's productivity level is also a function of the number of years that it has enjoyed peaceful development, the growth predictions yielded by the catch-up hypothesis and by the operational form of the Olson hypothesis are likely to be similar.'[7] Abramowitz also indicates that he would find it helpful to discriminate between catch-up *ab initio* (the case of a developing country which can imitate the practices of the advanced nations but has never enjoyed their capital-intensity or research activity) and catch-up following a once-for-all catch-down (the case of a developed country with cheap and plentiful credit, well-educated scientific and technological personnel and a healthy supply of entrepreneurial alertness which experiences a crisis and thereafter rebuilds) – as when he points out that 'the interwar years were marked by military preparations more in some countries than in others. The heavy industries of Germany and Japan were expanded, as were to a lesser extent those in Italy. These countries, therefore, could more easily revive heavy industry after the war.'[8] Such subtleties and qualifications, important though they undoubtedly are to an economist such as Abramowitz, are conspicuous by their absence from the approach to catch-up that is adopted by Mancur Olson. When all is said and done, Olson insists, the fact remains that Germany and Japan continued to grow faster than, say, postwar Britain even *after* wartime losses had been made up. Catch-up, he concludes, cannot in the circumstances be regarded as being of primary causal significance for the purposes of accounting for differences in growth-performance.

Second, France. Like Germany and Japan, France has enjoyed a high postwar rate of economic growth. Like Germany and Japan, moreover, France has experienced disruption of her special-interest groups. The French Revolution and the Napoleonic order demolished much of feudal culture; further revolutions and unstable political systems impeded the development of long-lasting coalitions and collusive arrangements; foreign invasion in the Second World War continued the tradition of reshuffle; and, as if the above were not enough, ideological and religious divisions have long split potentially large organisations such as unions into smaller groupings such as the socialist and the Catholic. The net result of these disruptive tendencies is a society relatively free from institutional hangovers and *loci* of monopolised power. The net result of such a social structure is an economy which is prone to grow economically at a relatively rapid rate. All of which is well and good, but also, in the eyes of some observers, rather simplistic. Two problems in particular would appear to present the greatest difficulties.

The first problem concerns time. It has been well encapsulated by Asselain and Morrisson in the following: 'It is difficult, on reading Olson's essay, to know precisely what period is under consideration, because the argument sometimes concerns a short period (from a historical point of view) of about twenty years, and sometimes a much longer period – several centuries in some cases. For instance, Olson refers to the social stability of England since the Middle Ages; in the United States, the length of times since statehood varies between sixty and 200 years; regarding Germany and Japan, we are concerned with the consequences of World War II, over about thirty years.'[9] Applied to the French case in question, Olson's adoption of the rubber measurement of time elapsed cannot but lend support to his hypothesis, that serious disruption (as in the case of the wars of the present century and the Revolution of the eighteenth) leads to rapid economic growth (as is demonstrated by accelerated French development in the period following the Second World War). Sadly, it cannot but lend support to virtually every other hypothesis as well – including that of the mischievous totalitarian who, modifying the lag-structure to suit himself, reaches the conclusion that it was not Revolution but Robespierre and Napoleon, not war but Hitler and Pétain, not shake-out, in short, but discipline that was most productive of the postwar boom. Olson's generous flexibility with respect to the use of calendar time is, of course, entirely appropriate in view of the fact that institutions can hardly be expected to evolve at some pre-specified and invariant pace. Appropriate though it undoubtedly is, there is one snag: it means that the evidence presented by the mischievous totalitarian and by Olson himself must be treated as being *a priori* of equal value. The epistemological sceptic welcomes such a conclusion as proof positive that social science theories cannot convincingly be falsified. The positive scientist returns to the drawing board.

The second problem involves the relationship between political upheaval and economic upheaval. Olson consistently argues as if the former were a good proxy for the latter. Other observers will argue, however, that the two modes of disruption are somewhat less intimately linked – as where, say, the replacement of one ruling elite by any other leads not to the disruption of existing groups and coalitions but to the reinforcement of their privileges, the new rulers wanting not so much to challenge the old economic order as to enlist its support in the defence of the new political regime. Such encouragement to interested organisations is particularly likely to obtain where their activities are believed to have contributed significantly to the healthy rate of economic growth already being enjoyed by the nation: where powerful unions given legislative protection are believed to have promoted high productivity of labour, where influential cartels sheltered by tariffs and stimulated by entry-restricting patents are believed to have placed themselves in the vanguard of risk-taking innovation and technological advance, it would be the study of the new set of citizen-pleasers not to threaten but rather to placate such valuable allies in the pursuit of progress. Since Olson treats it as all but axiomatic that pressure-groups resist change and are seen to frustrate growth, he does not regard it as necessary to make a significant theoretical distinction between those wars and revolutions which threatened growth-furthering groups and those upheavals which reinforced them. Even within the confines of his own model, however, there is no reason to think that every major non-economic dislocation will represent a serious breach with the economic *status quo*. Some will (the case of the revolution where, in the interests both of economic growth and political stability, the pillars of the *ancien régime* are deliberately destroyed). Some will not (the case of the palace coup where the faces at the top are changed but the overall structure of interlocking elites and interests remains unaltered). The student of the disruption-prone economy such as that of France would in the circumstances be well-advised not to generalise as Olson does but rather to proceed pragmatically, case by case.

Third, Sweden. The Swedish experience is a surprising one, generating as it does empirical evidence which would appear to be at variance with the main thrust of Olson's theory. Sweden has long enjoyed freedom of organisation and has in recent times been spared the disruptions of war, revolution or invasion. It has not relied so heavily on immigrants and guest-workers as to challenge in that way the unionisation of the labour-force. It has no restrictive clauses in its constitution (in contrast, say, to cautious Switzerland, which does) such as would limit the losses imposed on the community by special-interest groups by means of a multi-period convention prohibiting special-interest legislation. Sweden has, for all of these reasons, developed a number of strong special-interest groups. Yet it has also experienced a rate of economic growth that is surprisingly satisfactory when set against the backdrop of Olson's theory.

The contradiction is, as it happens, more apparent than real. It is easily resolved by looking at the precise nature of the Swedish organisations. They are large, inclusive and highly encompassing. Most unionised manual workers belong, in Sweden, to a single union; the counterpart employers' association also offers a comprehensive national service; and the society with large-scale organisations may reasonably be expected to grow at a faster rate *ceteris paribus* than will the society without. Large-scale organisations have, after all, a direct interest in measures and policies that boost efficiency and accelerate advance. The small-scale organisation which speaks for no more than, let us say, one-millionth of the income-generating capacity of the nation knows that the direct benefits it reaps from the furtherance of social objectives are effectively insignificant, and it accordingly sets its sights on redistribution rather than growth. Not so the large-scale organisation representing, for example, one-third of national capacity, of which the representative or typical member receives back one-third of the benefits accruing to any improvement he makes and suffers one-third of any losses experienced by the society in consequence of any course of action he pursues: 'Thus any effort to obtain a larger share of the national income for the clients of such an encompassing organization could not make sense if it reduced the national income by an amount three or more times as great as the amount shifted to its members.'[10] Which is the logic behind the growth-promoting policies of the encompassing organisations in Sweden: favourable to mobility and retraining-schemes in preference to the subsidisation of inefficient firms, friendly to the stimulus of international competition and sceptical about the growth-repressing protective tariff, organisations in Sweden have, precisely because they are large, made a

not-insignificant contribution to the relatively rapid growth-rate that
that country has been able to enjoy.

5.2.2 Organisations and slow growth

Olson's theory predicts that 'countries that have had democratic
freedom of organization without upheaval or invasion the longest will
suffer the most from growth-repressing organizations and combinations': 'This helps to explain why Great Britain, the major nation with
the longest immunity from dictatorship, invasion and revolution, has
had in this century a lower rate of growth than other large developed
democracies.'[11] Great Britain is, in Olson's view, a prime illustration
of the proposition that the inertial traditionalism of a powerful
network of special-interest groups tends *ceteris paribus* to repress
economic advance: 'In short, with age British society has acquired so
many strong organizations and collusions that it suffers from an
institutional sclerosis that slows its adaptation to changing circumstances and technologies.'[12] Much the same may be said of the older
areas in the United States which constitute the alternative illustration
that Olson proffers in support of his proposition.

First, then, Great Britain. The British interest-group, in contrast
to its more encompassing Swedish counterpart, tends to be relatively
narrow in its coverage – partly due, no doubt, to the fact that British
culture is more heterogeneous and more diversified than is that of the
smaller Scandinavian nation, and partly to the heritage of early
industrialisation in a stable society: the craft or trade basis of the
economy in those early days, the primitive nature of transportation
and communications, these and other causal influences from the past
help to explain the prevalence of small-scale coalitions in the Britain of
the present (despite the economies of large size that account for the
emergence of large-scale productive units in that country), and
therewith the widespread tendency to focus on redistributive issues at
the cost of concern with growth. More than twice as many professional
associations enjoyed an unbroken history in Britain as compared with
Germany over the period 1939–71, and the impact of institutional
ossification in place of institutional destruction is, in Olson's view, easy
enough to detect: Britain has experienced one of the slowest rates of
economic growth among the industrialised countries in the years since
the Second World War.

In Britain, unlike Sweden, the interest-group does not stand itself significantly to gain from growth, and has little incentive, therefore, to renounce inefficient practices and out-of-date rules in a bid to advance national prosperity. Even in Britain, however, the common interest of the group need not prove incompatible *ex post facto* with that of the nation as a whole – the case where countervailing power serves to annul existing distortions rather than to introduce new ones (as where, to take an example from another country, 'the construction lobby may oppose the usury law that keeps house buyers from getting credit, the farm organization may oppose a tariff on farm machinery').[13] Besides which, of course, rapid scientific and technological progress undermines the stable practices of existing coalitions; occupational, geographical and social mobility (including the greater equality of educational opportunity that is brought about by improved State education) has a similarly corroding impact upon traditional barriers; and optimistic developments such as these must inevitably offset, to some extent, the innovation-retarding, entrepreneurship-repressing conformism of existing habits and *status quo* institutions.

Clearly, to say that Britain has not exploited her full potential for growth is not to say that she has not grown at all. But the fact remains that Britain has grown at an abnormally slow pace, and that for the inhibition of her rate of growth her 'exclusive' organisations, her elitist school and universities, her persistent special pleaders must all, in Olson's view, shoulder their share of the blame: 'Consider the distinction between solicitors and barristers, which could not possibly have emerged in a free market.'[14] Military security and democratic stability, it would appear, have, in the British case at least, imposed a heavy tax upon the process of economic growth.

Second, the United States. Like Britain, the United States as a whole has experienced one of the slowest rates of economic growth among the developed democracies – and, never occupied by a foreign power, never torn apart by a revolution at home, still governed by the same constitution as in the eighteenth century, it has enjoyed, as a whole, the benefits of stability of institutions. As a new country, the United States had when created little or no tradition of feudal subordination; and at first income and wealth (and the opportunity to achieve them via conspicuous application) were distributed in a relatively even manner. As a new country, therefore, the United States was in the enviable position of starting off its historical journey without the encumbrance of groups and coalitions based upon class-consciousness and inherited identity such as had divided the older European countries and impaired their economic performance.

Stability of institutions over time put paid, however, to the advantage associated with the clean slate, at least for those regions settled first: they, after all, have had a longer span in which to accumulate special-interest organisations than have those settled later. Statistical evidence on the individual states in the postwar period bears out the hypothesis that there is 'a strong and systematic relationship between the length of time a state has been settled and its rate of growth of both per capita and total income'.[15] That relationship, needless to say, is negative: the longer the time, the stronger the groups, the slower the growth.

The economic impact of distributional coalitions in the United States is visible in a number of ways. One is the chaos and near-ungovernability of older cities such as New York which are burdened with a dense network of inflexible special-interest groups. Another is the slow rate of technological progress in the older industries such as coal and steel which, cartelised and unionised, substitute pay and perquisites for adaptation and advance. Yet another is the movement of 'footloose' labour and capital out of areas dominated by restrictive groupings such as unions (the latter a sensitive social indicator: 'Their membership should also serve as a proxy measure of . . . other coalitions that are harmful to local growth')[16] and into areas where the absence of distributional coalitions has led to a higher differential return (even within an identical industrial or occupational category). More controversial is the interpretation of the data on 'the number of lawyers per 100,000 of population, on the debatable assumption that the need for lawyers would probably show *some* tendency to increase with the extent of lobbying and the complexity of legislation and regulation it brings about'.[17] Most dramatic, perhaps, is the case of the Confederacy and the South.

The states that constituted the Confederacy at the time of the Civil War were old ones. The development of special-interest groups upon their territory was, however, discouraged by the war itself, by devastation and defeat, by occupation and outsiders, by divisive racial policies. Olson's theory predicts that such states should be growing (the usual allowance made for accelerated imitative catch-up on the part of the laggards) at a faster rate than the long-settled, more ossified, non-frontier areas with their accumulations of interest-groupings; and this would seem indeed to correspond to the facts. One is tempted to ask, of course, why the effect took from the 1860s to the 1960s to make itself felt – why, in other words, something like a century had to elapse before the disruptions of war were able at last to confer upon the South a relatively rapid pace of advance in a nation where the overall rate of economic growth was slow. Low wages and the absence of restrictive associations cannot, clearly, be the whole story: 'Something kept the rapid industrialization that occurred after World War II from happening earlier', Olson himself has observed, 'and we should not be completely confident of *any* explanation of postwar southern growth until we know what it was'.[18]

Reflecting further on the question of delayed impact, Olson has offered this account of the missing link in the chain of causation: 'Perhaps the most important reason why the South did not industrialize faster between the Civil War and World War II . . . is that transportation costs were too high, at least in the earlier part of this period. Transportation costs were not crucial for industries like textiles, and the textile industry and some others like it had in fact moved South earlier than other industries. Industries that needed to be near the larger markets, which were not in the South, or which needed to be near raw materials, often could not move South, and especially not to rural parts of the South, to take advantage of the lower wages. By the 1930s transportation costs had already fallen significantly, but there was naturally very little investment in new plants anywhere during the depression.'[19] Other economists, finding it less convincing than does Olson to explain growth in the 1960s with reference to the disruption of cartelisation fully a century earlier, have pointed to other causal variables which, in their view, account at least as well for observed facts. Some of those variables are indisputably regional in nature (the availability of surplus labour in low-productivity agriculture, for example, such as permits of significant shifts in local employment-patterns without simultaneously precipitating either a noticeable fall in the output of the donor-sector or a noticeable rise in the industrial remuneration).[20] Other causal variables are, however, potentially national (not primarily local or even state), as Frederick Pryor has made clear in his critical assessment of Olson's thesis: 'The relatively greater importance of defense industries in the southern and western states (the "newer" states) had a strong impact on growth during the decade of the Vietnam War, which Olson examined. Further, given the locational pattern of committee chairmen in Congress and the federal funds flowing to the states for the construction of growth-inducing social-overhead capital, it is not unusual that the southern and western states grew faster.'[21] There is, it would be fair to say, some disagreement as to the causes of rapid growth in the South of the sixties, and as to the extent to which Olson's thesis in fact explains that experience. What is not in doubt is Olson's personal conviction that stagnation and stability are just around the corner, that the normal American pattern of cartelisation and slow growth will ultimately reassert itself even in today's fast-growing regions – and that, 'in that sense, the South will fall again'.[22]

5.2.3 Organisations and jurisdictional integration

Consider the widening of markets that occurred at the end of the Middle Ages. In the old towns, the rule being that 'smaller groups are much more likely to organize spontaneously than large ones',[23] local merchants and craftsmen succeeded in uniting for purposes of collective action: limited and homogeneous groups, interacting socially, were able to generate the requisite selective incentives (of which avoidance of ostracism is an obvious candidate), deficient transportation restricted outside competition (and thereby protected collusive power from the ravages of price-flexibility), and the net result was technological stagnation and delayed adaptation, entry-barriers and apprenticeship-schemes, the inefficiencies of quotas and the privileges of monopolies. Even before the decline of the guilds in the towns, of course, entrepreneurs had circumvented the restrictions by 'putting out' materials to families dwelling in the countryside; but the ultimate blow to the older economic order only came with the move into 'jurisdictional integration'. Roads and canals reduced the cost of shipment and increased the scope for competition. The transfer of the law-and-order functions from decentralised authority to national government meant administration less in touch with local pressures and interests. The elimination of internal tolls and barriers diminished the ability of the cartel to control its area. In these ways and in others the market mechanism succeeded, at the end of the medieval period, in undermining the power of the groups.

The formation of the European Economic Community in the modern period had a not dissimilar impact upon the power of the special pleaders. It is well-known that the EEC was established for a wide range of reasons (the fear of the Soviet Union, the desire to reconcile old enemies, the ideal of a European United States), and that the expected economic benefits from free trade and factor mobility were, while significant, hardly the only considerations in the minds of its architects: 'Specialists have long known that a country could get most or all of the gains from free trade without joining a customs union simply by reducing its own barriers unilaterally, and would indeed often gain much more from this than from joining a customs union.'[24] The customs union by itself was not the principal reason for the formation of the EEC. Nor did the subsequent trade creation represent the principal cause of the rapid economic growth to which the creation of the Community rapidly led. The principal cause in question was the disruptive impact upon the distributional coalitions of the process of jurisdictional integration. Cartelisation is impeded internationally by differences in language and culture, as well as by the larger pool of competitors to which the abolition of tariffs, quotas and exchange-controls gives access. Lobbying is discouraged by the difficulties of securing special-interest legislation on a supranational basis: clearly, 'if a Common Market could put the power to determine the level of protection and to set the rules about factor mobility and entry of foreign firms out of the reach of each nation's colluding firms, the economies in question could be relatively efficient'.[25] Price-fixing is challenged by multi-national competition, and the same may be said of wage-fixing as well: a union which succeeded in imposing inefficient working-practices or an abnormally high level of pay upon home producers would be rewarded not merely with redundancies as foreign interlopers captured its markets, but perhaps also with wholesale shut-downs as domestic capitalists transferred their resources elsewhere within the single jurisdiction. All of which leads Olson to the conclusion that the formation of the EEC contributed significantly to the economic growth of the Six (the number of members in the years to which his evidence refers) in a manner which would not easily be identified by the non-institutional, non-dynamic methodology of the textbook neo-classical.

5.2.4 Organisations and cultural change

Olson is convinced that his theory explains a wide range of cultural phenomena – not least those of caste in India and *apartheid* in South Africa. His assumptions of self-interest and calculative rationality will inevitably cause his readers to question his generalisations – and even, rather uncharitably, to ask if it is not facile and exaggerated to model so much of human experience on what can best be described as the outlook on life of the twentieth-century American businessman. Be that as it may, Olson is confident that attitudes are sufficiently homogeneous to permit of the intercultural comparisons which he proceeds to make.

First, caste in India. The British discouraged the development of interest-groups in the Crown colonies of Singapore and Hong Kong (just as the Japanese invasion pulverised independent coalitions in Korea and Taiwan) – and rapid economic growth was an unintended but constructive subsequent outcome. In India, however, the British were more lenient towards the intermediate groupings which they identified as symbiotically linked with religious traditionalism, an ongoing social structure, and an established system of local rule – with the result that the economy stagnated precisely because the society was petrified. Caste is a case in point, since it restricted entry into occupations and lines of business, led to the fixing of prices and the keeping of secrets, repressed equality of opportunity, stimulated group action in place of the individual response. The reward for fidelity to the collective (frequently professional) ethic may be reincarnation rather than the semi-detached, but the economic efficiency is no less real because of the spiritual overlay. Olson is particularly impressed by the fact that most castes bear the names of occupations: while the economic is hardly the only explanation for the emergence of the groups, the idea that castes may be nothing other than ossified guilds clearly appeals to him. So, for that matter, does the economic logic of the prohibition on marriage to outsiders: no members of a group likes, after all, to think that future returns will go other than to his descendants.

Besides which, 'the multi-generational guild can be successful only if it can keep its membership from increasing faster than can be justified by an expansion in its market, which will depend on such things as the growth of population and income in the areas in which it is located'.[26] In the case of any reward-seeking group, 'the greatest distributional gains come from a minimum winning coalition'[27] and 'the only way the distributional coalition can retain its value over several generations is by restricting the children of members to marriages with one another or by disinheriting a large portion of children. I hypothesize that the Indian castes used mainly the first method. The English nobility used this method to a great degree and combined it with primogeniture as well.'[28] Olson's hypothesis concerning the exclusive group which restricts its membership in order to retain its gains applies to caste and class as well as to the cartel. In the absence of strong empirical evidence such as would unambiguously support or refute the theory, there is no test but the test of logic. Olson's logic is that of the economist conjecturing that girls are married out in order to limit the size of the group that shares in the assets and the benefits. Other theorists will no doubt wish to bring to the analysis of inter-generational mobility a logic that is less material and more spiritual in nature. Their right to employ an alternative logic simply cannot be denied them even by the most enthusiastic of Olson's followers; for the truth is that there is no known way of collecting the requisite evidence on historical motivation.

Second, apartheid in South Africa. As in the case of caste, for *apartheid* too Olson finds an economic explanation. Mine-owners needed labour and sought to recruit it from low-waged pools such as indigenous Africans and indentured Asians. Well-paid white workers resented this competition and there were strikes, leading to colour-bar acts and apprenticeship-rules such as, by excluding non-whites from skilled employment, raised pay for those allowed access to the trade and grade: thus did left-wing unionists make common cause with racists and conservatives in an attempt to pass on to the consumer the burden of their benefits. The blacks were not pleased with these arrangements. Neither, however, were the employers, all too aware of the extent to which discrimination and demarcation kept wages artificially high, eroded their profit-margins, and made it difficult for them to keep up with foreign competitors. Employers in South Africa are fully aware of the fact the 'employers could profit by hiring the low-wage victims of discrimination', that 'firms that refused to do so would eventually be driven out of business by their lower-cost competitors',[29] and that the *apartheid* system is simply another case where distributive inequities and allocative inefficiencies are brought about by the power of interest operating in non-free markets. Like the consumers and the blacks, it would appear, the employers in South Africa are led by the logic of their economic situation to demand an end to the group privileges of the white workers – and the white workers vociferously to defend the rigidities, the inflexibilities and the barriers from which they derive such outstanding rewards.

Visible differences, whether in South Africa or in any other society, both result from in-breeding and serve to encourage its perpetuation: 'It will be far easier for a racially, linguistically, and culturally distinctive group to maintain a multigenerational coalition. The linguistic and cultural similarities will reduce differences in values and facilitate social interaction, and . . . this reduces conflict and makes it easier to generate social selective incentives.'[30] Endogamy and racial purity are valuable tools in the hands of a special-interest group bent on the preservation of its privileges: visible differences discourage intermarriage by permitting quick identification of outsiders, while group prejudices help to make the coalition more inward-looking, less vulnerable to dilution on the part of interlopers. Professional associations and trades unions in modern Britain require a membership card. Ethnic groups reinforcing the blood-ties that called them into being are, as the South African case well serves to illustrate, frequently in a far more fortunate position.

5.2.5 Organisations and macroeconomic policy

Olson is convinced that not all unemployment is desired: 'Common sense and the observations and experiences of literally hundreds of millions of people testify that there is . . . involuntary unemployment, and that it is by no means an isolated or rare phenomenon. . . . Only a madman – or an economist with both "trained incapacity" and doctrinal passion – could deny the reality of involuntary unemployment.'[31] To that extent Olson is a Keynesian: he explains the phenomenon in question not in terms of search (much of which can be conducted from the safe haven of an existing job) nor in terms of erroneous expectations (Britain in the Depression never had less than a 10 per cent rate of unemployment, and the argument that this was brought about because the mistaken belief in the imminence of a drastic inflation caused people to refuse offers of work at the then-current rates 'is – to put it mildly – doubtful')[32] but in terms of the failure of workers and employers to make the mutually-advantageous contracts which both sides would very much like to have seen concluded. Where the textbook Keynesian would explain that failure with reference to some alleged deficiency of total demand, however, it is to microeconomics, special-interest groups and institutional ossification that Olson himself tends to turn: 'Because of increasing inflexibility of prices, as time goes on, a stable society suffers more unemployment and a greater loss of output for any given reduction in aggregate demand.'[33] More specifically, 'Keynes was . . . working out his dazzling ideas in Great Britain in the 1920s and 1930s. The society in which he wrote had accumulated far more special-interest organizations and collusions than any other society at that time.'[34] A child of difficult times that had bred and formed the imposition of tariffs rather than the removal of entry barriers, the product of a nation which had opted for the comfortable conservatism of fixprice in preference to the dynamic uncertainties of quick adaptability, Keynes formulated a theory of wage and price inflexibilities, output and input adjustments, such as was in effect to be expected, given the circumstances of the old society in which he lived: 'Had Britain emerged from World War I with the clean institutional slate that Germany had after World War II, Keynes would probably not have written the book.'[35] Keynes developed a theory of unemployment of resources and underutilisation of capacity such as was not inappropriate in the Britain of his own times. His times are not, however, all times. His *General Theory* is not general after all.

The Keynesian theory of market failure is not, Olson stresses, of universal applicability, but rather the reflection of specific institutional conditions and constraints. That being the case, Olson adds, the Keynesian approach is mistaken insofar as it exaggerates the importance for the maintenance of full employment of the level of total demand: 'Involuntary unemployment can only be explained in terms of interests and policies that rule out mutually advantageous bargains between those who have their own labor or other goods to sell and those who would gain from buying what is offered. A low level of income or even a drop in aggregate demand is neither a sufficient nor a necessary condition for involuntary unemployment.'[36] Even, indeed, with a high level of demand, involuntary unemployment can still result, where a network of distributional combinations has the power to block the reaping of the welfare gains from trade by means of setting real wages that are in excess of the market clearing vector.

Cuts in wages can obviate the problem of involuntary unemployment irrespective of the level of total demand, and have often done so in the past – in the Britain and the United States of the nineteenth century, for example: 'Broadly speaking, the longest period of peaceful growth in per capita income that the world has even seen took place in a period in which the price level was, more often than not, falling.'[37] Cuts in prices were evidently accompanied by cuts in wages, given that output and employment would appear to have performed with an unprecedented measure of success despite the deflationary pressures of the period. The growth of the coalitions since that time has made it that much less likely that the burden of a counterpart reduction in demand would today fall on nominal and not on real variables. Workers firmly ensconced in their trade see no reason why they should accept a cut in their pay in order that new entrants be enabled to find jobs: 'The main group that can have an interest in preventing the mutually profitable transactions between the involuntarily unemployed and the employers is the workers with the same or competitive skills.'[38] Existing workers have accordingly formed themselves into cartels, lobbies and similar organisations devoted to the exercise of collusive pressure in defence of present-day privilege. Members of each coalition have a strong incentive to defend the public good of the non-competitive wage; the unemployed, impressed by the artificially inflated levels of remuneration, are motivated to be exceptionally choosy; and the stagnation that is engendered by the rational calculus both of the ins and of the outs is accentuated by the crowded agendas and decision-making lags of all large groups.

Clearly, 'it takes a special-interest organization or collusion some time to go through the unanimous-consent bargaining or constitutional procedures by which it must make its decision';[39] and to the inconvenience of postponement must be added some acknowledge-ment of the cost of change. Time invested being a scarce resource, it is only to be expected that groups will economise via rigidity in nominal values, delegating to the residual accomodation of real variables the onerous task of the sensitive response. Collective bargaining agreements in the United States are normally concluded for three years at a time, spot values in competitive markets need last but a few seconds: 'Wage flexibility appears to be particularly great in temporary markets where organization is pretty much ruled out, as in the markets for seasonal workers, consultants, and so on.'[40] Faced with the choice between low pay and no pay when recession reduces demand, it is at least arguable that workers will rank rationing by price above institutionalised rigidities. So apparently, does Mancur Olson, whose conclusion on the Keynesian approach to stabilisation policies is unambiguous: 'Since inadequate demand is not the main or ultimate source of involuntary unemployment, continuous, fast-changing demand management with fine tuning does not make sense.'[41] Even if the authorities had the knowledge and the techniques requisite for the adjustments, Olson is arguing, what is really needed is not so much an increase in total demand as a decrease in the power of special-interest organisations to impose the tax of fixprice – and therewith of slow growth – on the national collectivity of which they are a part.

5.3 THE *LOGIC* AND THE *NATIONS*

Olson says of his *Rise and Decline of Nations* that 'the present book is an outgrowth of *The Logic of Collective Action* and in large part even an application of the argument in it'.[1] Indeed it is; and it will be the task of this section to demonstrate the relationship between the more empirically-orientated investigation into the impact of distributional coalitions upon differences in growth-rates on the one hand, the more abstract and theoretical account of the formation and cohesion of groups of different sizes on the other. Our conclusion will be that Olson's insightful blend of the game-theoretic orientation with the historico-developmental approach, his synthesis of the cultural values of the sociologist with the State intervention of the political scientist and the cost-benefit individualism of the orthodox economist, makes his work genuinely novel and original – and valuable, even were it nothing else, as a useful corrective to the over-simplified theories of competitive equilibrium that so often divert the attention of the non-institutional economist from an appreciation of the real issues.

Olson at one point asks the following question: 'Why complain vociferously about the rapidly increasing and harmful influence of government and the perniciousness of labor unions, but then build macro models on the assumption that the economy is essentially free of governmentally or cartelistically set prices, or is even perfectly competitive?'[2] Economists whose primary concern is real-world relevance and not merely elegance of expression are morally bound to answer Olson's important question, even if they themselves do not happen to accept the specific theoretical alternative that forms the substance of his two contributions to the theory of collective action. It is with the integration of those two contributions into a unified whole that the two parts of this section are concerned.

5.3.1 The nation as a club

Artificially-inflated remuneration is the public good that is available to all members of a club such as a trades union or an oligopolistic cartel in consequence of its having successfully coerced insiders into conformity while excluding potential new entrants from access to the privileges enjoyed by the minimum winning coalition. Universal immunisation against contagious diseases, a reliable system of refuse disposal, a standing army for purposes of collective defence, these and other public services are no different from the coalition's abnormal rewards, in that they too are public goods, available to all if on offer to any. The difference lies not in the definition of the public good *per se* but rather in the specification of the precise constituency that constitutes the club. In the case of the abnormal reward, the constituency is some sub-set dwelling within the confines of the wider society. In the case of universal immunisation, it is the nation as a whole, in a world of committed nation-states the maximum feasible encompassing unit.

The citizens of a nation look to their politicians for the delivery of desired public goods in the public sector where, irrespective of consensus, spillovers and free riders render commercial provision problematic – where, in other words, 'individuals are not rewarded for the external economies they provide, and accordingly produce too little with any given method of production.'[3] Each citizen in such a situation would be happy to pay for his children's education (thereby upgrading the quality of the labour-force of the future) and to abstain from the dropping of litter (thereby ensuring the provision of unspoilt roads and parks in the here-and-now), provided only, however, that he had some assurance that all others would likewise translate into practice that convergence which he believes to exist at the level of perception. The State provides that assurance by means of expedients such as compulsory taxation and legislated prohibition which coordinate expectations potentially inconsistent in a manner that serves to demonstrate the truth of William Baumol's seemingly paradoxical contention that coercion in certain circumstances is an essential concomitant of liberty: 'In those cases where the welfare of the various members of the economy is partly dependent on each other's activity, it is possible that persons in pursuit of their own immediate interests will be led to act in a manner contrary to the interests of others. To the extent that such a situation is general, the members of the economy may find themselves busily engaged in the frustration of each others' desires. In these circumstances it may be to their mutual advantage to restrict their activity so as to prevent this happening.'[4] In such circumstances, concord on the specification of objectives being unanimous or nearly so, each is likely to consider himself better-off in consequence of the regulation of all, and simultaneous restriction is likely therefore to be Pareto-optimal. Compulsory immunisation is a case in point – where a rational community consciously elects to wipe out a generally-acknowledged public bad by means of State intervention. Governmental action to eliminate the collective diswelfare represented by an artificially-depressed rate of economic growth is a second illustration of the same venerable proposition – that what each can do, in the large or latent group, all, sadly, cannot. In the case of growth impeded by coalitions as in that of health impaired by diseases, the problem would appear to be the familiar one of under-provision of some vital public good, the solution, no less familiar, that of the introduction of corrective measures by a socially responsible leadership on behalf of the popular constituency that is the national club.

Thus it is that Olson, apparently convinced that the community as a whole desires growth while each coalition within it perversely desires redistribution as well, tends to turn to the national government for the defence of the public interest: 'The efficiency of an economy may be increased either by making narrow special-interest groups weaker or by making the government stronger in relation to them. This logic must stand behind demands for political leaders with the popularity and resolve needed to "stand up to the vested interests".'[5] The whole of the community wishing to see economic growth, it is only right and proper that the government should seek to procure for its employers the advantages which it promised to secure in exchange for its mandate. The greater the gains from the reduction of inefficiencies, moreover, the greater the popularity of the political entrepreneur who promises to deliver the public good of improved allocation – and the greater the subsequent resentment in the society as a whole should he despite his undertaking nonetheless fail to narrow the perceived gap between the actual and the potential. The vote-motive is a powerful source of responsible leadership in the political democracy, Olson evidently is convinced, and therewith the basis for economic policies aimed at boosting the rate of economic growth.

Economic policies, it must be said, that would seem disproportionately to wear the minus sign of elimination in prefence to the plus of introduction and expansion. Readers better acquainted with theories of economic growth than they are with those of collective action will perhaps be surprised at the absence of the traditional cast of characters – government support to geographical mobility via transportation and housing policies, for example, or collective subsidisation of investment in research and development undertaken by thrusting innovators not yet in lobbies, or a State-maintained educational system designed to expand the supply of scarce skills – and its replacement by what is in effect the ghost-cast of repeal and withdrawal. Those readers must be reminded that Olson never sets out to provide a full account of economic growth. Rather, his concern is with something more modest, namely the relationship between differential rates of economic growth and the politico-economic phenomenon generally known as 'rent-seeking activity' – that institutionally-contingent non-market reward-maximising, in other words, which James Buchanan, following the usage of Anne Krueger, defines as being 'directly related to the scope and range of governmental activity in the economy, to the relative size of the public sector': 'Governmental licenses, quotas, permits, authorizations, approvals, franchise assignments – each of these closely related terms implies arbitrary and/or artificial scarcity created by government. . . . Persons will invest genuinely scarce resources in attempts to secure either the initial assignments of rights to the artificially scarce opportunities or replacement assignments as other initial holders are ousted from privileged positions. In either case, and despite individually rational investments *ex ante*, valuable resources will be wasted in the process.'[6] Devotion of time and other resources to the capturing of windfall gains in excess of opportunity cost by means of sovereign-pleasing devices such as 'promotion, advertising, flattery, persuasion, cajolery'[7] is, in the sense of Buchanan and Krueger, nothing other than the public bad of pure waste. That public bad of pure waste, in turn, is, in the political economy of Mancur Olson, a not insignificant contributing factor to the public bad of economic growth at a rate slower than the community taken as a whole would like to see. Thence the concern with economic policies that seem disproportionately to wear the minus sign of elimination.

Rapid change and growth would appear itself to be a vote in favour of rapid change and growth, precisely because it shakes up the sleepy and discourages the formation of groups. Too much instability is, of course, rather a disincentive than an incentive to sustained development. Olson's point is simply that the same must be said of too much stability as well; and that it might therefore be 'quite desirable' to examine 'the possibility that public policies occasionally could be designed to promote exceptionally discontinuous and rapid growth partly because this would reduce the significance of distributional coalitions and the social rigidities they help to engender'.[8] Public policies in the field of international trade, for example; since tariff-cutting (the contribution of the GATT) and economic integration (as in the case of the EEC) not only expand the number of market-participants (thereby rendering distributional coalitions that much more difficult to organise) but also, via the spur of increased competition, provide a stimulus to rapid change and growth (thereby undermining still further the tyranny of the *status quo*). Public policies, alternatively, orientated towards the rooting-out of restrictive practices such as collusive arrangements by means of direct action taking the form of anti-trust laws: not all goods and services being exchanged in world-wide markets, there are areas of 'institutional rheumatism'[9] which freedom of trade does not touch, and these it must be the task of public policy to make less inflexible and more responsive. The labour market is an obvious instance of such an area; and that is why Olson, reflecting on the unhealthy mix of ingredients (ranging from minimum wage laws to social conventions stigmatising wage-cutting unions by way of the settled level of aspirations and the economic cost of revising decisions) that combine to produce the unwholesome dish of involuntary unemployment, is moved to declare that 'the most important macroeconomic policy implication is that the best macroeconomic policy is a good microeconomic policy. There is no substitute for a more open and competitive environment. If combinations dominate markets throughout the economy and the government is always intervening on behalf of special interests, there is no macroeconomic policy that can put things right.'[10] There is in the circumstances a certain irony in Olson's declaration that 'macroeconomic policies by definition apply to the whole of an economy – a good macroeconomic policy is a public good for the relevant economy':[11] a good macroeconomic policy in the sense of Olson is, after all, nothing other than a good microeconomic policy, where a good microeconomic policy is nothing other than the elimination of special-interest legislation such as benefits the parts while victimising the whole.

The perspective of the nation as a club thus serves ultimately strongly to recommend State intervention with a negative sign to the attention of a rational collectivity bent on the acquisition of the public good of rapid economic growth – as is borne out by the historical evidence on progress without direction; 'If the analysis in this book is right, the growth in Germany and the United States before World War I was more the result of a widening of product and factor markets than it was of any special promotion or plan.'[12] Olson on the public good of rapid economic growth is clearly in favour of competition rather than control – an author, in effect, who would seem to be all but echoing the views of the celebrated Scotsman who wrote as follows about the wealth of nations: 'Every system which endeavours, either, by extraordinary encouragements, to draw towards a particular species of industry a greater share of the capital of the society than what would naturally go to it; or, by extraordinary restraints, to force from a particular species of industry a greater share of the capital of the society which would otherwise be employed in it; is in reality subversive of the great purpose which it means to promote. It retards, instead of accelerating, the progress of the society towards real wealth and greatness; and diminishes, instead of increasing, the real value of the annual produce of its land and labour.'[13] Olson on the public good of an unpolluted environment or a sound educational system is, however, somewhat more sympathetic to the notion of State involvement – a thinker who points out that the share of government in the national product was no greater in slow-growing Britain than the overall average for the developed democracies,[14] and who would seem to have a great deal of sympathy with the important insights of the distinguished interventionist who has written so vividly about the social imbalance that is 'private affluence, public poverty': 'The more goods people procure, the more packages they discard and the more rubbish that must be carried away. If the appropriate sanitation services are not provided, the counterpart of increasing opulence will be deepening filth. The greater the wealth, the thicker will be the dirt.'[15] The nation as a club thus requires, if Olson is correct, a government of truly singular sensitivity, able to deliver both the public good of rapid economic growth (which presupposes the elimination of special-interest legislation) and the public good of decent roads and litter-free parks (to the provision of which the insights of the interventionist would appear to be more relevant than are the views of the Scotsman).

Olson, basically an optimist with respect to human nature in politics, would no doubt wish to maintain that wise and expert leadership is without any insuperable difficulty to be found such as is capable successfully of delivering both the public good which requires the State to withdraw and the public good which requires the State to provide. His optimism, it would be fair to infer, is more likely to be shared by the distinguished interventionist who reserves so much praise for the 'rational view' of the 'men of goodwill'[16] than by the celebrated Scotsman whose observations on the historical workings of the visible hand are typified by the following: 'I have never known much good done by those who affected to trade for the public good.'[17] The celebrated Scotsman was, of course, writing in a society in which the franchise was severely restricted, while the distinguished interventionist was, like Olson, in a very real sense the product of a political democracy practising a system of one adult/one vote at regular intervals. The vote-motive must inevitably concentrate the leaders' mind wonderfully; and it is therefore, arguably, the perspectives of Downs on democracy which in the last analysis serve to legitimate those of Olson on the nation as a club.

5.3.2 Coalitions and change

The collectivity as a whole desires economic advance. Each

sub-collectivity within it desires redistribution as well. Redistribution means inefficiency, waste and delayed adaptation such as retard advance. The *Rise and Decline* seeks to show that retarded advance results from an accretion of coalitions, the *Logic* to explain how and why the coalitions come into being. The insights of the two books are thus unambiguously interrelated, complementary accounts of a multi-faceted social phenomenon, the inductions of the later work building on the deductions of the earlier one and serving in turn to illustrate their practical applicability.

The key concept is the establishment of the club, in the one case as in the other a social fact not unconnected with the size of the potential constituency: 'Large numbers not only raise what might be called the "transactions" cost of bargaining but also pose an additional problem. A large group can bargain with others only if it is organized, so that it can have representatives. But such an organization is itself a public good to the group it would help, and won't exist unless it enjoys the power of coercion or has some other way of giving its members an incentive on an individual basis, to support the organization.'[18] Small groups undeniably have certain advantages when it comes to collective action in support of common objectives, if only because each party knows that the quantity of the public benefit supplied is directly dependent on the magnitude of the private cost that he himself supports. The inference here would seem to be that it is small groups (and most notably so where the potential constituency is culturally most homogeneous and geographically least dispersed) that are most likely to form to secure special-interest legislation, to exercise the brake on growth.

Evidence illustrative of asymmetries of this nature is not difficult to find (the over-representation of the towns as opposed to the countryside in certain less-developed countries is one example, that of the manufacturing interest as opposed to the agricultural is another, that of the producers as opposed to the consumers is a third), but its significance must not be exaggerated: large or latent constituencies demonstrably form collective-action groups as well, of which professional associations and industry-wide trades unions are cases in point. The power of coercion and the presence of selective incentives are undeniably important in accounting for the concerted action of large groups, and so too, it must be added, is the fact that, large groups being so often made up of smaller sub-sets, 'social pressure can often be an effective selective incentive': 'Social incentives will not be very effective unless the group that values the collective good at issue interacts socially or is composed of subgroups that do. If the group does have its own social life, the desire for the companionship and esteem of colleagues and the fear of being slighted or even ostracized can at little cost provide a powerful incentive for concerted action.'[19] Even, therefore, if the small group does happen to have the edge over the large one in areas such as frequency of interaction and homogeneity of membership that keep down the costs of colluding, it would evidently be wrong to write off all latent groups as powerless – as incapable, in other words, of entering into distributional coalitions aimed at redistribution of income rather than at growth of production. The large group alongside the small, it must be concluded, is to be held responsible for that over-indulgence in transferring to the detriment of creating which is so significant a cause of slower economic growth in the more stable political democracy.

The *Logic of Collective Action* complements the *Rise and Decline of Nations* by providing a theoretical explanation for the decline and rise of groups. The earlier book also complements the later one by reminding the reader of the extent to which the public good of growth might be under-provided not because of excessive grouping but because of that inadequate coordination which results when groups fail to form. This central paradox of collective action is well illustrated by Olson's example of 'how involuntary employment, and also deep depression, can occur even when each decision-maker in the economy acts in accordance with his or her best interests':[20] *individual* self-interest and *individual* rationality evidently do not bring about the full employment payoff despite the fact that it is generally regarded as optimal by all, and for this failing not so much the strength of decision-makers as their dispersion and discreteness is very much to blame.

Olson, it is clear, could have proposed the banding together of isolated atoms into nationwide encompassing unions as a means of accelerating the speed of decision-making (in response, say, to a deflationary stimulus) and of reducing what monetarists call the 'natural rate' (by ensuring that relative pay is not affected by cuts in absolute rates); and, a national and permanent prices and incomes policy being capable as well of delivering the same mix of flexibility and coordination, he could even have opted for the strong social democratic option of increased State direction such as he is only too pleased to champion in the case of externalities such as congestion and public goods such as defence. Olson could have opted for *dirigisme*. Where groups and growth are concerned, however, the fact is that he opts instead for the free market – hardly Pareto-optimal in the textbook sense, he concedes, but superior nonetheless to any reasonable alternative: 'An economy can be dynamic and rapidly growing without at the same time being optimal or perfectly efficient. An economy with free markets and no government or cartel intervention is like a teen-aged youth; it makes a lot of mistakes but nonetheless grows rapidly without special effort or encouragement.'[21] Hence the proposals to reduce the intervention and the coercion, to increase the mobility and the adaptability, in an attempt to ensure the supply of a vital public good without which the very essence of civilised living would appear itself to be in jeopardy: 'In a society without growth or progress . . . what the winners in fights over policy won the losers, inevitably, would lose. So the fights, presumably, would be mighty rough.'[22] State intervention, the author of the *Logic* is saying, is indispensable if collective action is successfully to be taken in areas involving externalities and public goods – and market freedom, the author of the *Rise and Decline* would wish to add, is the *sine qua non* if the new policy-initiatives are to be financed peaceably out of growth in resources, not by means of the zero-sum scramble for shares in fixed availabilities with which the road to the *bellum* is inevitably paved.

For peace, Olson is insistent, is preferable to war, and definitely a commodity worth having. Thence the internal contradiction in his world-view, that he both welcomes and fears the permanent revolution that is economic evolution itself: 'The contradiction is between the desire for stability and peace and the desire to realize our full economic potential. For those, like this writer, who are so devoted to democratic freedoms and peace that they would retain them even at the cost of all further growth, this is a disturbing finding. To some degree, the contradiction is inescapable.'[23] Growth is revolution and revolution is instability. Growth is also greater private affluence combined with diminished public poverty. Growth to Olson, it is clear, is nothing other than the public good of economic advance married to the public bad of the radical divorce of present practices from past usages. Olson leaves his readers in no doubt that the bundle that he himself would most like to purchase would afford him a sound rate of economic advance packaged together with a generous *quantum* of social cohesion – or that such a bundle is the standard mix that is normally on offer to the citizens of the modern developed democracies as their nations continue to grow. The less sanguine observer, less optimistic than is Olson about the extent to which the benefits normally outweigh the costs will, however, wish, no doubt, to question the nature of that mix. Economic advance, such an observer will suggest, is productive not so much of cohesion as of conflict where the utilities that are increasingly in demand cannot, after all, significantly be increased in supply; while the depletion of moral resources that accompanies the process of material up-grading inescapably shunts the car of economic growth on to the line of convention-free *anomie* that leads directly to the *bellum*. Such an observer, convinced as he will be of the existence of *social* limits to economic growth, will hardly be able to share Olson's confident expectation that economic advance does not carry within itself self-negating forces potentially so powerful as to ensure that even the 'perennial gale of creative destruction' will one day blow itself out. No student of strategic interaction or of comparative performance would, however, wish to deny the impact upon his own thinking of Olson's influential contribution to the formulation and the testing of theories of collective action.

Part III
Hirsch

6 Social Limits and Collective Action

The argument in Fred Hirsch's controversial book *Social Limits to Growth* is both a simple and an important one: analogous to the much-discussed physical resources constraint on future growth in the GNP, there exists a parallel social resources constraint on expansion. The latter is more immediate, less 'distant and uncertain',[1] than the former, and has two dimensions. First, the adding-up problem that when it comes to social scarcity there exists a number of goods whose function is 'positional', whose income-elasticity of demand is high but whose price-elasticity of supply is either low or zero; Second, the ethical problem that a decay in friendliness, generosity and even honesty is likely to occur in a world where economic men see clearly and correctly that a sense of moral obligation bears no significant (or predictable) rate of return.

In this chapter we shall attempt an examination of Fred Hirsch's arguments concerning social limits to economic growth. In the first section we shall consider the adding-up problem; in the second section the problem of moral decline; in the third section some policy inferences; and, finally, in the fourth section, some criticisms and extensions of Fred Hirsch's important theory of collective action.

6.1 THE ADDING-UP PROBLEM

Economics has traditionally been concerned with that maximisation of collective welfare which results, as if guided by an invisible hand, when each member of society tries rationally but without central coordination to maximise his own individual or household welfare. Hirsch maintains, however, that 'the stage may now have been reached where the analytical framework that the economist has come to take for granted . . . has become a hindrance in understanding some key contemporary problems',[1] problems of which the sociologist has for long been aware and which include the following.

First, interdependence of preference-patterns. The satisfaction derived from the consumption of a commodity depends not only on the intrinsic utility yielded by the thing consumed but also on its symbolic function within the consumer's reference-group; for 'a part (but only a part) of satisfaction from positional goods relates to their scarcity as such, implying criteria of status that are inherently comparative'.[2] Both Veblen's theory of 'conspicuous consumption' and Duesenberry's 'relative income hypothesis' refer to cases of social scarcity and remind us that economic growth need not imply increased happiness to the extent that relative rather than absolute deprivation is concerned. The concept of interdependence applies not simply to consumer goods, moreover. Top jobs too, for instance, are a scarce social resource, for they serve as desirable means to the socially-valued end of high status: 'Even if you don't like performing as the boss, you may still want to show that you can, that you can have and do what others cannot have and do'.[3]

Second, interdependence of decisions made. Turning from considerations of social status to those involving purely individual utility, we once again encounter the problem of social scarcity, a dimension of excess demand over supply related not to the production of final utilities but to their absorption: 'The value to me of my education depends not only on how much I have but also on how much the man ahead of me in the job line has. The satisfaction derived from an auto or a country cottage depends on the conditions in which they can be used, which will be strongly influenced by how many other people are using them'.[4] Private consumption has in truth an inevitably social dimension in that the sum of individual decisions made differs substantially from that outcome that might reasonably have been anticipated had we focused exclusively on individual actions in isolation; for 'what each of us can achieve, all cannot'.[5]

The *implications* of the adding-up problem are as follows:

Firstly, reduction in amenity-value. Whilst I as an individual might be able to drive my car on a congestion-free highway to my weekend retreat surrounded by unspoiled countryside, I might nonetheless as a social actor be unable to do so where in a growing economy more and more people have cars and crowd the roads in an attempt to reach similar retreats in countryside progressively more overbuilt and aesthetically less pleasing.

Secondly, inflation. Economic growth is accompanied by a rise in the price of positional goods as part of the process of allocating limited supplies in conditions of excess demand. This in turn means a regressive windfall gain to current owners of scarce commodities, who acquired them before rising standards of living and the massification of consumption so dramatically increased their prices relative to the prices of those goods whose supply can be expanded (the price of, say, land suitable for holiday homes near a beauty-spot relative to the price of colour televisions, cars or basic foodstuffs). Since all cannot in the positional sector have what some can have, economic growth is then accompanied by a distributional struggle and exacerbated social tensions rather than by heightened social integration; and consequently accompanied by wage-inflation associated with a new beggar-my-neighbour code in the labour market. The increasing power of manual workers and their unions, and the escalated leapfrogging of claims and expectations, is, however, in Hirsch's view, a threat not simply to the 'harmony and anonymity of the market system' but perhaps to its 'stability and efficiency'[6] as well; for it means that unions increasingly compete with one another for the greatest successes in collective bargaining arenas (since, after all, 'the normal channel of self-improvement for workers in occupations with no career structures is through collective bargaining')[7] and yet do not see that even a successful if disruptive strike will still lead rather to bitterness than to *embourgeoisement* where such a strike yields the workers money but not the minority goods on which to spend it (since – and here Hirsch is insistent – 'the extension of middle-class objectives has outdistanced middle-class opportunities'[8] in a world of widening reference-groups).

Thirdly, frustration. What some can have, all cannot; and a distributional struggle orientated towards elbowing one's way nearer the front of the queue can never fully choke off total disappointment and false hopes (to say nothing of resentment and anxiety on the part of those already at the head of the queue who come to feel increasingly beleaguered in the face of onslaught after onslaught on relative place) simply because 'the sum of benefits of all the actions taken together is nonetheless zero'.[9] Furthermore, the distributional struggle is a struggle for more than money; hence the enormous resistance to the introduction of comprehensive schooling on the part of those parents whose children already attend superior schools, fearful of a reduction in relative social position as well as of an absolute fall in material standards of living.

Fourthly, waste. In a world of scarce positional goods, resources must be wasted on defensive consumption, as in the case of sprawling suburbs (where the desire of more and more people to live in the suburbs leads to reduced access to air and open space for the inhabitants of present suburbs, and consequently to an increasing wastage of time and petrol in an attempt to reach a destination ever more distant from the cultural and occupational opportunities of the town-centre) and the inflation of paper qualifications (where increased access to formal education has meant increased demand for screening-of-potential rather than primarily training or cultural-humanitarian reasons, educational certification being one of the principal requirements for access to well-paid, job-satisfying, prestigious but scarce positions of leadership and responsibility). Such cases are cases of waste which mean either *more* input for the *same* output (cases where 'the race gets longer for the same prize',[10] since 'if everyone stands on tiptoe, no one sees better'),[11] or even *more* input for an *inferior* output (as where a Ph.D. today yields less *entrée* to top jobs than an M.Sc. did yesterday, and is in addition skewed in its social distribution towards wealthy families best able to finance the lengthening obstacle-course of education).

The conclusion then follows: economic liberalism for success presupposes a modest level of absolute incomes (so that the market mechanism is chiefly allocating material rather than positional goods, and the latter sector remains uncrowded) and a stratified rather than a classless social structure (so that different groups seek different things). In a society where absolute incomes are high and the distribution of relative incomes is somewhat egalitarian, however, social constraints arise and constitute a problem for which decentralised decision-making mechanisms are simply incapable of providing a solution (a problem similar to that which arises in the Keynesian model, where rational pursuit of individual self-interest does not keep the economy at full employment and provides no alternative to explicit State management and coordination in the public interest): 'More wealth of the kind attainable by all paradoxically means an increased scramble for the kind of wealth attainable only by some. . . . It is now questionable whether the road to the carefree society can run through the market economy, dominated as it is by piecemeal choices exercised by individuals in response to their situation'.[12]

6.2 THE MORAL NEXUS

Hirsch identifies as a second social limit to growth the decline in friendliness and increase in selfishness which he believes to be associated once again with increasing affluence. Here two social facts are of primary causal significance:

First, the rising marginal cost of time associated with the increasing supply of material goods per hour worked means that 'time becomes scarcer in relation to goods',[1] men are under pressure 'to do more things in – and at – the same time',[2] and time-saving goods and services are developed as a means (a form of defensive consumption) of economising on the scarce resource of time. Since more time is needed for consuming more material goods, and since a further quantity of time is wasted in 'the scramble to acquire larger shares of fixed availabilities',[3] there is a decreased quantity of time available for the time-consuming activities of sociability and friendliness (including the search element of starting contacts which may not 'pay off').

Second, a market economy enlists and legitimates individual self-interest and focuses it on monetary exchanges. Commercial advertising, for example, directs its appeal to the consumer's greed rather than to altruistic concern for the welfare of unknown strangers ('Commercial advertising comprises a persistent series of invitations and imperatives to the individual to look after himself and his immediate family; self-interest becomes the social norm, even duty');[4] and the blandishments of advertisers are reinforced, albeit for different reasons, by the consumerist movement of Ralph Nader and others (where 'the individual is urged to secure maximum value for money for himself or herself. The approach is to the individual as maximising consumer, rather than as cooperating citizen').[5] Simultaneously, at the same time as material prosperity and consumption increase in importance, so contact, concern and sociability reveal themselves to be inferior goods; for they 'do not, by their nature, have the character of private economic goods: which is to say that the costs and benefits of specific actions do not fall primarily on those undertaking them.'[6] In a closely-knit community, bonds are those of reciprocity and mutual aid (as where gift and counter-gift directly imply one another, even if in the long run rather than the short run – the case, for example, of a lifetime friendship) and/or affects (as where, for emotional reasons, the partner's happiness adds to one's own rather than being irrelevant to it in the way that the exchange model presupposes). In a more loosely-articulated and mobile society, however, the gift is unlikely directly and bilaterally to yield a return-gift to the donor (since one has increasingly to deal with unknown strangers), contacts are in general too casual to generate lasting ties of mutual sympathy and genuine concern, and people find it tempting – and rational – to behave in the manner of free-riders with respect to public goods and to seek to take without giving.

The *implications* of moral decline are as follows.

Firstly, to the extent that altruistic conduct is a necessity rather than a luxury, its decay will bring with it negative externalities insofar as the community is underprovided as a result with free gifts such as healthful blood for transfusion, willingness to help a stranger attacked in the street, willingness to untie rather than to rob the bound Ulysses once the danger from the Sirens is past, or the security of mutual support in a marriage founded on something more durable than calculation of costs and benefits. In area after area of social life, Hirsch says, 'the Good Samaritan remedies a market failure';[7] and thus a decline in social involvement resulting from the tyranny of small decisions impoverishes each because it impoverishes all (since that which is a public good to all can easily become a public good to none where people become so money-minded that no citizen is prepared to budget time and effort for the unilateral transfer). Hence we encounter the phenomenon that friendship and sociability, being public goods whose benefits are diffuse rather than specific, tend to be under-supplied relative to demand in rich countries: 'We may want sociability more than ever; yet we cannot, individually and separately, express that want in a way that secures it. This analysis helps explain a frequent casual observation, which otherwise appears economically puzzling: that human contact in advanced economies is increasingly sought but decreasingly attained'.[8] Individuals *qua* individuals, in short, may be expected rationally to underproduce the amount of sociability they desire to consume.

Secondly, and turning from quantity to quality of relationships, here again a preoccupation with individual utility has a deleterious effect on the nature of the product. To take one instance, just as sex with a prostitute (bought sex) is inferior to sex based rather on congruence of emotions than exchange of equivalents, so a highly commercialised form of marriage contract based on rational calculation of costs and benefits is likely similarly to convert friends into merchants (if only because 'the more that is in the contracts, the less can be expected without them';[9] and because in any case 'orgasm as a consumer's right rather rules it out as an ethereal experience').[10] Again, the quality of treatment provided by a doctor in a system of bilateral exchange is likely both to be different from that treatment provided where the *quid pro quo* is not implicit (as where the doctor removes a healthy appendix purely in order to maximise his profits) and to be perceived to be different (witness the rise in malpractice suits in the United States, an indication of diminished trust in doctors on the part of patients). All of this reminds us that the characteristics of a good or service are closely correlated with its mode of provision, and that supplying and demanding are activities substantially dependent on the social environment within which they are situated (so that *what* we have may be no more important than *how* we obtained it).

Thirdly, many choices nowadays presuppose a collective intervention which may not be forthcoming; for the erosion in the moral nexus makes the formulation of effective social policy progressively more difficult. A society with a market bias tends to overproduce goods which can be packaged and sold and to underproduce those which must be consumed in common; but public goods can often be made available in no other way but via public provision, or at the very most via some mode of provision which alters their fundamental character for the worse as compared with those features which people would have chosen if only they had stopped to think (consider, for example, a museum charge which removes not only an entrance-fee from the pockets of users 'but also the pleasure derived by some visitors from the existence of part of the cultural heritage as common property available freely to all';[11] or a turnstile restricting access to a pub dartboard to those who have paid a fee, thereby narrowing a game to a small number of effective demanders which up to then had been 'inextricably bound up with open socializing').[12] The escalating pressures of positional competition (implying as they do both fear of losing one's place relative to others and greater selfishness in consequence) generate resentment on the part of the well-to-do towards subsidising poorer members of the community (e.g. 'Formation of new suburbs with homogeneous residents has been a well-documented means for richer residents of big cities to escape from supporting less fortunate citizens');[13] and greater mobility induces increased privatisation of facilities on the part of those best situated to pay for them (e.g. 'the substitution of the country club for the village common or city park, or of the effectively private school for the effectively public school'),[14] with a corresponding unwillingness to finance those still dependent on common access, non-exclusive environments and informal exchange. Such privatisation always harms the poor (since they are increasingly asked to pay for what previously was a free good or accept second-rate safety-net provision instead) and is yet another example of the preoccupation with self which characterises the affluent society: 'As general prosperity grows, the difficulty of arranging redistributive transfers through the national or local fiscal system does not diminish. On the contrary, it may even increase.'[15] In a world of crowding and commercialisation, in other words, the ratepayers' revolt is fully predictable.

Fourthly, at the very time that new externalities are being generated which can only be dealt with on a collective basis, the very selfishness which gave birth to those externalities is now acknowledged to extend to the political market as well, at least in the Downsian economic approach to political institutions that was examined earlier in this book. According to that approach, the consumer shops for a political leader with desired characteristics (which nowadays, as already noted, are increasingly likely, in the Hirschian model, to include a preference for the individual and the specific as opposed to the collective and the general) and the producer seeks to match policies supplied to policies demanded purely so as successfully to compete in the marketplace for votes (with the result that, precisely because it is in the interests of *each* citizen to do what is not in the interests of *all*, politicians will fear to tackle the adding-up problem lest this harm their personal promotion prospects). More generally, corruption and abuse of power are to be expected from politicians interested exclusively in the maximisation of their own utility; for honesty and a sense of responsibility repose on moral absolutes which both pre-date exchange society and are the precondition for it, but which are increasingly being threatened by the utilitarian perspective and the substitution for morality of rational self-interest. Should judges and politicians truly come to regard themselves as merchants selling their services to the highest bidder, then the 'logical error'[16] in the utilitarian system becomes immediately apparent: in a world where there are no higher values than market-determined costs and benefits, there the market system itself becomes unstable – since even private property itself is then not secure from 'the first entrepreneur to be able to raise enough credit to buy the judge'.[17]

Early liberalism (the liberalism, for instance, of Adam Smith) 'was predicted on an underlying moral-religious base'[18] which constrained self-interest by ethics as rigidly as others have said it ought to be constrained by laws and the police. Christianity, for example, enjoined altruistic behaviour, and this was a good thing: 'While such cooperation can, in some cases, be replaced by coercive rules, or stimulated through collectively imposed inducements to individuals' private interests, this will rarely be as practicable and efficient as when it is internally motivated'.[19] Christianity, moreover, provided external legitimation for absolute values, such as devotion to duty, restraint of passion, service to the collectivity, truthfulness and honesty, and these values then become public goods for the whole community – a useful spillover benefit since they are also 'necessary inputs for much of economic output'[20] in a mobile, anonymous, large-scale society where individual behaviour is free of the continuous scrutiny that characterises more traditional communities. Historically speaking, 'the market system was, at bottom, more dependent on religious binding than the feudal system, having abandoned direct social ties maintained by the obligations of custom and status';[21] and yet, ironically perhaps, it is the market system itself which has done most to undermine the unseen source of support that results from the internalisation of social norms over and above that of buying cheap and selling dear.

Early capitalism, in short, was able successfully to rely on the market mechanism precisely because early capitalism was buttressed by social values dating from an earlier stage of social development. Those values are now in decay, and the result is a moral vacuum. Hence the paradox: just at a time when 'the responses of isolated individuals to the situation that faces them have become a less sure guide to promoting the objectives of individuals taken together', yet 'the weakening of traditional social values has made predominantly capitalist economies more difficult to manage, that is, to guide by indirect state intervention'.[22] Management is today increasingly necessary; the individualistic ethos makes it increasingly difficult.

6.3 POLICY INFERENCES

Hirsch stresses that policy inferences concerning social limits to growth ought to be kept 'guarded and modest',[1] both because there is a restricted amount that we know and because there is a restricted amount that we can do.

At the level of *knowledge*, there is indeterminacy reflecting 'the lack of a precise criterion for economic efficiency through use of collective action' ('we do not have a firm grasp on the full implications of collective action') and also reflecting 'the lack of a quantitative dimension of the critique' ('it has not been found possible to estimate over what proportion of economic activity social limits to growth are in play').[2] This indeterminacy calls in turn for further research into the nature of social limits (and Hirsch emphasises that his book is 'little more than a starting point'[3] with 'no clear-cut implications for immediate policy'),[4] especially important since collective intervention imposes costs of its own. In connection with research, moreover, it must be noted with regret that the national accounts as yet provide no statistical measures of positional competition, just as they provide no measure of the 'bads' associated with, say, pollution; and yet, just as 'expenditure on extra laundry services made necessary by a smokier atmosphere'[5] only negates a previous deterioration in individual welfare and merely restores the *status quo ante*, so additional education acquired solely 'so as to safeguard one's access to a particular job at a time that general education expansion is raising the level of required credentials'[6] ought also to be netted out of value added so as to avoid double counting. All human activities do not yield satisfaction to oneself (the case of defensive consumption in the form of, say, extra time wasted in getting to work, the concomitant of the need to dwell in increasingly distant suburbs so as to enjoy constant benefits in terms of amenity); some activities generate dissatisfaction for others (the case of road-congestion); and a reconsideration of the link between statistical value added and psychic pleasure supplied (involving the development of additional social indicators) is urgently needed.

More generally, such knowledge as we have concerning social limits to economic growth ought to be more widely disseminated, so that members of the public come to appreciate the threat to individual welfare implied by the new adding-up problem and the decay of the moral nexus. One by-product of such awareness is in turn likely to be greater scepticism with respect to salesmanship, and this is a healthy development. After all, 'to the extent that marketing and advertising appeal to individuals to isolate themselves from . . . group or social effects – to get in ahead or to protect their positions – they are socially wasteful. They are then also socially immoral on the mundane level of the morality concerned with social stability and consistency. If all are urged to get ahead, many are likely to have their expectations frustrated.'[7]

At the level of *action*, there is a need for explicit central coordination of objectives in the field of positional goods, where the discrete, decentralised, piecemeal, marginal adjustments of the market mechanism simply cannot take into account the interactive effects of combined decisions and where each individual in consequence ends up with a social environment significantly different from that which he would have preferred. One course of action which the State can take is land-zoning so as to restrict access to the countryside for purposes of constructing new suburbs (and thus to prevent suburban sprawl and protect scenic beauty). Another course of action is social provision of goods and services in areas where all individuals benefit but no single individual can make the relevant rational decisions, as in the case of road-congestion brought about by the absence of a viable alternative mode of transport: 'As public transportation deteriorates, we are given an extra incentive to use our own private mode of transport which in turn results in further deterioration and a worsened position of public *vis-à-vis* private transportation'.[8] Negatively speaking, the public sector must guard itself against escalating claims for public services complementary to positional goods (roads, for example, or education in its screening role), such public services being (and here Hirsch disagrees with Galbraith) not a solution but 'a part of the problem':[9] 'The flaw in the affluent society lies not in the false values of affluence but in its false promise'.[10] Within the realm of social scarcity, in summary, individuals come closer to attaining their desired ends the less they seek to attain in isolation their goals: 'In this sense, a shift in the invisible hand from the private into the public or communal sector is needed. Rather than pursuit of self-interest contributing to the social good, pursuit of the social good contributes to the satisfaction of self-interest. The difficulty is that the latter pursuit needs to be deliberately organized under existing standards and instincts of personal behavior. So the invisible hand is presently unavailable where it is newly needed.'[11]

Collective means are now needed in many areas of social life if individual ends are to be attained, but the free market mechanism too has a role to play in solving the problems associated with positional goods. In the labour market, for example, top jobs ('the most important positional sector'[12]) might be allocated by what Hirsch terms a 'Dutch auction' (i.e. an auction which would, in his formulation, reduce, Marshall-like, the pay-differentials of those who in compensation have the greatest power, status and job-satisfaction in the community): although such a method of paring demand (a variable) down to supply (a constant) would be opposed by groups now in power (and their unions), in alliance with those who favour the career structure, the established pay hierarchy and the traditional differential, it would in truth have a valuable secondary function of reducing social tensions on balance by providing an ethical validation and justification for differences in the capacity to earn and spend. The reduction in differentials could result from the introduction of a totally free market for labour; but, perhaps more realistically, it could also come from discriminatory taxation of highly-paid jobs up to the point where demand equals supply and where those applicants who have not dropped out of the market in disgust are by a process of elimination those who want particular jobs for their intrinsic attractions and not those attractions *plus* the supplementary benefit of superior remuneration.

Reduction in differentials would in turn have beneficial effects for educational institutions, which could then concentrate on educational rather than allocative objectives: 'If education were made a less sure means to acquisition or perpetuation of financial advantages, there would be less reason to restrict competition and diversity within education on distributional grounds. People would then be more likely to choose a particular school or course of education because it fitted their individual needs, rather than as a fast track to high-paying jobs.'[13] And the revised function of educational institutions would then reduce that social waste represented by excessive investment in the acquisition of formal credentials and also have progressive implications for social policy (since the lengthening of time-periods spent in formal education naturally favours the children of past winners in possession of present wealth).

Sharing of advantages is necessary where supply of the scarce utility cannot significantly be expanded; and while the State can do much to equalise access (say, by the provision free of goods such as parks and beaches open to all regardless of income), nonetheless 'it is the haves who expect too much'[14] and who must learn to adapt to the new constraint of positional scarcity. One example of this adaptation is greater power-sharing at work, where (even at the cost of some material inefficiency, and recognising that 'the pains of subordinate status, and the pleasures of superior status, may thereby be reduced a little, with a corresponding diminution in excess demand for superior positions')[15] leadership roles might be more democratically exercised. A second example is integrated schooling. In a hypothetical society fragmented into an intellectual meritocracy on the one hand and a class of frustrated helots (the 'idiotariat')[16] on the other, resentments potentially capable of threatening the security of the whole collectivity could be averted should some of the favoured groups agree 'to give up their isolation and perhaps also some of their advantages';[17] and one form that this renunciation could take is the acceptance of the comprehensive school. Parents whose children now attend superior institutions will protest that comprehensivisation will reduce their child's life-chances, and they will be right; for, top jobs being positional goods, it is of value to those having access to superior entry-qualifications to protect their interests. Yet what is of advantage to some cannot, in this case, be of advantage to all; and people must come to accept the need to put social interest (in this case, the reduction of racial and class segregation) above private orientation (in this case, privileged access to a trade). This presupposes State organisation of the process, of course, so as to prevent free riders from abusing their neighbours' generosity ('People may be willing to put social interests first at a modest sacrifice of their individualistic interests, but they cannot act out this preference on their own'),[18] but it also presupposes, most importantly, a willingness to act with an eye to collective obligation and communal needs.

To some extent, this willingness can be justified in terms of rational recognition of interest ('Action that would entail a heavy cost to the individual if undertaken by himself alone could involve imperceptible costs, or even benefits, if similar action were taken by his fellows')[19] as where citizens all detesting litter all, independently, behave *as if* they care about the damage done by litter to others' contentment and decide rationally not to litter. Yet the internalisation of new moral norms must nonetheless accompany the self-interested altruism of *as if*, precisely because so much of social action takes place in situations where only internal (and not external) restraint is practicable and efficient ('The controllers usually have a large handicap of relevant information. Only *I* can see everywhere I litter').[20] It is not, of course, entirely clear whence these new moral norms are to spring: but Hirsch suggests they may be associated with a greater belief in the justice of the social system as a whole.

One thing, however, is, in Hirsch's view, certain: social limits to growth will not be eliminated by the mere process of material growth itself. Expansion may be an alternative to redistribution in the material sector of the economy (where technological progress permits of an increase in supply of goods and services without any deterioration in quality of product). It cannot be an alternative in the positional sector, where one man's gain remains another man's loss and relative as well as absolute values are central to the drama. Hence the dilemma: 'What the wealthy have today can no longer be delivered to the rest of us tomorrow; yet as we individually grow richer, that is what we expect. The dynamic interaction between material and positional sectors becomes malign. Instead of alleviating the unmet demands on the economic system, material growth at this point exacerbates them.'[21]

6.4.   HIRSCH AND COLLECTIVE ACTION

The argument in Fred Hirsch's important interdisciplinary synthesis of economy, society and polity is in three parts concerned, respectively, with the emergence of an adding-up problem, the decay of the moral nexus, and the policy inferences to be drawn from social limits to economic growth. Of these three parts, however, the second would appear central and the first and third essentially derivative from it. The central role of the common culture will become increasingly apparent from the criticisms and extensions of Hirsch's theses to be considered in the three parts of this, the concluding section in this book.

6.4.1   The adding-up problem

Anthony Crosland, like so many other social democrats of the 1950s and 1960s, welcomed the rapid economic growth which he saw around him in no small measure because of the equalisation which he believed it bred: 'A majority of the population is gradually attaining a middle-class standard of life, and distinct symptoms even of a middle-class psychology.'[1] Fred Hirsch, entirely favourable as he was to the emergence of a society characterised by a 'general *consciousness* of equal living standards',[2] desperately wished to share the confident optimism of the Great Growthman who had propounded the proposition, almost as a natural law, that '*seen and felt disparities in personal living standards are a function not only of income-distribution, but also of the absolute level of average real income.* That is, the higher the level of average income, the more equal is the visible pattern of consumption, and the stronger the subjective feeling of equal living standards . . . almost regardless of the distribution of total income.'[3] Fred Hirsch, exceptionally anxious as he was about the increasing significance of the zero-sum sector and the beggar-my-neighbour scramble for inclusion, was, however, prevented by his vision of a dragon in the path from sharing the social democrats' prediction of integrative consumption through economic growth: 'What each of us can achieve, all cannot',[4] he said ominously, and issued an unambiguous warning that beyond the Butskellism lay the *bellum* should the collectivity not change its course before the crash. Yet he also conceded that he had not himself been able to quantify the magnitudes involved in his diagnosis of social scarcity – and would have been quick to acknowledge that, conceptually speaking, the bulk of incremental demand in the foreseeable future might well be concentrated in the material rather than the positional sector. Were that to prove the case, of course, then the existence of positional goods would not represent a significant buffer to *embourgeoisement*.

The question is an empirical one, and the alternative hypothesis to that advanced by Hirsch would be the assertion that the status of positionality extends only to a small percentage of the utilities increasingly pursued in an affluent society. Until considerable evidence has been collected, it is not possible to discriminate between the theories – and somewhat premature, therefore, to conclude that there is an inevitable march or progression in the course of social evolution from the material to the positional economy on such a scale as to warrant the description of social limits when social pin-pricks might be more apposite. It is, in other words, somewhat misleading to compare the middle-class standard of life to a crowded ship about to dispose of its last ticket and sail into the distance never to return; since while some people undeniably do, as they become better-off, demand country cottages (which cannot be infinitely replicated), and others demand the Rembrandt original (a case where my gain is truly your loss, the commodity being in totally inelastic supply), still others demand colour televisions, cassette recorders, fitted kitchens, automatic dishwashers, restaurant meals, dormer windows, electric carving-knives, home computers and clothing which is distinctive rather than durable (all commodities which can be mass-produced without encountering social limits) – or simply choose to substitute leisure for work by refusing overtime or avoiding promotion in order to have more time to potter in the garden, enjoy a hobby, play with their children or entertain friends. All in all, in short, all people do not want precisely the same things in life even now; and this social pluralism is likely much to be encouraged by greater tolerance of alternative lifestyles and differential preference-patterns in an increasingly heterogeneous and complex future which even the most imaginative of social theorists cannot possibly foresee. The evidence that must be collected would appear to relate not only to today's cross-section of desires but, and more significantly, to tomorrow's as well; and this reminds us that the question of the income elasticity of positional goods, in addition to being in essence an empirical one, is also a question to which anyone but the most omniscient seer will find it fiendishly difficult to supply an answer.

Even where the demand for positional goods does rise as incomes rise, moreover, it would still be wrong to underestimate the extent to which effective supply can in practice be increased. Technology, for instance, while it admittedly cannot significantly increase the number of holiday-makers squeezed on to the fixedly Ricardian land-mass of Brighton Beach, can nonetheless open up to holidaymakers a wide range of other beaches throughout the world. Expense, of course, is thereby incurred, and Dahrendorf is quite right to point out that defensive consumption is far from being a free good: 'If everybody can spend their holidays in Italy, one has to go to Fiji to do something special. "The race gets longer for the same prize", though not, to be sure, for the same price.'[5] Expense is incurred, but the very fact that money successfully buys the services of defensive consumption can only be taken as a demonstration that the crowded beach is not after all a social limit to economic growth. It is, indeed, nothing other than the economic growth itself which brought the consumption-services of the less-crowded beach within the budgetary reach of more than merely the very rich: Britain, Anthony Crosland declared in 1956, is 'achieving a rate of growth which, if maintained, will double the standard of living in twenty-five years',[6] and thus does economic growth more than compensate its victims for the nuisance of expensive holidays which it imposes on those members of the community who aspire to a constant level of amenity-value with respect to beaches.

As with beaches, so with roads; since technology, while it undeniably cannot infinitely augment the number of private cars travelling in to the city-centre at the height of the rush-hour, can nonetheless provide alternative modes of transport (the easily-manoeuvrable small vehicle, the rapid and reliable bus service), alternatives to the use of transport (including devices such as the tele-copier and the video-telephone which transport not the workers to the work but the work to the workers and thereby allow people – perhaps the parents of small children, perhaps lovers of secluded countryside and/or of village life, perhaps mere energetic enthusiasts keen to fill the traditional three hours of leisure enjoyed at place of work by growing vegetables and baking bread – to carry on at home a full business life complete with all necessary office communication, and as a result without ever having to venture forth at all on to congested highways) – and, quite simply, a reasonable expansion in roads themselves (a case where, because demand precedes supply and the shoe is perceived to pinch for a time before a size larger is ordered, citizens may be led by the lag to confuse an as-yet uncorrected disequilibrium with an eternal bottleneck in a manner which is as wrong-headed as it is common).

Technological improvements clearly have the capacity in some measure to increase the effective supply of positional goods; and so, for that matter, do a wide range of social usages (actual and potential). Thus the staggering of holidays raises the annual productivity of

Brighton beach; the introduction of flexihours at work and of evening opening of shops reduces congestion on the roads; and the decentralisation of industry and trade does something to combat the problem of suburban sprawl. And there is sharing. Time-sharing (or, the moderately more socialistic alternative, renting instead of buying), which boosts access to the services of otherwise unemployed country cottages. Job-sharing, which ensures that each of us, should remunerative labour prove a positional good, nonetheless enjoys a refreshing dip, however short, in a tempting pool, however small. Power-sharing, which, via joint leadership, consultation at boards and meetings, the rotating chairmanship most of all, gives each diner a larger portion of the tasty dish than if he had been given none at all. Sharing is sequential consumption and an obvious case where the time-factor, as Dahrendorf makes clear, renders the physical limits to growth that much 'less circumscribed than Hirsch would have us believe': 'Hirsch likes to quote the fact that if everybody stands on tiptoe nobody can see anything; but if everybody goes to a luxury hotel once (or stands on tiptoe for one minute), there is quite a chance for many to luxuriate (or to see).'[7] The fact that many concerned citizens, aware of the nuisances associated with (even if not social limits to) economic growth, have already proposed measures along these lines shows a healthy recognition of the extent to which men are the masters, not the prisoners, of their social fate.

Recognition is not the same as acceptance, however, nor many the same as most; and for the effective supply of goods in practice to be increased via so radical a rethinking of social usages as to make every member of the society a king for a day and famous for fifteen minutes, the action required inevitably presupposes, at least within the non-authoritarian parameters of the political democracy, a high degree of cultural consensus with respect to the merits of the proposal. It is more likely to be today's rich than today's poor who will vociferously oppose the debasement in the characteristics of their consumables that is well illustrated by the substitution of the car-pool for the advantages of exclusivity; and it is therefore, one suspects, their agreement which will be the more difficult to secure for any significant assault on privilege.

Difficult to secure or easy to secure, the fact remains that the haves in the Hirschian model are in a minority – the very reason, as it happens, why an unsympathetic reader might well wish to accuse Hirsch of having unwittingly formulated, in his theory of positional goods, a strong case not so much against privilege as in its favour. The reason for such an accusation is that Hirsch is far stronger on the diminished utility of the few than he is on the augmented utility of the many that arises in the quasi-positional sector in the course of economic growth and change. Hirsch shows great understanding for the position of Jack, who feels marginally deprived at having now to share his previously unspoilt Greek island with other tourists in a manner which Anthony Crosland clearly grasped when he admitted without reservation that 'driving round the country was much pleasanter when the roads were nearly empty. Venice and Majorca have been ruined for the minority since the *hoi polloi* invaded in their charter flights and the local peasantry bought noisy Vespas.'[8] What Crosland did and Hirsch did not, however, was to incorporate the position of Jill as well, and to say that the marginal deprivation of the minority is no reason for questioning the extension of beauty and pleasure (even if slightly debased beauty and pleasure) to the majority which is increasingly clamouring for access: 'My working-class constituents . . . want package-tour holidays to Majorca, even if this means more noise of night flights and eating fish and chips on previously secluded beaches – why should they too not enjoy the sun?'[9] Crosland's criticism of middle-class social thinkers who, having themselves gone up in the world, then 'want to kick the ladder down behind them',[10] strikes perilously close to home in the case of Hirsch, who appears to write in places as if Jill had seized Jack's beach (a straightforward transfer of the zero-sum kind) when in fact she had only asked him to share it (a positive sum game, albeit one which Jack could imagine as being that much more positive if Jill did not play at all). Jill has gained access to the beach while Jack has not entirely lost the opportunity to derive utility from it; total happiness is likely to have increased (although one can never be certain where comparisons are being made between different persons with differing perceptions of what it is to be happy); and, while one does, like Hirsch, sympathise with Jack, it is hard to believe that his deprivation demonstrates that economic growth *on balance* yields disappointing fruits as more and more people seek to join the mainstream of advance.

As with beaches, so with roads; since, while Tom might indeed feel marginally deprived at no longer being able to drive unimpeded by congestion to his office in the City, there is a good chance that his deprivation is more than offset by the pleasure Dick now obtains from being able to drive home from a party rather than waiting in the rain for a bus, or the satisfaction which Harry now experiences of being able to motor with his family in the Highlands of Scotland rather than spending his holidays on Brighton beach. It is obvious that more means worse when seen from the perspective of Tom – and, too, that Tom is being compelled (without consultation, consent or compensation) to pay a private cost for a collective benefit in a manner which most observers would find deeply distressing were the diswelfares in question to involve not a merchant banker deprived of his traditionally-speedy right of way but rather a middle-aged coalminer with specialised skills made redundant when his fellow citizens opt to switch to the cheaper, cleaner substitute of nuclear power. Even merchant bankers have feelings and Tom's unhappiness is as real as would be the scholar's were the playground of an infants' school to be constructed on the previously vacant plot of land which abuts his study. Tom, however, is only one among three; and the fact that more means worse when seen from his perspective must inevitably be set against the not-unrelated fact that more means better when seen from the perspective of Dick and Harry.

Sadly, there is no known scientific technique which permits of the measurement of intensities without which the crucial next step of aggregation of feelings cannot meaningfully be undertaken, and interpersonal comparisons in the Hirschian world are doubly fraught with difficulties in view of the fact that they are intertemporal as well: Benedick, unable to gauge the precise amount of pleasure derived by Beatrice from watching with him a performance of *Much Ado About Nothing*, can hardly be expected to say for certain whether people were happier or less happy before new goods such as the television-set were invented, or how happy each or all of the three families today housed in a converted Victorian villa happen to be as compared with the single family and its staff which lived there a century ago. Things change, people change, and, as Hirsch would be the first to remind us, static analysis must not be applied to dynamic situations: 'No comparison of welfare can be made where tastes vary.'[11] Social development is slow and gradual, individual experience limited and contingent, and it is in practice meaningless to ask the Japanese tourist queuing today for an hour to see the Tower of London, if he was not in essence happier in 1850: he was not alive in 1850, the Tower of London was not then open to the casual visitor, and precious few Japanese tourists in any case had, in 1850, either the funds or the incentive to spend their holidays in London. One could, of course, ask the Japanese tourist what he himself feels as, for an hour, he queues rather than views. His answer, one would guess, will have much in common with the content (if not the formulation) of Jack's statement when he awoke to find Jill eating fish and chips on his previously secluded beach, of Tom's declaration when his breakfast toast came with the traffic jam caused by Dick and Harry racing about on noisy Vespas and crowding the streets of the City with the *hoi polloi*. No one wants to be included in a crush. But, then, no one wants to be excluded from the benefit that caused the crush. There's nowt so queer as folk.

In cases where positional goods do exist, action does itself in some cases generate the necessary reaction and set into motion, without State intervention, forces tending automatically to check the abuse. Hirsch himself gives two examples. The first concerns roads where, should access be left unregulated, 'the increased supply then entails a reduction in quality, in the sense that a congested road is of lower quality than a clear one, which is a restraining influence on demand. The classical example of this process in economic literature is the crowding of a new highway that proceeds to the point at which travel along it is no faster than on the old road.'[12] The second concerns top jobs and associated differentials: 'Some responsiveness in relative salary levels to shifts in potential supply and demand undoubtedly exists. The greater expansion in supply of college graduates in the United States in the 1950s and 1960s eventually led to a surplus, and between 1969 and 1973 the excess in average mean income of male college graduates over high school graduates was reduced from 50 to 41 per cent.'[13] Hirsch himself, as is shown by these two examples, was evidently aware of the power and potential of self-regulating corrective mechanisms unaided to diminish the attractiveness of positional goods. One might well wish to point out that allocation by price would fulfil the same function with respect to beaches and roads; and that entry-charges more closely attuned to supply and demand could even reduce waiting-times at the Tower of London.

More fundamentally, perhaps, any reference to *homeostasis* raises important question concerning a possible elasticity of substitution of material for positional goods. On the one hand we have the mass-produced article, cheapened by economies of scale and improved out of all recognition by the dynamic of competition and the Schumpeterian entrepreneur in a genial mood. On the other hand we have the positional good, its price rising more rapidly than the rate of inflation, its amenity-value sinking as the trickle-down of chauffeur-driven limousines increasingly prevents any from trickling past. In such a situation (although Hirsch does not explore this possibility), many if not most consumers would be tempted to substitute the loft-conversion for the Rembrandt original, the complete video-library of Doris Day films for the tranquillity of the country cottage, to an extent that would have been inconceivable had relative prices remain unaltered in the face of changes in the respective relationships between supply and demand. The automaticity of the self-regulating mechanism will not, needless to say, have the force of the self-evident *ought-to-be* for all observers – many of whom will warn, as Schelling puts it, that equilibrium emphatically does *not* mean that 'something is all right': 'The body of a hanged man is in equilibrium when it finally stops swinging, but nobody is going to insist that the man is all right.'[14] Desirable or not desirable, a realignment of relative prices as between the material and the positional sectors undeniably generates very strong temptations indeed to alter one's expenditure-patterns. Should those temptations then be translated into actions, the conclusion to be reached is that the market system already provides its own turning-points on a more extensive scale than is envisaged in the work of Hirsch.

Naturally, it might be objected that the existing system involves waste and frustration, and is for those reasons less acceptable on philosophical grounds than would be the administered alternative. Yet Hirsch's approach both to waste and to frustration is in truth problematical.

Regarding *waste*, Hirsch is compelled by the logic of his arguments to say why this is a bad thing, but only implicitly does so – when he rejects Galbraith's idea of the 'revised sequence' and defends economic growth in terms of consumer sovereignty, non-manipulated authentic desires, and genuine non-satiety. Such a defence of economising on the grounds of perceived scarcity does, of course, close the door to the argument that a viable alternative to recklessly expanding supply might be ascetically reducing demand (possibly via social control of advertising, on which Hirsch blames – not without internal inconsistencies – at least part of our contemporary commodity fetishism). Slower growth is an established policy-option in the economics of depletable (natural) resources but it is not an option which Hirsch is able to incorporate in view of his acceptance that even Crosland's 'working-class constituents' should not be *denied* their holidays in Majorca, let alone their Vespas, merely because of the fact that growth makes ever more acute the problem of positionality. Indeed, Hirsch, writing not in the environment of 'You've never had it so good' which was that of Crosland and Galbraith in the 1950s and 1960s but against the more sombre backdrop of high unemployment, deindustrialisation, and the revolution of falling expectations which was the experience of the mid-1970s, might usefully have said a good deal more about the extent to which slow growth is itself an independent *cause* of waste – as where, say, the girl graduate compromises on a secretarial post because slow or zero growth means *ceteris paribus* that the supply of attractive jobs is not as great as she had anticipated. The Hirschian world is perhaps best understood when seen as a world made up of precisely such compromises, as a transitional world in which utilities previously assumed to be material (paid employment, let us say) now rapidly become positional in the wake of some unexpected economic shock (the fourfold rise in the price of OPEC oil in 1973, for example), a sad world in which people have not yet learned to live with slower growth or faced up to the fact that their prospects are somewhat less enticing than previous experience had led them to expect. Slow growth causes waste, both in the case of the girl graduate who takes a job which underutilises her skills and in the case of the school-leaver who is unable to find a job at all; and the stagnation is exacerbated where the macroeconomic fall in total demand occurs at the same time as a microeconomic upheaval in the techniques of production. Even where automation accompanied by technological change ultimately creates as many jobs as it destroys, there is no doubt that old human capital must be scrapped and new human capital installed. That being the case, it is bitterly ironical that Hirsch, rather than focusing on the potential of training and re-training schemes for reducing wastage of human capital and stimulating the rate of economic growth, should have had far more to say about the paperchase and the screenings – about education as waste, in other words –than he did about the personal liberation and the proper start. Few readers will be entirely in sympathy with Hirsch's reluctance to draw a clear qualitative distinction between that waste which he associates with the process of competitive educational upgrading and that waste which he identifies with the cost of reaching increasingly distant country cottages. Both the extra year at university and the extra hour on the motorway are, by Hirsch, impounded in the 'deadweight element'[15] of defensive consumption, and yet few readers will be entirely willing to accept that the two phenomena are not significantly different. No one regards the extra hour on the motorway as anything other than a means to an end which cannot come too soon – but many students regard the extra year at university at least in part as a valued consumer good and a liberating experience in its own right. No one, moreover, would say that the extra hour on the motorway was likely to make his nation better-off at some time in the future – but many educators and economists would say that the extra year at university contained a significantly greater productivity-boosing component than would, to take an instance at random, the well-known practice of all standing at once on tiptoe. A growth-conscious government anxious to reduce waste would do well to tax rather than to subsidise the quaint but uneconomic custom of tiptoe-standing. A growth-conscious government anxious to reduce waste would be foolish indeed if it applied the same measures in the case of education.

Regarding *frustration*, Hirsch presents us with an image of a human nature so flawed that even a white rabbit, were he to retrain as an economist, would have no option but to declare that mankind only gets what mankind deserves. It is one thing to complain of physical crowding, the rabbit will point out, and quite another to bemoan the fact that one has been overtaken in the status-stakes by a better or a luckier contestant. An extra hour on the motorway, an extra year at university – persons who suffer these unwelcome disamenities, these frustrating diswelfares, are the innocent victims of the tyranny of small decisions and the legitimate object of social endeavours orientated towards releasing them from their unexpected prison. The expensive Angora cat bought to impress, however, the hideous diamond necklace designed to out-dazzle the Joneses', the inconvenient rural retreat acquired exclusively as a means of putting pecuniary prowess on public display – persons who enter into zero-sum games of which these counters are the chips, the rabbit will say, are in a somewhat different position where frustration is concerned; for persons who are attracted into struggles for dominance by jealous emulation and aggressive competitiveness ought to have the foresight to realise that they might lose as well as win, whatever the rules of the game and however small (or large) the prize. Put in other terms, the white rabbit will conclude, where positional goods are sought as status symbols rather than exclusively because of their own intrinsic properties and characteristics, the prison in which mankind is trapped is one which is endemic to the human condition. Fred Hirsch himself says as much, speaking of top jobs – a commodity which is in demand precisely because its consumption is conspicuous rather than promiscuous.[16] Jack will want to defeat Jill, Jill will want to defeat Jack, and for that reason the frustration of the victim – the counterpart to the distinction of the victor – is a function not of sustained economic growth so much as of flawed human nature. As John Gray correctly points out, there are therefore 'certain truisms about positional goods. It is clear that any imaginable human society will contain some positional goods.

Wherever a conception of physical beauty is found, the genetic lottery will advantage some people over others in respect of the necessarily scarce attributes graded by the notion of beauty. . . . . Any society stratified by reference to differences in prestige – that is, all known human societies – will contain competition for the roles or statuses conferring prestige.'[17] Even in a classless society with identical incomes and no physically-positional goods, it would appear, a sense of frustration is likely nonetheless to obtain – since, if it is personal standing which is the objective, what all persons want only some by definition can in the event have. It may be, in the circumstances, that flawed human nature is itself an insuperable barrier to the passage of mankind from the judgemental and evaluative standards of what Erich Fromm would term the patriarchal society to the all-embracing, all-accepting, non-distinguishing, non-ranking values of the matriarchy which he saw as the cultural mode of the future – to the development of an integrated society founded upon the perceived equality of a common citizenship and shared way of life that was the Jerusalem of T.H. Marshall, Richard Titmuss, and, most of all, R.H. Tawney. Tawney's confidence in collective purposiveness stemmed in no small measure from what he regarded as the socialistic values of High Church Christianity: 'The necessary corollary . . . of the Christian conception of man is a strong sense of equality',[18] he argued, and maintained that, precisely because each of us was created in God's image, therefore none of us has the right, with respect to any brother-toiler in the Father's vineyard, to 'look a gift cherub in the mouth'.[19] Alfred Marshall predicted that economic growth, because of occupational upgrading and improvements in conduct and character, would itself play a significant part in bringing about the equal respect for equal humanity which he, like Tawney, so much wanted to see, but which he related to evolutionary progress rather than to revealed religion: 'The question is not whether all men will ultimately be equal – that they certainly will not – but whether progress may not go on steadily if slowly, till the official distinction between working man and gentleman has passed away; till, by occupation at least, every man is a gentleman. I hold that it may, and that it will.'[20] Fred Hirsch was less sanguine about economic growth than was Marshall, significantly closer to the misanthropic Hobbesianism of Buchanan magnified by a sociology in which widening reference-groups meant multiplied opportunities for bulls to lock horns in the primordial, instinctual struggle for supremacy which brands the losers with the stigma of failure. The widespread sense of frustration, one would therefore anticipate, is likely to remain behind long after the last Japanese tourist of the summer has taken flight, and the only recommendation to be made must accordingly be a moral one – to accept that each man, regardless of his temporal estate, still merits sincere esteem by virtue of his fundamental humanity and because of the function which he performs (whatever it is) within the framework of the social organism. Those who have lost out in the conflict to acquire the nebulous but desirable benefits attached to positional goods sought primarily because of their status-giving properties will no doubt welcome this call for tolerance with considerable enthusiasm. Those who have won the contest and are subsequently invited *ex post facto* to share the subjective attributes of their prize with the losers, the also-rans and the found-wantings will presumably be less enthusiastic.

6.4.2 Policy inferences

The point of departure is self-interest and calculative rationality. Hirsch is convinced that the economically advanced societies of the present day are characterised by a 'ferment of continual rejection and violence'[21] so intense that no rational member of the privileged middle classes can now afford to turn a blind eye to the anger and resentment of those left behind as the rest of us rise: 'There is at least the possibility that society will be faced with the unpleasant choice between constant insecurity for all and a crackdown involving repression of individual liberties of all. To avoid a choice of this kind, some of the favored groups would prefer to give up their isolation and perhaps also some of their advantages.'[22] The appeal is to the well-educated and the well-informed, to men and women who studied books such as Hirsch's while at university, who are in the habit of discussing political questions on social occasions, who have the background knowledge mentally to associate newsreel footage of urban riots with stories of tumbrils and guillotines. The appeal is not to their compassion – to what Titmuss calls the 'biological need to help'[23] and T.H. Marshall describes as the 'urge to sociability within the group'[24] – but to their greed in the face of threatened outcomes which even Galbraith (whose great work on *The Affluent Society* stressed the beneficent functionality of economic growth as a solvent of social tensions) has increasingly come to describe as 'angry',[25] 'drastic and disagreeable':[26] "Perhaps the disadvantaged are now too few to make a revolution,' Galbraith warned the Californians in 1980 (two years after the budget-limiting

Proposition 13), 'but they could make life uncomfortable for all.'[27] The appeal is at the level of interest and the incentive to act nothing significantly more self-denying than the purchase of insurance: it may well be that 'it is the haves who expect too much',[28] but the reason for them voluntarily to revise their expectations downwards is simply that it is they (and not the have-nots) who would stand most heavily to lose 'if society broke down'.[29] The rational consumer buys a burglar-alarm in order to protect his stylish sports-car. The rational citizen votes for comprehensive schooling in order to protect his country cottage. Each spends a little to protect a lot and makes in that way an intelligent investment in the future of the mixed economy which is in the one case remarkably similar in intent and function to the other.

Given the apparent 'rejection' and even the 'violence' of the have-nots, however, the risk-averting reader is bound to wonder whether the Hirschian guns are really pointed in the right direction and whether the specific policy-inferences Hirsch draws are in effect relevant to the needs of a society which he seems to regard as moving ever nearer to anarchy than to the middle ground. It is not, one suspects, the two-income couple in their twenties who, appalled at the price of country-cottages within striking distance of the City, demonstrate their felt exclusion by means of casual mugging. Nor is it likely to be the middle manager passed over for a top job carrying a multiple-digit salary (and therewith the status symbols which large sums of money can buy) who stones police-vehicles and sets fire to shops. If the seeds of the 'violence' which is but the tip of the iceberg of 'rejection' are to be found, it is indeed rather misguided to look for them at all in the middle-class world of positional goods rather than plunging boldly into the darkest England of absolute deprivation – of the unemployed and the low-paid, the badly-housed and the physically handicapped, the ghetto black and the forgotten pensioner. While the unmarried mother is spectacularly under-represented in the statistics on armed robbery, the same cannot be said of the dead-ender from a rat-infested slum dwelling whose principal hope *ceteris paribus* of entering the acquisitive society is by means of a part-time job in a hamburger restaurant. If, therefore, the objective is genuinely to combat the 'violence' and even the 'rejection' of the have-nots, what would seem to be called for is a wide range of proposals aimed at granting the poorer members of the community heightened access not so much to the positional as to the material sectors of the economy – proposals such as improved State housing schemes, higher pensions and other cash benefits, more and better social workers, selective discrimination in favour of the worst-off, none of which Hirsch chooses to make. It may be that Hirsch was persuaded by the arguments of the ideologists of growthmanship which Titmuss (who, however, was never himself naive enough about the multiple causes of poverty to join their fraternity) encapsulates as follows: 'All will share, rich and poor, in the benefits of growth. By a natural process of market levitation all classes and groups will stand expectantly on the political right as the escalator of growth moves them up. Automation thus substitutes for the social protest.'[30] It may be, alternatively, that Hirsch fell victim to that mode of discourse which may be termed Manchester-Didsburyism and defined as the academic's perhaps rather endearing propensity to deny that there exist people in this world other than the educated middle classes who know a good Camembert when they see one. Whether his intellectual home was in the future (once the absolutely deprived have fattened up as individuals and withered away as a group) or in Manchester-Didsbury (where absolutely everyone is middle-class nowadays), what is clear is that Hirsch's policy inferences hardly deal as directly with the social blight of 'rejection and violence' as one would have expected from an author who writes in so many places, as does Buchanan, very much like a man surrounded by assassins.

Hirsch's policy inferences are surprising. They are also surprisingly limited. They may usefully be considered under two headings. The first is *Planning and sharing*. The second is *The labour market*.

(a) Planning and sharing

Hirsch regarded the 'subjugation of individual judgement on moral issues and behavioral choices to the thought of some Chairman Mao' with all the caution and reservation one would have expected from a social thinker deeply imbued with 'primary liberal values'.[31] An enthusiastic advocate neither of moral leadership exercised by a hectoring elite nor of centralised coordination by means of powerful computers and omniscient bureaucrats, Hirsch turned to the bitter medicine of direction only where and when he felt that the individualistic alternative was so disagreeable as to be totally unacceptable.

One such case is road-congestion, where Hirsch indicates that public transport should be provided publicly where it cannot be provided otherwise. What is not entirely clear is why the private sector has defaulted with respect to the supply of a commodity that is potentially so lucrative. The simple answer is that so many people can nowadays afford the amenity-value and the status-symbol of the private car that the bus and the Underground are then relegated by the course of economic evolution to the category of the second-rate service for the third-class citizen; and that is also the (demand-side) explanation which follows from the very logic of the argument concerning the positional good in the growing economy. A somewhat different answer, however, would make reference to entry-barriers, restrictions and regulations; and would point to the (supply-side) dilemma that much potential competition amongst differentiated alternatives priced according to the subjective value which consumers themselves choose to assign to different combinations of privacy and economies of scale is nowadays repressed by nothing other than public sector directive. Were this latter answer to have significant relevance, then it would perhaps be the case that it is as much from the repeal of obsolete laws as from any expansion in State activity that relief of pressure on the roads is to be expected. Just as some old laws might usefully be repealed, moreover, so some new laws might usefully be introduced – laws specifying that no car or taxi may enter the central business district in the rush hour which does not carry its full complement of four passengers, for example, or which ration access to roads, areas and parking-spaces on the basis of price. Proposals for collective action along these lines do, admittedly, depart from the strict letter of the Hirschian canon. Not, however, from the moderate and questioning pragmatism which constitutes the essence of its spirit.

A second case of State intervention has to do with the planned development of the rural environment; and here Hirsch recommends zoning-schemes in order to prevent the over-building of country-cottages in beauty-spots. The problem is a real one for the rich man forced to spend his weekends next door to another rich man where previously next door there was nothing but the occasional moose. In such a situation the Coasean will gently point out to the first rich man that he does not have a properly-specified property-right in the plot next door until such a time as he has acquired it; and that, desiring constant amenity-value as he does, his proper course of action must now be to secure a rearrangement of legal entitlements by means of recourse to market compensation. Of course the first rich man experiences subjective diswelfare imposed by the presence of the second, the Coasean will admit; but so too does the second experience psychic nuisance and felt harm at being made to understand that his hunting and fishing are ranked by the first below the perceived value of the representative moose. The position, the Coasean will say, is in every way analogous to that faced by the farmer ('It is true that there would be no crop damage without the cattle') and the cowman ('It is equally true that there would be no crop damage without the crops')[32] whom 'a smoothly operating pricing system' would convert via contracts and commerce into the best of friends: 'The cattle-raiser would be better off if the farmer would agree not to cultivate his land for any payment less than $3. The farmer would be agreeable to not cultivating the land for any payment greater than $2. There is clearly room for a mutually satisfactory bargain which would lead to the abandonment of cultivation.'[33] The Coasean will in the circumstances encourage the first and the second rich man to explore the possibilities for a similar compromise – but the Hirschian, neglecting altogether the option of improving allocation of resources through the voluntary exchange of rights for money, recommends instead that there be recourse to zoning-schemes. The second rich man, one is compelled to say, is somewhat less likely to be a Hirschian that is the first. Zoning schemes would, after all, not only exclude the *nouveaux arrivés* from the enjoyment of a commodity which they are by definition keen to acquire (despite the decrement in utility represented by the presence of bad neighbours and the loss of the moose) but also generate regressive windfall gains to the old rich already in possession of the scarce good (now artificially to be kept scarce by edict). Hirsch is aware of these gains. Yet he makes no proposals either for the expropriation of existing owners (so that, in a sense, they are to be allowed to pull up the drawbridge to amenity behind themselves, much as the residents of the Channel Islands can do at the present time) or for the inter-generational transmission of their head-start to be rendered more difficult (by a more intensive use being made, for example, of fiscal weapons such as death-duties, capital gains taxes and wealth taxes). Almost certainly aware of these difficulties, Hirsch does propose at one point that future access might be governed not by the price mechanism but by 'public allocation on a nonmarket basis'.[34] Almost certainly aware as well of the near-impossibility of securing any form of consensus for the idea of allocating country cottages as if they were council flats, or for the criteria which might in the present moral climate be applied, Hirsch then abandons his mysterious proposal for a collective view without further explanation. All of which is well and good but is unlikely to assuage the feelings of 'rejection' experienced by the second rich man or to prevent the 'violence' manifested by the third man who is not rich at all. These persons are likely to complain that Hirsch's policy-inferences in the case of zoning-schemes are nothing other than a defence of privilege and a means of ensuring that positional goods remain strictly positional for the foreseeable future.

A third case in which Hirsch turned away from the individualistic alternative and prescribed the bitter medicine of direction relates to public goods provided in the public sector – to the National Health Service, the State schools, the parks, the museums. Some if not all of these goods already being, in the modern mixed economy, freely available in the private sector to paying customers, Hirsch could not and did not maintain that the alternative to collective provision was no provision at all. What he did argue was that private provision in the areas which he enumerated (together with similar areas to which the eternal pragmatist would have hastened to apply the argument by analogy) was almost certainly condemned to be inferior provision. Economically inferior – as is shown by the inadequate supply and the contaminated nature of blood for transfusion which Hirsch believed to be endemic to a profit-motivated system of commercial blood-banking. Socially inferior most of all – as is illustrated by the small step away from true publicness that was taken by the British Government when in 1973 it introduced an entry-fee for access to museums: 'This charge removed not only 10 pence from the pocket but also the pleasure derived by some visitors from the existence of a part of the cultural heritage as common property available freely to all.'[35] The change in the mode of delivery, in other words, may – precisely because individual action is social action and individuals' preference-patterns interdependent – be said to possess the capacity significantly to alter the characteristics of (and thus the utility yielded by) a good or service: 'The crucial limitation in the conventional analysis is that it does not allow for a change in the nature of the product according to the method of provision.'[36] Before the charge was introduced, Henry Dubb and the Lady of the Manor experienced a strengthening of their citizenship-based solidarity and cohesion as a perceived consequence of their shared appreciation of a common culture. After the charge was introduced, they did not and the museum thereby came to offer a debased product as compared with the previous one: the culture remained but the common was gone, and no raising of revenue or reducing of congestion can justify such a loss. Tickets and fees in such a case are 'detrimental to the poor, by removing what to them (though not of course to society) was a free good';[37] and Henry Dubb is likely to experience 'rejection' at this *de facto* frustration of his freedom of choice to enjoy the sight (if not the possession) of our limited national stock of positional goods such as Rembrandt originals which by virtue of the charges become ever more the preserve of the privileged. Fortunately, the Lady of the Manor, in an integrated and consensual society such as was Britain in the 1950s and 1960s (Hirsch's own formative years), is likely to come to his aid and to manifest 'violence' at the polling-station against the candidate who committed this act of injustice against the poor and the powerless. Indeed, Hirsch would argue, the very integration and consensus which provoked this defence of public goods provided in the public sector is a direct product in no small measure of the feelings of fellowship which those institutions themselves help to promote. The model is the National Blood Transfusion Service, which mobilises free gifts for unknown strangers and in that way both emanates from and fosters the common bonds of belonging – a school for altruists, in effect, and thus a fine school which, in Titmuss's view, must not be allowed to be crowded out by the expensive and nasty substitute: 'The commercialization of blood', Titmuss wrote, 'is discouraging and downgrading the voluntary principle. Both the sense of community and the expression of altruism are being silenced.'[38] The commercialisation of blood, Titmuss warned, is not a thing apart but rather, and insidiously, the thin end of the wedge: 'It is likely that a decline in the spirit of altruism in one sphere of human activities will be accompanied by similar changes in attitudes, motives and relationships in other spheres.'[39] A wedge of self-interest and calculative rationality, he had stated in his early Fabian pamphlet of 1959 on *The Irresponsible Society*, which is a veritable stake pointed directly at the heart of the body politick: 'More prosperity and more violence may be one of the contradictions in a system of unfettered private enterprise and financial power oblivious to moral values and social objectives.'[40] Neither Titmuss nor Hirsch, it must be stressed, was resistant on principle to the market capitalist system, and both quite rightly welcomed the important contribution which it had made and was making to the economic growth which *inter alia* augmented State revenues without the need to put up tax rates. Simply, each made a clear distinction in his own mind between that which properly belonged in the realm of Mammon and that which properly belonged in the realm of community; and each therefore staunchly opposed the transfer (partial or complete) into the private sector of those goods and services of which the true home is in the public.

Hirsch opposed the commercialisation of the State-owned museum;

and there his model was Titmuss on the gift of blood. He also opposed the commercialisation of the private-sector public good of sociability; and in this second instance of formalisation – that of individualisation, as opposed to that of privatisation – his references to the country-club and the dartboard show him to have been influenced by Scitovsky on 'the lively, social atmosphere of pubs'.[41] There are, Scitovsky had written in 1976 (with, it must be added, that considerable degree of naivety which is the rootless intellectual's normal travelling-companion in his ongoing search for a home), 'innumerable pubs thickly strewn all over London and dotting the English countryside. Every noon and evening you will find all of them full of people and animated talk. Socializing rather than drinking is clearly most people's main occupation there, although a half-pint of beer is to talk as a bed is to making love – one can do without but does better with.'[42] People go to pubs in England, Scitovsky had revealed, most of all because of psychological imperatives such as cause them to seek there the twin stimuli of novelty and togetherness which are also enjoyed in places of communal conviviality by their cousins across the Channel ('The French do much of their talking in cafés')[43] but which are sadly inaccessible to their brothers across the sea: even the physical layout of the American bar, Scitovsky had indicated, is anti-social, 'conducive to the ordering and silent consumption of one's drink, not to conversation',[44] for the fact is that the American bar is designed in such a way that the customers face the barman and do not have to face one another. Hirsch was obviously impressed by this symbolic denial of human gregariousness[45] but evidently saw in it not so much the indelible shadow of the Puritan hostility to idle chat (that having been Scitovsky's own explanation) as the invisible hand of acquisitive free enterprise, which had taught the practical and rights-minded Americans to purchase no more of personal relationships than they rationally required and to target their interactions at self-selected groups with specific interests in common. Scitovsky's pub was to Hirsch the private-sector equivalent of Titmuss's bloodmobile, the co-bibulous community the comprehensive school of the responsible adult. The country-club, on the other hand, was to Hirsch the private-sector equivalent of the national museum with the user-charge, the collective facility that encouraged the Lady of the Manor to come in while making absolutely clear to Henry Dubb that he did not warrant inclusion.

Hirsch opposed the commercialisation of the State-owned museum and drew specific policy inferences such as indicate that, with respect to that public-sector public good and to others like it, the bitter medicine of direction is unambiguously to be ranked above the individualistic alternative. He also opposed the commercialisation of the private-sector public good of which spontaneous sociability may be taken as a case in point; but here, the enemy in this case being not privatisation but individualisation, Hirsch carefully resisted the temptation to mobilise the powerful instrumentality of State direction in an attempt to build political dams against encroaching formalisation. Brothels could be closed in order to discourage the substitution of sex exchanged for money for love exchanged for love. Country-clubs could be required to generate a membership-list statistically representative of the surrounding community. Bad Samaritans who refused to assist confused old ladies to cross the road could be fined for polluting and littering, broadly defined. Much could clearly be done to defend even private-sector publicness by means of State direction. Hirsch, however, first and foremost a moderate social thinker strongly committed to 'primary liberal values', preferred to leave the war against individualisation to be waged by the socially responsible moral attitudes of an integrated community.

The very same moral attitudes, one is bound to reflect, which underlie his explicit recommendations for State intervention as well. For public goods provided in the public sector – since without an other-orientated ethos the member of the country-club who lives in an elegant suburb is likely to resent and resist the collective provision of parks and schools in inner-city ghettoes populated by colourful characters with whom he himself would not want to drink even a half-pint of beer. For the planned development of the rural environment – since without a shared conviction that beautiful surroundings are a part of our nation's wealth and must be defended, the slum tenant inhabiting a sub-standard property rendered artificially expensive by the cessation of building for letting consequent upon state controls will resent and resist the capital gains made by the rich from the sale of their country-cottages once zoning schemes had artificially boosted the price of their positional good. For shared transport in preference to individual transport – since without a widespread desire collectively to alleviate the common blight of road congestion, the privileged classes are likely to resent and resist overcrowded buses that must be waited for, commuter-carriages where one's fellow-passengers smell of garlic and wet dog and talk far too loudly, and are likely to call instead for more and wider roads, for high tolls to ration access to fast lanes, for taxes on vehicle-usage so punitive as to restore numbers to the levels that obtained before the *hoi polloi* were permitted by economic growth to debase amenity-value via noisy Vespas. It should not in the circumstances come as any great surprise that Hirsch was prepared to leave the war against individualisation to be waged by the socially-responsible moral attitudes of an integrated community: it is precisely those moral attitudes, after all, which inform all the other policy inferences which he, with respect to Planning and Sharing, in the event chose to make.

(b) The labour market

Top jobs stand at the very centre of the discussion. They are positional goods in their own right, both in the strictly physical sense (the notion of superordination being inseparable from that of hierarchy) and in the sense of conferring social status (it being generally assumed that it is the cream, not the scum, that rises to the top). They are in addition the means to the end represented by yet other positional goods; for the simple truth is that they are frequently exceptionally well remunerated relative to the average within the society as a whole as well as within a single organisation. Positional goods in their own right, the gatekeeper via superior incomes to yet other positional goods, top jobs constitute, within the framework of the Hirsch model, a problem which simply must be solved if societies as they become richer are not also to become more divided, more polarised and more antagonistic.

The problem is one of popular legitimation and, specifically, of the need to find some 'conscious justification of the distribution of economic rewards'.[46] The man-made solution is the planning of wages and salaries (accompanied, perhaps, by directives influencing the absolute and relative levels of those other forms of income – rents, interest, dividends, profits – about which Hirsch has somewhat less to say than he does about earnings from labour). Incomes policies embodying information collected via large-scale attitudinal surveys and imposed via demand-led democratic politics are undeniably regarded in some quarters as the most socially-sensitive means for institutionalising, in the vital area of *who* gets *what*, the requisite perceptions of what most people most regard as just desserts and merited rewards. Not, however, in all quarters; and certainly not by classical liberals committed to the adoption of the individualistic, non-administered alternative wherever possible. Such liberals would point to the existence of a natural solution, alongside the man-made solution, to the problem of popular legitimation of economic rewards;

and would argue that, taking but restraint away, the invisible hand of the free market would then establish differentials based upon supply and demand such as would be far more likely than any other policy-instrument to provide the justification needed to defuse potentially explosive social tensions and resentments. Hirsch, elsewhere so much the social democrat, was here more nearly the monetarist; for it was the natural and not the man-made solution that in the event had the greater appeal for him.

Whether automaticity is indeed widely perceived to equal social justice is, of course, the key question to which no one can be sure of the answer. Supply and demand tells us nothing about need (a point which advocates of transfers to the poor in work via the negative income tax are quick to make). Nor do market valuations come pre-corrected for inherited status (and therewith the unearned advantages of informal education, familial expectations and gifted ownership of non-human resources). Then there is the eternal conundrum of the rent of ability (a cause of considerable cleavage between the intelligent and the talented on the one hand, the diligent but the plodding on the other). The unique requirements of the unskilled labourer with the disabled wife, the intergenerational transmission of class and privilege, the genetic endowment which permits the idle layabout to command higher earnings than the exhaustively-trained surgeon provided only that the former was born with an outstanding bass voice – these variables muddy the clear waters of supply and demand and suggest that, to some members of the community at least, justice is simply not seen to be done where differentials are determined by that which the traffic will bear and by no other standard of right and wrong.

Hirsch would no doubt be surprised to find any widespread rejection of the market mode of legitimation. The market embodies, after all, a set of Buchanan-like constitutional rules and there is intuitive logic in associating fairness with a veil of unknowledge so impenetrable that no participant can predict in advance of play if he himself will be awarded the disabled wife or the outstanding bass voice. The market represents, moreover, a network of coordinated contracts and structured flexibilities such as improve allocative efficiency and stimulate individual effort – and thereby boost the rate of economic growth. Negatively speaking, finally, the natural solution obviates the need to rely upon the man-made alternative – and since, as Hirsch puts it, 'the controllers usually have a large handicap of relevant information',[47] perhaps this too is good grounds for expecting that market will generate popular legitimation of income-differentials where plan will not. Expecting is not the same as finding, however; and the simple fact is that no one knows with any degree of certainty what, precisely, it is that breeds the 'conscious justification of the distribution of economic rewards' that represses bitterness and fosters attachment.

Assuming that automaticity and legitimation are widely accepted, however, as being organically linked, then Hirsch's suggestion that differentials should be set by the unimpeded forces of supply and demand is likely to prove an eminently attractive one. Most persons have, after all, at some stage in their lives reflected that top jobs seem to carry with them top status, top power, top fringe-benefits and top satisfaction *as well as* top pay; and have even gone so far as to wonder if many recipients of so generous a package might not in practice actually be *over*-compensated relative to the minimum reward which would just retain them in the post. Few persons can, of course, do much more than reflect and wonder: given the present-day paucity of hard facts concerning marginal rewards and executives' surplus, no one is capable actually of proving that senior staff are currently overpaid (as Hirsch would assert) rather than underpaid (as the incumbents themselves have been known to hint). A major complication in this context is the important fact that no two persons are identical; that each of us has an absolute monopoly in a unique bundle of characteristics; that you and I are not as perfectly interchangeable, as effortlessly substitutable, as would be, let us say, two Treasury Bills of the same denomination and maturity-date. Yet no serious advocate of of the Dutch auction method of reducing payment for the performance of a top job up to the point at which the marginal supplier is just willing at that rate to supply his labour, would deny that the technique is an acceptable one in economic terms only where lumps of labour are homogeneous. Insofar as they are not, however, the danger exists that as incentives are pared away the best brains and skills might drop out of the relevant market altogether, opting perhaps for less arduous employment, or to start their own business, or to go abroad. There is no *a priori* reason to assume that the man or woman just willing to accept a top job at a low rate of pay is also the person most likely to perform it with maximal efficiency (although, naturally, there is also no *a priori* reason to assume the opposite); and to the extent that human potential is widely differentiated rather than highly standar-dised the choice the community might have to make could well lie not between Tweedledum and Tweedledee but between the well-paid accountant on the one hand, the second-rate accountant on the other.

Hirsch, presumably, would want to deny the real-world relevance of this choice, insisting instead that it is leadership positions alone, and not born leaders, that are in limited supply. To the extent that the choice is a real one, however, it then has five important implications for economic policy. *First*, if differential pay is an incentive essential to secure the services of scarce meritocrats, then an economically rational community will remain obliged to pay an economic reward even to the owner of inherited intelligence such as to put him well ahead in the race to acquire country-cottages – a clear case where considerations of equity (in the sense of justice-as-fairness as if behind a thick Rawlsian veil) and of efficiency (in the sense of high output of desired commodities per unit of productive input) both point in the direction of continuing inequalities of income and consumption. *Second*, the relationship between efficiency and equality is likely to remain what Arthur Okun has called 'our biggest socioeconomic tradeoff'[48] and thus an ongoing cause of concern to the believer both in market capitalism (a system of rewards and penalties awarding unequal prizes that 'allow the big winners to feed their pets better than the losers can feed their children')[49] and in the viability of democratic institutions (a set of structures and conventions inextricably linked with notions of equal political rights and equal moral worth) who is also all-too-aware that any attempt to transcend the double standard would imperil economic growth: 'Any insistence on carving the pie into equal slices would shrink the size of the pie'.[50] *Third*, there is no reason to suppose that a substitution of the *tâtonnement* and the auctioneer for the administered rigidities of collective bargaining would in any real sense generate lessened disparities in levels of remuneration: the invisible hand might simply reshuffle existing inequalities, unchanged save in that the prime trophies are taken from doctors and transferred to dustmen (or, of course, vice versa: in view of the not-inconceivable surplus of workers prepared to supply their labour for low pay and the present-day shortage of key professionals, redistribution via the market mechanism might actually work to the net disadvantage of the poor in a manner hardly likely to win Hirsch the complete confidence of the relatively deprived). *Fourth*, the possibility that the market might redistribute without levelling is bound to be a source of reassurance to the Hirschian anxious about the implications for the positional sector of a greater equality in purchasing power: as it stands, the proposal for more perfect competition might conceptually shift high incomes from the managing directors to their exhausted subordinates performing dirty jobs but need not, once we acknowledge that human potential is widely differentiated rather than highly standardised, exacerbate (or, indeed, resolve) the problems associated with the caucus-race for a limited supply of country-cottages. *Fifth*, if all children expect to grow up equal in all respects, then some are doomed to have their expectations frustrated and their hopes dashed precisely because their ambitions are unrealistic in the light of their specific endowments – and this even in a free labour market presided over by nothing less than the unimpeded forces of supply and demand.

Automaticity need not be linked with perceived legitimacy. Automaticity need not be productive of greater equality. Automaticity need not, finally, be all that easy to establish. The administered labour market of present times is undeniably a highly imperfect one, and there cannot be many members of the community who would find much 'conscious justification' for pay-structures in modes of bargaining such as reward the powerful union and the disruptive strike to the detriment of the weak, the moderate and the unrepresented. Union leaders are, however, hardly likely to welcome with any real enthusiasm social reforms which challenge the privileges of their members through the continuous realignment of differentials and which also, by implication, challenge the power of giant organisations to defend those privileges in the face of some more broadly-based conception of the social interest. Their reluctance to cooperate is entirely comprehensible within the parameters of the Hirschian model, given that positional goods and distributional struggles are bound to go together in an overloaded economic system characterised by frenzied competition for increasing shares in fixed availabilities and by the awareness of an ever-widening 'gap between aspirations and the means of fulfilling them'.[51] Besides that, many union leaders, greedy enough to call for the walk-out of ambulance men or power-workers at the height of a snowstorm and conceited enough to believe that Peter Wiles was right when he stated that, because of cost-push, the price-level today is theoretically indeterminate ('It depends', Wiles said so memorably, 'on what numbers the trade union leaders pick out of the air when they make wage-claims')[52], will find silly, soppy and sentimental Hirsch's plea to them to extract less than the maximum possible benefits for their members (on the grounds that the full use of their potential powers would be 'inimical to the general welfare)':[53] no one, they will say, would demand of the peasant farmer or the manufacturer of soap that he should altruistically charge less than the traffic will bear, and it is in any case not their job to correct for 'the erosion of the social underlay of a stable capitalist order (and more generally of any market or contractual society) set in train by the value system of the market society'.[54]

Their case is not an easy one to answer. With respect to positional goods, there is always the defence of calm and rational contracting (as opposed to the accelerating free-for-all and the aggressiveness of competitive leap-frogging) that there is no reason to fear that the shop will be empty by the time the tail of to-day's queue becomes tomorrow's head: top jobs and status symbols undoubtedly constitute a cause for concern but goods positional in some more concrete and objective sense we have already dismissed, in opposition to Hirsch's contention, as more of a footnote *curiosum* (like the Giffen Good) than a major social problem (like unbridled avarice in an antinomian culture). One is tempted to add that the failures of capitalism in the positional sector are far less important than its successes in the material sphere of mass production; to observe that unions are likely therefore to be more reluctant to show voluntary restraint or accept less than they could wrest when their members are experiencing stagnating standards of living combined with diminished promotion prospects than when the economy is buoyant and growing rapidly; and to stress that, at least in connection with labour-market militancy, alongside social limits to economic growth there also exist economic limits to social growth.

With respect to the moral dimension of the debate, however, the assertion of union leaders that they are self-interested individualists, not other-regarding communitarians, and see no good reason to sacrifice the potential welfare of their members in order to benefit unknown strangers, points to a case which is less easily answered. Hirsch, speaking of the need for responsible attitudes in such conflictual situations, says: 'Containment of the latent distributional struggle without financial instability requires either sufficient authority, or sufficient consensus, on the values or principles underlying the distribution of income and other aspects of welfare.'[55] Authority being undeniably undemocratic, coercion a threat to liberty (as well as inviting evasion – the normal experience with incomes policies), Hirsch clearly had a bias for consensus, for background moral values involving self-restraint – and for the identification of 'conscious justification' for *who* gets *what* with the unfettered forces of supply and demand. Union leaders, for their part, are likely to reply that self-restraint and supply and demand are as ill-matched a couple as Iago and Juliet; that in the market muscles speak louder than morals;

and that if a free labour market means an end to their pooled power then they will strongly resist any move to introduce a regime of automaticity where there now reigns administration. Hirschian man withdraws frustrated and saddened at this demonstration that market capitalism once again appears to breed its own transcendence – in this case an anomic collective consciousness born of liberal individualism, as to Smith the eventual evaporation of investment opportunities, to Ricardo the unstoppable diminution of returns in agriculture, to Marx the development of the revolutionary proletariat, to Schumpeter the bureaucratisation of the entrepreneurial spirit.

Hirschian man attributes the increasing selfishness of the union leaders to the evolutionary displacement of pre-capitalist by capitalist values. This essentially sociological diagnosis is profoundly depressing (in the sense that it is not easy to turn back the clock of historical determinism). It is made more depressing still by the insistence of thinkers such as Veblen that conspicuous power and dominance put on show are today themselves valued ends having much of the character of true positionality. Scitovsky in particular appears to adopt a psychology of behaviour able so easily to incorporate the aggressive risk-lovers of the original *bellum* as to suggest that peaceloving introverts do indeed have grounds for concern with respect to the blood lust of zero-sum confrontationalists. Novelty and challenge are preferred to boredom, Scitovsky says; 'danger and the fear of danger are exciting; excitement within limits is pleasant'[56] – and economic growth does nothing to cordialise the incessant search for stimulus: 'The idle rich born into that state or reaching it young are prone to take up dangerous sports and become involved in reckless adventures. . . . Perhaps the increasing violence of our increasingly affluent society can be similarly explained.'[57] If an under-socialised union leader is not likely to heed Hirsch's plea for freedom of markets in preference to administered values reflecting power-positions, it is not easy to see why an aggressive union leader should do so: red in tooth and claw and green with envy, he will present himself as the captain of a team out to win and will make rude suggestions concerning the future develop-ment of the pre-capitalist values to which a reply is not easily found by Hirschian man without speaking in the very code which he seeks to eradicate.

The vested interest of powerful unions is an obstacle to the institutionalisation of automaticity in the labour-market. So too, needless to say, is the vested interest of the well-paid; but to them Hirsch is at least in a position to direct his appeal not to a benevolence which he evidently regards as a vestigial organ but to a concern with self which he clearly situates at the very centre of the capitalist value system. Specifically, he is able to encourage the rich to accept diminution of privilege and narrowing of differentials through the Dutch auction by reminding them none too delicately that they are 'much farther from the incomes they could rely on if society broke down than are the laborer and the craftsman'.[58] Such a statement being a truism, it is unlikely that the rich will be much impressed by it: society, they will say, is certainly changing and perhaps even decaying but hardly breaking down, and long before anarchy sets in citizens with a vested interest in the *status quo* will press not for Dutch auctions to redistribute their rewards so much as for the Leviathan of law and order to defend what they have against the envious many whose initiative and effort are economic goods notable for their scarcity. Hirsch's optimism was possibly premature, but there is no mistaking the nature of his prediction – that the well-paid will voluntarily accept the *de facto* discrimination associated with competitive labour markets, and will do so for fear of finding something worse.

Where competitive labour markets genuinely cannot be established (and market imperfections such as large corporations and civil service monopsonies do present obstacles on the side of demand for the factor such as reinforce those on the side of supply with which Hirsch is principally concerned), there the well-paid, Hirsch anticipates, will accept the second-best solution of planned redistribution of earned income *ex post facto* through progressive income taxation: technocrats and administrators cannot, of course, be certain of the precise equilibrium levels that would have been set by some non-existent allocative process, but a step in the right direction (a measure of levelling *as if* by a free market) would, once its 'rightness' had been confirmed by the hoped-for lack of response in quantity of labour supplied, nonetheless provide some if not all of the 'conscious justification' which is a part if not the whole of the antidote to the 'rejection and violence' that Hirsch regards as a growing threat to the stability and tranquillity of the market system. Largely because of that threat, incidentally, Hirsch is able to predict that the rich will also voluntarily accept two further reforms which he proposes. The first is power-sharing – where each employee is given the opportunity to enjoy yet another characteristic of the top job, either as part of a collective (the departmental meeting) or sequentially (the rotating headship). The second is comprehensive schooling – where each child is given an equal opportunity to become unequal and no child is allowed to purchase enhanced life-chances by virtue of having selected wealthy parents.

And there are other reforms which Hirsch does not himself propose but which are fully in keeping with the objectives of his grand design. One is selective discrimination or compensatory variation in favour of the less advantaged – a principle of redress which Rawls expresses as follows: 'To provide genuine equality of opportunity, society must give more attention to those with fewer native assets and to those born into the less favorable social positions.'[59] Another is the quota – since equality of educational opportunity is not (for the black, say, or the female or the handicapped) the same as equality of access to the top job, let alone equality of access to the first job or, indeed, to any job at all. Then there is non-credential appointment – since selection for employment exclusively on the basis of track-records and aptitude tests in total ignorance of paper qualifications in effect breaks the link between two positional goods and thereby reduces the wastefulness of unnecessary screening through formal education. Finally, there is decentralisation and devolution – since, quite simply, the multiplication of bodies means the multiplication of heads. These reforms which Hirsch does not himself propose serve the same function as those reforms with respect to the labour market which figure so prominently in his work. That function is the defence of social cohesion. Hirsch believes that cohesion to be under threat from the have-nots – but also believes that the haves will perceive the threat and hasten to plug the leak lest the dam subsequently burst. Thence the curious asymmetry in his model that the unions are asked to give up some of their privileges because of the pre-capitalist premium on altruism while the well-paid are expected to do likewise because of the rational capitalist's propensity to invest and insure.

Whether automaticity in the labour market is or is not capable of providing the 'conscious justification' that is needed if the tide of 'rejection and violence' is to be stemmed, one thing is clear: intellectual constructs can only work their magic if translated into practical policies, and there is accordingly an important role to be played in the drama of social change by the sensitive politician with a commitment to reform. That is why it is in a sense surprising that Hirsch is evidently so hostile to the Schumpeter-Downs model of the political as an economic market, as a structure of exchanges in which suppliers passively provide that which demanders most want to consume and receive an acceptable *quid pro quo* as compensation for the disutility they experience. Such a self-interested and calculatively rational orientation is, after all, precisely what is called for if automaticity is to be actualised and social cohesion thereby strengthened: given adequate popular support for the restructuring of differentials, it is clearly the ambitious power-seeker who will move most rapidly to implement the requisite reforms, while in the absence of such popular support it is not unlikely that any attempt by the moral absolutist to bring present-day practices into line with pre-capitalist values will become an independent cue for 'rejection and violence' in its own right. There is therefore a very real sense in which the true Hirschian ought positively to welcome the amoral politician; and should concentrate his own efforts as a thinker and a writer not so much on castigating the selfish as on creating a groundswell of opinion with which the selfish will then inevitably have to identify themselves. Such would perhaps be the attitude of the true Hirschian but it is not the attitude of Hirsch, who, concerned with purity of motive as well as with optimality of outcome, tends to regard the merchanting of that which is in truth a civic duty as a depressing indicator of moral decay in its own right. Selfishness leads to greed, Hirsch reasoned, and even to bribery, corruption, nepotism and flagrant rule-breaking; and no one – not even Schumpeter and Downs – would actually want to live in a society in which the men of Watergate were the rule and not the exception.

On a more limited scale, Hirsch accepted, politicians have already become involved in what Samuel Brittan has termed the 'competitive wooing of the electorate'[60] and have all-too-frequently offered bribes in the form of policies (both interventions and abstentions) which most of us would regard as profoundly immoral if offered in the form of cash. Brittan says quite bluntly that the two 'endemic threats to liberal representative democracy' are, first, 'the generation of excessive expectations in the political market place' and, second, 'the disruptive effects of the pursuit of group self-interest'.[61] It was quite clearly the same socially-lethal cocktail of government failure and union irresponsibility which Hirsch had in mind when he denied that inflation is always and everywhere a monetary phenomenon: 'There is no such thing as a dominant technical monetary policy outside the socio-political context.'[62] Friedman and Buchanan would, as it happens, be entirely happy with the logic that underlies this statement and with the controversial interpretation of the historical record to which it points – that democratically-elected politicians have in the past often, perhaps normally, been prepared to buy votes through an inflationary expansion of the money-supply in support of projects which the nation cannot afford and in validation of wage-claims for which the principal justification has not uncommonly been concentrated power to disrupt. Convinced monetarists would then propose, however, that the socio-political context be cut loose altogether from the realm of technical monetary policy by means of the non-discretionary money-supply rule (the Ulysses strategy with respect to the sirens of *akrasia*); whereas Hirsch would continue to look for solutions in the general area not of legal precommitment of socio-political usages so much as of the remoralisation of these usages.

Thus Hirsch calls upon politicians to show a disinterested devotion to duty in preference to the pursuit of short-run popularity – even if such action then costs them their own jobs and power and leads to the election of an opposition party whose policies they regard as profoundly undesirable. Similarly, he calls upon unions to demonstrate moderation and practise restraint – even if the incidence of the burden represented by such voluntary limitation must be borne by subscription-paying members without any known attachment to the pre-capitalist value system. In the case of the well-paid at least, Hirsch's appeal would appear to be couched in the language of self-interest and calculative rationality, directed as it is not to the benevolence of the rich so much as to the precautionary sensibilities of the seasoned shareholder. Certainly the appeal is directed to the concern with self on the part of the privileged, but even here there is an element of other-regarding self-denial simply by virtue of the inter-temporality of family and class rewards. One rich man invests and insures today, future cohorts of rich men pocket the profits tomorrow, and the lesson is clear – that wherever we look in Hirsch's political economy, there we find morality.

6.4.3   The moral nexus

Fred Hirsch, surveying the social scene from anarchy to Leviathan, took the view that the internalisation of the shared moral convention remains, even in the age of the lawmaker and the maximising economist, a topic of paramount importance. He reached the followng conclusion on the position of self-policing normative constraint in the course of an exceptionally ambitious account of 'functionally necessary social cooperation' which begins with religion ('Christianity sets great store by altruistic behavior') and ends with rubbish ('Only *I* can see everywhere I litter'): 'While such cooperation can, in some cases, be replaced by coercive rules, or stimulated through collectively imposed inducements to individuals' private interests, this will rarely be as practicable and efficient as when it is internally motivated.'[63]

It would probably be fair to say that not every economist would share Hirsch's conclusion or, indeed, assign any significant place at all to the public good of moral attitudes within the context of the modern market economy. That some economists would do so is not, however, in dispute. Kenneth Arrow, for one, who states that 'the categorical imperative and the price system are essential complements',[64] or Albert Hirschman in his appeal for a 'rehabilitation of benevolence': 'It has become increasingly clear that, in a number of important areas, the economy is in fact liable to perform poorly without a minimum of "benevolence".'[65] Robin Matthews, similarly, reaches the conclusion that a market economy requires a mixed ethos and, specifically, a freedom to exchange that is not unlimited but is subject to 'conventional notions of commercial morality': 'The doctrine of the hidden hand is correct in its assertion that an economic system will not work efficiently if the prescribed code of conduct is complete altruism, or, for that matter, complete adherence to the Kantian categorical imperative. On the other hand, a competitive system will not work efficiently either, unless the pursuit of self-interest is constrained by a moral code.'[66] A mixed ethos is, of course, an untidy ethos, requiring a kind of deliberate schizophrenia on the part of actors trading in the economic market. Untidy it may well be, Matthews concedes, but also, and for that very reason, eminently suitable for the economic reality of an untidy world. On the one hand, Matthews argues, the total absence of self-interested utility-maximisation in the economic sphere can truly lead to 'absurd results', to situations such as the following in which complete altruism breeds nothing less than complete indeterminacy: 'I am selling you a house. Your utility ranks equally with mine, both in my eyes and in yours. So the price is a matter of indifference to both of us. £10 000 more to me, £10 000 more to you – there is nothing in it. As a result, no market signals emerge.'[67] On the other hand, he says, a significant number of market malfunctions can and do result from self-interested utility-maximisation (not least where abuse of superior knowledge is a threat, as in the doctor – patient relationship) and these can best be contained by 'a very limited, not to say commonplace, moral code, which can be summed up as honesty and trust':[68] 'Moral sanctions are capable of being more all-pervasive than legal ones. They can conduce to better observance of the law in cases where enforcement is difficult and they can extend to areas on which it is not practicable to legislate at all. Indeed, in the absence of *some* moral sanctions, it is doubtful whether a competitive system could work at all.'[69] Matthews's defence of the mixed ethos and of *some* moral sanctions is one with which Hirsch would have been pleased to associate himself. It also serves as a reminder that Hirsch, in emphasising the moral input in the market capitalist production function, was unquestionably in a minority, but hardly in a minority of one.

Hirsch, a *conservative* social democrat in this respect, drew attention to the functionality in contemporary conditions of shared moral conventions inherited from the past: 'Truth, trust, acceptance, restraint, obligation – these are among the social virtues grounded in religious belief which are . . . now seen to play a central role in the functioning of an individualistic, contractual economy.'[70] The reference is to religious belief, but it could just as easily be to the Kantian universal law as to the Christian Golden Rule so long as the normative standard in question is rooted in the fundamental truth that what one can do, all cannot: thus lying and stealing are bad and no one should lie or steal since, if one person were to lie or steal and if others were then to adopt the same practice, human relations based upon private property would ultimately be impossible, Ego would come to regard Alter as means rather than end, no one would be treated in the way that he would like to be treated and – to borrow a phrase from Hirsch on the tyranny of small decisions – the market product 'comes out flawed'.[71] As is so easily the case, given the contemporary ethos of self-interest and the entirely accurate perception of the individual free rider that rational action for all is the antithesis of rational action for each: 'Elemental personal values of honesty, truthfulness, trust, restraint and obligation are all necessary inputs to an efficient (as well as pleasant) contractual society, but all are without significant direct pay-off to the individuals providing them.'[72] What all can do, one cannot – and the result is a serious underinvestment in the supply of an essential public good.

The moral nexus is the centrepiece of Fred Hirsch's contribution to theories of collective action, the decay in the moral nexus the more worrying of the social limits to economic growth. The *real* social limit is the moral one, and there is much in Hirsch's assertion that an exchange society is in an unstable state so long as it is deficient in built-in restraint of a quasi-religious or an ethical nature. As Hirsch puts it, 'in the absence of a "private" sanction such as that furnished by religious belief, cooperation can be expected only on the basis of some directly "felt" sense of duty or obligation'.[73] Yet in a large-scale, mobile and anonymous national society one does not have at all times a vested interest in a good reputation or feel vulnerable to informal sanctions; one does have a vested interest in conformity to the dominant value system of commercialism by, wherever possible, rationally acting the free rider; and one is increasingly aware that a society unable without prohibitive expense to enforce its laws and statutes in so many areas of social life (shoplifting and fare-dodging, to name but two) is not likely to be conspicuously successful in reforming conventions and practices involving, let us say, greater courtesy shown to strangers and a diminution in spitting in public places. It is *anomie* rather than the rush hour that presents the greatest threat to late utilitarianism.

Hirsch's justification of cooperation in terms of *as if* is thus in a significant sense as depressing as the disease he identifies. It speaks the language of the enemy insofar as it focuses on right conduct rather than moral intent (I am asked not to litter lest I be littered upon, not because the voluntary imposition of such an externality is illegitimate in itself). It seeks to replace pre-commercial by mercantile ethics through its attempt to derive normative constraint from self-interest (I am asked to assist a stranger in distress as a form of social insurance against the risk that I should myself one day be in a similar situation). In addition, it is unenforceable: I am asked not to push my way to the head of a queue comprised entirely of old ladies I am never likely to see again but am also informed with the greatest of clarity that the rejection of expediency on my part bears no personal return whatsoever while any conspicuous selfishness will attract no punitive sanction. Above all, it is internally inconsistent: I am asked to donate my own *as if* here and now in implicit exchange for the collective *as ifs* of unknown others at unnamed times and unspecified places – which is to say that I am asked to show confidence in the rule-governed other-directedness of seers who correctly recognise a sucker but simply will not allow a nice guy to finish last – which is to say that the shared moral conventions are still in force. Not needed when it is viable, not viable when it is needed, the *as if* is not a genuine substitute for the authentic *ought-to-be*. Nor is the authentic *ought-to-be* anything less than indispensable if the evolutionary processes that throw up social limits to economic growth are significantly to be smoothed by means of a remoralisation of social usages. Three authentic *ought-to-bes*, as it happens most of all.

(a) *Willingness to share*

One obvious *ought-to-be* in the over-crowded conditions of the Hirschian present-day has to do with tolerant acceptance and a sharing propensity. Hirsch makes proposals for public galleries (as opposed to private sitting-rooms), for commuter trains (in contrast to the one adult-one car system of anarchic individualism), for power-sharing (a democratic alternative to the one boss/one voice rule of the hierarchical organisation), comprehensive schooling and unrestricted conviviality (the non-exclusive counterpart of the private school and the country-club), all of them not only compatible with the sharing propensity but unthinkable without it. Status-symbols present greater problems, however, involving as they do standards of evaluation that are inherently comparative. Many women can follow mass-produced fashions but only the very rich can afford the Paris originals; many runners can enter the New York marathon but only the fleetest can win the coveted prizes; and in these intrinsically zero-sum cases the sharing of status is tantamount to downgrading if not eliminating it. While that may in itself be no bad thing, it is not a proposition one would wish to dispute with alleycat obsessives clawing their way to the top of an executive ladder, let alone with heavyweight boxers battling for trophies and more hostile to 'rejection' than they are to 'violence'.

If the winner/loser relationship is indeed the archetypical mode of human intercourse, then the normative injunction to share is unlikely to have the same attraction that it would to a peaceful colony of well-integrated fellow-citizens deeply concerned about the physical availability of country-cottages. Even so, however, the sharing propensity could ultimately provide the solution to the winner/loser as well as to the physical availability problem. In the latter case, that solution involves alternative *foci* and *loci* – the idea being that if Jill takes her holidays in summer while Juliet takes hers in winter, if Jack opts for the mountains while Romeo opts for the seaside, it is their very differences and not their similarities which at the end of the day prevent these high-spirited English people and foreigners from getting on each other's nerves and riding roughshod over one another's personality. In the former case, reasoning analogously, the sharing propensity leads to a multiplication of the number of games in town – the outcome being that the highly-competitive Iago, bad at physics and worse at music, comes to win second prize in the ballroom dancing championship and ultimately discovers in the billiards room that he is the greatest snooker-player since Ghengis Khan. In the one case as in the other, of course, all proposals for greater plurality of experience must be weighed against the potential threat which greater diversity of lifestyles represents for the central value system and the moral consensus; but there is no particular reason to regard that threat as a major one provided that there exist adequate defences of the common culture in the form, if not of a common religion, then at least of common educational institutions and very common television programmes.

All in all, therefore, the *ought-to-share* is health-giving normative medicine which could with great profit be taken by a body politick experiencing a bout of social limits. Whether the community will do so is a separate matter. You can lead a nation to medicine *and* you can make it drink – but only if you are either a charismatic prophet or a bloodthirsty dictator. Within the more mundane constraints of democratic normality, the probability that the syrupy linctus of the sharing propensity will eventually be swallowed must remain indeterminate at best: Clarence has a Rembrandt, Richard wishes to acquire one, you propose that Clarence and Richard should share one and the same Rembrandt by means of situating it in the National Gallery, and it does not require the wisdom of Solomon to grasp that your final seat might not be upon the Woolsack but rather in the butt of Malmsey.

(b) *Honesty*

One obvious *ought-to-be* in the Hirschian world involves tolerant acceptance and a sharing propensity. A second involves truth-telling and honest reliability – such, indeed, as most of us take for granted in our dealings with policemen, magistrates, and civil servants in a manner which Hirsch perceptively captures in the negative answer which he obviously expects to the following question concerning bribery: 'The trust-busting officials are to maximize their salaries and promotion prospects in all legal ways; but does this include the most lucrative way, which is to change sides?'[74] Clearly it does not and it cannot; for, should public officials begin to think of themselves as profit-maximising merchants rather than as gentlemen imbued with devotion to civic duty, then not one of us could sleep soundly in his or her bed for fear of 'the first entrepreneur to be able to raise enough credit to buy the judge'.[75] The judge, most of us are entirely happy to accept, is the trustworthy servant of absolute obligation which transcends the law of supply and demand and vanquishes the law of the jungle; and this curious constant in a world of flexibilities is undeniably a source of confident reassurance to all but the first entrepreneur to try to buy that which simply is not for sale.

The personal morality which most of us would expect from the judge, however, few of us would expect from the seller of the used car, whom most of us would probably expect actually to exploit our inferior knowledge of the quality of his vehicle by playing up its good points while papering over its shortcomings. Knowing the troughs of our own ignorance as well as the peaks of other men's greed, most of us tend therefore to discount claims made as exaggerated, to trim the vendor's asking price smartly – and thereby, however, unintentionally, either to cheat truth-telling vendors (by underpricing their fine and trustworthy cars on the assumption that the normal vendor is an unrepentant liar) or to drive them out of the market altogether in a manner which Akerlof has described as a special case of 'Gresham's Law': 'Dishonest dealings tend to drive honest dealings out of the market. There may be potential buyers of good quality products and there may be potential sellers of such products in the appropriate price range; however, the presence of people who wish to pawn bad wares as good wares tends to drive out the legitimate business. The cost of dishonesty, therefore, lies not only in the amount by which the puchaser is cheated; the cost also must include the loss incurred from driving legitimate business out of existence.'[76] Since bad would not drive out good were truth-telling and honest reliability to be the norm, the inference is that the economic welfare of the community is diminished by the lack of personal morality in the market for used cars in precisely the same way as the standard of High Court verdicts would be debased were they to be auctioned off in High Street premises to high-income shoppers. The inference is that personal morality has no close substitutes in the marketplace for used cars.

An inference, as it happens, which not all economists would be prepared to draw. Some would point to functional equivalents in the form of legal sanctions imposed where the vendor's exaggerations exceed pre-specified bounds (the model being the Weights and Measures and Sale of Goods Acts which exist to contain the potential depredations even of the most venal of publicans and greengrocers). Others would stress the valuable work performed by the established car-entrepreneur with a reputation in iterated transactions to defend which is in itself a consumers' guarantee: the dealer-expert trades in so many used cars that he becomes accustomed to detecting quality-variations, and indeed earns a monopoly-rent precisely because of the confidence which his skill in the proportioning of price to product comes to command. The law, of course, is not always in a position to adjudicate (as in the case of disputes where one party swears the gaskets were faulty before sale and the other party swears they were as unimpeachable as the brakes); all recourse to the brand-name of a professional risk-absorber with financial interest in future merchanting costs money; and that is why economists such as Akerlof draw their inference concerning the necessity and the functionality of self-motivated truth-telling and honest reliability.

Economists such as Akerlof – and Hirsch, who, much impressed by Akerlof's 'pioneering exposition'[77] of sub-optimality in markets where 'lemons' are more common than trustworthiness, return the model inspired by Gresham's Law to its original home in the City of London. A place, it appears, where, once Bagehot's *Lombard Street* in 1873 had codified the convention that the bankers' bank had a duty to lend freely when no other lender would do so, no central banker would have been able to sleep soundly in his or her bed for fear of 'moral hazard' had it not been for the existence of an informal mechanism 'closer to the understanding of the sociologist than of the modern neo-classical economist thinking in terms of optimisation subject to a budget, but not social, constraint'.[78] What the sociologist understands, the schoolboy representing his home, his House and his School in the annual Charterhouse versus Rugby cricket-match understands even better, than the non-discretionary right of access to a discount-window which never shuts carries with it a non-statutory obligation to avoid irresponsible practices (excessive commitment to high-return, high-risk, low-liquidity assets is a standard example, insider-trading and speculation against the pound more controversial ones) such as might bring the open-access privilege into disrepute. Bagehot's advice need not, therefore, cause any central banker to lose any sleep in view of the fact that, in the City of London at least, the Bank of England's acceptance of unlimited potential liability finds its counterpart in the 'informal controls and inculcation of a club spirit among the commercial banks to play the game according to the established conventions which are seen to be in the interests of all participants. In return for the insurance premium of responsible behaviour, insurance cover is comprehensive and assured.'[79] The system is, admittedly, somewhat more conducive to conservative cartelisation than it is to thrusting new entry and dynamic banking efficiency: 'Participation in such an arrangement must obviously be limited to those who can be trusted to be responsible – call them gentlemen. This will mean excluding those not known to be gentlemen; and they will be those not known to existing gentlemen. So entry will be socially controlled, and competition discouraged.'[80] Still, nothing in economics (nothing, indeed, in life itself) is ever perfect, and the my-word-is-my-bondism of the Reform Club in office hours has at least this to recommend it, that it is, on economic grounds alone, unambiguously superior to any viable alternative.

The private market, obviously, cannot be expected to provide insurance against the contingencies of default and failure: to do so would be positively to invite the substitution of destabilising and irresponsible practices for soundness, prudence and good management. Nor are legal requirements on the nature and distribution of assets (whatever might be their role in normal times) of any great value in the panic conditions of threatened bankruptcies: the whole economy would be disrupted by the collapse of a banking giant (even if in truth a giant lemon) and this fact is sufficient in itself to blackmail the central bank into relieving the scoundrels. The blackguards might even take precautionary action through mergers in advance of premeditated naughtiness being committed, acting on the not unreasonable assumption that a concentrated and oligopolised industry is better placed to bully the central bank (by means of the dreaded threat of 'your money or *my* life') than would be a banking industry comprised of a large number of tiny institutions. Concentration without the eyeball-to-eyeball pressures of gentlemen upon gentlemen, cartelisation with and because of those pressures – the invisible hand of *competitive* capitalism hardly gets a look-in. The problem being 'the dependence of well-functioning markets on certain individual behavioural characteristics, such as telling the truth and keeping one's word', the cartelised mode of provision of these 'collective intermediate goods' is undeniably the best attainable in present-day conditions – since, as is no great secret, 'co-operation is technically easier to organise in a small group of like-minded individuals and institutions than in an open group'.[81] *In present-day conditions*, however, and not in those vastly superior conditions which would be ushered in by a remoralisation of social usages: then shared moral conventions would constitute moral capital accessible to all, and large-group competition among perfect gentlemen would become an eminently desirable possibility.

(c) *Justice*

There is a third and final *ought-to-be* which, alongside the sharing propensity and honest reliability, would appear indispensable if economic growth is indeed to proceed smoothly and without encountering significant social limits. That obvious *ought-to-be* involves justice – and justice most of all in the Rawlsian sense of perceived fairness. It comes as no surprise that Hirsch, so deprecatory of those who wish to divorce the social from the moral sciences (those who would say, with Harold Macmillan, that 'if people want morality let them get it from their Archbishops'), is so full of praise for the ambition and success of *A Theory of Justice*: 'The great significance of this work rests on its attempt to face the problem of political obligation within the context of a liberal market economy, and its acceptance that the basis of such obligation must be the justice of the politico-economic system, in the sense of fairness. . . . All are agreed on the importance of the undertaking itself. Rawls has brought the moral issue back to a system that had earlier hived off the issue as belonging to a separate and higher sphere.'[82]

The Rawlsian idea is one of neutrality and impartiality, stability and impersonality. The first step is to decide, situated behind a thick veil of ignorance such as obscures our own particular characteristics and interests, the procedures to be applied when faced as a group with some future eventuality – as in Schelling's example of a ceiling imposed by a collectivity on what it regards as excessive expenditure on health care: 'If we could sit down together at an early age in good health and legislate our relation to each other, specifying the entitlements we wished to obtain between us, recognizing equal likelihood of being beneficiaries or benefactors, we could elect to eschew exorbitant claims.'[83] The second step is consciously to abstain from what Buchanan calls 'behavioral pollution' ('the polluting of the sociobehavioral environment'),[84] to 'abide by the minimal behavioral precepts' of the rules-governed order, to 'refrain from lapsing into the role of moral anarchist'[85] – voluntary adherence to agreed-upon patterns of conduct, in other words, such as one would, indeed, legitimately expect from a decision-maker and a stake holder who accepts that the legal-political order is the product of proper process and has no doubts that 'all persons are effectively required to play by the same rules'.[86] Both steps in the Rawlsian line of reasoning are implicit in the Hirschian approach to justice – and explicit in the occasional *dictum* such as the following: 'In a fair game, I obey the spirit as well as the letter of the rules.'[87] In that *dictum* the Rawlsian bedrock is picked up by the words 'fair game' and 'letter of the rules', the Hirschian superstructure by 'spirit'. The message is clear: a social framework which actualises the vital *ought-to-be* of justice as fairness can reasonably expect its citizens to donate their blood as well as their conformity, to supply the minimum required and then to run the lap of honour in addition. Justice as fairness is sometimes regarded as coldly legalistic. In Hirsch's perspective it is warmly legalistic, the source of an affectual commitment which breeds other-regarding team-spirit and fosters moral sentiment including charity and belonging.

Consider the case of the political market. The fact is that 'the great majority of people do vote', and this suggests to Hirsch that the Downs model is internally inconsistent and essentially incomplete: 'The predication of private maximization cannot be easily transposed from its original market home to the politico-social arena. . . . Something else is necessary to elicit independent support for society's rules and conventions.'[88] That 'something else' he regards as 'some minimum area of social obligation'[89] – a recognition, in effect, that you and I opted for the democratic system and that you and I are therefore morally bound to make it work. The spirit of the law, Hirsch would reason, condemns abstention even where the letter of the law permits it; and, just as no self-respecting member of the Reform Club would contemplate hiring a mercenary to father his child purely to purchase himself additional hours in the shop, so no one but a blackguard or a scoundrel would set up a game that requires players and then refuse himself to make one. Similar considerations apply to the choice of the product. Hirsch had strong reservations about any model in which party politics is reduced to 'an extension of the department store', to a shopping-centre situation where the problem is simply 'to find the managers who can undersell the rest of the street'.[90] Behind those reservations lies not the lack of faith in inter-party competition, still less the elitist's belief that voters should be denied the policies they demand, but rather the familiar emphasis on the 'spirit' in supplementation of the 'letter' of the law. The letter of the law would allow unscrupulous and irresponsible office-seekers to market a political product of which the principal selling-point was free gin financed through crippling inflation. The spirit of the law, however, calls out to buyers that they must look their gift gin in the mouth, while instructing sellers that they must bridle their ambitions. Provided only that the procedural rules of the democratic order conform to the *ought-to-be* of justice, its voice will be heard – since, 'in a fair game, I obey the spirit as well as the letter of the rules'.

Consider now the economic market. Hirsch, as we have seen, is convinced that popular perceptions are such as would situate the automaticity of the supply and demand mechanism within the broad church of the fair game. Perhaps they are; but that will be a cause for regret not only to the powerful union (asked in the interests of fairness to show moderation and restraint) but the low-paid labourer in poor health as well (informed as he will be by the market that equity and equality, perceived fairness and perceived success, point in his case in opposite directions). Nor is it by any means certain that supply and demand actually represent the solution to the problem of dissensus: the very concept of a solution in such a context presupposes the pre-existence of an ongoing consensual pool of ideals and essences, and in a society characterised by a decay of the moral nexus, consensual legitimation even of supply and demand might be found to be most wanting just at the time when it is most wanted. Supply and demand are, more fundamentally perhaps, themselves not only a mode of resolving conflict in the Hirschian model but an independent cause of excessively self-seeking conduct in their own right – a menace to altruism of intent which Allen Buchanan has encapsulated in the following observation; 'It is something of a platitude that one factor which accelerates the expansion of market relations is the recognition that there is a market and that we are exchangers in it. In other words, to the extent that we come to view our interactions as market transactions they may actually come more closely to approximate the model by which we seek to explain them.'[91]

In seeking to cast the values of the economic market in the roles both of his friend (the fair game) and of his enemy (the egotistical orientation), Hirsch is demonstrating his devotion to the mixed ethos which characterises his work. What he does not prove is that the justice brought about by the friend will be sufficient to arrest the weakening of collective ties caused by the enemy, or say how to reassert the external moral constraint and sense of purpose that are essential for the process of social intercourse itself. Hirsch takes the view that internalised ethical values are more efficient in supplying the essential public good of rule-bound conduct than is the calculation of individual costs and benefits under the sound supervision of laws, lawyers and policemen. If he is right that we are truly living off a depleting legacy acquired in a common cultural childhood, then his warning must be taken seriously. Hirsch would assert that we today will avoid activities such as burglary, bullying and deceit (despite the fact that they do in certain circumstances constitute the most rational means for the attainment of a particular end) not simply out of fear but because of the inner voice of a man within who came to dwell long before we learned the art of buying cheap and selling dear. Hirsch would warn that, to the extent that that voice is now becoming muted, to the extent that the sitting tenant of ethics is being evicted that his empty room might be converted into a counting house, to that extent the deadweight burden of law-enforcement is likely to rise, together with a widepread sense of disillusionment associated with the failure adequately to secure the desired conformity to rules. Hirsch asks, in sum, how long a given society (and this quite irrespective of whether or not it also suffers from positional goods) can continue to make progress through an ethical vacuum, to dance on the graves of dead philosophers and half-forgotten prophets.

All of this is exceptionally worrying to anyone interested in theories of collective action; and it is bound to cause him to wonder if it is not even rather optimistic to talk of social limits to economic growth when the real question must surely be social limits to civilised survival. A less apocalyptic but possibly more valuable ending to this book is, however, the following: a society in which internalised normative constraint is assigned a significant role to play may or may not be more efficient than one in which functional equivalents are sought, but it is likely to be infinitely more pleasant, and that is important too. The Rousseauist natural man, the *enfant sauvage*, Wild Peter of Hanover, all three stole away from their lonely isolation to join us in society. No doubt they did so because they liked our colour televisions if not our Spaghetti Junctions, our Marks and Spencer's if not our Northern Line. But perhaps they did so as well because they liked us as people, because the liked the way in which we relate to one another when we interact. Our economic institutions in no small measure breed and form our character-patterns and make us the people that we are. Our economic institutions ought therefore themselves to be shaped and tailored in such a way as to ensure that we remain nice as we become rich.

Social limits or social decency, it is the great merit of Fred Hirsch's important contribution to theories of collective action that he reminds the reader of the extent to which the choice of the institutional framework is the choice of something else as well, of something which is as distinct from the wealth of nations as it is superior to it. That something, as Alfred Marshall consistently maintained, is nothing less than man himself: 'For man's character has been moulded by his every-day work, and the material resources which he thereby procures, more than by any other influence unless it be that of his religious ideals; and the two great forming agencies of the world's history have been the religious and the economic.'[92] If, therefore, religious ideals are now in decay, the burden placed upon economic institutions would seem to be that much greater. So too would seem to be the social responsibility of the political economist, standing as he must upon the shoulders of Downs, Olson and Hirsch, to take an active interest in theories of collective action.

Notes and References

2 DEMOCRACY AND CONSENT

1. A. Smith, *The Wealth of Nations* (1776), ed. by E. Cannan (London: Methuen, 1961), Vol. I, p. 18.
2. Ibid., Vol. II, pp. 49–50.
3. See, for example, P. A. Samuelson, *Foundations of Economic Analysis* (Cambridge, Mass.: Harvard University Press, 1947), pp. 203–53 and his 'Social Indifference Curves', *Quarterly Journal of Economics*, Vol. 70, 1956, pp. 1–22.
4. K. E. Boulding, 'Economics as a Moral Science', *American Economic Review*, Vol. 59, 1969, p. 8. Note also Boulding's reminder (ibid., p. 10) that the economic mode at times breeds and forms some very unpleasant character-traits indeed: 'No one in his senses would want his daughter to marry an economic man, one who counted every cost and asked for every reward, was never afflicted with mad generosity or uncalculating love, and who never acted out of a sense of inner identity and indeed had no inner identity even if he was occasionally affected by carefully calculated considerations of benevolence or malevolence. ' Boulding's observation is a salutary corrective to the approach of 'economics imperialism' which he is criticising. It is important to remember, however, that there is a clear distinction to be made between discouraging one's daughter from marrying an economic man and refusing oneself to enter into a trading relationship with such an individual; and that even Boulding would appear to assign pride of place to economic man in specifically *economic* affairs, narrowly defined.
5. J. A. Schumpeter, *Captialism, Socialism and Democracy* (1942) (London: George Allen & Unwin, 1976), p. 287.
6. B. Frey, *Modern Political Economy* (London: Martin Robertson, 1978) pp. 5, 6. Since Frey says there is 'little evidence' for believing A, it is not clear why he says 'it must rather be assumed' with respect to B.
7. G. Tullock, *The Vote Motive* (London: The Institute of Economic Affairs, 1976) pp. 5, 25.

2.1 Methodology

1. C. B. Macpherson, 'Market Concepts in Political Theory', in his *Democratic Theory: Essays in Retrieval* (Oxford: Clarendon Press, 1973), p. 189.
2. J. F. J. Toye, 'Economic Theories of Politics and Public Finance', *British Journal of Political Science*, Vol. 6, 1976, p. 434.
3. Macpherson, 'Market Concepts', *op. cit.*, p. 192.
4. J. M. Buchanan and G. Tullock, *The Calculus of Consent* (Ann Arbor: University of Michigan Press, 1962), p. 306.

5. A. Downs, *An Economic Theory of Democracy* (ETD) (New York: Harper and Row, 1957), p. 27.

6. G. Tullock, *The Politics of Bureaucracy* (Washington, DC: Public Affairs Press, 1965), p. 65.

7. *ETD*, p. 292.

8. *ETD*, p. 30.

9. Jo Grimond, in J. M. Buchanan et al, *The Economics of Politics* (London: Institute of Economic Affairs, 1978), p. 66.

10. W. Rodgers, 'The Political Process: Market Place or Battleground?', in R. C. O. Matthews (ed.), *Economy and Democracy* (London: Macmillan, 1985), p. 117.

11. Interestingly enough, James Buchanan – while not sharing Rodgers' confidence in the ease with which the 'right' can in practice be identified by the practical politician – lends unexpected support to the line of argumentation which Rodgers is pursuing, that politicians have intellectual objectives such as transcend the narrow egotism and the selfish hedonism which clearly enjoy pride of place in the Downs model. Of course one can find passages in Buchanan where he demonstrates the nervous libertarian's debt to Hobbes and fear of fallen man – the following, for example, taken from his *Academia in Anarchy* (New York: Basic Books, 1970), p. 36, written in collaboration with Nicos Devletoglou: 'Individuals enjoy power. They relish opportunities to control the lives of others, and there are few exceptions to this generalization . . . The producer begins, all too naturally, to enjoy his role as chooser. ' Elsewhere, however, Buchanan has made absolutely clear that it is not merely power in general but power to do something in particular to which politicians frequently aspire – one reason, indeed, why they become politicians and not, let us say, business executives or military officers. As he puts it in his important *Limits of Liberty* (Chicago: University of Chicago Press, 1975), p. 157: 'Those persons who place relatively high values on the ability to influence collective outcomes, and who do so in the genuinely incorruptible sense of desiring to 'do good' for the whole community, are quite likely to be those who seek to accomplish their own preferred social objectives through collective or governmental means.' While Buchanan would prefer the politicians to follow the revealed preferences of the citizenry whereas Rodgers sees it as their proper role to take a lead, both would maintain – in contrast to Downs – that the opportunity to 'do good' is a significant part of the politician's psychic income and a significant source of utility to him in its own right. Gordon Tullock, however, takes a more cynical (and a more Downsian) view of the 'conviction politician'. See, for instance, *The Vote Motive*, p. 25, where he writes: 'Wilson, Nixon, Johnson and Heath are examples of politicians who reached the top, and we doubt that anyone will claim they are highly motivated by devotion to a consistent set of policies. It is true they normally talk in terms of policies, but the policies they favour changed depending on where political support was to be found. '

12. Rodgers, 'The Political Process', in *Economy and Democracy*, op. cit., p. 118.

13. J. Plamenatz, *Democracy and Illusion* (London: Longman, 1973), pp. 149, 153.
14. R. C. O. Matthews, 'Competition in Economy and Polity', in Matthews (ed.), *Economy and Democracy*, op. cit., p. 11.
15. Ibid., p. 12.
16. *ETD*, p. 276.
17. *ETD*, p. 275.
18. *ETD*, p. 7.
19. *ETD*, p. 7.
20. *ETD*, p. 34.
21. *ETD*, p. 7.
22. Matthews, "Competition in Economy and Polity", in *Economy and Democracy* op. cit., p. 6.
23. Ibid., p. 9.
24. Ibid.
25. Ibid.
26. Schumpeter, *Capitalism, Socialism and Democracy*, op. cit., p. 263.
27. Ibid., p. 253.
28. B. Barry, *Sociologists, Economists and Democracy* (Chicago: University of Chicago Press, 1978), p. 127.

2.2 Policies Supplied

1. A. Downs, 'Why The Government Budget Is Too Small In A Democracy', *World Politics*, Vol. 12, 1960, p. 541. This paper may also be found in an abridged form in E. S. Phelps (ed.), *Private Wants and Public Needs*, 2nd ed. (New York: W. W. Norton, 1965).
2. K. J. Arrow, *Social Choice and Individual Values*, 2nd ed. (New York: John Wiley & Sons, Inc., 1963), p. x.
3. *ETD*, p. vii.
4. H. Hotelling, 'Stability in Competition', *Economic Journal*, Vol. 39, 1929, p. 44.
5. Ibid., p. 53.
6. Ibid., p. 54.
7. Ibid., p. 57.
8. Ibid., p. 55.
9. A. Smithies, 'Optimum Location in Spatial Competition', *Journal of Political Economy*, Vol. 49. 1941, p. 423.
10. Ibid.
11. *ETD*, p. 100.
12. Rodgers, 'The Political Process', in *Economy and Democracy*, op. cit., pp. 124–5.
13. D. Black, *The Theory of Committees and Elections* (Cambridge: Cambridge University Press, 1958), p. 113.
14. Ibid., p. 125.
15. See Black, *The Theory of Committees*, op. cit., Part II, for a historical account of the early development of the mathematical theory of committees and elections. See also Arrow, *Social Choice*, op. cit., esp. pp. 93–6.

16. Arrow, *Social Choice*, op. cit., pp. 109 and 109n.
17. A. Downs, 'In Defense of Majority Voting', *Journal of Political Economy*, Vol. 69. 1961, p. 195.
18. Ibid.
19. Ibid., p. 192.
20. G. Tullock, 'Reply to a Traditionalist', *Journal of Political Economy*, Vol. 69. 1961, p. 203.
21. Arrow, *Social Choice*, op. cit., pp. 29, 30.
22. A. Bergson, 'On the Concept of Social Welfare', *Quarterly Journal of Economics*, Vol. 68, 1954, p. 239.
23. W. Nordhaus, 'The Political Business Cycle', *Review of Economic Studies*, Vol. 42, 1975, p. 184.
24. M. Olson, 'Evaluating Performance in the Public Sector', in M. Moss (ed.), *The Measurement of Economic and Social Performance* (New York: National Bureau of Economic Research, 1973), p. 358.
25. Ibid.
26. Ibid.
27. Plamenatz, *Democracy and Illusion*, op. cit., p. 184.

2.3 Policies Demanded

1. *ETD*, p. 270.
2. *ETD*, p. 261.
3. *ETD*, p. 267.
4. *ETD*, p. 268.
5. *ETD*, p. 270.
6. *ETD*, p. 267.
7. Tullock, *The Politics of Bureacracy*, op. cit., p. 85.
8. Downs, 'Why The Government Budget Is Too Small In A Democracy', loc. cit., p. 530. It is a fine philosophical question if something can be *too small* where the costs of being properly informed are *too high*. Nor is it clear that all rational citizens, even if fully informed, would reveal the same preference as Downs himself. It is uncharacteristic for Downs to confuse the subjective with the objective but he clearly does so in the present context.
9. Ibid., p. 544.
10. See on this Buchanan and Tullock, *op. cit.*, *The Calculus of Consent*, Chapter 10, and D. A. Reisman, *The Political Economy of James Buchanan* (London: Macmillan, 1989), Chapter 4.
11. Downs, 'In Defense of Majority Voting', loc. cit., p. 195.
12. Downs, 'Why The Government Budget Is Too Small In A Democracy', loc. cit., p. 562.
13. Ibid., p. 544.
14. Ibid., p. 551.
15. Ibid., p. 561.
16. G. Tullock, *Towards a Mathematics of Politics* (Ann Arbor: University of Michigan Press, 1967), p. 118.
17. *ETD*, p. 186.
18. *ETD*, p. 199.

19. H. G. Johnson, 'The Economic Approach to Social Questions', *Economica*, Vol. 35, 1968, p. 12.
20. Ibid.
21. Ibid., p. 11.
22. Ibid., p. 6.
23. Ibid., p. 1.

3 ORGANISATIONS AND INTERESTS

1. The kind of socio-political (as opposed to economic) approach that is most often coupled with the name of Max Weber.

3.1 Methodology

1. A. Downs, *Inside Bureaucracy* (*IB*) (Boston: Little, Brown and Company, 1967), p. 79n.
2. *IB*, p. 28n.
3. W. Niskanen, *Bureaucracy and Representative Government* (Chicago: Aldine, 1971), p. vi.
4. *IB*, p. 41.
5. *IB*, p. 2.
6. *IB*, p. 82.
7. *IB*, p. 37.
8. *IB*, p. 85.
9. *IB*, p. 84.
10. *IB*, p. 84.
11. *IB*, p. 84.
12. Tullock, *The Politics of Bureaucracy*, op. cit., p. 29.
13. *IB*, p. 84.
14. *IB*, p. 84.
15. *IB*, p. 85.
16. I. Illich, *Deschooling Society* (Harmondsworth: Penguin Books, 1973), p. 44.
17. Ibid., p. 45
18. J. K. Galbraith, 'Foreign Policy: The Stuck Whistle', *The Atlantic*, February 1965, p. 65.
19. *IB*, p. 84.
20. *IB*, p. 168.
21. *IB*, p. 87.
22. *IB*, p. 96–7.
23. *IB*, p. 97.
24. *IB*, p. 102.
25. *IB*, p. 109.
26. *IB*, p. 103.
27. M. Weber, 'Bureaucracy', in H. H. Gerth and C. W. Mills (eds), *From Max Weber: Essays in Sociology* (London: Routledge and Kegan Paul, 1948), pp. 228, 197.
28. *IB*, p. 111.

29. Tullock, *The Politics of Bureaucracy*, op. cit., p. 15.
30. Niskanen, *Bureaucracy*, op. cit., pp. 38, 41.
31. A useful overview and analysis of these theories may be found in O.E. Williamson, *The Economics of Discretionary Behavior: Managerial Objectives in a Theory of the Firm* (New York: Prentice-Hall, 1964).
32. R. M. Cyert and J. G. March, *A Behavioral Theory of the Firm* (New York: Prentice-Hall, 1963), p. 30.
33. H. A. Simon, *Models of Man* (New York: John Wiley & Sons, 1957), p. 167.
34. *IB*, p. 2.
35. *IB*, p. 3.
36. *IB*, p. 3.
37. H. A. Simon, *Administrative Behavior*, 2nd ed. (Glencoe: The Free Press, 1965), p. 65.
38. Ibid., p. xxiv.
39. Ibid., p. xxv.
40. Ibid.
41. G. J. Stigler, 'The Economics of Information', *Journal of Political Economy*, Vol. 69, 1961, p. 214.
42. Ibid., p. 213.
43. Ibid., p. 215.
44. H. A. Simon, 'Rationality as Process and as Product of Thought', *American Economic Review*, Vol. 68, 1978, p. 10.
45. Simon, *Models of Man*, op. cit., p. 257.
46. Simon, 'Rationality as Process and as Product of Thought', loc. cit., p. 10.
47. Ibid., p. 5n.
48. *IB*, pp. 168–9.
49. *IB*, p. 171.
50. Smith, *The Wealth of Nations*, op. cit., Vol. I, p. 18.
51. Weber, 'Bureaucracy', *loc. cit.,* p. 199.

3.2 The Bureau: Responsibility and Responsiveness

1. *IB*, p. 24.
2. *IB*, pp. 24–5.
3. *IB*, p. 25.
4. *IB*, p. 25.
5. Niskanen, *Bureaucracy*, op. cit., p. 15.
6. Ibid., p. 16.
7. *IB*, p. 30.
8. *IB*, p. 37.
9. Niskanen, *Bureaucracy*, op. cit., p. 20.
10. Ibid., p. 9.
11. Ibid., p. 20.
12. Ibid., p. 8.
13. *IB*, p. 77.
14. *IB*, p. 126n.
15. *IB*, p. 118.

16. *IB*, p. 130.
17. Cyert and March, *A Behavioral Theory*, op. cit., p. 34.
18. *IB*, p. 172.
19. *IB*, p. 98.
20. *IB*, p. 216.
21. *IB*, p. 99.
22. *IB*, p. 109.
23. *IB*, p. 100.
24. *IB*, p. 87.
25. *IB*, p. 173.
26. *IB*, p. 172.
27. *IB*, p. 196.
28. *IB*, p. 159.
30. Niskanen, *Bureaucracy*, op. cit., p. 8.
31. *IB*, p. 106.
32. *IB*, p. 104.
33. *IB*, p. 109.
34. *IB*, p. 109.
35. *IB*, p. 143. Emphasis deleted.
36. *IB*, p. 57.
37. *IB*, p. 12.
38. *IB*, pp. 217–18.
39. *IB*, p. 181.
40. *IB*, p. 179. Emphasis added.
41. *IB*, p. 180.
42. *IB*, pp. 180–81.
43. *IB*, p. 182.
44. *IB*, p. 181.
45. *IB*, p. 181.

3.3 The Bureau: Accountability and Action

1. *IB*. p. 163.
2. *IB*, p. 7.
3. *IB*, p. 104.
4. *IB*, p. 104.
5. *IB*, p. 199.
6. *IB*, p. 258.
7. *IB*, p. 35.
8. *IB*, p. 163.
9. *IB*, p. 132.
10. *IB*, p. 245.
11. *IB*, p. 248.
12. *IB*, p. 248.
13. *IB*, p. 251.
14. *IB*, p. 12.
15. *IB*, p. 164.
16. *IB*, p. 35.

17. A. Wildavsky, *Budgeting: A Comparative Theory of Budgetary Processes* (Boston: Little, Brown and Company, 1975), p. 4.
18. *IB*, p. 219.
19. See, for example, C. E. Lindblom, *The Intelligence of Democracy* (New York: The Free Press, 1965), esp. Part Four.
20. See on this C. E. Lindblom, 'The Science of "Muddling Through"', *Public Administration Review*, Vol. 19, 1959.
21. The parallel is drawn explicitly in A. O. Hirschman and C. E. Lindblom, 'Economic Development, Research and Development Policy-Making: Some Converging Views', *Behavioral Science*, Vol. 7, 1961.
22. A. Wildavsky, 'Does Planning Work?', *The Public Interest*, Vol. 33, 1973, p. 89.
23. J. K. Galbraith, *Economics and the Public Purpose* (Harmondsworth: Penguin Books, 1975), p. 176.
24. *IB*, p. 105.
25. *IB*, p. 119.
26. *IB*, p. 121.
27. *IB*, p. 23.
28. *IB*, p. 29.
29. *IB*, p. 257.
30. *IB*, p. 259.
31. *IB*, p. 259.
32. R. H. Tawney, *The Radical Tradition* (Harmondsworth: Penguin Books, 1966), p. 169.
33. *IB*, p. 32.
34. *IB*, p. 35.
35. *IB*, p. 34.
36. *IB*, p. 33.
37. The term is from Titmuss. See in particular R. M. Titmuss, 'The Social Division of Welfare' (1955), reprinted in his *Essays on 'The Welfare State'*, 2nd ed. (London: George Allen and Unwin, 1963).
38. *IB*, p. 34.
39. M. and R. D. Friedman, *Free to Choose* (Harmondsworth: Penguin Books, 1980), p. 230.
40. Ibid., p. 229.
41. Ibid., p. 10.
42. *IB*, p. 34.
43. *IB*, p. 32.
44. *IB*, p. 38.
45. *IB*, p. 38.
46. *IB*, p. 38.
47. *IB*, p. 38–9.
48. *IB*, p. 256.
49. *IB*, p. 256.
50. D. Bell, *The Coming of Post-Industrial Society* (Harmondsworth: Penguin Books, 1976), p. 157.
51. H. Leibenstein, 'Allocative Efficiency vs. X-Efficiency', *American Economic Review*, Vol. 56, 1966, pp. 392, 395.

52. H. Leibenstein, 'Competition and X-Efficiency: Reply', *Journal of Political Economy*, Vol. 81, 1973, p. 767.
53. K. J. Lancaster, 'A New Approach to Consumer Theory', *Journal of Political Economy*, Vol. 74, 1966, p. 133.
54. Ibid.
55. Leibenstein, 'Competition and X-Efficiency: Reply', loc. cit.
56. Cyert and March, *A Behavioral Theory*, op. cit., p. 36.
57. M. Friedman, 'The Methodology of Positive Economics', in his *Essays in Positive Economics* (Chicago: University of Chicago Press, 1953), p. 22.
58. Simon, *Administrative Behavior*, p. xx.
59. *IB*, p. 74.
60. *IB*, p. 108.
61. *IB*, p. 225.
62. *IB*, p. 124.
63. *IB*, p. 126.
64. *IB*, p. 126.
65. *IB*, p. 57.
66. *IB*, p. 124.
67. *IB*, p. 124.
68. *IB*, p. 124.
69. *IB*, p. 57.
70. *IB*, p. 58.
71. *IB*, p. 67.
72. H. G. Brennan and J. M. Buchanan, *The Reason of Rules* (Cambridge: Cambridge University Press, 1985), p. 3.
73. *IB*, p. 69.
74. *IB*, p. 150.
75. *IB*, p. 151.
76. *IB*, p. 58.
77. *IB*, p. 223.
78. *IB*, p. 223.
79. *IB*, p. 237.
80. *IB*, p. 229.
81. R. Milliband, *The State in Capitalist Society* (London: Quartet Books, 1974), p. 59.
82. K. Marx and F. Engels, *The Communist Manifesto* (1848) (Harmondsworth: Penguin Books, 1967), p. 82.
83. Leibenstein, 'Competition and X-Efficiency: Reply', loc. cit., p. 768.
84. *IB*, p. 235.
85. *IB*, p. 240–41.
86. *IB*, p. 227.
87. *IB*, p. 227.
88. *IB*, p. 227.
89. J. M. Buchanan, 'Foreword', in Tullock, *The Politics of Bureaucracy*, op. cit., p. 2.
90. A. Downs, 'The Public Interest: Its Meaning in a Democracy', *Social Research*, Vol. 29, 1962, p. 31.
91. Ibid.

92. Ibid.
93. D. C. Mueller, *Public Choice* (Cambridge: Cambridge University Press, 1979), pp. 1–2.
94. A. Marshall, 'The Present Position of Economics' (1885) in A. C. Pigou (ed.), *Memorials of Alfred Marshall* (1925) (New York: Augustus M. Kelley, 1966), p. 160.
95. *ETD*, p. 37.
96. Downs, 'The Public Interest: Its Meaning in a Democracy', loc. cit., p. 31.
97. Ibid., p. 24.
98. Ibid., p. 30.
99. Ibid.
100. O. E. Williamson, *The Economic Institutions of Capitalism* (London: Collier Macmillan, 1985), p. 47.
101. O. E. Williamson, *Markets and Hierarchies* (New York: The Free Press, 1975), p. 14.
102. Williamson, *The Economic Institutions of Capitalism*, op. cit., p. 49.
103. P. M. Jackson, *The Political Economy of Bureaucracy* (Deddington: Philip Allan, 1982), p. 205.

4. FREE RIDERS AND FREE MARKETS

1. D. Hume, *A Treatise of Human Nature* (1739–40), ed. by E. C. Mossner (Harmondsworth: Penguin Books, 1969), p. 590.
2. A. L. Stinchcombe, 'Is the Prisoners' Dilemma all of Sociology?', *Inquiry*, Vol. 23, 1980, p. 190.

4.1 Methodology

1. M. Olson, *The Logic of Collective Action*, (LCA) (Boston: Harvard University Press, 1965), p. 59.
2. *LCA*, p. 60.
3. *LCA*, p. 13.
4. *LCA*, p. 63n.
5. *LCA*, p. 61n.
6. *LCA*, p. 160n.
7. *LCA*, p. 61n.
8. Mancur Olson, 'The Relationship Between Economics and the Other Social Sciences', in S. M. Lipset (ed.), *Politics and the Social Sciences* (New York: Oxford University Press, 1969), p. 142.
9. *LCA*, p. 174.
10. *LCA*, p. 173.
11. *LCA*, p. 161.
12. *LCA*, p. 2.
13. *LCA*, p. 87.
14. *LCA*, p. 13.
15. *LCA*, p. 15.
16. *LCA*, p. 159.

17. *LCA*, p. 20.
18. *LCA*, p. 161n.

4.2 Group Size

1.   *LCA*, p. 49.
2.   *LCA*, p. 37.
3.   *LCA*, pp. 40–41.
4.   *LCA*, p. 50.
5.   *LCA*, p. 29. But there are exceptions: 'During periods of all-out war or exceptional insecurity, it is likely that defense is (or is nearly) a superior good, and in such circumstances alliances will not have any tendency toward disproportionate burden sharing. The amount of allied military capability that Great Britain enjoyed in World War II increased from 1941 to 1944 as the United States mobilized, adding more and more strength to the allied side. But the British war effort was maintained, if not increased, during this period.' See M. Olson and R. Zeckhauser, 'An Economic Theory of Alliances', *Review of Economics and Statistics*, Vol. 48, 1966, p. 270. The British, it would be fair to say, could not reasonably have been excluded from enjoying the public good represented by the defeat of the Germans. The fact that they chose not to ride piggy-back on the American defence capability but increased their own war effort accordingly suggests that there is, even to Olson, sentiment and/or obligation such as transcends the rational-choice model which he presents.
6.   *LCA*, p. 35.
7.   *LCA*, p. 50.
8.   *LCA*, p. 43.
9.   *LCA*, p. 64.
10. *LCA*, p. 48.
11. *LCA*, p. 50.
12. *LCA*, p. 166.
13. *LCA*, p. 58.
14. *LCA*, p. 103.
15. *LCA*, p. 108.
16. *LCA*, p. 110.
17. *LCA*, p. 172.
18. *LCA*, p. 173.
19. *LCA*, p. 143.
20. *LCA*, p. 148.
21. *LCA*, p. 163. Note the attribution of rational choice at a conscious level in the words 'they recognize'.
22. *LCA*, p. 91.
23. Barry, *Sociologists, Economists and Democracy*, op. cit., p. 29.
24. Ibid.
25. D. Marsh, 'On Joining Interest Groups: An Empirical Consideration of the Work of Mancur Olson, Jr.', *British Journal of Political Science*, Vol. 6, 1976, p. 264.
26. Olson does not, in fact, compare the size of contribution with the stream

of benefits expected from membership in groups – a surprising neglect of an opportunity to compare marginal costs and marginal revenues in the manner than Downs does when discussing the act of voting as if it were an inexpensive form of insurance against non-provision.

27. D. Marsh, 'More on Joining Interest Groups', *British Journal of Political Science*, Vol. 8, 1978, p. 384. His argument is weaker than it appears, however, when one reflects how often the decision to join is taken not by profit-seeking owners but by salaried managers: in order properly to understand why firms join, it is likely to be helpful to disaggregate results so as to distinguish the 'capitalistic' from the 'bureaucratised' organisation. The inclusion of a control-group of non-joiners would in addition have strengthened confidence in Marsh's conclusions: joiners and non-joiners might be differently motivated, and were that to be the case a sample drawn from either group would not be representative of British businessmen as a whole. It would, finally, have been interesting for the study to have sought to identify and explain particular changes over time: the elasticity of demand for membership with respect to variation in the quantity supplied of selective incentives would seem to be a particularly useful line of inquiry to follow up.

28. G. S. Becker, 'Irrational Behavior and Economic Theory', *Journal of Political Economy*, Vol. 70, 1962, p. 1.

29. F. Hirsch, *Social Limits to Growth* (SLG) (London: Routledge & Kegan Paul, 1977), p. 136.

30. *LCA*, p. 58.

4.3 The Prisoner's Dilemma

1. R. Sugden, *The Economics of Rights, Co-operation and Welfare* (Oxford: Basil Blackwell, 1986), p. 1.

2. T. C. Schelling, *The Strategy of Conflict* (Cambridge, Mass.: Harvard University Press, 1960), p. 57.

3. T. C. Schelling, *Micromotives and Macrobehavior* (New York: Norton, 1978), p. 24.

4. A. Schotter, *The Economic Theory of Social Institutions* (Cambridge: Cambridge University Press, 1981), p. 149.

5. See my *The Political Economy of James Buchanan*, op. cit., Chapter 2.3, for a further discussion of this theme.

6. This example is taken from Schelling's *Strategy of Conflict*. While the character of Grand Central Station has no doubt altered significantly since 1960, one thing has not changed: people still go (and are known to go) to Grand Central Station in order to meet other people. Schelling's point is that it is precisely such an association of ideas that causes persons lost in the City to think first of the Station. Not only was he able to establish this result by means of direct questioning, he also found that, when asked to predict how a coin would land, more respondents chose 'heads' than said 'tails' – although the statistical probability of each outcome's occurrence is, of course, the same. From this Schelling concludes that random does not mean random where the individual psychology of socially-conditioned human beings is concerned.

Schelling's emphasis on non-rational elements within rational action is a useful corrective to the undeniable temptation to treat all of human action as the product of consciousness and deliberation.

7. G. Hardin, 'The Tragedy of the Commons', *Science*, 13 December 1968, p. 1244.
8. F. A. Hayek, *Law, Legislation and Liberty*, Vol. 3 (London: Routledge & Kegan Paul, 1979), p. 164.
9. See, for example, his *First Principles*, 5th ed. (London and Edinburgh: Williams & Norgate, 1890).
10. Hayek, *Law, Legislation and Liberty*, Vol. 3. pp. 156–7.
11. Ibid., p. 157.
12. Ibid., p. 155. Which is not to say that the 'acting individuals' do not make the relevant choices merely because they do not actually understand the concrete functions of the 'learnt rules'. On the contrary: they do and they must, since it is people and not depersonalised structures that alone can take decisions. What the evolutionary holist who is also a methodological individualist would, however, maintain, is that those decisions are frequently not random but patterned, the result both of childhood socialisation and personal learning-by-doing in a historically-delimited social setting. A child taught by his parents to be assiduous who himself subsequently learns from experience that hard work is correlated with success in a way that laziness is not, retains, of course, the freedom to develop habits other than those that are so evidently expected of him. There is good reason to think, however, that he will not do so. In that sense the prisoner's dilemma is not a real dilemma – since each prisoner must individually make a conscious choice, but his or her action is not set in a social vacuum that provides no guidelines. Needless to say, the solution that is passed on by convention is more likely to be the cooperative than the conflictual strategy: serious conflict is incompatible with social stability and society would therefore continue to adapt until a different standard had evolved. All of which is to say that 'acting individuals' with freedom of choice might not have quite as much freedom, in prisoner's dilemma-type situations, as they think they do – and as Mancur Olson thinks they do.
13. Hirsch, *Social Limits to Growth* (*SLG*), op. cit., p. 179.
14. A. Marshall, *Principles of Economics* (1920) (London: Macmillan, 1949), p. 253.
15. Ibid.
16. Ibid., p. 29.
17. Ibid., p. 19.
18. Smith, *Wealth of Nations*, op. cit., Vol. I. p. 433.
19. M. Weber, *The Protestant Ethic and the Spirit of Capitalism* (1904–5), trans. by T. Parsons (London: George Allen & Unwin, 1930), p. 177.
20. F. Knight, 'The Ethics of Competition' (1923), in his *The Ethics of Competition and Other Essays* (1935) (Freeport, New York: Books for Libraries Press, 1969), p. 72.
21. R. H. Tawney, 'A Note on Christianity and the Social Order' (1937), in his *The Attack and Other Papers* (London: George Allen & Unwin, 1953), p. 170.
22. Ibid., pp. 176–7.

23. *The Gospel According to Saint Luke*, 6:14.

24. *The Gospel According to Saint Matthew*, 6:16.

25. *Luke*, 6:14.

26. *Matthew*, 21:3. Passages such as these are highly reminiscent of the Old Testament, where God nowhere reveals himself more clearly as a contractarian than in the Covenant described in *Exodus* 34:9. Witness the force of the 'if' in the following part of the pact proposed to Moses and his followers: 'When I have dispossessed the nations for you and extended your frontiers, no one will covet your land, if you present yourselves three times in the year before Yahweh your God.' All passages are cited from *The Jerusalem Bible* (London: Darton, Longman and Todd, 1966).

27. E. Durkheim, *The Division of Labour in Society* (1893), in *Emile Durkheim: Selected Writings*, ed. and trans. by A. Giddens (Cambridge: Cambridge University Press, 1972), p. 101.

28. Durkheim, *Division of Labour*, in *Emile Durkheim: Selected Writings*, p. 127.

29. E. Durkheim, 'L'individualisme et les intellectuels' (1898), in *Emile Durkheim: Selected Writings*, p. 147.

30. Durkheim, *Division of Labour*, in *Emile Durkheim: Selected Writings*, p. 102.

31. Durkheim, *Division of Labour*, in *Emile Durkheim: Selected Writings*, p. 121.

32. E. Durkheim, book review (1887), in *Emile Durkheim: Selected Writings*, p. 220.

33. Durkheim, *Division of Labour*, in *Emile Durkheim: Selected Writings*, p. 222.

34. T. H. Green, *Lectures on the Principles of Political Obligation* (*circa* 1879) (London: Longmans, Green and Co., 1941), pp. 123–4.

35. Sugden, *The Economics of Rights, Co-operation and Welfare*, op. cit., p. 106.

36. T. C. Schelling, *Choice and Consequence* (Cambridge, Mass.: Harvard University Press, 1984), p. 55.

37. G. S. Becker, 'A Theory of Social Interactions', *Journal of Political Economy*, Vol. 82, 1974, p. 1078.

38. A. Smith, *The Theory of Moral Sentiments* (1759) (New York: Augustus M. Kelley, 1966), pp. 465–6.

39. Ibid., p. 466.

40. Ibid., p. 328.

41. Ibid., p. 321.

42. Ibid.

43. Ibid., p. 326.

44. Ibid., p. 192.

45. Schelling, *Choice and Consequence*, op. cit., p. 115.

46. R. M. Titmuss, *The Gift Relationship* (Harmondsworth: Penguin Books, 1973), p. 223.

47. J. M. Buchanan, 'An Economic Theory of Clubs', *Economica*, Vol. 32, 1965, p. 2n.

48. A. O. Hirschman, *Shifting Involvements* (Oxford: Basil Blackwell, 1982), pp. 90, 91.

49. D. Collard, *Altruism and Economy* (Oxford: Martin Robertson, 1978), p. 180
50. A. K. Sen, *Choice, Welfare and Measurement* (Oxford: Basil Blackwell, 1982), pp. 98, 99.
51. A. K. Sen, *Collective Choice and Social Welfare* (San Francisco: Holden-Day, 1970), p. 195.
52. Hirschman, *Shifting Involvements*, op. cit., p. 103.
53. Ibid., p. 107.
54. R. M. Axelrod, *The Evolution of Cooperation* (New York: Basic Books, 1984), p. 87.
55. Ibid., p. 54.
56. Ibid., p. 173–4.
57. Ibid., p. 132.
58. Smith, *Moral Sentiments*, op. cit., p. 127.
59. Ibid., p. 170.
60. Ibid., p. 166.
61. Ibid., p. 167.
62. Ibid., p. 429.
63. Hardin, 'The Tragedy of the Commons', loc. cit., p. 1244.
64. Ibid., p. 1248.
65. Ibid., p. 1247.
66. Schelling, *Choice and Consequence*, op. cit., p. 33.
67. See Schelling, *Microeconomics and Macrobehavior*, op. cit., Ch. 7.
68. Schelling, *Choice and Consequence*, op. cit., p. 58.
69. Ibid., p. 93.
70. J. Elster, *Ulysses and the Sirens* (Cambridge: Cambridge University Press, 1979), p. 37.
71. Ibid., p. 45.
72. Schelling, *Microeconomics and Macrobehavior*, op. cit., p. 50.
73. Hardin, 'The Tragedy of the Commons', loc. cit., p. 1244.
74. M. Lipton, 'The Prisoners' Dilemma and Coase's Theorem', in Matthews (ed.), *Economy and Democracy*, op. cit., p. 92.
75. Buchanan, *The Limits of Liberty*, op. cit., p. 144.
76. Ibid., p. 128.
77. Elster, *Ulysses*, op. cit., p. 94.
78. A. Marshall, *Industry and Trade*, 4th ed. (London: Macmillan, 1923), p. 822.
79. P. A. Samuelson, 'Diagrammatic Exposition of a Theory of Public Expenditure', *Review of Economics and Statistics*, Vol. 37, 1955, p. 351.
80. P. A. Samuelson, 'The Pure Theory of Public Expenditure', *Review of Economics and Statistics*, Vol. 36, 1954, p. 387.
81. Ibid.
82. H. Demsetz, 'The Exchange and Enforcement of Property Rights', *Journal of Law and Economics*, Vol. 7, 1964, p. 20.
83. R. H. Coase, 'The Problem of Social Cost', *Journal of Law and Economics*, Vol. 3, 1960, p. 15.
84. Ibid., p. 2.
85. Ibid., p. 26.
86. Ibid., p. 2.

87.   Ibid., p. 17.
88.   Ibid., p. 2.
89.   Ibid., p. 9.
90.   Ibid.
91.   Schelling, *Choice and Consequence*. op. cit., p. 55.

5.   COLLECTIVE ACTION AND ECONOMIC GROWTH

1.   M. Olson, *The Rise and Decline of Nations* (*RDN*) (New Haven and London: Yale University Press, 1982), p. x.
2.   *RDN*, p. 215.
3.   *RDN*, p. 129.
4.   B. Barry, 'Some Questions about Explanation', in 'Symposium: Mancur Olson on the Rise and Decline of Nations', *International Studies Quarterly*, Vol. 27, 1983, p. 20.
5.   Ibid., p. 19.
6.   *RDN*, p. 161.
7.   *RDN*, p. 129.
8.   *RDN*, p. 8.
9.   C. Kindleberger, 'On the Rise and Decline of Nations', in 'Symposium', loc. cit., p. 5.

5.1   Groups and Growth

1.   *RDN*, p. 74.
2.   J. K. Galbraith, *American Capitalism*, rev. ed. (Harmondsworth: Penguin Books, 1963), p. 127.
3.   *RDN*, p. 37.
4.   *RDN*, p. 37.
5.   *RDN*, p. 74.
6.   *RDN*, p. 23.
7.   *RDN*, p. 165.
8.   *RDN*, p. 165.
9.   J. de Vries, 'The Rise and Decline of Nations in Historical Perspective', in 'Symposium', loc. cit., p. 12, Alongside the political and the economic upheaval, it is worth mentioning yet another species of shock – the cultural upheaval as is exemplified by the impact of Carnaby Street in the Britain of the 1960s, Vietnam on America a decade later. Cultural shocks too are capable of shaking up interest-groups and other economic actors who have got into a rut; and of stimulating growth through change in that way. There is clearly more to upheaval than is captured by Olson's wars and revolutions.
10.   *RDN*, p. 74.
11.   *RDN*, p. 74.
12.   *RDN*, p. 47.
13.   *RDN*, p. 44.
14.   *RDN*, p. 74.
15.   *RDN*, p. 51.
16.   *RDN*, p. 74.

17. *RDN*, p. 74.
18. *RDN*, p. 65.
19. J. S. Coleman, *The Asymmetric Society* (Syracuse: Syracuse University Press, 1982), p. 27.
20. Durkheim, *Division of Labour*, in *Emile Durkheim: Selected Writings*, p. 186.
21. M. Olson, 'The Political Economy of Comparative Growth Rates', in D.C. Mueller (ed.), *The Political Economy of Growth (PEG)* (New Haven and London: Yale University Press, 1983), p. 22n.
22. Ibid.
23. M. Olson, 'On the Priority of Public Problems' in R. Marris (ed.), *The Corporate Society* (London: Macmillan, 1974), p. 319.
24. Ibid.
25. M. Olson, 'The Plan and Purpose of a Social Report', *The Public Interest*, Vol. 15, 1969, p. 87.
26. Ibid., p. 88.
27. Ibid., p. 86.
28. Ibid., p. 90.
29. Ibid., p. 86. In the era of the women's movement, growing concern with the environment, unrest among blacks in the inner cities, it would be foolish to forget how many issues besides growth *per se* are now on the national agenda. A cultural conservative would say that the upheaval of growth itself should be one of these: if a public bad, then it should be accounted for as a *minus* in the data on national welfare.
30. M. Olson, 'The Treatment of Externalities in National Income Statistics', in L. Wingo and A. Evans (eds), *Public Economics and the Quality of Life* (Baltimore and London: Johns Hopkins University Press, 1977), p. 219.
31. M. Olson, 'Introduction', in M. Olson and H. Landsberg (eds), *The No-Growth Society* (New York: Norton, 1973), p. 13.
32. Ibid., p. 3.
33. E. J. Mishan, *The Costs of Economic Growth* (Harmondsworth: Penguin Books, 1969), pp. 171, 175, 196, 197.
34. J. M. Buchanan, *Liberty, Market and State* (Brighton: Wheatsheaf Books, 1986), p. 116.
35. Ibid., p. 108.
36. *RDN*, p. 74.
37. *RDN*, p. 74.
38. *RDN*, pp. 69–70.
39. *RDN*, p. 72.
40. *RDN*, p. 72.

5.2 Illustrations and Implications

1. *RDN*, p. 141.
2. Olson, 'On the Priority of Public Problems', in Marris, *The Corporate Society*, op. cit., p. 307.
3. M. Olson and C. Clague, 'Dissent in Economics', *Social Research*, Vol. 38, 1971, p. 776.

4. *RDN*, p. 10.
5. *RDN*, p. 82.
6. Olson, 'The Political Economy of Comparative Growth Rates', in *PEG*, p. 27.
7. M. Abramowitz, 'Notes on International Differences in Productivity Growth Rates', in *PEG*, p. 83.
8. Ibid., p. 86.
9. J.-C. Asselain and C. Morrisson, 'Economic Growth and Interest Groups: The French Experience', in *PEG*, p. 157.
10. *RDN*, p. 48.
11. *RDN*, p. 77.
12. *RDN*, p. 78.
13. Olson, 'The Political Economy of Comparative Growth Rates', in *PEG*, p. 19.
14. *RDN*, p. 78.
15. *RDN*, p. 97.
16. *RDN*, p. 105.
17. *RDN*, p. 105.
18. M. Olson, 'The South Will Fall Again: The South as Leader and Laggard in Economic Growth', *Southern Economic Journal*, Vol. 49, 1983, p. 924.
19. Ibid., p. 932. But Olson elsewhere states (*RDN*, p. 110) that resistance to change in the South based upon 'the old pattern of coalitions' was eroded by 'adaptation to new technologies and methods of production'. This admission of reverse causation is hardly comforting to the supporter of his theory: if slow growth can foster coalition-building and rapid growth can undermine it, the inference is that the lines of causation can go *from* growth *to* groups and not *vice versa*, as Olson would suggest, based on a correlation-coefficient which would apparently be an ambiguous indicator.
20. This line of argumentation owes much to W.A. Lewis, 'Economic Development with Unlimited Supplies of Labour', *Manchester School*, Vol. 22, 1954. It has also figured prominently in the explanation provided by Edward Denison and other economists of why France enjoyed so rapid a rate of economic growth in the postwar period. Olson makes no effort to integrate the surplus labour argument into his account of why growth-rates differ. Nor does he correct his data on growth to allow for differential growth in the population or in participation-rates (say, of married women). It would have been useful if he had tested his hypothesis using per capita data and/or data on growth of production per person who is *economically active*, as opposed to using data on national income aggregates.
21. F. L. Pryor, 'A Quasi-test of Olson's Hypotheses', in *PEG*, p. 91.
22. Olson, 'The South Will Fall Again', loc. cit., p. 932.
23. *RDN*, p. 91.
24. *RDN*, p. 142.
25. *RDN*, p. 131.
26. *RDN*, p. 158.
27. *RDN*, p. 158.

28. *RDN*, p. 158–9.
29. *RDN*, p. 173.
30. *RDN*, p. 159.
31. *RDN*, p. 195.
32. *RDN*, p. 190.
33. *RDN*, p. 224.
34. *RDN*, p. 224.
35. *RDN*, p. 225.
36. *RDN*, p. 229.
37. *RDN*, p. 221.
38. *RDN*, p. 201.
39. *RDN*, p. 203.
40. *RDN*, p. 204.
41. *RDN*, p. 230.

5.3 The Logic and the Nations

1. *RDN*, p. 18.
2. *RDN*, p. 232.
3. M. Olson, 'The Efficient Production of External Economies', *American Economic Review*, Vol. 60, 1970, p. 516.
4. W. J. Baumol, *Welfare Economics and the Theory of the State*, 2nd ed. (London: G. Bell and Sons, 1965), p. 180.
5. Olson, 'The Political Economy of Comparative Growth Rates', in *PEG*, p. 23.
6. J. M. Buchanan, 'Rent Seeking and Profit Seeking', in J. M. Buchanan, R. D. Tollison and G. Tullock (eds), *Towards a Theory of the Rent-Seeking Society* (College Station: Texas A & M University Press, 1980), p. 9. The two seminal contributions to the literature on rent-seeking are reprinted in this volume. They are G. Tullock, 'The Welfare Costs of Tariffs, Monopolies and Theft' (originally published in the *Western Economic Journal*, Vol. 5, 1967) and A. O. Krueger, 'The Political Economy of the Rent-Seeking Society' (*American Economic Review*, Vol. 64, 1974).
7. Ibid., p. 8.
8. *RDN*, p. 254n.
9. *RDN*, p. 254n. It must be stated, however, that not *all* of the measures demanded by the coalitions are in fact antithetical to growth and efficiency. Thus some will press, no doubt, for resale price maintenance and the perpetuation of the conveyancing monopoly, but others will call for more start-up capital and lower interest-rates to promote new investment. Clearly, some groups will demand policies that are *favourable* to economic progress. The real question then becomes the Downs question of why one group succeeds where another fails – and not the Olson question of what can be done about coalitions *per se*.
10. *RDN*, p. 233.
11. M. Olson, 'Environmental Indivisibilities and Information Costs: Fanaticism, Agnosticism, and Intellectual Progress', *American Economic Review* (*Papers and Proceedings*), Vol. 72, 1982, p. 265.

12. *RDN*, p. 176.
13. Smith, *Wealth of Nations*, op. cit., Vol. II, p. 208.
14. *RDN*, p. 81.
15. J. K. Galbraith, *The Affluent Society*, 2nd ed. (Harmondsworth: Penguin Books, 1970), pp. 210–11.
16. J. K. Galbraith, 'Reflection on the Asian Scene', *Journal of Asian Studies*, Vol. 23, 1964, p. 504.
17. Smith, *Wealth of Nations*, op. cit., Vol. I, p. 478.
18. M. Olson, 'The Principle of "Fiscal Equivalence": The Division of Responsibilities among Different Levels of Government', *American Economic Review (Papers and Proceedings)*, Vol. 59, 1969, p. 481.
19. *RDN*, p. 85.
20. *RDN*, p. 8.
21. *RDN*, p. 177.
22. M. Olson, H. Landsberg and J. Fisher, 'Epilogue', in Olson and Landsberg, eds., *The No-Growth Society*, op. cit., p. 241.
23. Olson, 'The Political Economy of Comparative Growth Rates', in *PEG*, p. 44.

6 SOCIAL LIMITS AND COLLECTIVE ACTION

1. Hirsch, *Social Limits to Growth (SLG)*, p. 4.

6.1 The Adding-Up Problem

1. *SLG*, p. 2.
2. *SLG*, p. 113.
3. *SLG*, p. 22.
4. *SLG*, p. 3.
5. *SLG*, p. 5.
6. *SLG*, p. 172.
7. *SLG*, p. 172.
8. *SLG*, p. 173.
9. *SLG*, p. 7.
10. *SLG*, p. 67.
11. *SLG*, p. 5.
12. *SLG*, p. 26.

6.2 The Moral Nexus

1. *SLG*, p. 73.
2. *SLG*, p. 73.
3. *SLG*, p. 71.
4. *SLG*, p. 82.
5. *SLG*, p. 82.
6. *SLG*, p. 78.
7. *SLG*, p. 79.
8. *SLG*, p. 81.

9. *SLG*, p. 88.
10. *SLG*, p. 101.
11. *SLG*, p. 91.
12. *SLG*, p. 90.
13. *SLG*, p. 103.
14. *SLG*, p. 103.
15. *SLG*, p. 103.
16. *SLG*, p. 140.
17. *SLG*, p. 143.
18. *SLG*, p. 137.
19. *SLG*, p. 139.
20. *SLG*, p. 141.
21. *SLG*, p. 143.
22. *SLG*, p. 118.

6.3 Policy Inferences

1. *SLG*, p. 178.
2. *SLG*, p. 181.
3. *SLG*, p. vii.
4. *SLG*, p. 10.
5. *SLG*, p. 57.
6. *SLG*, p. 57.
7. *SLG*, p. 109.
8. *SLG*, p. 18.
9. *SLG*, p. 106.
10. *SLG*, p. 110.
11. *SLG*, p. 178.
12. *SLG*, p. 183.
13. *SLG*, p. 187.
14. *SLG*, p. 188.
15. *SLG*, p. 42.
16. *SLG*, p. 126.
17. *SLG*, p. 149.
18. *SLG*, p. 151.
19. *SLG*, p. 150.
20. *SLG*, p. 139.
21. *SLG*, p. 67.

6.4 Hirsch and Collective Action

1. C. A. R. Crosland, *The Future of Socialism* (1956) (London: Jonathan Cape, 1963), p. 216.
2. Ibid., p. 215.
3. Ibid., p. 208.
4. *SLG*, p. 5.
5. R. Dahrendorf, 'The Limits of Equality: Some Comments on Fred Hirsch', *Journal of the Royal Society of Arts*, June 1980, p. 412.
6. Crosland, *Future of Socialism*, op. cit., p. 218.

7. Dahrendorf, 'The Limits of Equality', loc. cit., pp. 414–15.
8. C. A. R. Crosland, 'A Social-Democratic Britain' (1971), in his *Socialism Now* (London: Jonathan Cape, 1974), p. 79.
9. Ibid.
10. Ibid., p. 78.
11. *SLG*, p. 62.
12. *SLG*, p. 31.
13. *SLG*, p. 43.
14. Schelling, *Micromotives and Macrobehavior*, op. cit., pp. 26–7.
15. *SLG*, p. 64.
16. *SLG*, p. 22.
17. J. Gray, 'Classical liberalism, positional goods, and the politicization of poverty', in A. Ellis and K. Kumar, eds., *Dilemmas of Liberal Democracies* (London: Tavistock Publications, 1983), p. 178.
18. Tawney, 'A Note on Christianity and the Social Order', in *The Attack*, op. cit., p. 182.
19. J. M. Winter and D. M. Joslin (eds), *R. H. Tawney's Commonplace Book* (1912–14) (Cambridge: Cambridge University Press, 1972), pp. 53–4.
20. A. Marshall, 'The Future of the Working Classes' (1873), in Pigou (ed.), *Memorials of Alfred Marshall*, op. cit., p. 102.
21. *SLG*, p. 149.
22. *SLG*, p. 149.
23. Titmuss, *The Gift Relationship*, op. cit., p. 239.
24. T. H. Marshall, *The Right to Welfare and Other Essays* (London: Heinemann Educational Books, 1981), p. 73.
25. J. K. Galbraith, 'A Pioneer Approach to Affirmative Action' (1971), in his *A View from the Stands* (London: Hamish Hamilton, 1987), p. 28.
26. Ibid., p. 33.
27. Galbraith, 'Two Pleas for Our Age' (1980), in *A View from the Stands*, op. cit., p. 5.
28. *SLG*, p. 188.
29. *SLG*, p. 185.
30. R. M. Titmuss, 'Social Welfare and the Art of Giving' (1965), in B. Abel-Smith and Kay Titmuss (eds), *The Philosophy of Welfare: Selected Writings of Richard M. Titmuss* (London: Allen & Unwin, 1987), p. 118.
31. *SLG*, p. 180.
32. Coase, 'The Problem of Social Cost', loc. cit., p. 13.
33. Ibid., p. 4.
34. *SLG*, p. 185.
35. *SLG*, p. 91.
36. *SLG*, p. 93n.
37. *SLG*, p. 92.
38. Titmuss, *The Gift Relationship*, op. cit., p. 177.
39. Ibid., p. 224.
40. R. M. Titmuss, 'The Irresponsible Society' (1959), in his *Essays on 'The Welfare State'*, 2nd ed. (London: George Allen & Unwin, 1963), p. 218.
41. T. Scitovsky, *The Joyless Economy* (New York: Oxford University Press, 1976), p. 240.

42. Ibid., p. 241.
43. Ibid., p. 241.
44. Ibid., p. 244.
45. See *SLG*, p. 89.
46. *SLG*, p. 177.
47. *SLG*, p. 139.
48. A. M. Okun, *Equality and Efficiency: The Big Tradeoff* (Washington, DC.: The Brookings Institution, 1975), p. 2.
49. Ibid., p. 1.
50. Ibid., p. 48.
51. F. Hirsch, 'The Ideological Underlay of Inflation', in F. Hirsch and J. H. Goldthorpe (eds), *The Political Economy of Inflation* (London: Martin Robertson, 1978), p. 272.
52. P. Wiles, 'Cost Inflation and the State of Economic Theory', *Economic Journal*, Vol. 83, 1973, p. 392.
53. *SLG*, p. 145.
54. Hirsch, 'The Ideological Underlay of Inflation', loc. cit., p. 273.
55. Ibid., p. 276.
56. Scitovsky, *The Joyless Economy*, p. 41.
57. Ibid., p. 74.
58. *SLG*, p. 185.
59. J. Rawls, *A Theory of Justice*, (Oxford: Oxford University Press, 1972), p. 100.
60. S. Brittan, 'The Economic Contradictions of Democracy', *British Journal of Political Science*, Vol. 5. 1975, p. 130.
61. Ibid., pp. 129. 130.
62. Hirsch, 'The Ideological Underlay of Inflation', loc. cit., p. 275.
63. *SLG*, p. 139.
64. K. J. Arrow, 'Gifts and Exchanges', in E. S. Phelps (ed.), *Altruism, Morality and Economic Theory* (New York: Russell Sage Foundation, 1975), p. 24.
65. A. O. Hirschman, *Essays in Trespassing* (Cambridge: Cambridge University Press, 1981), p. 299.
66. R. C. O. Matthews, 'Morality, Competition and Efficiency', *The Manchester School*, Vol. 49, 1981, p. 306.
67. Ibid., p. 291.
68. Ibid., p. 294.
69. Ibid., p. 292.
70. *SLG*, p. 141.
71. *SLG*, p. 54.
72. Hirsch, 'The Ideological Underlay of Inflation', loc. cit., p. 274.
73. *SLG*, p. 145.
74. *SLG*, p. 131.
75. *SLG*, p. 143.
76. G. A. Akerlof, 'The Market for "Lemons"; Quality Uncertainty and the Market Mechanism', *Quarterly Journal of Economics*, Vol. 84, 1970, p. 495.
77. F. Hirsch, 'The Bagehot Problem', *The Manchester School*, Vol. 45, 1977, p. 245.

78. Ibid., p. 249.
79. Ibid., p. 251.
80. Ibid.
81. Ibid., p. 243.
82. *SLG*, p. 134.
83. Schelling, *Choice and Consequence*, op. cit., pp. 10–11.
84. Buchanan, *The Limits of Liberty*, op. cit., p. 122.
85. Buchanan, *Liberty, Market and State*, op. cit., p. 114.
86. Ibid.
87. *SLG*, p. 145.
88. *SLG*, p. 136.
89. *SLG*, p. 143.
90. *SLG*, pp. 93–4.
91. A. Buchanan, *Ethics, Efficiency and the Market* (Oxford: Clarendon Press, 1985), p. 103.
92. Marshall, *Principles*, op. cit., p. 1.

Index

abstention in elections 46–7
abuse, bureaucratic 102–3, 128
  checks on 104, 117–18, 120, 126
  and recruitment 128
accountability of bureaus 95–137
action
  altruistic 183
  collective, *see* collective action;
    also democracy and consent;
    growth, economic; free
    riders; organisations and
    interests; social limits
  individual 150, 162; constraints
    on 1; precommitment of 195,
    203–5
  and policy 268
activists, party political 17
activity–pace–quality–time 115–16
adding-up problem 259–62, 266,
  268, 271, 272–83
advertising 263
advocate 68, 70, 71, 92, 119
Akerlof, G. A. 308–9
akrasia 196, 203–5
alienation 184
altruism 15–16, 65, 132, 147–8, 163,
  303
  and Christianity 266, 302
  decay of 264, 289
  and self-interest 2, 13, 131, 271
  and social responsibility 54, 130,
    181–3
amenity value 260
anarchy 284
  see also instability, social; violence
anomie 256, 298, 305
apartheid 243–4
apathy 154
Arrow, K. J. 24–5, 219, 303
  and paradox of voting 37, 39,
    40–1, 42–3, 44
Asia, Eastern 210
assessment in bureaus *see*
  performance indicators

asymmetry and groups 212–13
authority 21, 72
  of all over each 173, 174, 175
  and bureaucrats 78, 90, 98, 125
automaticity 293–6, 298, 300
Axelrod, P. B. 186–7

Bagehot, W. 309
Barry, B. 23–4, 158–9, 211
Baumol, W. 248
Becker, G. 59, 110, 159, 178
Bell, D. 114
Bergson, Abram 42
Black, D. 29, 40
blood donation 181, 288, 289
Boulding, K. E. 8, 289
brainwashing 22
Brittan, S. 301
Buchanan, A. 313
Buchanan, J. M. 12, 111, 128, 282,
  285, 293
  on budget 58
  on coercion 192, 199
  on conventions 122, 168, 169,
    226–7, 311
  on democracy 54, 301
  on groups 182
  resource allocation 249–50
  on self-interest 130, 134,
budget
  of bureau 70, 90, 91, 97, 100, 101
  in democracy 54, 55, 56–7, 58,
    97
bureaus
  abuse and 102–3, 104, 117–18,
    120–1, 126, 128
  accountability of 95–137
  altruism of bureaucrat 15, 65
  behaviour of bureaucrats 62–74,
    78
  budget of 70, 90, 91, 97, 100, 101
  competition between 104–5
  conflict resolution 121–30, 135
  and costs 83, 84, 85

339

bureaus *cont.*
definition 79–81
expansion of 90–3, 99–113
and freedom 108
hierarchy in 119–20
inertia in 85–93, 117–18, 136
and information 83–5, 117, 120–1
and law and order 109
output of 80–1, 82
promotion in 122–3, 127
reform of 96, 135, 137
risk aversion in 95, 105
survival of 96–7
see also organisations and
interests

calculative rationality 3–4, 11, 19, 98–9
and bureaus 73, 90
defined 18
in economic theory 7–8, 10
and information 74, 75–6, 77–8
and voters 19–20, 21–4
capitalism 11, 172, 267, 298, 304,
contradictions of 154, 199
and growth 289, 297
and inequality 53, 295
Carroll, Lewis 37
caste 242–3
catch-up growth 232–3, 238
Chamberlin, E. H. 24
change 168, 171, 172, 220, 250
in behaviour of bureaucrats 89
in bureaus 118–20
and costs 229
differential 230–40
and groups 230–1
choice
individual 1, 2, 22, 149
and normative constraint 14
and prisoner's dilemma 160–1
public 132, 133, 134
rationality of 23
and resources 56, 159
Christianity 172–3, 176–7, 266, 282,
302, 304
class, social 228
and information 49–50
and promotion 127
solidarity 153–4
and voters 47

climber 66–7, 70, 71, 83–4, 106
and continuity 118
and inertia 87–8, 89, 92
club 182–3
nation as 252, 253
co-operation 186–8
coalition 31, 36–7
Coase, R. H. 206–8, 286–7
coercion 156, 192, 196, 213, 253,
254
by consent 193
collective 160
and liberty 248, 297
Coleman, J. S. 221
Collard, D. 184
collective action, precommitment of
193–4, 195–6, 198, 205
collective discipline 221–2
collective good *see under* good
collective intervention 56, 265, 267
competition 25, 152, 250
and bureaus 103–5
and coalitions 31
and elections 8, 21, 37
and growth 251
and information sources 105–7
and privatisation 116–17
and strategy 36–44
complexity and groups 228–9
conflict and bureaus 121–30, 135
conscience 198
consensus 36, 37, 38, 44
and bureaucracies 64
goal 126, 128, 129, 130, 136
group 143
minimal 133, 134
social 130
consent, unanimity of 199
conservatism
in bureaus 86, 90, 127
of group 219
conserver 67, 70, 71, 83, 84, 100,
106
and calculative rationality 73
and continuity 118, 119–20
and inertia 87, 88, 89, 91, 92,
126
constraint 1
moral 46
normative 14, 129, 175, 206, 305

consumer
  and economic policy 51–2, 53,
    employee 115–16
  rational 20–1, 115
consumption
  defensive 273–4, 280
  sequential 275
contract, political 21, 22, 57, 61
conventions
  shared 164–8, 169–70, 173–4,
    202; enforcement of 189–90,
    192, 201; moral 173, 206,
    302, 305, 310
convergence 24–30
costs and bureaus 83, 84, 85
crime 227
  see also instability; violence
Crosland, C. A. R. 272, 274, 276,
    279
crowds 162, 166, 174
culture 170–1, 231, 241, 242–4, 306
  common, and interests 131
Cyert, R. M. 72–3, 86, 116

Dahrendorf, R. 272, 275
de Borda, Jean Charles 37
de Tocqueville, A. 25
de Vries, Jan 214
decision-making 30, 120–1, 212
  of bureaucrats 66, 84, 85, 101,
    115
  and calculative rationality 74,
    76–8
  collective 42
  and consensus 133
  and information 136
  of legislators 98
  of voters 29, 42; delegated 57;
    see also preferences, voting
decisions, interdependence of 260
demand-pull inflation 153
democracy 8–9, 14, 22, 134, 156,
    220, 301
  and economic policy 51–9
  paradox of 199
  and preferences 9, 18, 26–7, 28,
    58, 98
democracy and consent 7–59, 133
  methodology 9–24, 143, 145;

calculative rationality 18–24;
  self-interest 12–18
policies demanded 44–59;
  democracy and economic
  policy 51–9; information
  without investment 49–51;
  investment in information
  47–9; voting decision 45–7
policies supplied 24–44;
  competition and strategy
  36–44; convergence and
  divergence 24–30;
  distributions 32–6
multi-party system 30–2
Democrats 25–6
Demsetz, H. 203
differentials in labour market 293–5
discipline, collective 221–2
distribution of rewards 293
distributions 32–6
diswelfare 111, 248
divergence 24–30
division of labour, and bureaus 81,
    82, 83, 113
Dodgson, C. L. 37
Donne, John 181
Downs, A. 2, 153, 154–5, 191, 228,
    252, 266, 300–1, 311
  see also democracy and consent;
    organisations and interests
Duesenberry, J. 86, 260
Durkheim, Emile 173–5, 222

economic approach and politics
    8–9, 11, 27, 59, 60
economic policy and democracy
    51–9
education 109, 114, 123–4, 249
  as source of advantage 262, 268,
    270, 299–300
efficiency
  and equality 295
  social 216
egoism 2, 60, 63–5, 66, 131, 132,
    163
elections 33–4
  abstention in 46–7
  and calculative rationality 19–24
  and uncertainty 30, 48
  see also voting

electoral promises 23, 42
Elster, J. 194, 196, 199
encompassing organisation 217–18
enforcement *see* sanctions
Engels, F. 127
European Economic Community
    240–1, 250
exclusivity and groups 227–8
expectations 165, 168

fairness 190, 293, 311
France 210, 214, 215, 233, 290
free market 269, 295
    see also under free riders
free riders 3, 46, 109, 304
    and free markets 141–209; group
        size 149–60; methodology
        142–9; *see also* prisoner's
        dilemma
    rationality of 263
    and self-interest 131, 132
    and State intervention 271
    and voting 35, 48
freedom 192
    bureaucratisation and 108
Frey, Bruno 8
Friedman, M. 86, 110, 116, 211,
    301
friendliness 262–3
Fromm, Erich 282
frustration 261, 279, 281, 282

Galbraith, J. K. 57, 65, 102, 212,
    269
    on budget 58
    on growth 279, 283
Germany 210, 230–3, 236, 251
goals
    of bureaucrats 73, 119, 122
    common 143–4
    consensus 126, 128, 129, 130, 136
good
    collective 150–1, 152, 155–6, 159,
        162
    material 262
    public 131, 143, 144, 145, 200–1;
        and politicians 248
    and rational consumer 115

goods
    material 262
    positional 270, 272, 278–80, 283,
        292, 296–7; and State
        intervention 286–7, 292
Gray, J. 281
Green, T. H. 175
Grimond, Jo 15, 16
group(s) 98, 159, 215, 219
    complexity 228–9
    influence of 156, 212
    interest 214, 215–16, 218, 221,
        222, 230–44
    intermediate 152
    large 3, 20, 152–60, 162, 164,
        174, 217, 253–4
    latent 162
    of one 149
    size 149–60
    small 3, 150–2, 162, 174, 253–4
    values 159
    see also under growth
growth 224–5, 226
    collective action and economic,
        210–56; groups 212–29
    illustrations and implications
        229–46; the *Logic* and the
        Nations 246–256
    and diswelfare 248
    and political instability 233–6

Hardin, Garret 170, 192, 197
Harsanyi, J. C. 168
Hayek, F. A. 170, 171
hierarchy in bureaus 119–20
Hirsch, Fred 4, 159, 171, 259–314
    see also social limits and
        collective action
Hirschman, A. O. 183, 184–5,
    303
Hobbes, Thomas 130, 132–3
honesty 208, 307–8
Hotelling, H. 24–7
Hume, David 141, 142

ideology 28
    and bureaucrats 65, 128–9
    of politicians 15, 42
    ignorance 56, 57, 99, 113

Illich, Ivan 65
imbalance
    information 99–100, 123
    probable 50–1, 53
incentives
    in bureaus 70–3
    selective 157–7, 158–9, 213, 240,
        243; and group action 253
incomes 272
    redistribution of 32, 35, 52–3,
        216, 217, 218; and bureaus
        81, 109–10
incrementalism 100–1
India 242
indicators, performance 102, 105,
    106, 123–5, 129
individual
    action 1, 150, 162;
        precommitment of 195,
        203–5
    and rationality 20
    self-determination 184
individualisation 291
indoctrination in bureaus 128
inefficiency and groups 215–17
inequality
    of rewards 293–6
    see also imbalance; incomes
inertia 85–93
    in bureaus 85–93, 117–18
inflation 260, 310
information 47–51, 56, 57, 225
    and bureaus 83–5, 117, 120–1
    and calculative rationality 74,
        75–6, 77–8
    competition between sources
        105–7
    imbalance 99–100, 123
    impactedness 135–6
    and investment 47–51
innovation 89
instability
    political, and growth 234
    social 213–4, 250; and growth 255
    see also violence
interest
    public 63, 64, 68, 69, 72, 130,
        249
    social 270

vested, and bureaus 83, 84, 85,
    100
interest-groups 98, 214, 215–16,
    218, 221, 222
    and growth 230–44
intermediate group 152
intervention
    collective 56, 265, 267
    State 111–13, 154–5, 224, 248,
        251–2, 255, 288; and free
        riders 271; guidance by 267;
        and moral attitudes 290–2
    and positional goods 286–7, 291;
        and scarce utilities 270
investment and information 47–51
irrelevance, personal 221
Italy 232

Jackson, P. M. 137
Japan 210, 230–3, 242
Johnson, H. G. 58–9
justice *see* fairness

Kant, I. 63, 303, 304
Keynes, J. M. 197, 211, 244–6, 262
Kindleberger, C. 212
Knight, F. H. 172, 173
knowledge 267, 268
    abuse of superior 303
    as power 75
    see also information
Krueger, Anne 249–50

labour
    division of 81, 82, 83, 113
    market 269
Lancaster, K. J. 115
law and order 109, 145, 299
    see also instability; violence
leadership 160
Leibenstein, H. 114–15, 125, 128
Lindblom, C. E. 101
Lipton, M. 197
lobbying 223, 228, 238, 241
    see also groups; special interest
love see sentiment
loyalty of bureaucrats 64, 78, 79,
    88, 118

MacIntyre, A. 211
Macmillan, H. 310
Macpherson, C. B. 11
majority 18
  interests 51, 54–5
  view of voters 37, 38–9, 40–1
March, J. G. 72–3, 86, 116
market
  control 103–17
  failure 197
  free 141–209, 269
  redistribution by 295
Marsh, David 158–9, 325–6n
Marshall, Alfred 28, 200, 269, 282, 314
  on altruism 132
  on honesty 171
Marshall, T. H. 282, 283
Marx, Karl 11, 173
  on bourgeois interests 54, 127 153–4
  on class struggle 212, 298
material goods, allocation of 262
Matthews, R. C. O. 17–18, 21, 22, 303,
Milliband, R. 127
Mills, C. Wright *see* Wright Mills
minority 18
  interests 51, 54–5
  view of voters 37, 40
Mises, L. 62, 82
Mishan, E. J. 226–7
monopolies, regulation of 110
moral/morality 136, 144, 222, 262–7, 291, 302–14
  and bureaus 130–7
  constraint 46, 313
  conventions 173, 206, 302, 305, 310
  decline 4, 227, 263, 265, 268, 271, 301, 304
  personal 134, 307
  of politicians 15–16
  and prisoner's dilemma 169–77
  social 208
  values 297
motivation 159
  of bureaucrats 66–70
Mueller, D. C. 132

multi-party system 30–2
  see also democracy; elections; voting

Nader, Ralph 263
Nanson, E. J. 37
Niskanen, W. 61–2, 70–1, 80, 81–2, 90
Nordhaus, W. 43
normative constraint 14, 129, 175, 206, 305
  and choices 14
norms
  institutionalised 164, 166–7, 171, 185
  internalised 167, 267, 271, 314

obligation, social 312
Okun, A. 295
Olson, M. 2–3, 141–256
  see also growth, collective action and economic; free riders and free markets
opinions
  altered 29
  see also preferences
opportunism 135, 136
organisational slack 116
organisations and interests 60–137
  bureaucracies: accountability and action 95–137; conflict resolution 121–30; internal reorganisation 117–21; market control 103–17
  bureaucracies: responsibility and responsiveness 79–95; inertia 85–93
  information distortion 83–5
  methodology 61–79; calculative rationality 18–24; self-interest 62–73
  see also bureaus; growth; collective action

paradox of voting 37–41, 43–4
Pareto, V. 36
party
  differential 48
  political, activists 17

patriotism 147–8, 181
performance indicators 102, 105, 106, 123–5, 129
personality types in bureaus 66–71, 83–4, 91–2, 100
Plamenatz, J. 17, 44
policies
  demanded 44–59
  supplied 24–44
policy and action 268
political
  control and bureaus 96–103
  market 2; self-interest in 8–9, 16–17
  parties *see* democracy; elections; voters
  party activists 17
politicians 29, 39
  altruism of 15–16
  and calculative rationality 19–23
  rational 2
  self-interest of 13–14, 16, 17, 134
politics and economic approach 8–9, 11, 27, 59, 60
positional goods *see under* goods
power 212
  of bureaucrats 70
  electoral 32
  of groups 215
  of individual 149
  inequality of 223
  knowledge as 75
  sharing 299
  see also authority
preferences, 22, 32–3, 55, 116, 199
  and democracy 9, 18, 26–7, 28, 58, 98
  differential 273
  interdependence of 1, 259–60
  revealed: and calculative rationality 18; constraints on 1; of voters 12, 18, 28–9, 37–43
prejudice of voters 48
pressure group 98
prisoner's dilemma 131, 160–209, 163, 178, 205, 209, 226
  and choices 160–1
  convention 164–9

formalisation 200–9
morality 169–77
sanctions 185–209; legal 191–200; self-policing 185–8; social 188–91
sentiment 177–85
and truth 163
privatisation 107–17, 204, 289, 291
privilege and groups 150
producers, and economic policy 51–2, 53
promises, electoral 23, 42
promotion in bureaus 122–3, 127
proportional representation 30
  see also voting rule
Pryor, F. 239
public good *see under* good
public interest 63, 64, 68, 69, 72, 130
  State and 249
pubs 290

quality of utilities 264

rational
  bureaucrats 2
  citizens 45–6
  consumer 115
  employee 115
  politicians 2
  voters 2, 47, 51
rationality
  of voters 2, 30, 39, 48
  see also calculative rationality
Rawls, J. 168, 300, 310–11
recruitment, selective 126–7
redistribution by market mechanism 295
rejection 284–5, 287, 299, 300–1
religion 172–3, 175–7, 266, 282, 302, 304
'rent-seeking activity' 249
reorganisation of bureaus 117–21
Republicans 25–6
resources 27
  and calculative rationality 74
  and choice 56, 159
  depletion 226–7

resources *cont.*
 influences on allocation 32, 58
 saving of scarce 167
responsibility of bureaus 79–95
restrictive practices 250
revealed preferences *see*
 preferences
Ricardo, D. 298
risk 137
risk-aversion
 in bureaus 95, 105
 in capitalism 53
Robinson, Joan 24
Rodgers, W. 15–16
Rousseau, J.-J. 7
rules
 established 165, 170, 312, 313
 see also norms

Samuelson, P. A. 8, 200
sanctions 185–209
 cost of 198–9
 free riders and self-policing 185–8
 legal 191–200, 303, 308
 social 46, 156, 188–91
scarce utilities 270
Schelling, T. C. 181, 193–4, 197,
 279, 311
 on conventions 165, 167, 168
 on morality 177, 208
Schotter, A. 167
Schumpeter, J. A. 8, 23, 298, 300–1
Scitovsky, T. 289–90, 298
selective recruitment 126–7
self-determination, individual 184
self-interest 3, 4, 57, 132, 159, 269
 and altruism 271
 and bureaucracies 62, 84, 90,
 130–1
 of citizens 55
 and competition 103–4
 constraints on 63–4, 266
 in economic theory 7–8, 10
 and market economy 263
 and normative constraint 305
 and opportunities 136
 of politicians 8–9, 13–14, 17, 60,
 134
 and prisoner's dilemma 161, 205

of shareholders 153
 of voters 13, 17, 60, 98–9, 184
self-policing 4, 131, 192, 200, 302
 see also normative constraint;
 sanctions
selfishness 262, 265–6, 305
Sen, A. K. 184
sentiment 177–85
shareholders 153
Simon, H. A. 73, 74–5, 76–7, 117
size and power of groups 215
Smith, Adam 171–2, 197, 251, 252,
 266, 298
 on self-interest 7, 62, 78
 on society 188–9, 190
 on sympathy 180–1
Smithies, A. 27
sociability 263, 264
social
 efficiency 316
 obligation 312
 sanctions 46, 156, 188–91
 values 267
 welfare 8, 12, 42, 155
social limits and collective action
 259–314
 adding-up problem 259–62,
 272–83
 Hirsch on 217–314
 moral nexus 262–7, 302–14;
 honesty 307–10; justice
 310–14
 willingness to share 305–7 policy
 inferences 267–71, 283–302;
 labour market 292–302;
 planning and sharing 285–92
social welfare 8, 12, 42
socialisation 128, 167, 170, 191, 313
socialising 290
South Africa 243
Soviet Union 88, 128, 158
special interest group *see* interest
 group
Spencer, H. 170
Spinoza, B. 132
Sraffa, P. 24
stabilisation of economic activity
 111
stability and groups 213–15

State intervention *see* intervention, State
statesman 69–70, 71, 92, 119
status and imbalance 50–1
Stigler, G. J. 59, 75–7, 111
Stinchcombe, A. L. 141
Sugden, R. 165, 176
superman syndrome 94–5
Sweden 214, 235–6
Switzerland 214
sympathy 180–1

Tawney, R. H. 108, 172, 173, 282
taxes 56, 58, 156, 157, 299
  visibility of 55
technological progresss 220, 221, 274, 280
tensions, social *see* instability
time 42, 168
  and growth 233–4, 275
Titmuss, R. M. 181, 282, 283, 284, 289
Toye, F. J. 11
trades unions 157–8, 261, 296, 297, 302
Truman, President H. 133–5
trust 208
truth 135, 307, 308
  and prisoner's dilemma 163
Tullock, G. 61–2, 69–70, 111
  and democracy 8, 12, 46, 54, 58
  and majority rule 40–1
  and self-interest 13, 57, 64, 130
two-party system 219

uncertainty
  as constraint 1
  in democracy 57–8
  and elections 30, 48
unemployment 244–6
United Kingdom 21, 158, 288, 290
  growth 210, 215, 231–3; and groups 214, 217, 236–7, 242, 244–5
United States 11, 21, 25, 133–4, 264, 290

growth 110, 210, 233, 236, 237–8, 245, 251; and groups 218, 220, 236, 246
superpower concept 65
trade unions 157
utility 33–4
  and distributions 32
  maximising by bureaucrats 62–3
  see also preferences

values
  group 159
  moral 297
  social 267
Veblen, T. 11, 260, 298
violence 283–5, 287, 289, 299, 300–1
  see also instability, social
Virginia School 40, 54–5
vote 8, 131
  as investment 49
  maximising policies 16, 17, 24, 26, 36, 40
  selling 35
  value 47–9, 141, 158
vote-maximising, by politicians 12, 16, 17, 33
voters 48
  and calculative rationality 19–20, 21–4; *see also* preferences
  Downs on 10, 184
  minority view 37
  prejudice of 48
  rational 2, 30, 39, 48
  self-interest of 13, 17, 60, 98–9, 184
  and uncertainty 30
  and utility 33–4
voting
  majority 54
  paradox of 37–41, 43–4
  rule 30, 40; majority 18, 40
  strategic 48–9

waste 261, 279, 280–1
Weber, Max 20, 66, 69, 78, 80, 88
  on capitalism 172

welfare
  individual 259
  perceived 198
  social 8, 12, 42, 155
Wicksell, K. 18, 54, 199
Wildavsky, A. 100, 101
Wiles, P. 296

will, weakness of 196, 203–5
Williamson, O. E. 135–6
Wright Mills, C. 127

zealot 68, 70, 71, 83, 91–2, 119
  and calculative rationality 74